About the Author

David L. Hudson Jr., J.D. is the author, co-author, or co-editor of more than 40 books, including several in the "Handy" series: *The Handy Supreme Court Answer Book, The Handy Law Answer Book, The Handy Presidents Answer Book* (2nd edition), and *The Handy History Answer Book* (3rd edition). He serves as the Director of Academic Affairs for the Nashville School of Law. He also teaches classes at the Nashville School of Law, Vanderbilt Law School, and Belmont University Law School. He earned his undergraduate degree from Duke University and his law degree from Vanderbilt. Hudson lives in Nashville with his wife, Carla, who assists him with her excellent research skills.

Also from Visible Ink Press

The Handy African American History Answer Book
by Jessie Carnie Smith
ISBN: 978-1-57859-452-8

The Handy Anatomy Answer Book, 2nd edition
by Patricia Barnes-Svarney and Thomas E. Svarney
ISBN: 978-57859-542-6

The Handy Answer Book for Kids (and Parents), 2nd edition
by Gina Misiroglu
ISBN: 978-1-57859-219-7

The Handy Art History Answer Book
by Madelynn Dickerson
ISBN: 978-1-57859-417-7

The Handy Astronomy Answer Book, 3rd edition
by Charles Liu
ISBN: 978-1-57859-190-9

The Handy Bible Answer Book
by Jennifer Rebecca Prince
ISBN: 978-1-57859-478-8

The Handy Biology Answer Book, 2nd edition
by Patricia Barnes Svarney and Thomas E. Svarney
ISBN: 978-1-57859-490-0

The Handy Chemistry Answer Book
by Ian C. Stewart and Justin P. Lamont
ISBN: 978-1-57859-374-3

The Handy Civil War Answer Book
by Samuel Willard Crompton
ISBN: 978-1-57859-476-4

The Handy Dinosaur Answer Book, 2nd edition
by Patricia Barnes-Svarney and Thomas E. Svarney
ISBN: 978-1-57859-218-0

The Handy English Grammar Answer Book
by Christine A. Hult, Ph.D.
ISBN: 978-1-57859-520-4

The Handy Geography Answer Book, 2nd edition
by Paul A. Tucci
ISBN: 978-1-57859-215-9

The Handy Geology Answer Book
by Patricia Barnes-Svarney and Thomas E. Svarney
ISBN: 978-1-57859-156-5

The Handy History Answer Book, 3rd edition
by David L. Hudson, Jr.
ISBN: 978-1-57859-372-9

The Handy Hockey Answer Book
by Stan Fischler
ISBN: 978-1-57859-569-3

The Handy Investing Answer Book
by Paul A. Tucci
ISBN: 978-1-57859-486-3

The Handy Islam Answer Book
by John Renard, Ph.D.
ISBN: 978-1-57859-510-5

The Handy Law Answer Book
by David L. Hudson, Jr.
ISBN: 978-1-57859-217-3

The Handy Math Answer Book, 2nd edition
by Patricia Barnes-Svarney and Thomas E. Svarney
ISBN: 978-1-57859-373-6

The Handy Military History Answer Book
by Samuel Willard Crompton
ISBN: 978-1-57859-509-9

The Handy Mythology Answer Book,
by David A. Leeming, Ph.D.
ISBN: 978-1-57859-475-7

The Handy Nutrition Answer Book
by Patricia Barnes-Svarney and Thomas E. Svarney
ISBN: 978-1-57859-484-9

The Handy Ocean Answer Book
by Patricia Barnes-Svarney and Thomas E. Svarney
ISBN: 978-1-57859-063-6

The Handy Personal Finance Answer Book
by Paul A. Tucci
ISBN: 978-1-57859-322-4

The Handy Philosophy Answer Book
by Naomi Zack
ISBN: 978-1-57859-226-5

The Handy Physics Answer Book, 2nd edition
By Paul W. Zitzewitz, Ph.D.
ISBN: 978-1-57859-305-7

The Handy Politics Answer Book
by Gina Misiroglu
ISBN: 978-1-57859-139-8

The Handy Presidents Answer Book, 2nd edition
by David L. Hudson
ISB N: 978-1-57859-317-0

The Handy Psychology Answer Book
by Lisa J. Cohen
ISBN: 978-1-57859-223-4

The Handy Religion Answer Book, 2nd edition
by John Renard
ISBN: 978-1-57859-379-8

The Handy Science Answer Book, 4th edition
by The Carnegie Library of Pittsburgh
ISBN: 978-1-57859-321-7

The Handy Supreme Court Answer Book
by David L Hudson, Jr.
ISBN: 978-1-57859-196-1

The Handy Technology Answer Book
by by Naomi Balaban and James Bobick
ISBN: 978-1-57859-563-1

The Handy Weather Answer Book, 2nd edition
by Kevin S. Hile
ISBN: 978-1-57859-221-0

Please visit the "Handy" series website at www.handyanswers.com.

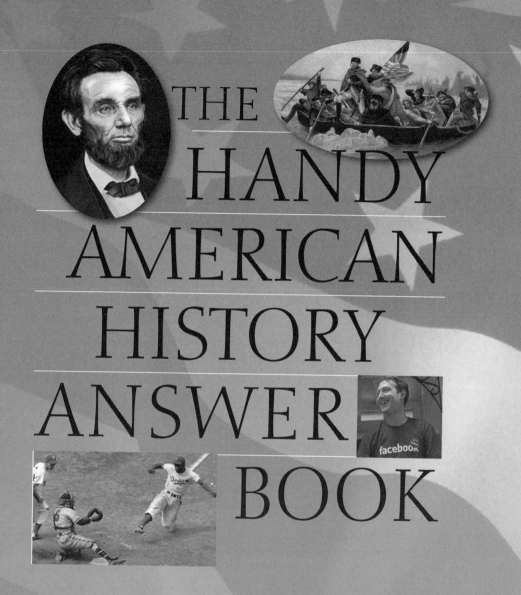

THE HANDY AMERICAN HISTORY ANSWER BOOK

David L. Hudson, Jr., JD

VISIBLE INK PRESS

Detroit

THE HANDY AMERICAN HISTORY ANSWER BOOK

Visible Ink Press®
43311 Joy Rd., #414
Canton, MI 48187–2075
Visible Ink Press is a registered trademark of Visible Ink Press LLC.

Most Visible Ink Press books are available at special quantity discounts when purchased in bulk by corporations, organizations, or groups. Customized printings, special imprints, messages, and excerpts can be produced to meet your needs. For more information, contact Special Markets Director, Visible Ink Press, www.visibleink.com, or 734–667–3211.

Managing Editor: Kevin S. Hile
Art Director: Mary Claire Krzewinski
Typesetting: Marco DiVita
Proofreaders: Paul Cain and Shoshana Hurwitz
Indexer: Larry Baker

Cover images: background flag, Washington in boat, Mark Zuckerberg, and San Francisco gay pride parade–all Shutterstock. Jackie Robinson–Associated Press.

**Cataloging–in–Publication data
is on file at the Library of Congress.**

Printed in the United States of America

10 9 8 7 6 5 4 3 2 1

Contents

Acknowledgments

I would like to thank Roger Jänecke of Visible Ink Press for his vision in creating the Handy series and allowing me to participate as an author; Kevin Hile of Visible Ink Press for his expert editing; and my wife, Carla Harris Hudson, for her superb research skills. I also wish to thank all of my students through the years at Southeastern Paralegal Institute, Middle Tennessee State University, the Nashville School of Law, and Vanderbilt Law School for supporting me as an educator.

Photo Credits

David Bjorgen: p. 66.

Dr. Dennis Bogdan: p. 203.

Ron Cogswell: p. 111.

HJPD: p. 2.

Leena Krohn: p. 237.

Library of Congress: p. 123, 160, 162, 211, 214, 215, 217, 285, 338.

Stuart Milk: p. 206.

National Aeronautics and Space Administration: p. 228, 230, 231.

Fred Palumbo: p. 295 (R).

Ivo Shandor: p. 96.

Shutterstock: p. 14, 32, 92, 197, 257, 260, 262, 269, 272, 275, 276, 279, 281, 290, 298, 300, 302, 304, 309, 312, 313, 315 (L and R), 317, 327, 329, 330, 332, 340, 343, 345, 348, 350, 352, 358, 360, 361, 364.

Gloria Steinem: p. 207.

Toastydave: p. 192.

Wystan from Ann Arbor: p. 169.

Public domain: pp. 5, 7, 11, 16, 19, 21, 23, 25, 30, 34, 37, 39, 42, 44, 46, 48, 51, 53, 57, 60, 64, 68, 69, 71, 74, 76, 78, 79, 81, 83, 86, 88, 97, 99, 101, 102, 103, 106, 108, 114, 116, 119, 125, 128, 130-131, 135, 137, 139, 141, 143, 147, 149 (L and R), 151 (L and R), 152, 154, 156, 158 (L and R), 164, 170, 171, 173, 175, 180, 183, 185, 188, 190, 194, 202, 209, 224, 226, 234, 240, 242, 244, 249, 251, 253, 264, 266, 283, 284, 288, 291, 293, 295 (L), 306, 320, 322, 326, 344, 357.

Introduction

History always interested me more than all other subjects in school. I couldn't find enough information about different historical figures, battles, movements, and eras. While I later took courses on ancient Greek and Roman history, Russian history, and modern European history, my favorite was American history.

That is one reason why I remain grateful to Roger Jänecke of Visible Ink Press because he gave me the opportunity to write a book on American history. When he asked if I would like to write this book for the "Handy Answers" series, I couldn't help but say "yes."

The "Handy Answers" series provides information on important subjects in an accessible, easy-to-read format. Previously, I have worked on several works in the series— *The Handy Supreme Court Answer Book, The Handy Law Answer Book, The Handy Presidents Answer Book* (2nd edition), and *The Handy History Answer Book,* (3rd edition). *The Handy American History Answer Book* is a natural extension of the series.

Hopefully, the *Handy American History Answer Book* will supplement high school or community college courses on American history. Students in the United States need more education on history and civics. The book also can provide a starting point for those who simply want to refresh their memory or learn more about the subject.

The difficulty with such a work is determining what material most merits inclusion. But that is a great problem to have because it leads to more reading, more research and more writing. It helps satisfy the thirst for more knowledge. If you don't find what you are looking for, let us know and we will consider it for the next edition. It is impossible to include every fascinating detail of America's story in one book, so the intention of this work is to provide a solid overview of this nation's history, hitting the high points and illuminating the most significant events and people of the last couple hundred years.

I truly hope you enjoy reading this book as much as I enjoyed working on it.

Timeline of
U.S. Events

Date	Event
1513	Spanish explorer Ponce de León sights Florida.
1587	Sir Walter Raleigh founds a British colony in Roanoke, Virginia.
1607	On May 14, John Smith and others found the Jamestown settlement in modern-day Virginia.
1626	On May 6, Dutch explorer Peter Minuit purchases Manhattan Island from American Indians.
1631	John Winthrop becomes the first governor of Massachusetts.
1633	On June 19, Lord Cecil Baltimore obtains a charter for Maryland.
1634	On March 25, the first English settlers arrive at present-day Maryland.
1636	Harvard University is founded.
1642	On June 14, Massachusetts passes the first compulsory education law.
1649	On April 21, the Toleration Act is passed in Maryland, providing for religious freedom.
1652	On May 18, Rhode Island passes a law declaring slavery illegal.
1662	On April 23, Connecticut is chartered as a British colony.
1664	On June 24, the colony of New Jersey is established.
1665	On June 12, the Dutch colony of New Amsterdam becomes a British territory and is named New York after the English Duke of York.
1681	On March 1, William Penn receives a charter to start a colony in what would become known as Pennsylvania.
1682	On June 18, William Penn founds the city of Philadelphia.
1701	Yale University is founded.
1718	The city of New Orleans is founded.
1721	On May 21, South Carolina becomes a royal colony.
1733	James Oglethorpe begins the colony of Georgia.

1734	New York printer John Peter Zenger is arrested for seditious libel (he is later acquitted).
1746	Princeton College receives its charter.
1749	On May 19, King George II authorizes the Ohio Company to settle the region that became known as the Ohio Valley.
1751	On May 11, Pennsylvania Hospital is founded—the first hospital in what would become the United States of America.
1752	On May 10, Benjamin Franklin conducts his famous kite-flying, lightning experiment.
1765	On March 22, the British Parliament enacts the Stamp Act, which imposes a host of taxes on American colonists.
	On August 4, colonists in Massachusetts plant the first liberty tree in protest of what they perceive as autocratic British rules.
	On October 7, the Stamp Act Congress begins meeting in New York.
1769	On June 7, Daniel Boone begins exploring in what is now known as Kentucky.
1770	On March 5, British soldiers fire into a crowd of angry American colonists in what became known as the "Boston Massacre."
1774	On June 13, Rhode Island becomes the first colony to ban the importation of slaves.
1775	On March 23, Virginia politician Patrick Henry delivers his famous "Give me Liberty or Give me Death" speech.
	On April 14, the first abolitionist group forms in Philadelphia.
	On April 18, Paul Revere rode during nighttime hours to warn colonist in Concord of a pending attack by the British.
	On April 19, the Battle of Lexington takes place—the first battle of the Revolutionary War.
	On May 24, John Hancock is elected president of the Continental Congress.
	On June 15, George Washington becomes the commander of the Continental Army.
	On June 17, the Battle of Bunker Hill takes place.
1776	In January, Thomas Paine's work Common Sense is published. It provides support for the cause of American independence.
	On June 10, the Continental Congress forms a committee to work on creating what became known as the Declaration of Independence. The committee consists of Thomas Jefferson, John Adams, Benjamin Franklin, Roger Sherman, and Roger Livingstone.
	On July 4, the Continental Congress approves of the Declaration of Independence drafted principally by Thomas Jefferson. The document includes a series of grievances against English King George III and famously declares that "all men are created equal."
1777	On November 15, the Articles of Confederation is released. This document establishes the structure of the American government.
1778	France signs a treaty with the American forces, becoming its ally in the Revolutionary War against Great Britain.
1781	The British army, under the direction of Lord Charles Cornwallis, surrenders at Yorktown.

1783   The United States and Great Britain sign the Treaty of Paris, ending the Revolutionary War.

1787   On June 19, Oliver Ellsworth of Connecticut introduces a proposal at the Constitutional Convention to call the country the United States.

On Dec. 7, Delaware is admitted as the first state.

On Dec. 12, Pennsylvania is admitted as the second state.

On Dec. 18, New Jersey is admitted as the third state.

1788   On Jan. 2, Georgia is admitted as the fourth state.

On January 9, Connecticut is admitted as the fifth state.

On Feb. 6, Massachusetts is admitted as the sixth state.

On April 28, Maryland is admitted as the seventh state.

On May 23, South Carolina is admitted as the eighth state.

On June 21, New Hampshire is admitted as the ninth state.

On June 25, Virginia is admitted as the tenth state.

1789   On April 1, the U.S. House of Representatives holds its first meeting.

On April 30, George Washington is inaugurated as the first president of the United States.

On June 8, U.S. Representative James Madison (VA) introduces his proposed bill of rights in what is called "The Great Rights of Mankind" speech.

On July 26, New York is admitted as the eleventh state.

On December 21, North Carolina is admitted as the twelfth state.

1790   On May 29, Rhode Island is admitted as the thirteenth tate.

1791   On March 4, Vermont is admitted as the fourteenth state.

1792   On June 1, Kentucky is admitted as the fifteenth state.

1796   On June 1, Tennessee is admitted as the sixteenth state.

1802   On May 3, Washington, DC, is incorporated as a city.

On June 9, the U.S. Academy at West Point is founded.

1803   On February 24, the U.S. Supreme Court decides *Marbury v. Madison*, establishing that the Supreme Court has the power of judicial review and can invalidate acts of Congress that are unconstitutional.

On March 1, Ohio is admitted as the seventeenth state.

On April 30, American ambassador Robert Livingstone and future President James Monroe sign the Louisiana Purchase Treaty, acquiring a huge tract of land of more than 828,000 square miles that covers parts of fifteen present-day states. President Thomas Jefferson announces the treaty to the American public on July 4.

1804   On May 14, Meriwether Lewis and William Clark commence the so-called "Lewis and Clark expedition," heading west from St. Louis.

On July 11, Aaron Burr shoots and kills Alexander Hamilton in a duel in Weehawken, New Jersey.

1806   Future President Andrew Jackson kills Charles Dickinson in a duel after Dickinson insulted Jackson's wife, Rachel.

1807	On March 2, Congress abolishes the African slave trade.
1812	On April 30, Louisiana is admitted as the eighteenth state.
	On December 12, the U.S. declares war on Great Britain, beginning the War of 1812.
1816	On December 11, Indiana is admitted as the nineteenth state.
1817	On December 10, Mississippi is admitted as the twentieth state.
1818	On December 3, Illinois is admitted as the twenty-first state.
1819	On December 14, Alabama is admitted as the twenty-second state.
1820	On March 6, President James Monroe signs the Missouri Compromise. It establishes the dividing lines where slavery is legal and illegal.
	On March 15, Maine is admitted as the twenty-third state.
1821	On August 10, Missouri is admitted as the twenty-fourth state.
1823	On December 2, President James Monroe delivers his annual message to Congress. In the address, he announces his foreign policy positions in statements that are known as "The Monroe Doctrine."
1836	On June 15, Arkansas is admitted as the twenty-fifth state.
1837	On January 6, Michigan is admitted as the twenty-sixth state.
	On May 10, the Panic of 1837 ensues with the failure of many banks.
1840	On May 7, a tornado kills more than 300 people in Natchez, Mississippi.
	On June 20, Samuel Morse patents the telegraph.
1845	On March 3, Florida is admitted as the twenty-seventh state.
	On December 29, Texas is admitted as the twenty-eighth state.
1846	On December 28, Iowa becomes the twenty-ninth state.
1848	On May 29, Wisconsin is admitted as the thirtieth state.
1851	On June 2, Maine passes the first prohibition law on alcohol.
1852	On March 6, the U.S. Supreme Court rules that slaves are property and denies Dred Scott his freedom.
1853	On June 24, President Franklin Pierce signs a measure approving the Gadsden Purchase (much of modern-day New Mexico and part of Arizona) from Mexico.
1858	On May 11, Minnesota is admitted as the thirty-second state.
1859	On February 14, Oregon is admitted as the thirty-third state.
1860	On December 20, South Carolina secedes from the Union.
1861	On Jan. 29, Kansas is admitted as the thirty-fourth state.
	On February 9, the Confederate States are formed with Jefferson Davis installed as President.
	On April 12, Confederate forces fire on the federal garrison Fort Sumter. This is often cited as the beginning of the American Civil War.
	On April 27, President Lincoln suspends the writ of habeas corpus.
	On May 8, Richmond, Virginia, is designated as the capital of the Confederacy.
1862	On April 16, slavery is abolished in the District of Columbia.
	On May 19, the Homestead Act is passed.

1863	On January 1, President Abraham Lincoln issues the Emancipation Proclamation. It proclaims that all persons held as slaves in the rebellious states are freed.
	On June 20, West Virginia is admitted as the thirty-fifth state.
	From July 1–3, the Union army defeats the Confederates at the bloody Battle of Gettysburg.
	On November 19, President Lincoln delivers the Gettysburg Address.
1864	On October 31, Nevada is admitted as the thirty-sixth state.
1865	On January 1, Congress approves the Thirteenth Amendment to the U.S. Constitution, which outlaws slavery and involuntary servitude.
	On April 9, Confederate General Robert E. Lee surrenders to Union General Ulysses S. Grant at Appomattox Court House in Virginia. The Civil War ends a few months later.
	On April 14, John Wilkes Booth assassinates President Lincoln.
	On December 6, the Thirteenth Amendment is ratified by the required number of states.
1866	On April 9, the U.S. Congress passes the Civil Rights Bill of 1866.
1867	On March 1, Nebraska is admitted as the thirty-seventh state.
	On March 30, U.S. Secretary of State William Seward signs a treaty with Russia to purchase the land that forms the state of Alaska. It is called "Seward's Folly."
1868	On February 24, President Andrew Johnson is impeached.
	On May 16, the Senate fails to have enough votes to convict President Johnson of impeachment charges.
	On May 22, the Great Train Robbery takes place in Reno, Nevada. The perpetrators steal nearly $100,000.
1869	On May 15, the National Woman Suffrage Association is formed in New York City.
1875	On June 2, Alexander Graham Bell successfully makes the first electronic transmission of sound.
1876	On August 1, Colorado becomes the thirty-eighth state.
1881	On July 2, President James A. Garfield is assassinated by Charles Guiteau. Vice President Chester A. Arthur succeeds him.
1882	On April 3, notorious outlaw Jesse James is shot and killed by Robert Ford.
	On May 6, Congress passes the Chinese Exclusion Act, ending Chinese immigration.
1885	On February 28, *The Adventures of Huckleberry Finn* is published by author Mark Twain.
1888	On May 7, inventor George Eastman patents his Kodak box camera.
1889	On May 31, the Johnstown Flood leads to death of more than 2,000 in Pennsylvania.
	On November 2, North and South Dakota are admitted as the thirty-ninth and fortieth states.
	On November 8, Montana is admitted as the forty-first state.
	On November 11, Washington is admitted as the forty-second state.
1890	On May 12, Louisiana legalizes the sport of boxing, or prizefighting, as it was commonly called.
	On July 3, Idaho becomes the forty-third state.

1893	The Panic of 1893 begins, highlighted by a severe drop in the New York Stock Exchange.
1894	On May 16, a devastating fire in Boston destroys nearly 200 buildings.
1896	On January 4, Utah is admitted as the forty-fifth state.
	On May 18, the U.S. Supreme Court upholds a Louisiana law mandating racial segregation on railways. The Court justifies the law by the so-called "separate but equal" doctrine.
1899	On April 10, the U.S. and Spain sign the Treaty of Paris, ending the Spanish–American War. As a result of this treaty, Puerto Rico comes under U.S. control.
1900	On April 30, the United States annexes Hawaii.
1901	On September 6, President William McKinley is shot by anarchist Leon Czolgosz. President McKinley dies several days later.
1902	On May 20, the U.S. ends its military occupation in Cuba.
1903	On December 17, brothers Orville and Wilbur Wright complete the first successful airplane flight in Kitty Hawk, North Carolina.
1905	On May 15, the city of Las Vegas, Nevada, is founded.
1906	A horrific earthquake in San Francisco kills more than 450 people.
1907	On November 16, Oklahoma is admitted as the forty-sixth state.
1909	On February 12, the National Association for the Advanced of Colored People (NAACP) forms.
	On April 6, American explorers Robert Peary and Matthew Henson reach the North Pole.
1912	On January 6, New Mexico is admitted as the forty-seventh state.
	On February 4, Arizona is admitted as the forty-eighth state.
1913	On May 31, the Seventeenth Amendment, providing for the direct election of U.S. Senators, is ratified.
1915	On June 9, Secretary of State William Jennings Bryan resigns his cabinet position.
1916	On June 15, the Boy Scouts of America is formed.
1917	The United States enters World War I.
	On April 2, Jeannette Rankin (R, MT) serves her first day in the U.S. House of Representatives.
1918	President Woodrow Wilson outlines his "Fourteen Points" for peace.
1919	On June 4, the Senate passes a women's suffrage measure.
1920	The Eighteenth Amendment (Prohibition amendment) is ratified.
	On August 18, the Nineteenth Amendment is ratified, giving women the right to vote.
1924	On May 10, J. Edgar Hoover is appointed the head of the Federal Bureau of Investigation.
1925	On May 5, teacher John Scopes is arrested in Dayton, Tennessee, for teaching evolution.
1929	On February 14, the Valentine's Day Massacre occurs as a result of a gangland war between gangsters Al Capone and Bugs Moran. Capone orders a hit on Moran's headquarters.
	On May 16, the first Academy Awards ceremony is held.

On October 24, the New York Stock exchange collapses in a day known as "Black Thursday."

1931   On March 19, the Nevada legislature votes to legalize gambling as a way to combat the Great Depression.

1933   On March 12, President Franklin D. Roosevelt broadcasts his first fireside chat to the American public.

On May 18, President Roosevelt signs the Tennessee Valley Authority Act, authorizing the building of damns.

1934   On June 6, the Securities and Exchange Commission (SEC) is established.

1937   On May 3, Margaret Mitchell wins the Pulitzer Prize for her book *Gone with the Wind*.

On May 30, Chicago police fire on striking steel workers in what came to be known as the "Memorial Day Massacre."

1939   On May 16, the U.S. government first issues food stamps.

1940   On May 15, the first McDonald's restaurant is opened in San Bernardino, California.

1941   On June 18, heavyweight champion Joe Louis rallies and knocks out Billy Conn to retain his world heavyweight title.

On December 7, Japanese aircraft bomb U.S. ships docked in Pearl Harbor in Hawaii. This attack led the U.S. to enter into World War II.

1945   On February 23, 1945, U.S. troops display the American flag at Iwo Jima after a brutal battle with Japanese forces.

On August 6, the U.S. drops an atomic bomb over Hiroshima, Japanese. More than 140,000 people died from this attack.

On August 9, the U.S. drops an atomic bomb over Nagasaki, Japan.

1947   On March 12, President Harry Truman announces the so-called "Truman Doctrine" in a message before Congress.

On April 15, Los Angeles Dodger Jackie Robinson becomes the first African American to break the color barrier in major league baseball.

On June 5, Secretary of State George Marshall introduces the so-called "Marshall Plan" to assist West Berlin, which had become surrounded by the USSR occupation of East Germany.

1950   On April 25, Chuck Cooper becomes the first African American to play in an NBA game.

1952   On April 8, President Truman seizes the nation's steel mills to avoid a strike.

1954   On May 17, the U.S. Supreme Court unanimously rules in *Brown v. Board of Education* that segregation in secondary public schools in unconstitutional and violates the Equal Protection Clause of the Fourteenth Amendment.

On June 9, Joseph Welch, head counsel for the U.S. Army, famously asks U.S. Senator Joseph McCarthy "Have you no decency, sir?" during Senate hearings.

1955   On April 10, Dr. Jonas Salk successfully tests a vaccine for the deadly disease polio.

1956   On April 27, Rocky Marciano retires from boxing. The heavyweight champion ended his career with an undefeated record of 49-0.

1959   On January 3, Alaska becomes the forty-ninth state admitted into the United States.

On May 4, the first Grammy Awards are held.

On Aug. 21, Hawaii becomes the fiftieth state.

1961   On March 1, President John F. Kennedy establishes the Peace Corps.

On May 1, Harper Lee wins the Pulitzer Prize for Literature for her book *To Kill a Mockingbird*.

On May 14, a bus carrying the Freedom Riders is attacked and burned in Alabama.

1962   On March 2, Wilt Chamberlain scores 100 points in a professional basketball game.

1963   On April 12, the Children's Crusade in Birmingham, Alabama, receives nationwide attention after the police use fire hoses and dogs on black children protesting civil rights abuses.

On June 10, President Kennedy signs the Equal Pay Act.

On August 28, Dr. Martin Luther King Jr. delivers his historic "I Have a Dream" speech during the March on Washington. Several other civil rights leaders delivered speeches, but Dr. King's is the one that has had the most historic significance.

On November 22, President John F. Kennedy is assassinated while riding in a motorcade in Dallas, Texas.

1964   On February 25, Cassius Marcellus Clay—later known as Muhammad Ali—defeats Charles "Sonny" Liston to win the world heavyweight title.

On July 2, President Johnson signs into law the Civil Rights Act of 1964, arguably the most important civil rights bill of the twentieth century.

1965   On February 21, Malcolm X is assassinated in New York City.

On May 25, Muhammad Ali successfully defends his heavyweight title in Lewiston, Maine, with a first-round stoppage of former champion Sonny Liston. Some claim that Liston took a dive.

1967   On April 27, heavyweight boxing champion Muhammad Ali refuses induction into the U.S. Army and is stripped of his title.

On May 19, the U.S. bombs Hanoi.

On June 3, Aretha Franklin, the so-called "Queen of Soul," hits #1 with her signature song *Respect*.

On June 13, President Johnson nominates Thurgood Marshall as the first African American to serve on the U.S. Supreme Court.

1968   On March 16, 1968, a platoon of American soldiers kills hundreds of unarmed civilians in the so-called Mai Lai Massacre.

On April 4, Dr. Martin Luther King Jr. is assassinated in Memphis, Tennessee, while on the balcony of the second floor of the Lorraine Motel.

On June 3, the Poor Person's March on Washington takes place.

On June 6, Democratic presidential candidate Robert F. Kennedy dies from gunshot wounds at an assassin's hands the previous evening.

1969   On July 20, 1969, *Apollo 11* lands on the Moon. Neil Armstrong becomes the first human to walk on the Moon, followed by crew member Buzz Aldrin. Fellow astronaut Michael Collins remains in orbit in the command spacecraft.

August 15–18, the Woodstock music festival is held in Bethel, New York. It is arguably the high point of the 1960s rock music and hippie era.

1970   On May 1, four students are shot to death by national guardsmen during a disturbance at Kent State University.

On June 22, President Nixon signs the 26th Amendment, lowering the voting age from 21 to 18.

1972   On June 22, President Nixon signs into law Title IX, prohibiting gender discrimination in college sports.

1973   On January 22, the U.S. Supreme Court strikes down a Texas law that criminalized abortion in *Roe v. Wade*.

1974   On April 8, Henry Aaron of the Atlanta Braves hits his 715th career home run, breaking the record of former New York Yankee great Babe Ruth.

On August 8, President Nixon resigns because of fallout from the Watergate scandal. He is the first (and as of now, only) U.S. president to resign from office.

1975   On April 4, Bill Gates and Paul Allen form Microsoft.

1976   On April 1, Stephen Wozniak and Steve Jobs found Apple Computer.

1977   On April 18, Alex Haley wins a Pulitzer Prize for his book *Roots*.

1978   On June 9, Larry Holmes defeats Ken Norton via split decision over 15 rounds to win the world heavyweight championship—a title he would hold until 1985.

1979   On June 18, President Jimmy Carter and Soviet leader Leonid Brezhnev sign the SALT II treaty limiting nuclear weapon.

1980   On June 23, David Letterman's late night show—"The Letterman Show"—debuts on network television.

1981   On January 30, John F. Hinckley Jr. shoots President Ronald Reagan, who later recovers from his wounds.

On May 1, tennis star Billie Jean King announces that she is in a relationship with another woman.

1982   On April 19, Sally Ride becomes the first female astronaut in U.S. history.

On June 21, a jury finds John Hinckley Jr. not guilty by reason of insanity in the shooting of President Ronald Reagan.

On June 24, the Equal Rights Amendment is defeated.

1983   Alice Walker wins the Pulitzer Price for *The Color Purple*.

1986   On January 28, the space shuttle *Challenger* explodes.

On April 20, Chicago Bull guard Michael Jordan scores 63 points in a playoff game against the Boston Celtics.

1991   On May 1, Oakland As star Rickey Henderson steals his 993th base, breaking Lou Brock's all-time record.

1992   On April 29, a state jury in California acquits four officers in the beating of African American motorist Rodney King. This announcement leads to rioting in the city.

1994   On June 17, L.A. police chase a bronco down the freeway carrying legendary football star O.J. Simpson, who is later tried and acquitted for the deaths of his ex-wife, Nicole Brown Simpson, and a companion named Ronald Goldman.

1995   On April 19, the federal office building in Oklahoma City is bombed, killing 168 people and injuring more than 500.

1998	On May 18, the United States and 20 states file an anti-trust action against Microsoft.
1999	On February 12, President Bill Clinton is acquitted in his impeachment trial before the U.S. Senate.
	On April 20, two high school students—Eric Harris and Dylan Klebold—kill 12 other students and one teacher at Columbine High School in Colorado. The two students also kill themselves.
	On May 21, daytime soap opera star Susan Lucci finally wins a Daytime Emmy after 19 previous nominations.
2001	On September 11, 2001, terrorists fly planes into the World Trade Towers in New York City, killing thousands. A second plane crashes into the Pentagon, while a third crashes near Shanksville, Pennsylvania, after passengers try to thwart the highjackers.
2004	Massachusetts becomes the first state to legalize same-sex marriage.
2005	On May 9, the website *The Huffington Post* is formed, featuring a variety of left-leaning commentaries.
	On May 31, a *Vanity Fair* article reveals that former FBI official Mark Felt was the "Deep Throat" source for the Watergate reporting.
2007	On April 16, Virginia Tech student Seung-Hui Cho engages in a deadly massacre, killing more than 30 people on campus before killing himself.
2008	On November 4, Barack Obama is elected the nation's first African American president.
2011	On May 2, U.S. special forces kill 9/11 terrorist leader Osama Bin Laden in Abbottabad, Pakistan.
	On May 25, Oprah Winfrey airs the last episode of her award-winning talk show, *Oprah*.
2012	President Barack Obama announces his support for same-sex marriage.

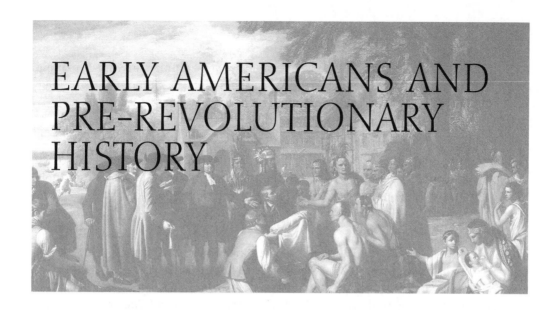

EARLY AMERICANS AND PRE-REVOLUTIONARY HISTORY

EARLY AMERICANS

Who were the first people to inhabit North America?

There is no sure answer to this question, but many historians or paleontologists believe the first people to inhabit what is present-day North America crossed near the Bering Sea, which connects Asia with Alaska. There is a piece of land known as the Bering Strait, which is less than sixty miles long. Many believe that during the Ice Age—sometime between 34,000 B.C.E. and 30,000 B.C.E.—many people crossed the Bering Sea or Bering Strait when it was a land mass to reach North America. While scientists agree that the first people crossed the Bering Strait during the Ice Age, they do not know the identity of these first peoples.

Most scholars also agree that there were several discrete, and perhaps isolated, movements of various peoples from Asia to the Americas. The migrations might have been prompted by population increases in the tribes of central Asia, which impelled some to move eastward in search of food sources—animals. As game moved across the Bering Strait, hunters followed.

Who are the Native Americans?

Native Americans is a term often used to describe American Indians, widely believed to be the first peoples to inhabit the Americas, including North America. Some historians have claimed that at one time there were sixty million Native Americans living on the continent. Their population declined dramatically when they came into contact with Europeans and diseases or epidemics Europeans transmitted.

1

Around 5,000 B.C.E., the disappearance of large game animals in both North and South America produced a series of regional developments, culminating in the emergence of several great civilizations, including the Inca, Maya, and Aztec.

Is there much evidence of these early peoples?

Not much, as it was so long ago. However, archaeologists have found numerous artifacts dating back to at least 12,000 or 10,000 B.C.E. in parts of North America. For example, artifacts from that time period have been found in Alaska, Oregon, and New Mexico.

Who are the Anasazi?

The Anasazi refer to an ancient Pueblo Indian tribe that inhabited parts of the southwestern United States during 10,000 to 5,000 B.C.E. Anasazi is roughly translated to "ancient ones." This ancient Pueblo culture featured adobe buildings and beautiful baskets. They are sometimes referred to as the "Basket Makers." The ancient Pueblo peoples were also known for their mastery of pottery.

What were mounds?

Mounds, also known as earthworks, were man-made piles of land and/or rocks created by early Indians in the United States. There is evidence of mounds in Louisiana and Florida dating back to at least 3,000 B.C.E. There is a mound complex known as Watson

The Escalante pueblo in Colorado is an example of ruins left behind by the Anasazi people, who occupied it in the twelfth century.

Brake in Louisiana that is believed to be the oldest mound complex in North America. Historians date this complex to around 3,500 B.C.E.

What was the environment of the first Americans?

The original people of North America lived in many different types of environments. On the eastern side of North America, Native Americans lived in woodlands, hunting elk and deer. On the grass plains of the Midwest, Native Americans hunted camel and other mammals—some of whom are extinct on this continent. In the desert regions of the Southwest, Native Americans relied on the gathering of seeds and smaller animals. In the Arctic north, there was much more hunting and fishing.

What were the first crops developed by the early Indian cultures?

The earliest crops were squash and chili in the southwestern United States. The Native Americans also developed corn, or maize, as an early crop. They then started cultivating various types of beans.

THE FIRST EUROPEANS
TO REACH AMERICA

Who was the first European to reach North America?

Many believe the first European to reach North America was a Norse explorer named Leif Ericsson (970–1020), who arguably reached North America around 1,000 B.C.E.—more than 400 years before Christopher Columbus. He established a small Norse settlement known as Vinland in what is now modern-day Newfoundland in Canada. Ericksson was born in Iceland and was the son of the famous explorer Erik the Red (950–1003).

About 1001, Ericsson set out from Greenland with a crew of thirty-five men and probably landed on the southern end of Baffin Island, due north of the province of Quebec. The expedition likely made it to Labrador, Newfoundland (on the northeastern North American mainland), and later landed on the coast of what is today Nova Scotia or Newfoundland, Canada; this landfall may have been at L'Anse aux Meadows (on Newfoundland Island). Ericson and his crew spent the winter of 1001–1002 at a place he called Vinland, which was described as well wooded and produced fruit, especially grapes. He returned to Greenland in the spring of 1002.

Who was Christopher Columbus?

Christopher Columbus, or Christoforo Columbo (1451–1506), was an Italian-born explorer best known for his multiple voyages to the Americas, or the so-called "New World." Columbus studied maps and had a fascination for seafaring exploration. He initially approached King John II of Portugal about funding his explorations to the New World that Columbus knew existed. King John rejected his proposals after asking sev-

How did America get its name?

America is derived from the name of Italian navigator Amerigo Vespucci (1454–1512), who took part in several early voyages to the New World. Vespucci had been a merchant in service of the Medici family in Florence. He later moved to Spain, where he worked for the company that outfitted the ships for Christopher Columbus's (1451–1506) second and third voyages. He sailed with the Spaniards on several expeditions (in 1497, 1499, 1501, and 1503).

Though scholars today question his role as an explorer, in a work by German mapmaker Martin Waldseemüller (c. 1470–c. 1520) published in 1507, the author credited Vespucci with realizing that he had actually arrived in a New World—not in the Far East, as other explorers (including Columbus) had believed. Thus, Waldseemüller suggested the new lands be named America after Amerigo Vespucci. For his part, Waldseemüller was led to believe this by Vespucci himself, who had written to Lorenzo de Medici in 1502 or 1503, relaying his discovery of a new continent and vividly describing it.

The designation "America" was used again in 1538 by Flemish cartographer Gerardus Mercator (Gerhard Kremer; 1512–1594). Today the term in the singular refers to either continent in the Western Hemisphere and sometimes specifically to the United States. In the plural, it refers to all the lands of the Western Hemisphere, including North and South America and the West Indies.

eral of his expert advisors, who cautioned that the distance to this new land had been underestimated by Columbus. The explorer again asked King John, but the king became more interested in explorations to Africa, as Portugese explorer Bartolomeu Dias (1451–1500) had just sailed by the southernmost point of the African continent. King John wanted to focus exploratory activities in that region.

Columbus then presented his plans to the monarchs of Spain—King Ferdinand II of Aragon (1452–1516) and Queen Isabella of Castile (1451–1504). They eventually approved Columbus's exploits. They designated Columbus with the title "Admiral of the Seas," although it is speculated that they expected him to not be successful and return to Spain.

Where did Christopher Columbus first land in the New World?

Columbus set sail from Palos, in southwest Spain, on August 3, 1492, and he sighted land on October 12 that year. Going ashore, he named it San Salvador, alternately called Watlings Island (a present-day island in the Bahamas). With his fleet of three vessels, the *Nina*, the *Pinta*, and the *Santa Maria*, Columbus then continued west and south, sailing along the north coast of Cuba and Haiti (which he named Hispaniola). When the *Santa Maria* ran aground, Columbus left a colony of about forty men on the Haitian coast where they built a fort, which, being Christmastime, they named La Navidad ("Christmas" in Spanish).

In January 1493, Columbus set sail for home, arriving back in Palos on March 15 with a few "Indians" (Native Americans), as well as some belts, aprons, bracelets, and gold. News of his successful voyage spread rapidly, and Columbus journeyed to Barcelona, Spain, where he was triumphantly received by Ferdinand and Isabella.

On his second voyage, which he undertook on September 25, 1493, he sailed with a fleet of seventeen ships and some fifteen hundred men. In November he reached Dominica, Guadeloupe, Puerto Rico, and the Virgin Islands. Upon returning to Haiti (Hispaniola), Columbus found the colony at La Navidad had been de-

Although famed explorer Christopher Columbus made multiple treks to the New World, he never actually landed in North America.

stroyed by natives. In December 1493, he made a new settlement at Isabella (present-day Dominican Republic, the eastern portion of Hispaniola), which became the first European town in the New World. Before returning to Spain in 1496, Columbus also landed in Jamaica.

On his third voyage, which he began in May 1498, Columbus reached Trinidad, just off the South American coast. On his fourth and last trip, he reached the island of Martinique before arriving on the North American mainland at Honduras (in Central America). It was also on this voyage, in May 1502, that he sailed to the Isthmus of Panama—finally believing himself to be near China. But Columbus suffered many difficulties and in November 1504 returned to Spain for good. He had, of course, never found the westward sea passage to the Indies in the Far East. Nevertheless, the Caribbean islands he discovered came to be known collectively as the West Indies. And the native peoples of North and South America came to be known collectively as "Indians."

Why does controversy surround Christopher Columbus?

History wrongly billed Columbus as "the discoverer" of the New World. The native peoples living in the Americas before the arrival of Christopher Columbus truly discovered these lands. It is more accurate to say that Columbus was the first European to discover the New World, and there he encountered its native peoples.

But it was for his treatment of these native peoples that Columbus is a controversial figure. Columbus was called back from the New World twice (on his second and third voyages) for investigation regarding his dealings with the Native Americans, including charges of cruelty. The first inquiry (1496–1497) turned out favorably for the explorer. His case was heard before the Spanish king, and charges were dismissed. However, troublesome rumors continued to follow Columbus, and in 1500 he and two of his brothers (Bartholomeo and Diego) were arrested and sent back to Spain in chains.

Though later released and allowed to continue his explorations (making one final trip to the New World), Columbus never regained his former stature, lost all honor, and died in poverty in the Spanish city of Valladolid in 1506.

SPANISH CONQUERORS AND EXPLORERS

Who were the Conquistadors?

Conquistador is the Spanish word for conqueror. The Spaniards who arrived in North and South America in the late 1400s and early 1500s were just that—conquerors of the American Indians and their lands. In many cases, the Spaniards were the first Europeans to arrive in these lands, where they encountered native inhabitants including the Aztec of Mexico, the Maya of southern Mexico and Central America, and the Inca of western South America. By the mid–1500s these native peoples had been conquered, their populations decimated by the conquistadors. The conquest happened in two ways: First, the Spaniards rode on horseback and carried guns, while their native opponents were on foot and carried crude weapons, such as spears and knives; second, the European adventurers brought illnesses (such as smallpox and measles) to which the native populations of the Americas had no immunities, causing the people to become sick and die.

By 1535 conquistadors such as Francisco Pizarro (c. 1475–1541), Hernéan Cortés (1485–1547), and Vasco Núñez de Balboa (1475–1519) had claimed the southwestern United States, Mexico, Central America, and much of the West Indies (Caribbean islands) for Spain.

Who was Ponce de León?

Juan Ponce de León (1474–1521) was a Spanish conquistador who explored Puerto Rico for the Spanish crown and who also ventured into modern-day Florida. De León became the first governor of Puerto Rico and the first Spanish explorer to "discover" Florida. De León actually named the "Sunshine State" *La Florida*, translated as "Flowery Land."

De León traveled to Florida in search of the mythical Fountain of Youth. De León had traveled with Christopher Columbus in his second (1493) mission to the New World. During Columbus's missions, the Spanish established a colony called Hispaniola. De León would later serve in a leading capacity in that region under Governor Nicolas de Ovando.

Ovando later named De León governor of Puerto Rico in 1509. Spanish King Ferdinand II convinced De León to explore other lands, leading De León to his voyage to

Florida. He led an expedition of three ships—including the *Santiago*, the *San Christobal*, and the *Santa Maria*—on the mission.

A tiny town in Holmes County, Florida, called Ponce de León, is named after the famous explorer.

What areas of present-day America did Hernando de Soto explore?

Spanish explorer Hernando de Soto (c. 1500–1542) ventured throughout the Southeast before he caught fever and died along the banks of the Mississippi River.

Having been part of a brutal expedition that crushed the Inca Empire (in present-day Peru), in 1536 de Soto returned to Spain a hero. But he sought to return to the New World and got his wish when King Charles I (1500–1558) appointed him governor of Cuba and authorized him to conquer and colonize the region that is now the southeastern United States.

Arriving in Florida in the winter of 1539, de Soto and an army of about six hundred men headed north during the following spring and summer. In search of gold and silver, they traveled through present-day Georgia, North and South Carolina, and the Great Smoky Mountains, and into Tennessee, Georgia, and Alabama. After defeating the Choctaw leader Tuscaloosa in October 1540 in south-central Alabama, the Spaniards headed north and west into Mississippi. They crossed the Mississippi River on May 21, 1540, and de Soto died later that same day. Since he had shown no mercy in his con-

Spanish explorer Hernando de Soto was the first European to see the Mississippi River, which he discovered in 1541, as portrayed in this 1853 painting by William Henry Powell.

The European explorers brought with them many things that were previously unknown in the Americas. When Christopher Columbus landed at Hispaniola in 1492, he carried with him horses and cattle. These were the first seen in the Western Hemisphere; the American Indians had no beasts of burden prior to the Europeans' arrival. In subsequent trips, Europeans introduced horses and livestock (including cattle, sheep, pigs, goats, and chickens) throughout South and North America. They later carried plants from Europe and the East back to the Americas, where they took hold. These included rice, sugar, indigo, wheat, and citrus fruits—all of which became established in the Western Hemisphere and became important crops during colonial times. With the exception of indigo (which was used as a fabric dye), these nonindigenous crops remain important to the countries of North and South America.

quests of the native peoples, de Soto's troops sunk his body in the river so it would not be discovered and desecrated by the Indians. Then his army continued on without him; under the direction of Luis de Moscoso, they reached Mexico in 1541.

What was the claim to fame of Balboa?

Vasco Núñez de Balboa (1475–1519) was a Spanish explorer best known for laying claim as the first European to lead an expedition to see the Pacific Ocean. He set sail for the New World, eventually landing in modern-day Colombia. He established the first colonial settlement established by the conquistadors in mainland America at Santa Maria la Antigua del Darren. Balboa became governor of the area. He also crossed the Isthmus of Panama and "discovered" the South Sea.

Were the Spaniards the first Europeans to reach North America after the Vikings?

No, that distinction goes to explorer John Cabot (c. 1451–1498), who in 1497 sailed westward from Bristol, England, in search of a trade route to the East. Cabot's story began in 1493, when Columbus returned to Spain from his New World voyage, claiming to have reached Asia. From the accounts of the trip, Cabot, who was himself a navigator, believed it was unlikely Columbus had traveled that far. He did, however, believe it was possible (as did subsequent explorers) to find a route—a northwest passage—that ran north of the landmass Columbus had discovered and by which Asia could be reached. In 1495 the Italian Cabot—born Giovanni Caboto—took his family to England, and in March 1496, appealed to King Henry VII (1457–1509) for his endorsement to pursue the plan. For his part, King Henry, well aware of the claims made by the Spanish and

Portuguese who had sponsored their own explorations, was eager to find new lands to rule. Accordingly, he granted a patent authorizing Cabot's expedition.

Later that year, Cabot set sail, but problems aboard the ship and foul weather forced him to turn back. On May 20, 1497, he sailed again, in a small ship christened "Matthew." The crew of twenty included Cabot's son, Sebastian. On June 24, they sighted land, and Cabot went ashore. While he saw signs of human habitation, he encountered no one. From reports of the trip, scholars believe Cabot reached the coasts of present-day Maine, Nova Scotia, and probably Newfoundland. He then sailed home, returning to England on August 6, 1497. He reported to the king six days later and was given both a reward and authorization for a more sizeable expedition, undertaken in May 1498. Cabot set sail with five ships in his command, but the expedition was not heard from again.

COLONIAL AMERICA

What were the Spanish holdings in the New World?

New Spain comprised many of the Spanish possessions in the New World during the colonial period. At its height, New Spain included what are today the southwestern United States; all of Mexico; Central America to the Isthmus of Panama; Florida; much of the West Indies (islands in the Caribbean); and the Philippines (in the Pacific Ocean). The viceroyalty (province governed by a representative of the monarch) was governed from the capital at Mexico City beginning in 1535. In 1821, a Mexican rebellion ended Spanish rule there, and the colonial empire of New Spain dissolved. By 1898, after Spain lost the Spanish–American War, Spain had ceded all its possessions in North America. Its last holdings were the islands of Cuba, Puerto Rico, Guam, and the Philippines.

During the colonial period, Spain also claimed other territories in the New World—in northern and western South America. Most of these holdings fell under the viceroyalty of Peru, which was administered separately from the viceroyalty of New Spain. These possessions were also lost by Spain by the end of the 1800s.

What were the French holdings in the New World?

The French possessions in North America, called New France, consisted of the colonies of Canada, Acadia, and Louisiana. The first land claims were made in 1534 by French explorer Jacques Cartier (1491–1557) as he sailed the St. Lawrence River in eastern Canada. In 1604, Sieur de Monts (Pierre du Gua; c. 1568–c. 1630) established a settlement at Acadia (in present-day Nova Scotia, Canada), and French claims later extended the region to include what are today the province of New Brunswick, Canada, and the eastern part of Maine. After founding Quebec in 1608, explorer Samuel de Champlain (c. 1567–1635) penetrated the interior (present-day Ontario) as far as Georgian Bay on Lake Huron, extending French land claims westward.

In 1672, French-Canadian explorer Louis Jolliet (1645–1700) and French missionary Jacques Marquette (1637–1675) became the first Europeans to discover the upper part of the Mississippi River. Ten years later, French explorer Sieur de La Salle (1643–1687) followed the Mississippi to the Gulf of Mexico, claiming the river valley for France and naming it Louisiana. While the French expanded their North American claims, the majority of French settlers lived in Canada. France lost Canada to Great Britain in the Seven Years' War (1756–1763). Louisiana changed hands numerous times before it was finally sold to the United States in 1803 as part of the Louisiana Purchase; it was France's last claim on the North American mainland. French culture and influence in these areas remains prevalent today.

In 1635, the French also claimed the West Indies islands of Martinique and Guadeloupe (and its small surrounding islands, including Saint Barthélemy). In 1946, the French government changed the status of these islands from colonies to "overseas departments."

Who was the proprietor of French-owned Louisiana in the early eighteenth century?

Antoine Crozat (1655–1738) was a wealthy French businessman (merchant) who effectively ruled French-owned Louisiana in the early eighteenth century. In 1712, French King Louis XIV gave Crozat a trade monopoly in the Louisiana territory. The monopoly lasted until 1717.

What was the "Lost Colony"?

It was the second English colony established in America. Set up in 1587 on Roanoke Island, off the coast of North Carolina, by 1590 it disappeared without a trace. Theories surround the disappearance, though it is not known for certain what happened. Some speculate the colonists fell victim to disease. Others have posited that perhaps some hostile Indians killed the colonists.

Roanoke Island had also been the site of the first English colony, set up in 1585 by about 100 men sent there by Sir Walter Raleigh (1554–1618). Raleigh had perceived the island to be a good spot for English warships (that were then fighting the Spanish) to be repaired and loaded with new supplies. But the plan was unsuccessful: The land wasn't sufficiently fertile to support both the colonists and the Indians living nearby, and because the surrounding sea proved too shallow, ships could not get close enough to the island. The colonists returned to England in 1586. In the meantime, Raleigh dispatched a second group of colonists from England. They arrived at Roanoke just days after the original settlers left. Seeing that the site had been abandoned, all but fifteen of the colonists opted to return to England.

In the spring of 1587, Raleigh sent a third group of colonists to America, but these ships were headed for areas near Chesapeake Bay, farther north (in present-day Virginia). Reaching the Outer Banks in July, the ships' commander refused to take the colonists to their destination and instead left them at Roanoke Island. The colonists' leader, John White, who had also been among the first settlers at Roanoke, returned to

England for supplies in August 1587. However, a war between England and Spain prevented his return until three years later. Arriving back at Roanoke in August 1590, he expected to be met by family members and the hundred or so settlers (including some women and children). Instead, he discovered the colony had been abandoned.

The only clue White found was the word CROATOAN engraved on a tree. The Croatoan, or Hatteras, were friendly Indians who lived on an island south of Roanoke Island. White set out to see if the colonists had joined the Indians, but bad weather prevented the search, and his expedition returned to England instead.

Two theories explain what might have become of the lost colonists. Since the shore of Chesapeake Bay was their original destination, the colonists might have moved there but, encountering resistance, perished at the hands of the Indians. Other evidence suggests that the colonists became integrated with several Indian tribes living in North Carolina. Either way, no European ever saw them again.

What was Jamestown?

Jamestown, Virginia, is considered the first permanent English colony in the New World. In April 1607, a group of settlers under the auspices of the Virginia Company arrived at the James River and created the Jamestown settlement. They arrived by three ships: the *Susan Constant*, the *Godspeed,* and the *Discovery*. The settlers searched in vain for gold and suffered through what historian Robert V. Remini calls "the starving season."

Led by military leader Captain John Smith (1579–1631), the colonists managed to survive. The colonists interacted with a powerful Indian chief named Wahunsonacock,

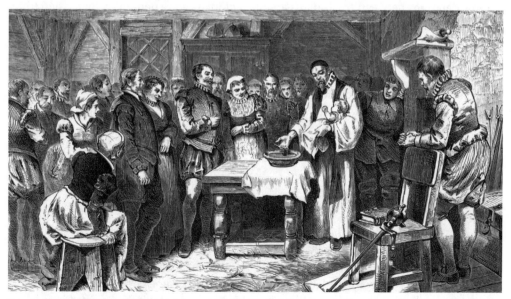

Born to Eleanor and Ananias Dare on August 18, 1587, Virginia Dare was the first person born to English parents in the New World. She disappeared along with the rest of the Roanoke colony.

or Powhatan (?–1618). Relations were uneasy at times, but the colonists and the Indians managed to carve out a largely peaceful existence. This was helped by the marriage of Powhatan's daughter, Pocahontas (1595–1617) to English planter John Rolfe (1585–1622), the first recorded interracial marriage in North America. Rolfe was best known for successfully cultivating tobacco.

After whom was the colony of Jamestown named?

It was named after the English king at the time, James I (1566–1635), the first of the Stuart kings. He was King James VI of Scotland before the Scottish and English crowns were united. His mother was Mary, Queen of Scots. He succeeded Elizabeth I (1533–1603), who was also known as the Virgin Queen. Because Elizabeth I had no children, the crown passed to James. King James disliked tobacco and even wrote a treatise entitled *A Counterblaste to Tobacco* (1604), in which he called tobacco a "filthy habit."

What happened to John Rolfe?

He traveled back to Virginia after losing Pocahontas. He began farming and working on his plantation. He remarried Jane Pierce, with whom he had a daughter. Unfortunately, Rolfe died in 1622 after an attack by Native Americans. It is unknown whether Rolfe died directly during the attack or from an illness contracted shortly afterward.

What was the Jamestown Massacre?

The Jamestown Massacre, or the Indian Massacre of 1622, was an attack by the Powhatan Indians on the Jamestown colony that led to more than 340 deaths suffered by the colony. Relations between the Indians and the colonists were generally good when Chief Powhatan was alive. However, after Chief Powhatan's death in 1618, his half-brother, Chief Opechancanough (1554–1646), led a series of attacks upon the colony. Under his reign, Opechancanough participated in the Second and Third Anglo-Powhatan Wars.

What happened to Chief Opechancanough?

Chief Opechancanough lived more than ninety years. Some historians list his age as more than one hundred. During the Third Anglo-Powhatan War, begun in 1644, the colonists captured him. A soldier assigned to guard the chief allegedly shot and killed him.

How did Pocahontas die?

Most historians believe Pocahontas contracted smallpox, causing her death at only twenty-two. In 1716, Rolfe and Pocahontas traveled to England, where Pocahontas was treated very well. In 1717, the couple boarded a ship and planned to return to Virginia. En route to Jamestown, Pocahontas became very ill. She was taken ashore and died a few days later. She was buried in Gravesend's St. George Church.

What legislative body was created in Jamestown?

The Virginia House of Burgesses was created in Jamestown, becoming the first legislative body of elected members in North America. It held its first meeting on July 30, 1619. It was the governing body of the colony of Virginia until it was replaced by the Virginia House of Delegates in 1776.

THE PILGRIMS AND THE PURITANS

Were the Pilgrims explorers?

The Pilgrims were early settlers who sought religious freedom and self-government in the New World. Since theirs was a religious journey, they described themselves as pilgrims. In fact, they were Separatists, Protestants who separated from the Anglican Church to set up their own church. In 1609, they fled their home in Scrooby, England, settling in Holland. Fearing their children would lose contact with their own culture (becoming assimilated into the Dutch culture), the group decided to voyage to America to establish their own community. In 1620, they arrived on the rocky western shore of Cape Cod Bay, Massachusetts. Their transatlantic crossing aboard the *Mayflower* took sixty-six days. Two babies were born during the passage, bringing the number of settlers to 102. Only some thirty-five were Pilgrims; the rest were merchants. On November 21, 1620, the Pilgrims drafted the Mayflower Compact, an agreement by which the forty-one signatories (the men aboard the *Mayflower*) formed a body politic authorized to enact and enforce laws for the community. The Compact's members elected religious leader John Carver (1576–1621) governor. Although their colonial charter from the London Company specified they were to settle in Virginia, the Compact's members decided to establish their colony at Cape Cod, well outside the company's jurisdiction. By December 25, 1620, the Pilgrims had chosen the site for their settlement and began building at New Plymouth.

During the first year, the Pilgrims faced many hardships: thirty-five more colonists arrived aboard the *Fortune*, straining already limited resources; sicknesses such as pneumonia, tuberculosis, and scurvy claimed many lives, including that of Governor Carver; and the merchants in the group challenged the purity of the settlement. Having secured a new patent from the Council of New England in June 1621, the lands of New Plymouth Colony were held in common by both the Pilgrims and the merchants. However, this communal system of agriculture proved unsuccessful. In 1624, William Bradford (1590–1657), who succeeded Carver as governor, granted each family its own parcel of land. The Wampanoag Indians, who had previously occupied the land settled by the Pilgrims, proved friendly and helpful advisers in agricultural matters. In 1626, the Pilgrims bought out the merchants' shares, claiming the colony for themselves. Although inexperienced at governing before arriving in America, and despite a lack of formal education, the Pilgrims successfully governed themselves according to the Scriptures. Ply-

A reconstructed village designed to be historically accurate as to what the settlement of Plymouth looked like is run by the Plimoth Plantation museum in Massachusetts. It serves as an education center for people to learn both about the Pilgrims and the native peoples they encountered.

mouth Colony remained independent until 1691, when it became part of the Massachusetts Bay Colony—founded by the Puritans.

How were the Puritans different from the Pilgrims?

The Puritans who founded Massachusetts Bay Colony were, like the Pilgrims, religious Protestants (both sects "protested" against the Anglican church). But while the Pilgrims separated from the church, the Puritans wished to purify it. Their religious movement began in England during the 1500s, and they were influenced by the teachings of reformer John Calvin (1509–1564). They also had strong feelings about government, maintaining that people can only be governed by a contract (such as a constitution) that limits a ruler's powers. When King James I (1566–1625) ascended the throne of England, he was the first ruler of the House (royal family) of Stuart. The Stuart monarchs, particularly James's successor, King Charles I (1600–1649), tried to enforce absolute adherence to the High Church of Anglicanism and viewed the Puritan agitators as a threat to the crown's authority.

Persecuted by the throne, groups of Puritans fled England for the New World. One group was granted a corporate charter for the Massachusetts Bay Company (1629). Unlike other such contracts, which provided the framework to establish colonies in America, this one did not require its stockholders to hold their meetings in England. Stockholders who made the voyage across the Atlantic would become voting citizens in their own settlement; the board of directors would form the legislative assembly; and the company president, Puritan leader John Winthrop (1588–1649), would become governor. In 1630, they settled in present-day Boston and Salem, Massachusetts, establishing a Puritan Commonwealth. By 1643, more than twenty thousand Puritans arrived in Massachusetts during what was called the Great Migration. Puritans also settled in Rhode Island, Connecticut, and Virginia during the colonial period.

What were the Salem Witch Trials?

The Salem Witch trials were a series of trials in colonial Massachusetts in 1692 and 1693 that resulted in the execution of many women (and one man) accused of witchcraft. The trials did not occur only in Salem but also in surrounding towns. Many of those charged were women who were a little different, who did not subscribe to the tenets of the Puritan Church and who were all outcasts of some sort. Some of the women wore black clothing and allegedly lived an immoral lifestyle.

The Salem Witch Trials today are seen as a form of mass hysteria, of community judgment gone overboard, and as exemplifying the lack of due process and fair trial procedures. For example, Bridget Bishop (1632–1692) was the first person charged in the Salem Witch Trials. She was indicted and tried on June 2, 1692, and executed on June 10. Much of the testimony of people who claimed to have been afflicted by the defendants was very dubious.

Who was Roger Williams?

Roger Williams (1603–1683) was an English theologian best known for his early defense of religious freedom and for the principle of separation of church and state. Williams learned under the great English jurist Sir Edward Coke (1552–1634). Williams later traveled to the Puritan colony of Massachusetts. However, Williams ran afoul of authorities in Salem, particularly after he questioned the close ties between the Puritan church and the Church of England. He was charged and convicted of heresy and sedition. He managed to escape to a new land that he called Providence, where he believed God had guided him to establish a new church and community. Williams is considered the founder of Rhode Island. He also opposed slavery and believed in treating Indian tribes with respect for their cultures.

Who was Anne Hutchinson?

Anne Hutchinson (1591–1643) was a Puritan religious leader who was banished from the Massachusetts Bay Colony for her dissident religious views. She preached a so-called "covenant of grace," emphasizing the importance of individual communication with God and the importance of divine grace. This offended many orthodox Puritans, who adhered to a view that emphasized the importance of religious figures and of good works. Hutchinson was referred to as an antinomian, a person who believes that one can achieve salvation through grace alone. Gender bias also played a role in Hutchinson's treatment, as she ruffled the feathers of some male religious leaders. After being expelled from the colony in 1638, she fled to Rhode Island. She and her family were killed by Siwanoy Indians in the so-called "Hutchinson Massacre."

Who was Thomas Hooker?

Thomas Hooker (1586–1647) was a religious leader in the Massachusetts Bay Colony who inspired jealousy and ire among other religious leaders. A popular preacher, Hooker left the Massachusetts Colony rather than face expulsion. He and a group of his followers formed the colony of Connecticut; Hooker is called "the Father of Connecticut." He contributed greatly to the written founding document of the Connecticut colony, "the Fundamental Orders of Connecticut," a progenitor to later written constitutions. Some consider it the first written constitution in colonial America. The Orders provided for expanded suffrage and more freedom than existed in Massachusetts.

DUTCH AND SWEDISH COLONISTS

What were the Dutch colonial holdings?

New Netherlands was the only Dutch colony on the North American mainland. It consisted of lands surrounding the Hudson River (in present-day New York) and, later, the lower Delaware River (in New Jersey and Delaware). Explorers from the Netherlands first settled the area around 1610. In 1624, the colony of New Netherlands was officially founded by the Dutch West India Company. On behalf of the company, in 1626 Dutch colonial official Peter Minuit (1580–1638) purchased the island of Manhattan from the

An etching depicting English explorer Henry Hudson meeting Indians at Sandy Hook, New York, in 1609.

What were the Swedish colonial holdings?

The Swedish possessions consisted of a small colony called New Sweden, established in 1638 at Fort Christina (present-day Wilmington), Delaware. The Swedes gradually extended the settlement from the mouth of the Delaware Bay (south of Wilmington) northward along the Delaware River as far as present-day Trenton, New Jersey. The settlers were mostly fur traders, although there was farming in the colony as well. In 1655, the territory was taken by the Dutch in a military expedition led by Director-General of New Netherlands, Peter Stuyvesant (c. 1610–1672). For nine years, the territory was part of the Dutch colonial claims called New Netherlands. In 1664, the English claimed it and the rest of New Netherlands. Delaware was set up as a British proprietary colony and remained so until the outbreak of the American Revolution (1775–1783).

American Indians for an estimated $24 in trinkets. The colonial capital of New Amsterdam (present-day New York City) was established there. The Dutch held the colony until 1664, when it was conquered by the English under the direction of King Charles II's brother James II, the Duke of York (1633–1701). The English sought the territory since New Netherlands separated its American holdings. While under British control, the area was divided into two colonies: New Jersey and New York.

During the colonial period, the Netherlands also claimed the West Indies islands of Aruba, Bonaire, and Curaçao (the present-day Netherlands Antilles), which were administered separately from New Netherlands on the North American mainland.

Who was Henry Hudson?

Henry Hudson (1560–1611) was an English-born explorer whose most notable exploits were carried out under the banner of the Dutch East India Company. Hudson sailed mainly in North America, originally to find a passage in the Northwest that would take him to present-day China. Unsuccessful in those attempts, Hudson did discover many areas in North America in the present-day New York region. For the Dutch East India Company, he established Dutch claim to many lands in New York. The Hudson River, which runs through eastern New York, bears his name.

What are the origins of slavery in America?

The roots of slavery in North America date back to about 1400, when the Europeans arrived in Africa. At first, the result of African contact with Europeans was positive, opening trade routes and expanding markets. Europeans profited from Africa's rich mineral and agricultural resources and for a while abided by local laws governing their trade; Africans benefited from new technologies and products brought by the Europeans. But the relationship between the two cultures soon turned disastrous as the Europeans cast their attention on

17

a decidedly different African resource—the people themselves. As the Portuguese in West and East Africa began trading in human lives and the Dutch in South Africa clashed with the native people who—once displaced by the wars—became servants and slaves, other Europeans began calculating the profits that could be made in the slave trade.

By the end of the 1400s, Europeans had landed in the New World. Soon Europe's established and emerging powers vied to control territories in the new lands of North and South America and the West Indies. The Spaniards, Portuguese, Dutch, English, and Swedes all made claims in the Western Hemisphere and began setting up colonies.

By the mid–1600s, triangular patterns of trade emerged. The most common route began on Africa's West Coast, where ships picked up slaves. The second stop was the Caribbean islands—predominately the British and French West Indies—where the slaves were sold to plantation owners and traders, who used the profits to purchase sugar, molasses, tobacco, and coffee. These raw materials were then transported north to the third stop, New England, where a rum industry was thriving. There, ships were loaded with the spirits before traders made the last leg of their journey back across the Atlantic to Africa's West Coast, where the process began again. Other trade routes operated as follows: 1) manufactured goods were transported from Europe to the African coast; slaves to the West Indies; and sugar, tobacco, and coffee back to Europe, where the route began again; and 2) lumber, cotton, and meat were transported from the colonies to southern Europe; wine and fruits to England; and manufactured goods to the colonies, where the route began again. There were as many possible routes as there were ports and demand for goods.

The tragic result of the triangular trade was the transport of an estimated ten million Africans. Sold into slavery, these human beings were often chained below deck and allowed only brief—if any—periods of exercise during the transatlantic crossing, which came to be called the Middle Passage. Conditions for the slaves were brutal, improving only slightly when traders realized that should slaves perish during the long journey across the ocean, it would adversely affect their profits upon arrival in the West Indies. After Caribbean economies crashed at the end of the 1600s, many slaves were sold to plantation owners on the North American mainland, initiating another tragic trade route. The slave trade was abolished in the 1800s, putting an end to the forced migration of Africans to the Western Hemisphere.

When did the first Africans arrive in the British colonies of North America?

In 1619, a Dutch ship carrying twenty Africans landed at Jamestown, Virginia. They were put to work as servants, not as slaves. Though they had fewer rights than their white counterparts, they were able to gain their freedom and acquire property, which prompted the development of a small class of "free Negroes" in colonial Virginia. For example, there is record of one Anthony Johnson arriving in Virginia in 1621 as a servant. He was freed one year later, and about thirty years after that he imported five servants himself, receiving from Virginia 250 acres of land for so doing.

OTHER ENGLISH COLONISTS

Who founded Pennsylvania?

William Penn (1644–1718), a prominent English real estate magnate and son of a British admiral, founded the province of Pennsylvania with the permission of King Charles II in 1681. He later founded the city Philadelphia, Greek for "brotherly love." Penn, a Quaker, wanted to found a colony in which Quakers could live in peace and not be prosecuted. Penn sometimes referred to his plan as the "Holy Experiment." King Charles II named the area Pennsylvania after Penn's father. Penn created a charter of liberties that included freedoms later found in the U.S. Bill of Rights—individual liberties such as the right to an impartial trial and trial by jury.

In what publication did William Penn establish an early constitution?

Penn wrote *Frame for Government*, a detailed plan for the government of Pennsylvania. It provides for a representative body of officials who accept or reject legislation from the council of the government. It provided for freedom of worship and limited the death penalty to only the most violent of crimes. It also provided for a bicameral form of government and is viewed as an important precursor to American democracy.

Who were the Carolinas named after?

Both North Carolina and South Carolina were named after English King Charles II (1630–1685). The two were initially one British territory or province. However, in 1712 the two officially split into separate British provinces. By 1729, both provinces became royal colonies.

Who founded the colony of Georgia?

General James Oglethorpe (1696–1785) founded the colony of Georgia with the permission of King George II of England—for whom the colony was named. Oglethorpe petitioned to create this colony to house many who were imprisoned for debt in England and also for some Protestants persecuted for their religious beliefs. Oglethorpe landed in South Carolina and moved his settlers to present-day Savannah, Georgia, in 1733. The colony of Georgia served as a buffer of sorts between the English colonies to the north and the Spanish-held Florida.

William Penn was the founder of Pennsylvania, as well as the city of Philadelphia.

What were the different types of early colonial governments?

The three forms of early colonial government were royal, corporate, and proprietary. A royal colony was one where the English government set up a royal governor, who directly ruled the colony in the name of the Crown. Several early American colonies were royal colonies, including Georgia, Maryland, New Hampshire, New Jersey, and New York.

Corporate colonies were colonies established by a trading company that received permission from the Crown to set up a colony in the form of a charter. Connecticut and Rhode Island were corporate colonies.

Proprietary colonies were colonies established by one or two landowners who served as the primary ruler of such lands. Pennsylvania was an example of a proprietary colony, as William Penn was granted the province by charter. The Carolinas were other examples of proprietary colonies.

MOVEMENTS AND REBELLIONS

What was Bacon's Rebellion?

Bacon's Rebellion was an armed uprising of Virginia settlers beginning in 1674 against the rule of Colonial Governor William Berkeley (1605–1677). The rebellion was named after Nathaniel Bacon (1647–1676), a Cambridge graduate who had to leave England after marrying a woman who had been betrothed to someone else. Bacon settled in Jamestown, where he worked with Governor Berkeley. However, Governor Berkeley favored reconciliation and appeasement with Native American tribes. Bacon, whose farm had been attacked by Native Americans, wanted to respond by attacking the Native Americans. This difference culminated in Bacon's being in armed rebellion against Governor Berkeley. In 1676, Bacon and his followers issued a Declaration of the People of Virginia to the governor, criticizing Berkeley for failing to protect settlers from the Native Americans and for corruption in his government. Bacon's forces actually burned Jamestown to the ground in September 1676. English forces were dispatched from overseas to quell the rebellion. Bacon died of dysentery in October 1676 before facing the English forces. After Bacon's death, the rebellion floundered. Governor Berkeley re-established control and had many of the members of the rebellion hanged for their conduct.

However, British officials were not pleased with Berkeley's performance and ordered him to return home.

What was the First Great Awakening?

The First Great Awakening was a religious movement in the American colonies, particularly in Massachusetts and other parts of New England, that led to a renewed revitalization in personal commitment to religion. Ministers such as Jonathan Edwards (1703–1758) and George Whitefield (1714–1770) led revivals at their churches, urging their parishioners to dedicate themselves to a renewed sense of personal responsibility and morality. Edwards delivered one of the best-known sermons in American history known as "Sinners in the Hands of an Angry God." Whitefield traveled the colonies preaching with messianic zeal, urging that all achieve salvation by confessing their sins and accepting God. The First Great Awakening was a major social event that transformed numerous Protestant denominations and posed a serious threat to the traditional Puritan church structure.

Protestant preacher and major theologian of his day, Jonathan Edwards was one of the key figures in the First Great Awakening in the eighteenth century.

Were there other Great Awakenings?

Yes, there have been at least two others. The Second Great Awakening started around 1790 and lasted throughout much of the first half of the nineteenth century. The Third and Fourth Awakenings (occurring in the latter part of the nineteenth century and from 1960 to 1980, respectively) are often viewed by historians as more hypothetical and indicative of the promotion of an agenda by certain Protestant leaders. Each Great Awakening has been marked by a return to piety and a call by Protestant denominations to return to a purer form of Christianity marked by proselytizing and social activism, such as support for the abolition of slavery and prohibition of alcohol.

Which colony first passed an anti-slavery law?

Rhode Island passed an anti-slavery law in 1652—the first by any colony in North America. However, the demand for inexpensive labor remained great, and the law largely remained unenforced. Rhode Island did not pass an anti-slavery law with real force until the 1780s.

What Boston judge wrote against slavery in 1700?

Boston judge Samuel Sewall (1652–1730) wrote an anti-slavery piece called *The Selling of Joseph*. He termed slavery an "atrocious crime" and said that "liberty is in real value next unto life: none ought to part with it themselves or deprive others of it." Sewall based many of his objections to slavery on Biblical principles. Sewall is also known for his participation in the Salem Witch Trials, for which he later apologized. Sewell served for many years as chief justice of the leading Massachusetts court. Sewall has been called the only abolitionist in early eighteenth-century Massachusetts.

What anti-slavery law was passed in Virginia in 1670?

The Virginia assembly passed a law prohibiting lifelong slavery for those African slaves who became Christians before arriving in the colony. The bill was inspired by those who believed it was unlawful to enslave fellow Christians. However, the Virginia assembly later repealed the law in 1682.

What is the official church of Maryland?

In May 1692, the Anglican Church was declared the official church of the Maryland colony. This is somewhat counterintuitive, as Maryland was originally set up as a haven for Catholics. However, most of the inhabitants of the colony were Protestants. The Anglican Church remained the official church of Maryland until 1776.

Maryland was not the only colony with strong ties and allegiance to the Anglican Church; it had a stronghold in several colonies. For example, South Carolina passed a law in 1704 providing that non-Anglicans could not hold positions in the assembly. The British parliament rejected the law two years later.

WARS AND CONFLICTS

What was King Philip's War?

King Philip's War was a conflict between several Native American tribes and English colonists in New England. The war was fought between 1675 and 1678 in present-day Massachusetts, Connecticut, Rhode Island, and Maine. The war is named after an Indian chief named Metacom, or King Philip (1639–1676), leader of the Wampanoag. The conflict allegedly began when a farmer killed an Indian who was stealing his cattle. Metacom believed this amounted to murder and demanded retribution. When the local colonists denied his claim, Metacom took matters into his own hands, killing the farmer and several other settlers.

During the conflict, the Wampanoag were assisted by several other tribes, including the Nipmuck, Podunk, Narragansett, and Nashaway. However, some Native American tribes served as allies to the colonists, including the Mohegan and Pequot tribes. Metacom died during the conflict at the hands of an Indian named John Alderman, who had converted to Christianity. The conflict was bloody, leading to the death of more than three thousand Indians.

What was Queen Anne's War?

Queen Anne's War, also known as the Third Indian War, was the North American component of the larger conflict known as the War of the Spanish Succession. It took place between 1702 and 1713. The larger conflict featured Spain and France battling against England. Different Indian tribes fought on each side. The war was fought on several fronts, including in Carolina, Florida, New England, and Newfoundland, Canada.

The British got the best of the military conflicts overall and ultimately obtained certain French settlements during the treaty that ended the conflict. The treaty, however, failed to resolve the interests of different Indian tribes, nor did it result in a significant defeat for the French, who maintained an active presence in North America.

Queen Anne (1665–1814) ruled England from 1702 to 1707 and was the last monarch of the House of Stuart. Queen Anne's War involved England's territorial disputes in North America with France and Spain.

What was the War of Jenkins's Ear?

The War of Jenkins's Ear refers to a military conflict between Great Britain and Spain that technically lasted from 1739 to 1748. It is so named because Robert Jenkins, an English captain, had his ear cut off by Spanish officials who boarded his vessel in 1731. The war was largely fought by ships, but in 1742 the Spanish attempted to invade the colony of Georgia. General Oglethorpe successfully defeated the Spanish at two successive battles at Bloody Marsh and Gully Hole Creek to repel the invaders.

What was King George's War?

King George's War was the North American component of the War of Austrian Succession and a conflict sometimes referred to as the third of the four French and Indian Wars. It was fought between 1744 and 1748 between French and British colonial interests. The war failed to solve the tensions and enmities between the two powers, which resulted in the fourth French and Indian War a decade later. Much of the conflict occurred in New England, particularly Massachusetts.

What was the Siege of Louisbourg?

The Siege of Louisbourg was a key battle in King George's War in which New England colonial forces captured Louisbourg, a French stronghold in present-day Cape Breton Island in North America. A significant British success, the victory helped Britain bargain to obtain peace. However, the British ceded Louisbourg back to the French in the 1848 treaty that ended the war.

What was the French and Indian War?

The French and Indian War was the name for the armed conflict of the Seven Years' War between Great Britain and France fought on North American soil. Some of the Seven Years'

War was waged in other parts of the world, including Europe. The war was waged between 1754 and 1763. The war featured Great Britain and a couple of Indian tribes—the Iriquois, Catawba, and Cherokee against France and a host of Indian tribes. On North America, the war was fought from Virginia up into present-day Canada. Great Britain far outnumbered the French, leading to the French enlisting the aid of numerous Indian tribes.

The war featured the emergence of a young military leader from Virginia named George Washington (1732–1799), who led a group of Virginia militia into armed conflict. The war finally ended with the Treaty of Paris in 1763. The treaty was a magnificent victory for Great Britain and an ignoble loss for France, ceding Louisiana to Spain and the rest of her North American holdings to Great Britain. However, Great Britain suffered severe financial losses incurred during the French and Indian War. This led to increased taxation on the colonies, which ultimately led to the American Revolution or the Revolutionary War.

What was the Stono Rebellion?

The Stono Rebellion was a slave rebellion that began on September 9, 1739, about twenty miles from Charleston, South Carolina. Twenty slaves broke into a store, stole guns, and killed the storeowners. They left the heads of the storeowners on the front porch of the store. They then moved south, killing other whites along the way. A large group of white planters confronted the group and subdued them with a larger force. Historians estimate that approximately twenty-one whites and forty-two blacks were killed in the rebellion and its suppression. The rebellion is named the Stono Rebellion because it took place near the Stono River. It is sometimes called Cato's Rebellion. Scholar and former federal appeals court Judge Leon Higginbotham writes in *In the Matter of Color: Race and the American Legal Process* (1978): "The Stono Rebellion was the most serious outbreak of the colonial period."

The next year South Carolina enacted the 1740 Slave Code. The South Carolina general assembly stated: "the extent of … power over … slaves ought to be settled and limited by positive law so that the slave may be kept in subjection and obedience." The preamble to the law provided that slaves were "subject of property in the hands of particular persons." The law also prohibited teaching slaves how to read and write, a common feature of slave laws in the colonies.

FAMOUS AMERICAN
INDIAN LEADERS

Who was Squanto?

Squanto (1585–1621) was an American Indian of the Patuxet Tribe who is best known for his amicable relations with Pilgrim leaders in the early seventeenth century. Squanto befriended the Pilgrims during their first brutal winter in the New World. He helped teach the Pilgrims to grow corn and how to better hunt and fish in the area. Squanto was able to communicate effectively with the Pilgrims because he had been trained in English and had been to England years earlier. A testament to Squanto's good works can be seen in how Massachusetts colonial leaders felt when he died. William Bradford wrote of his passing: "His death was a great loss."

Who was Samoset?

Samoset (1590–1653) was an American Indian who made early contact with the Pilgrims in Massachusetts in 1621. Samoset surprised the Pilgrims at Plymouth by coming into the Pilgrims' camp and greeting them in English. He likely was helpful in ensuring peace between the Pilgrims with the Indian leader Massasoit (1581–1661), the leader of the Wampanoag Confederacy.

Who was Neolin?

Neolin, or the "Delaware prophet," was an eighteenth-century Indian leader who urged his people to reject European goods and influences, which he viewed as corrupting. He urged Indians to return to their original or traditional way of living. One of his followers was Pontiac (1720–1769), an Ottawa war chief who organized a military effort against British occupation of the Great Lakes area.

Tamanend negotiates a peaceful treaty with William Penn in this 1772 oil painting by Benjamin West.

Who was Tamanend?

Tamanend (1625–1701) was an Indian leader who advocated for peaceful relations with European settlers in the Pennsylvania and Delaware area in the seventeenth century. He helped bring about peaceful relations with Pennsylvania leader William Penn, who believed strongly in good relations with the Indians. Tamanend is also known as "the Patron Saint of America" for his good works and efforts on behalf of peace.

EARLY EDUCATIONAL INSTITUTIONS

What American college was founded in October 1636?

Harvard College—later named Harvard University—was founded in October 1636 by the Great and General Court of the Massachusetts Bay Colony. It was initially called the New College. In 1638, the college was named after a Charleston, Massachusetts, minister named John Harvard (1607–1638), who left his library of more than four hundred books and half of his estate to the school. Harvard is the first institution of higher learning in the United States. It provided a sound education in the classics. It is associated with Congregationalism.

What was the second college founded in what became the United States?

The second oldest college in what became known as the United States is William & Mary in Williamsburg, Virginia, founded in February 1693. It was named after the reigning British rulers, King William III and Queen Mary II. The original plans for the college were made in 1618, which would have made it the oldest institution of higher learning in the United States. The first president of the University (sometimes called the founder of the college) was James Blair (1656–1743), a Scottish-born clergy of the Church of England.

What was King William's School?

King William's School was a preparatory school founded in 1696 in Maryland. It was designed as a sort of feeder school to William & Mary, the institution of higher learning founded five years earlier. It later became St. John's College in Annapolis, Maryland, in 1784. Today the school has two campuses—one in Annapolis and the other in Santa Fe, New Mexico.

What college was founded in October 1701?

Yale College was founded in October 1701 in Saybrook, Connecticut, a town at the mouth of the Connecticut River. It was originally known as the Collegiate School of Saybrook. However, in 1716 the college moved to its current location in New Haven. In 1718, it was renamed Yale University after wealthy merchant Elihu Yale (1649–1721). Yale amassed a fortune working for the British East India Company and later helped religious leader Cotton Mather fund the college. Like Harvard, Yale is affiliated with the religion of Congregationalism.

What was Princeton's original name?

Princeton University was originally known as the College of New Jersey, founded in Elizabeth, New Jersey, in 1746. It moved to Newark in 1747 and then to its current location in Princeton in 1756. It was renamed Princeton University in the late nineteenth century. Jonathan Dickinson (1688–1747) was the college's first president, but he died shortly after assuming the post. Its most prominent early president was John Witherspoon (1723–1794), who signed the Declaration of Independence and served as president from 1768 until his death.

THE REVOLUTIONARY PERIOD

GROWING DISCONTENT

Why did the British colonies in America become discontented with the government of King George III?

King George III (1738–1820, r. 1760–1820) was one of Great Britain's longest-ruling monarchs. While he enjoyed successes during his reign, such as leading England's victory in the Seven Years' War and, later, the defeat of Napoleon Bonaparte, his tight grip on the American colonies caused the settlers there to bristle. The king supported a number of economic burdens imposed upon the Colonies by the British Parliament because the Americans were proving financially successful, and their taxes helped England. At least until the Americans rebelled.

What was the Stamp Act?

The Stamp Act of 1765 was a direct tax imposed by the British Parliament upon the American colonies. Under it, the colonies had to pay taxes on much printed paper created in London. Basically, the colonists had to pay taxes on everything written or printed. The measure was a revenue-generated measure designed to pay expenses associated with British troops stationed in North America to protect the colonies in battles against the French and some Indian tribes, a conflict collectively known as the Seven Years' War. The colonies viewed the Stamp Act as oppressive and unfair. The colonies believed the taxes were particularly unfair because they had no voice in Parliament. The phrase "taxation without representation" encapsulated some colonists' reactions to the Stamp Act.

Colonists from several states sent representatives to a meeting in New York known as the Stamp Act Congress. This body approved a resolution, stating that only the colonial legislatures could tax the colonists. One of the measures read: "That is inseparably essential to the freedom of a people, and the undoubted rights of Englishmen, that no taxes should be imposed on them, but with their own consent, given personally, or by their own representatives." Another read: "That the only representatives of the people of these colonies are persons chosen therein, by themselves, and that no taxes ever have been or can be constitutionally imposed on them but by their respective legislatures."

Parliament repealed the Stamp Act in 1766, causing widespread celebration in the colonies. But the British Parliament then passed the Declaratory Act, which reaffirmed Parliament's resolve to pass other tax measures on the colonies. Parliament also passed the Townshend Acts.

What were the Townshend Acts?

The Townshend Acts were a series of laws designed to raise revenue for the British crown by taxing the colonists. Charles Townshend (1725–1767), the Crown's Chancellor of the Exchequer, proposed the revenue laws that—like the Stamp Act—sought to tax the colonists to raise money for the British Crown. Townshend and others believed that colonial opposition to the Stamp Act arose primarily because the Stamp Act was a direct and internal tax. The Townshend Acts imposed taxes on products imported into the United States—such as lead, paper, print, and glass. However, colonists opposed the Townshend Acts, believing them to violate the basic principle of "taxation without representation."

What was the New England Restraining Act?

The New England Restraining Act was a law approved by King George III in March 1775, forbidding the New England colonies from trading with any countries except England. In April, the law was extended to apply to several other colonies in the Mid-Atlantic region, including Maryland, New Jersey, and others. The law was a direct response to the colonists' efforts to boycott British goods. It was also an attempt to put a stranglehold on the rising tides of rebellion in certain parts of New England.

What was "salutary neglect"?

Salutary neglect was the name given to the longstanding British policy of taking a hands-off approach to the American colonies. This policy lasted from the early seventeenth century through the bulk of the eighteenth century—until the 1760s, when the British crown needed revenue to pay for the expense of fighting wars in North America.

Charles Townshend was a son of a viscount. As a politician, one of his important positions was exchequer, during which he proposed raising taxes on the American colonists.

The term is traced to Edmund Burke (1729–1797), a political theorist who served for many years in the House of Commons. In a 1775 speech, Burke said that "through a wise and salutary neglect, a generous nature has been suffered to take her own way to perfection." Historians explain that salutary neglect in part contributed to the Revolutionary War because for many years colonists had been able to govern themselves largely free from the Crown's influence or direct control. When the British Parliament began to impose laws directly controlling the colonists, they reacted unfavorably. Burke urged his colleagues in the Parliament to treat the colonists with respect or face armed rebellion. "Great empires and little minds go ill together," he said.

EARLY SPARKS OF REBELLION

What was *Letters from a Farmer in Pennsylvania*?

Letters from a Farmer in Pennsylvania was a series of essays authored in 1767 and 1768 under the pen name "A Farmer," which objected to "excesses and outrages" of the British crown. The author was Pennsylvania legislator and lawyer John Dickinson (1732–1808). Dickinson believed the British monarchy exceeded its authority by passing tax laws such as the Stamp Act and the Townshend Acts. Dickinson opposed the British policies but did not advocate violence against the British.

What was the Boston Massacre?

The Boston Massacre refers to a killing on King's Street in Boston on March 5, 1770. British soldiers had been sent to Boston to maintain order amidst the growing unpopularity of British measures, such as the Townshend Acts. Many colonists viewed the British soldiers with resentment and suspicion. In March 1770, a group of British soldiers were guarding the local customs house. Several young colonists began shouting at the soldiers. Apparently feeling threatened, the soldiers fired into the growing throng of people. They killed five people and injured six others. The event came to be known as the Boston Massacre.

What colonial lawyers defended the British soldiers?

The British soldiers—including Captain Thomas Preston—were successfully defended by Boston lawyers John Adams (1735–1826), the future second president of the United States, and Josiah Quincy (1744–1775). Adams and Quincy secured an acquittal for Preston, who was alleged to have given the order to fire into the crowd.

What was the Boston Tea Party?

The Boston Tea Party was a protest organized by a group of protestors in Massachusetts known as the Sons of Liberty. Organized by Boston political leader Samuel Adams, the men protested the Tea Act of 1773, which culminated in their boarding ships and dump-

The Boston Tea Party museum offers a full range of historical experiences for visitors, including films and the chance to participate in a reenactment of the dumping of the tea into Boston Harbor.

ing the tea they contained into Boston Harbor. This caused an intense crackdown by the British authorities with a series of even more restrictive measures, known as the Intolerable Acts. The Boston Tea Party is seen as the act of protest that ultimately led to the Revolutionary War. John Adams called the event an "epoch in history."

Parliament responded with a series of laws, called "Intolerable Acts" by the colonists. One of these—called the Quartering Act—empowered British officials to quarter, or house, soldiers in colonists' homes. This law inspired the later passage of the Constitution's Third Amendment. Another act prohibited Massachusetts colonists from electing members to the upper house of their legislature.

Who started the Boston Tea Party?

Many believe that on December 13, 1773, patriot Samuel Adams (1722–1803) gave the signal to the men, who may have numbered more than one hundred and were dressed as Indians, to board the ships in Boston Harbor and dump the tea overboard. Whether or not it was Adams who started the Tea Party, about this there can be no doubt: He was most certainly a leader in the agitation that led up to the event. The show of resistance was in response to the recent passage by the British parliament of the Tea Act, which allowed the British-owned East India company to "dump" tea on the American colonies at a low price, and also required the colonists to pay a duty for said tea. Colonists feared the Act would put local merchants out of business and that if they conceded to pay the duty to the British, they would soon be required to pay other taxes as well.

Once the ships carrying the tea arrived in Boston Harbor, the colonists tried to have them sent back to England. But when Governor Thomas Hutchinson (1711–1780) of Massachusetts refused to order the return of the ships, patriots organized their show of resistance, which came to be known as the Boston Tea Party.

Who was Thomas Paine, and why were his philosophies important to the American Revolution?

English political philosopher and author Thomas Paine (1737–1809) believed that a democracy is the only form of government that can guarantee natural rights. Paine arrived in the American colonies in 1774. Two years later he wrote *Common Sense*, a pamphlet that galvanized public support for the American Revolution (1775–1783), which was already underway. Published in July 1776, more than 100,000 copies of it were sold that year. Paine wrote that "we have it in our power to begin the world over again." He wrote passionately about the importance of freedom in society. He accused the British king of engaging "in a long and violent abuse of power." In *Common Sense*, he waxed eloquently about the need for freedom. He concluded:

> These proceedings may at first appear strange and difficult; but, like all other steps which we have already passed over, will in a little time become familiar and agreeable; and, until an independence is declared, the continent will feel itself like a man who continues putting off some unpleasant business from day to day, yet knows it must be done, hates to set about it, wishes it over, and is continually haunted with the thoughts of its necessity.

Common Sense may have been Paine's most well-known publication, but it was not his only contribution. During the struggle for independence, Paine wrote and distributed a series of sixteen papers, called *Crisis*, upholding the rebels' cause in their fight. Paine penned his words in the language of common speech, which helped his message reach a mass audience in America and elsewhere. "We have it in our power to begin the world over again," Paine wrote in language that resonated with many colonists.

He soon became known as an advocate of individual freedom. The fight for freedom was one that he waged in letters. In 1791 and 1792, Paine, now back in England, released *The Rights of Man* (in two parts), in which he defended the cause of the French Revolution (1789–1799) and appealed to the British people to overthrow their monarchy. For this he was tried and convicted of treason in his homeland. Escaping to Paris, the philosopher became a member of the revolutionary National Convention. But during the Reign of Terror (1793–1794) of revolutionary leader Maximilien Robespierre (1758–1794), Paine was imprisoned for being English. An American minister interceded on Paine's behalf, insisting that Paine was actually an American. Paine was released on this technicality. He remained in Paris until 1802 and then returned to the United States. Though he played an important role in the American Revolution by boosting the morale of the colonists, he nevertheless lived his final years as an outcast and in poverty. Historian Joseph Ellis writes in his highly readable history *American Creation*: "Paine was an indispensable ally in the cause of American independence. But the combination of his utopian convictions and his brilliant pen also made him the most dangerous man in America once his independence was declared." (p. 44)

What two colonial-era leaders founded the first abolitionist society in the colonies?

Benjamin Franklin (1706–1790) and Dr. Benjamin Rush (1746–1813) of Pennsylvania founded the Society for the Relief of Free Negroes in Philadelphia in April 1775. In 1784, the society changed its name to the Pennsylvania Society for Promoting the Abolition of Slavery and the Relief of Free Negroes Unlawfully Held in Bondage. Franklin added clout to the organization by serving as its first president. Many members of the organization were Quakers who had a strong opposition and moral revulsion to slavery.

What congressional body formed in response to the Intolerable Acts?

Colonist leaders formed the First Continental Congress in Philadelphia in 1774. The leaders elected delegates to this body, which publicly condemned the Intolerable Acts as null and void. The Continental Congress also urged the creation of militias in the different colonies, understanding the need to arm themselves and protect their interests from possible further British incursions. The Continental Congress adopted the Suffolk Resolves, a series of resolutions opposed to British measures—such as the Intolerable Acts. These resolves not only opposed the Intolerable Acts but also called for Massachusetts and others to arm themselves.

Fifty-six men from twelve different colonies (all of the original thirteen except Georgia) attended the First Continental Congress, which first convened on September 5, 1774. The Congress debated whether to engage in armed conflict or seek reconciliation with the British crown. The Continental Congress supported a boycott of British goods. The First Continental Congress also called for the creation of a second Congress, which met in May 1775.

What luminaries in American history attended the First Continental Congress?

George Washington (1732–1799) and John Adams (1735–1826), the first two presidents of the United States, attended the

The First Continental Congress met here at Carpenters' Hall in Philadelphia in 1774.

34

Who said "Give me liberty or give me death"?

Patrick Henry (1736–1799) uttered this famous revolutionary phrase on March 23, 1775, in the Virginia House of Burgesses. Henry spoke these words upon learning that the British Parliament refused to repeal the Intolerable Acts. Henry believed the colonists needed to revolt in order to obtain freedom from the repressive measures of the British government. Henry was an attorney who also served as governor of Virginia. Henry is considered one of the leaders of the American Revolutionary War effort. He had earlier gained acclaim for his opposition to the Stamp Act and his drafting of the so-called Virginia Resolves against the Stamp Act.

First Continental Congress. Other famous attendees included John Jay (1745–1829), the first U.S. Supreme Court chief justice; Roger Sherman (1721–1793), the author of the "Great Compromise" that saved the U.S. Constitution; Sam Adams (1722–1803), the architect of the resistance in Boston against British rule; and John Dickinson, author of the *Letters from a Pennsylvania Farmer*.

Who was James Otis?

James Otis, Jr. (1725–1783) was a Massachusetts lawyer most famous for challenging writs of assistance and for uttering the slogan "Taxation without representation is tyranny." Writs of assistance were general search warrants that British officials used to search colonial ships to determine whether the ships were engaged in smuggling. Opposition to these writs of assistance led to the adoption of the protections found in the Fourth Amendment to the U.S. Constitution, which prohibits government officials from engaging in unreasonable searches and seizures.

Otis gained renown for representing a group of Boston merchants who challenged the fairness and constitutionality of writs of assistance. Otis's passion in argument for his clients made him a popular man in revolutionary circles. Otis also wrote a series of tracts challenging British policies on taxation. Otis also showed forward thinking on race relations, particularly for his time period.

Who were the Loyalists?

Loyalists were American colonists who remained loyal to the British crown and opposed the American Revolutionary War effort. They were also called Tories or King's Men. Historians have estimated that at least fifteen percent of the colonial population considered themselves Loyalists. Many Loyalists avoided actual military conflict. Some Loyalists actively joined the British military cause, particularly if British officials came to their particular town.

WAR BREAKS OUT

What were the first battles of the Revolutionary War?

The first battles were the Battles of Lexington and Concord, Massachusetts, fought on April 19, 1775. British forces led by General Thomas Gage learned that some colonists were storing weapons in Concord. Gage led a group of British forces to march upon Concord, disarm the colonists, and arrest colonial leaders Samuel Adams and John Hancock. The British forces marched toward Concord and engaged in gunfire first at Lexington. More heavy fighting took place at Concord.

Who were Paul Revere and William Dawes?

Paul Revere (1734–1818) was a silversmith best known for riding by horseback through Massachusetts to warn leaders in different cities that British forces were marching toward Lexington and Concord. Gage's wife Margaret warned Dr. Joseph Warren (1741–1775) of the impending plan. Warren in turn told Revere and enlisted him to go on his famous ride to warn colonial leaders of the impending assault. Revere became famous in part because of Henry Wadsworth Longfellow's poem "Paul Revere's Ride."

Revere was not the only midnight rider. The other was William Dawes (1745–1799), who also was instructed by Dr. Warren to warn John Hancock and Samuel Adams of their impending arrest. Dawes has been ignored in American history. Author Michael Farquhar calls Dawes "the other Midnight Rider" in his book *A Treasury of Foolishly Forgotten Americans*. He writes that "William Dawes had the misfortune of being at the right place but with the wrong rhyme."

Who was Joseph Warren?

Joseph Warren was a doctor in Boston who played a leading role in the American Revolution, particularly in the early days in Boston. He served as president of the Massachusetts Provincial Congress and wrote "A List of Infringements and Violations of Rights" at a Boston town meeting in November 1772 that aroused the passions of others.

Warren fought bravely in the Revolutionary War, eschewing his own personal safety. He told his mother, who pleaded with him to avoid further conflict: "Where danger is, dear mother, there must your son be. Now is no time for any of America's children to shrink from any hazard. I will set her free or die."

Who were the Minutemen?

The Minutemen were a group of men from Massachusetts drawn from the state's militia who engaged British forces at the Battles of Lexington and Concord. They were called the Minutemen because allegedly they could be prepared for battle immediately—or in a minute.

Who was Ethan Allen?

Ethan Allen (1738–1789) was a Revolutionary War hero and later one of the founders of Vermont. Allen and Benedict Arnold captured the British garrison at Fort Ticonderoga on May 10, 1775. In September 1775, Allen was captured at the Battle of Longue-Pointe. Allen led a band of fighting men from the colonies and Canada in an attempt to capture Montreal from British forces. Unfortunately, the Canadian and British militia had a stronger force, defeating Allen. He was not released from captivity until several years later. He later wrote a memoir about this time in captivity.

What was Bunker Hill?

Bunker Hill was the name of a significant early battle in the Revolutionary War—known as the Battle of Bunker Hill in Charleston, Massachusetts. Fought in June 1775, American militia were able to inflict heavy casualties on British forces, although the Americans eventually had to repeat. Most of the actual combat at the Battle of Bunker Hill actually took place on Breed's Hill. The Americans suffered casualties in the combat too, however, including Dr. Joseph Warren.

At the battle, William Prescott led about twelve hundred colonial troops in battle against a larger British force led by General William Howe (1729–1814). Some historians have said Prescott uttered the famous phrase "don't fire until you see the whites of

An illustration depicting the 1775 Battle of Bunker Hill, which actually mostly occurred on Breed's Hill.

their eyes." Colonial forces repelled the first two assaults by British troops. The British were able to capture Bunker Hill on their third assault, obtaining a technical victory. However, the victory was often seen as a Pyrrhic victory, in part because the British suffered more casualties than their colonial opponents.

Why were there two Continental Congresses?

Both meetings were called in reaction to the British Parliament's attempts to assert its control in the American colonies. When colonial delegates to the First Continental Congress met, they developed a plan but were obviously prepared for it not to work, since even before dismissal they agreed to reconvene if it were necessary to do so. In short, the First Continental Congress developed Plan A; the Second Continental Congress resorted to Plan B (one last appeal to King George) and then to Plan C (finally declaring independence from Britain).

The First Continental Congress convened on September 5, 1774, in Philadelphia, Pennsylvania. The meeting was largely a reaction to the so-called Intolerable Acts (or the Coercive Acts), which Parliament had passed in an effort to control Massachusetts after the Boston Tea Party. Sentiment grew among the colonists that they would need to band together in order to challenge British authority. Soon twelve colonies dispatched fifty-six delegates to a meeting in Philadelphia. (The thirteenth colony, Georgia, declined to send representatives but agreed to go along with whatever plan the others developed.) Delegates included Samuel Adams (1722–1803), George Washington (1732–1799), Patrick Henry (1736–1799), John Adams (1735–1826), and John Jay (1745–1829). Each colony had one vote. When the meeting ended on October 26, the Congress petitioned the king, declaring that Parliament had no authority over the American colonies; that each colony could regulate its own affairs; and that the colonies would not trade with Britain until Parliament rescinded its trade and taxation policies. The petition stopped short of proclaiming independence from Britain, but the delegates agreed to meet again the following May—if necessary.

But King George III was determined that the British Empire be preserved at all costs. He believed that if the empire lost the American colonies, then there might be a domino effect, with other British possessions encouraged also to demand independence. He feared these losses would render Great Britain a minor state, rather than the power it was. Britain was unwilling to lose control in America, and in April 1775 fighting broke out between the Redcoats and the Patriots at Lexington and Concord, Massachusetts. So, as agreed, the colonies again sent representatives to Philadelphia, convening the Second Continental Congress on May 10. Delegates—including George Washington, John Hancock (1737–1793), Thomas Jefferson (1743–1826), and Benjamin Franklin (1706–1790)—organized and prepared for the fight, creating the Continental Army and naming Washington as its commander in chief. With armed conflict already underway, Congress nevertheless moved slowly toward proclaiming independence from Britain: On July 10, two days after issuing a declaration to take up arms, Congress made another appeal to King George, hoping to settle the matter without further conflict. The attempt failed, and the following summer the Second Continental Congress approved the Declaration of Independence, breaking off all ties with the mother country.

What does the Declaration of Independence say?

The Declaration of Independence, adopted July 4, 1776, has long been regarded as history's most eloquent statement of the rights of the people. In it, not only did the thirteen American colonies declare their freedom from Britain, they also addressed the reasons for the proclamation (naming the "causes which impel them to the separation") and cited the British government's violations of individual rights, saying "the history of the present King 'George III' of Great Britain is a history of repeated injuries and usurpations," which aimed to establish "an absolute tyranny over these States."

The opening paragraphs go on to state the American ideal of government, an ideal that is based on the theory of natural rights. The Declaration of Independence puts forth the fundamental principles that a government exists for the benefit of its people and that "all men are created equal." As chairman of the Second Continental Congress committee that prepared the Declaration of Independence, Thomas Jefferson (1743–1826) wrote and presented the first draft to the Second Continental Congress on July 2, 1776.

The most frequently cited passage is:

> We hold these truths to be self-evident, that all men are created equal, that they are endowed by their Creator with certain unalienable Rights, that among these are Life, Liberty, and the Pursuit of Happiness. That to secure these rights, Gov-

Artist John Trumbull's famous oil depicting the signing of the Declaration of Independence on July 4, 1776.

ernments are instituted among Men, deriving their just powers from the consent of the governed. That whenever any Form of Government becomes destructive of these ends, it is the Right of the People to alter or to abolish it, and to institute new Government, laying its foundation on such principles and organizing its powers in such form, as to them shall seem most likely to effect their Safety and Happiness.

The Declaration then contained a lengthy list of abuses committed by King George, including:

He has refused his Assent to Laws, the most wholesome and necessary for the public good.

He has forbidden his Governors to pass Laws of immediate and pressing importance, unless suspended in their operation till his Assent should be obtained; and when so suspended, he has utterly neglected to attend to them.

He has refused to pass other Laws for the accommodation of large districts of people, unless those people would relinquish the right of Representation in the Legislature, a right inestimable to them and formidable to tyrants only.

He has called together legislative bodies at places unusual, uncomfortable, and distant from the depository of their public Records, for the sole purpose of fatiguing them into compliance with his measures.

He has dissolved Representative Houses repeatedly, for opposing with manly firmness his invasions on the rights of the people.

He has refused for a long time, after such dissolutions, to cause others to be elected; whereby the Legislative powers, incapable of Annihilation, have returned to the People at large for their exercise; the State remaining in the meantime exposed to all the dangers of invasion from without, and convulsions within.

He has endeavoured to prevent the population of these States; for that purpose obstructing the Laws for Naturalization of Foreigners; refusing to pass others to encourage their migrations hither, and raising the conditions of new Appropriations of Lands.

He has obstructed the Administration of Justice, by refusing his Assent to Laws for establishing Judiciary powers.

He has made Judges dependent on his Will alone, for the tenure of their offices, and the amount and payment of their salaries.

He has erected a multitude of New Offices, and sent hither swarms of Officers to harrass our people, and eat out their substance.

He has kept among us, in times of peace, Standing Armies without the Consent of our legislatures.

He has affected to render the Military independent of and superior to the Civil power.

He has combined with others to subject us to a jurisdiction foreign to our constitution, and unacknowledged by our laws; giving his Assent to their Acts of pretended Legislation:

For Quartering large bodies of armed troops among us:

For protecting them, by a mock Trial, from punishment for any Murders which they should commit on the Inhabitants of these States:

For cutting off our Trade with all parts of the world:

For imposing Taxes on us without our Consent:

For depriving us in many cases, of the benefits of Trial by Jury:

For transporting us beyond Seas to be tried for pretended offences:

For abolishing the free System of English Laws in a neighbouring Province, establishing therein an Arbitrary government, and enlarging its Boundaries so as to render it at once an example and fit instrument for introducing the same absolute rule into these Colonies:

For taking away our Charters, abolishing our most valuable Laws, and altering fundamentally the Forms of our Governments:

For suspending our own Legislatures, and declaring themselves invested with power to legislate for us in all cases whatsoever.

He has abdicated Government here, by declaring us out of his Protection and waging War against us.

He has plundered our seas, ravaged our Coasts, burnt our towns, and destroyed the lives of our people.

He is at this time transporting large Armies of foreign Mercenaries to compleat [sic] the works of death, desolation and tyranny, already begun with circum-

What was the Olive Branch petition?

The Olive Branch petition was a document created by the Second Continental Congress in July 1775 as an attempt to avoid full-scale, armed conflict with the British monarchy. John Dickinson wrote the petition, signifying the colonists' loyalty to the British crown, and calling on the King to avoid further hostilities. King George rejected the petition and sought to bring the colonies back into a mode of obedience to the Crown.

stances of Cruelty & perfidy scarcely paralleled in the most barbarous ages, and totally unworthy the Head of a civilized nation.

He has constrained our fellow Citizens taken Captive on the high Seas to bear Arms against their Country, to become the executioners of their friends and Brethren, or to fall themselves by their Hands.

He has excited domestic insurrections amongst us, and has endeavoured to bring on the inhabitants of our frontiers, the merciless Indian Savages, whose known rule of warfare, is an undistinguished destruction of all ages, sexes and conditions.

When did the Second Continental Congress form?

The Second Continental Congress formed after the conflict at Lexington and Concord. It began meeting in May 1775. This congress called for the creation of a continental army. The congress believed a continental army would be superior to state militias. The Second Congress also nominated George Washington of Virginia to serve as general of the Continental Army. It acted as the basic leading governmental body for the colonists during the conflict.

Who was Richard Henry Lee?

Richard Henry Lee (1732–1794) was a leading Revolutionary War-era leader from Virginia who signed the Declaration of Independence, attended the First Continental Congress, and created a resolution in the Second Continental Congress calling for American independence. The famous Lee Resolution provided: "That these United Colonies are, and of right ought to be, free and independent States, that they are absolved from all allegiance to the British Crown, and that all political connection between them and the State of Great Britain is, and ought to be, totally dissolved."

Who was Nathan Hale?

Nathan Hale (1755–1776) was an American soldier from Connecticut in the Revolutionary War who was in New York at the time of conflict with British soldiers. The British nearly destroyed Washington's armies, but much of the Army managed to retreat and avoid capture. Hale was on an espionage mission in New York when the British captured him. British General William Howe ordered him hanged. Allegedly, Hale then uttered these famous words: "How beautiful is death when earned by virtue! Who would not be that youth? What pity is it that we can die but once to serve our country."

"The Last Words of Nathan Hale" (1858) by Scottish artist Alexander Hay Ritchie.

GEORGE WASHINGTON AND THE FIRST YEARS OF THE REVOLUTIONARY WAR

Who was George Washington?

George Washington (1732–1799) was the son of Augustine Washington, a well-to-do Virginia landowner and slaveowner who passed away when George was only eleven. After being educated by tutors and by Anglican clergymen in Fredericksburg, Virginia, at age seventeen he began work as a land surveyor in Culpeper County. Family connections later helped get him appointed a major in the Virginia Militia in 1753. During the Seven Years' War, Washington showed great valor at the Battle of Monongahela (1755). That same year, he was promoted to Colonel of the Virginia Regiment, commanding all the military forces in the colony. In Virginia, Washington became increasingly politically active, opposing the Stamp Act in the Virginia Assembly. In 1775, he was appointed general and commander in chief of the Continental Army. An arduous war soon followed, but Washington led the Americans to victory in 1783. Four years later, he attended the Constitutional Convention and was made president of that convention. He was elected the first president of the newly formed United States, serving admirably from 1789 to 1797. Refusing to run for a third term, he retired to his home for the remaining two years of his life.

What colonial defeat led to the capture of Fort Washington?

British forces captured Fort Washington at the aptly named Battle of Fort Washington on Manhattan Island in November 1776. British forces under General William Howe had superior numbers and used them to their advantage to capture Fort Washington, leading to the capture of more than twenty-eight hundred colonial soldiers. This defeat caused a serious retreat on Washington's part. He moved his troops through New Jersey into Pennsylvania and then Delaware.

Where did Washington begin to turn colonial fortunes around in the war?

Washington and his troops suffered defeats at the Battles of White Plains and Fort Washington. This had caused Washington to retreat through New Jersey. However, Washington managed to pull a few surprises and raise the morale of his troops. A prime example occurred at the Battle of Princeton on January 3, 1777. Washington managed to attack a smaller British force, obtaining a victory that was more significant in terms of morale than actual military impact in the conflict. The battle helped the colonists to increase recruitment efforts to their cause.

What was the significance of Valley Forge?

Valley Forge, Pennsylvania, was the site of the Continental Army's military camp during the bitter winter of 1777–1778. General George Washington chose this site for his men to try to recuperate from the superior British forces who had taken over Philadel-

General George Washington leads the Continental Army to Valley Forge in this 1883 painting by William B. T. Trego. Their survival through the winter of 1777–1778 was a true test of the determination of Washington's troops.

phia, less than thirty miles away. Many of the American forces barely survived the brutal weather and lack of adequate food supplies. But the men managed to survive and eventually prevailed in the conflict.

Who was appointed the first surgeon general of the Continental Army?

Dr. Benjamin Church (1734–1788) was appointed the first surgeon general of the Continental Army in July 1775. Church had been active in the Sons of Liberty movement and resistance in Boston. However, Church was court-martialed in October 1775 for "criminal correspondence with the enemy." Church had sent a letter to one Major Cane of the British forces, which did not disclose military secrets, but did declare his allegiance to the British crown. He remained imprisoned until 1778.

What American diplomat sought aid for the Revolutionary cause from France and was later branded a traitor?

Silas Deane (1737–1789) served as an American diplomat to France when the Continental Congress appointed him to serve as a colonial representative to try to secure military and financial aid from France in March 1776. Deane, however, later revealed his Loyalist ties and support of the British government. Many branded him a traitor. After the war, when he traveled back to the United States, he died under suspicious circumstances.

Who was Thomas Hickey?

Thomas Hickey (d. 1776) was a soldier who originally came to North America as part of a British force to fight the colonial Revolutionary War forces. However, Hickey deserted to the colonial side, managing to serve as part of General George Washington's Life Guard, or Commander in Chief Guard, a special unit tasked with the purpose of protecting Washington.

Hickey was later charged with treason for allegedly conspiring to turn over Washington to the British. He was hanged in public on June 27, 1776—the first person executed for treason in the United States.

Who was Henry Knox?

Henry Knox (1755–1806) was George Washington's chief artillery officer during the Revolutionary War. Knox owned a bookstore in Boston at the beginning of the conflict. He directed colonial cannon fire at the Battle of Bunker Hill. While not a soldier by trade, Knox acquired a deep interest in artillery. George Washington was impressed with Knox's bravery and mental acumen in artillery matters. When Washington became president, he named Knox his secretary of war.

Who was Friedrich Wilhelm von Steuben?

Baron von Steuben (1730–1794) was a Prussian military leader who served as George Washington's chief of staff during the last years of the American Revolutionary War. A military expert, von Steuben is credited with increasing the discipline of the American forces at Valley Forge. He also taught the men the art of fighting with bayonets. He authored the *Revolutionary War Drill Manual* and became a major general for his efforts. Washington learned of von Steuben from Benjamin Franklin, who met von Steuben in France. Paul Lockhart authored an aptly named biography of von Steuben *The Drillmaster of Valley Forge*.

What was the significance of the Battles of Saratoga?

The Battles of Saratoga are viewed as the key turning point in the Revolutionary War. There were two battles fought on September 19 and October 7, 1777, near Saratoga, New York. British General John Burgoyne (1722–1792) attacked American forces led by General Horatio Gates (1727–1806) and won the battle despite enduring heavy casualties. However, Burgoyne pressed his luck on the second battle, suffering an ignominious defeat. Historians consider the second Battle of Saratoga as the key event that caused France officially to support the colonial cause. France's foreign minister Charles Gravier believed the colonists' victory showed they could win the war.

General Gates claimed credit for the victory, but General Benedict Arnold (before he defected to the British) may have been more instrumental for the American victory.

What other American military leader participated in the Battle of Saratoga and later became the country's secretary of war?

General Benjamin Lincoln (1733–1810) played a significant role in the Battle of Saratoga in addition to other major battles in the Revolutionary War. He also participated in the

45

Battle of Charleston in 1780, losing many casualties to British forces. Lincoln had to surrender to British forces after this battle. Lincoln earned a measure of redemption later in the war, as he was one of the American leaders who surrounded British commander Lord Cornwallis (1738–1805) at Yorktown.

Who was John Paul Jones?

John Paul Jones (1747–1792) was the fiery naval war hero for the colonies during the Revolutionary War. Born in Scotland, Jones entered the British maritime service at age twelve. He served on numerous ships through the years, rising through the ranks. For his exploits, he earned the moniker "Father of the U.S. Navy." He served as lieutenant, commanding the ship *Alfred* for the Continental Navy. He later commanded the ship *U.S.S. Ranger* into battle with British naval forces. During a

Scottish-born John Paul Jones became known as the "Father of the U.S. Navy."

naval battle, Jones and the *Ranger* captured the British ship *HMS Drake*. He then commanded the ship *Bonhomme Richard* as its captain. He famously proclaimed, "I have not yet begun to fight" during the Battle of Flamborough Head, a naval battle during the Revolutionary War. He earned a Congressional gold medal in 1787.

Who was Daniel Morgan?

Daniel Morgan (1736–1802) was an American Revolutionary War leader known for his tactical skills and victories in battle during the Revolutionary War. He led an elite fighting force known as Morgan's Riflemen. He fought for the British during the French and Indian War. During that conflict, he punched one of his superiors and was severely punished. This left him with a bitter distaste for the British. After distinguishing himself at the Battle of Lexington with his riflemen, Morgan led a group of forces to repel British troops in Canada. Perhaps his greatest victory occurred at the Battle of Cowpens in January 1781 in South Carolina. In 1790, he received a medal from Congress for his battle planning and tactics at Cowpens. A few years later, he helped suppress the Whiskey Rebellion.

What country was a key ally for the colonists in the Revolutionary War?

France served as a key ally for the colonists during the American Revolutionary War. Benjamin Franklin worked his diplomatic skills effectively as U.S. Ambassador to France to produce the so-called French alliance. In 1778, France recognized the colonists as a sovereign nation and gave much monetary and military aid to the colonists in their battle with Great Britain. That year, France and the United States entered into something known as the Treaty of Alliance. Under this agreement between French King Louis XVI and leaders of the Second Continental Congress, France agreed to provide military support in case the colonists faced continued military attack by the British.

Who was the Marquis de Lafayette?

Marquis de Lafayette (1756–1834) was a French military officer who earned fame for his valiant service for the American Revolutionary War effort, beginning in July 1777. Lafayette was motivated in part by a desire to avenge the death of his father, who had died at the hands of the British in the French and Indian War. He volunteered to fight for the American cause without pay and served as a major-general under George Washington's Continental Army. He participated in numerous battles in the Revolutionary War, including the Battle of Brandywine, the Battle of Barren Hill, and the Battle of Monmouth. He suffered alongside many of Washington's troops during Valley Forge. For his efforts, the Continental Congress praised him officially for his "gallantry, skill and prudence."

In February 1779, he returned to France. He named his son after George Washington. He returned to America in 1780, serving at the Battles of Green Spring and Yorktown. When he returned to France in 1781, he was honored as a hero. He worked with Thomas Jefferson to set up trade agreements between the United States and France. He survived some difficult moments during the French Revolution. Many years later, in 1824 and 1825, he returned to the United States at the invitation of President James Monroe (1758–1831) as an honored guest and a symbol of the American Revolution.

THE WAR CONCLUDES

Why did General Benedict Arnold betray the United States?

Benedict Arnold (1741–1801) was an American general who fought for the colonists in the Continental Army but then defected to the British. In the early stages of the Revolutionary War, he proved himself to be a brave leader, helping to capture Fort Ticonderoga in 1775 and contributing to the success at Saratoga. However, Arnold was a spendthrift, finding himself in substantial debt. He also resented the fact that a number of officers of lower rank had been promoted ahead of him. After being placed in command of West Point in 1780, he decided to become a turncoat. Talking with the British in secret, he asked for money and a prominent role in the British Army; in return, he would turn over the fort at West Point to the British. But the plot was discovered, forcing Arnold to flee to the other side. He was put in command of British troops, fighting in Virginia and Connecticut against his former comrades. After the war, he lived in London, England, in semi-obscurity.

General Benedict Arnold's name has become synonymous with "traitor" in the American lexicon, but before 1780 he was actually considered a brave and heroic military leader.

What battle effectively ended the Revolutionary War?

The Battle of Yorktown resulted in British commander Lord Cornwallis surrendering to General George Washington and other colonial forces. The battle took place in September and October 1781 as American army and naval forces surrounded Cornwallis's troops. Colonial forces captured more than seven thousand British troops during the conflict. With the surrender of Lord Cornwallis, British officials realized they needed to end the costly war.

What song did the British drummers play after the surrender at Yorktown?

British drummers played the song "The World Turned Upside Down" as they headed with their American captors. Many of the British probably believed the lyrics of the song had come true.

What treaties ended the Revolutionary War?

The Peace of Paris officially ended the conflict between the British and American colonies. In September 1783, representatives of King George and American leaders met in Paris and signed the Treaty of Paris. Other treaties were needed to end the entire conflict, as the war also involved other world powers—including France and Spain. Under the agreements, Britain recognized the independence of the American colonies. Furthermore, Britain agreed that Florida would go to Spain, and Senegal would fall under the control of France. Diplomatic leaders signed the Treaty of Paris on September 3, 1783. The Second Continental Congress ratified the treaty on January 14, 1784.

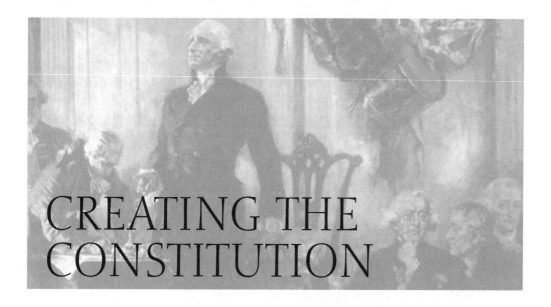

CREATING THE CONSTITUTION

Who are considered the Founding Fathers of the United States?

The term is used to refer to a number of American statesmen who were influential during the revolutionary period of the late 1700s. Though definitions vary, most include the authors of the Declaration of Independence and the signers of the U.S. Constitution among the nation's Founding Fathers.

Of the fifty-six members of the Continental Congress who signed the Declaration of Independence (July 4, 1776), the most well-known are John Adams (1735–1826) and Samuel Adams (1722–1803) of Massachusetts, Benjamin Franklin (1706–1790) of Pennsylvania, John Hancock (1737–1793) of Massachusetts, and Thomas Jefferson (1743–1826) of Virginia.

The thirty-nine men who signed the U.S. Constitution on September 17, 1787, included notable figures such as George Washington (1732–1799), who would go on, of course, to become the first president of the United States; Alexander Hamilton (1755–1804), who, as a former military aide to George Washington, went on to become the first U.S. secretary of the treasury; and James Madison (1751–1836), who is called the "Father of the Constitution" for his role as negotiator and recorder of debates between the delegates. At age eighty-one, Benjamin Franklin was the oldest signer of the Constitution and was among the six statesmen who could claim the distinction of signing both it and the Declaration of Independence; the others were George Clymer (1739–1813), Robert Morris (1734–1806), George Read (1733–1798), Roger Sherman (1721–1793), and James Wilson (1742–1798).

Patriots and politicians conspicuous by their absence from the Constitutional Convention of 1787 were John Adams and Thomas Jefferson, who were performing other government duties at the time, and would each go on to become U.S. president; Samuel Adams and John Jay (1745–1829), who were not appointed as state delegates but who continued in public life, holding various federal and state government offices (including governor of their states); and Patrick Henry (1736–1799), who saw no need to go beyond the Articles of Confederation (1777) to grant more power to the central government. Henry's view on this issue foreshadows the discontent that crested nearly one hundred years later, when twelve southern states (including Virginia) seceded from the Union, causing the Civil War (1861–1865) to break out.

Adams, Franklin, Hancock, Jefferson, Washington, Hamilton, Madison, Jay, and Henry: These names come to mind when the words "Founding Fathers" are uttered. Each of them had a profound impact in the political life of the United States—even beyond their starring roles as patriots and leaders during the American Revolutionary era. However, it is important to note that in many texts and to many Americans, the term "Founding Fathers "refers only to the men who drafted the U.S. Constitution since that document —more than two hundred years after its signing—continues to provide the solid foundation for American democratic government.

THE ARTICLES OF CONFEDERATION

What was the Articles of Confederation?

The Articles of Confederation was the initial constitution created by the original thirteen states of the fledgling United States of America. Created in 1777 by the Continental Congress, the Articles were not ratified until 1781. The Articles created a legislative branch—a Congress—that had many powers, including the power to wage war, deal with foreign nations, and borrow money.

But the Articles created a weak central government. The central feature of the Articles of Confederation was that "each state retains its sovereignty, independence, and freedom." It created no judicial or executive branches. It allowed individual states often to prevent action by Congress. On many important matters, nine of thirteen states had to approve a matter before it could become law or approved policy. In sum, the Articles of Confederation created a relatively weak central government that was not equipped to deal with intrastate rivalries and conflicts.

Which states were the original thirteen?

In order of admission, they are:

1. Delaware
2. Pennsylvania
3. New Jersey
4. Georgia
5. Connecticut
6. Massachusetts

What man is said by some historians to have been, technically, the first president of the United States?

Samuel Huntington (1731–1796) was a leading early American statesman from Connecticut. He served as chief justice of the Connecticut Supreme Court and as governor of Connecticut—his last public office. But Huntington was also the first president of the Continental Congress when the Articles of Confederation were ratified. Thus, some have made the claim that Samuel Huntington was technically the first president of the United States.

7. Maryland
8. South Carolina
9. New Hampshire
10. Virginia
11. New York
12. North Carolina
13. Rhode Island

Vermont was fourteenth and the first free state (without slavery).

What significant piece of legislation impacting the future growth of the country passed under the Articles of Confederation?

Probably the finest achievement of the government under the Articles of Confederation was the passage of the Northwest Ordinance in July 1787. It created a territory of land that eventually became the states of Ohio, Indiana, Illinois, Wisconsin, Michigan, and Minnesota. The law provided a process by which these individual territories could eventually become states.

The Northwest Ordinance provided that none of the territories could allow slavery. It also provided for a great measure of religious freedom, providing: "No person, demeaning himself in a peaceable and orderly manner, shall ever be molested on account of his mode of worship, or religious sentiments, in the said territory."

What caused some leaders to want a new constitution?

It became apparent that a stronger central government was needed to protect the interests of the country as a whole. The economic interests of the Northern states clashed with the economic interests of the Southern states. Some states feuded over navigational rights over rivers. Congress could not force states to contribute money and funds needed to address emergency circumstances.

Other leaders saw the need for a strong central government after Shay's Rebellion in Massachusetts in 1786–1787. A group of economically desperate farmers—led by former Revolutionary War veteran Daniel Shays (1747–1825)—marched on the county courthouse to protest and prevent the courts from issuing foreclosure notices on farmers. The Massachusetts government, led by governor James Bowdoin and General Benjamin Lincoln, organized a state militia and crushed the rebellion.

What meetings of states caused even more discontent with the Articles?

In March 1785, representatives from Virginia and Maryland met to discuss navigational rights and other issues surrounding the Potomac River. The delegates met at Mount Vernon, the home of General George Washington. The representatives from the so-called Mount Vernon conference agreed that more states needed to be involved in the discussions.

This led to the Annapolis Convention, which met in 1786. Every state was invited to send representatives, but representatives from only five states—Virginia, Pennsylvania, New Jersey, Delaware, and New York—attended. The attendees agreed that there should be a national convention called to address problems with the Articles of Confederation. This led directly to the Philadelphia Convention of 1787.

THE U.S. CONSTITUTION

What was the stated purpose of the Philadelphia Convention?

The stated purpose of the Philadelphia Convention was to "revise the Articles of Confederation." Instead, the delegates eventually scrapped the Articles of Confederation entirely and created a new system of government—what became known as the United States Constitution.

Who were the leaders of the Philadelphia Convention?

There were many leaders of the Philadelphia Convention—a group of men whom Thomas Jefferson referred to as an "assembly of demigods." The delegates who attended the Convention unanimously selected George Washington—the hero of the Revolutionary War—as the president of the Convention. Washington's presence brought confidence to the others and established the proceedings as legitimate in the eyes of many.

Another leader in the Convention was James Madison, who is sometimes called "the Father of the Constitution." Madison, a politician from Virginia, fervently believed the nation needed a strong central government to help guard against sectional divisions and other problems between the states. He came to the Convention early and prepared an outline of such a structure of government. He wrote a memorandum, "Vices of the Political Systems of the United States." His planned structure of government was known as the Virginia Plan. Madison also took detailed notes during the Convention.

George Washington's presence at the Philadelphia Convention comforted the attendees that this was a legitimate proceeding in the formation of the government (painting by Howard Chandler Christy [1873–1952]).

What exactly was James Madison's role in the Philadelphia Convention?

James Madison (1751–1836) played a key role in the Philadelphia Convention. He arrived early, and had prepared well for the Convention. A month before the Convention opened, Madison published a document called "Vices of the Political Systems of the United States," in which he criticized many aspects of the Articles of Confederation.

At the Convention, he introduced several resolutions to provide for a stronger central government. His most famous contribution in terms of resolutions was the so-called Virginia Plan. Though sometimes referred to as the Randolph Plan because Edmund Randolph formally introduced it, Madison wrote the essence of the measure. Madison's plan consisted of a bicameral legislature—a House of Representatives and a Senate. The number of representatives in each house would be determined by the state's population. Under this plan, the people would elect members to the House of Representatives, but then members of the House would elect and vote on membership to the Senate. The Virginia Plan also included plans for a national (or federal) judiciary.

He also took a detailed set of notes about the proceedings of the Convention. Historians emphasize that without Madison's notes, we would know little about the historic meetings in Philadelphia that eventually led to the United States Constitution. Madison instructed that his detailed notes of the Convention not be released until the last delegate at the Convention died. Ironically, that last delegate was Madison, who died in 1836 at age eighty-five.

Madison also played a key role in persuading fellow Virginian George Washington to attend the proceedings. The delegates elected Washington as chairman of the meeting. Washington's presence was important, given his leadership and popularity after the Revolutionary War.

What did Madison do to help ratify the Constitution?

Madison knew the delegates' work was not complete simply because they had finished and signed the new Constitution. They had to convince the states to ratify this new constitution, which radically changed the power of the central government.

Using pseudonyms, Madison—along with Alexander Hamilton and John Jay— drafted a series of essays called *The Federalist Papers* which advanced forceful arguments for the necessity of the new Constitution. Madison also argued in the Virginia legislature for Virginia to ratify the Constitution. Madison argued directly against Virginia governor Patrick Henry.

What was the Virginia Plan?

The Virginia Plan, introduced on May 29, 1787, formed the basis of the Convention and was debated word by word. The plan contained fifteen resolves. It was the first plan introduced in the Convention and the one that most closely resembled the Convention's final product. It proposed that the powers of the federal government should be expanded to accomplish three goals: "common defence [sic], security of liberty, and general welfare." Resolve number three provided for two houses of Congress, or a bicameral legislature. Under the Virginia Plan, the people would elect the first branch. Then the members of the first branch would elect the second branch of the "National Legislature."

Under the Virginia Plan, the U.S. Congress would possess great power. Resolve number six granted Congress the power to negate, or veto, any laws passed by state legislatures. Resolve number seven provided Congress the power to appoint the "National Executive" or leader of the country. Thus, under this plan, Congress—not the people— would select the national leader. Resolve number nine provided for a "National Judiciary," or a set of judges that could hear cases throughout the country.

The Virginia Plan envisioned the structure of the new United States government under the new Constitution discussed in the Philadelphia Convention. Under the Virginia Plan, there would be three branches of government— legislative, executive, and judicial branches. It also called for a bicameral legislature composed of a House and a Senate. It determined that each house would be selected based on the population of the respective states, meaning that the larger, more populous states would have more representatives and senators. The Virginia Plan also called for a very strong national government.

With what other plan did the Virginia Plan compete?

The other major plan for the structure of the new Constitution was the so-called New Jersey Plan, proposed by William Paterson. This plan called for a weaker national government, only one house of Congress, and equal representation in the legislative branch. It also called for executive and judicial branches, but they would clearly be less powerful than the one-house legislature.

On June 15, 1787, Paterson introduced his plan. "Can we, as representatives of independent states, annihilate the essential powers of independency?" Paterson said when introducing his proposal. He wanted a weaker central government.

The New Jersey Plan contained many features, including a multiperson executive. Under the New Jersey Plan, Congress could act only on certain matters. Congress would elect the members of the federal executive. Congress could remove the persons of the federal executive if a majority of state leaders voted such action necessary.

Interestingly, the New Jersey Plan contained language providing that the laws of the U.S. Congress "shall be the supreme law of the respective States." This formed the basis for the supremacy clause of the U.S. Constitution. The supremacy clause provides that the laws of the national, or federal, government are the supreme law of the land, trumping the laws of the various states.

What was the Great Compromise?

The Great Compromise of 1787 was a measure articulated by Roger Sherman (1721–1793) of Connecticut that created the ultimate form of the U.S. Congress. It combined features of both the Virginia Plan and the New Jersey Plan. It allowed representatives from the larger states and the smaller states to agree on the composition of Congress. Under the Great Compromise, one house—the U.S. House of Representatives—is based on proportional representation. This meant that the larger states would have more representatives. The other house—the U.S. Senate—was based on equal representation, as each state would have two senators. Each side received something from the Great Compromise: the larger states received proportional representation in the House, but the smaller states received equal representation in the Senate.

How precarious was the Great Compromise and its ultimate success?

It was a very precarious time, and the Convention almost divided irreparably over this issue of legislative representation. Fortunately, delegate Roger Sherman of Connecticut proposed a measure that eventually saved the Constitution.

Roger Sherman was an influential politician with a distinguished political career. Sherman has the distinction of signing several great American documents—the Declaration and Resolves of 1774 (a document where the colonists declared their resolve to oppose British power), the Declaration of Independence, the Articles of Confederation, and finally the United States Constitution.

55

Sherman played an influential role in the Convention, but he is most remembered for his compromise that saved the Convention and the Constitution. Under this so-called "Great Compromise," the states would be represented equally in the Senate, and the states would be represented proportionally in the House of Representatives based on population. This proposal reflects our current system. In the House of Representatives, a state's number of representatives is based on the state's population. In the Senate, each state has two senators.

However, Sherman's proposal was voted down 6–5 when it was first introduced. The delegates continued to argue over the issue of proportional versus equal representation. On July 2, the states voted 5–5 on the question of equal representation in the Senate. The states of Connecticut, New York, New Jersey, Delaware, and Maryland favored equal representation. The states of Massachusetts, Pennsylvania, Virginia, North Carolina, and South Carolina opposed equal representation. The state of Georgia could have broken the tie, but the two Georgia delegates present—William Houstoun and Abraham Baldwin—split.

Four delegates from Georgia were present at the Convention. However, two of the members—William Few and William Pierce—left the convention for New York to vote on pressing matters in Congress. Few and Pierce would have voted against equal representation. The Convention hung in the balance. The small states would have lost the question of equal representation were it not for the vote of Abraham Baldwin. Baldwin lived in Connecticut virtually his whole life, having moved to Georgia only three years before the Convention. Some historians assert that Baldwin saved the Constitution because he split the Georgia votes, saving the small states from defeat. They argue that Baldwin voted the way he did because he knew the small states would collapse the Convention if they lost the equal representation question in the Senate.

The Convention then agreed to allow a committee of one person from each of the eleven states to be formed to explore the question of how to organize the Congress. The states voted 10–1 in favor of such a committee. The committee was composed primarily of individuals in favor of a senate chosen by equal representation. On July 5, the committee read its report to the entire delegation, calling for proportional representation in the House and equal representation in the Senate. Many of the delegates who had wanted proportional representation in both houses had conceded this issue, realizing that the delegates from small states might leave if they did not get their way.

Did all fifty-five delegates sign the final product of the Philadelphia Convention?

Several delegates left before the Convention convened in September. These included William Richardson Davie, Oliver Ellsworth, William Houston, William Houstoun, John Lansing, Jr., Alexander Martin, Luther Martin, James McClurg, John Francis Mercer, William Pierce, Caleb Strong, George Wythe, and Robert Yates.

Additionally, three members of the Convention stayed until the end but refused to sign the document: Elbridge Gerry, Edmund Randolph, and George Mason IV.

Who were the fifty-five Founding Framers of the Philadelphia Constitutional Convention?

The following table lists the states of the framers and their names:

Framers of the Constitution

State	Framers
Connecticut	Oliver Ellsworth, William Samuel Johnson, Roger Sherman
Delaware	Richard Bassett, Gunning Bedford, Jacob Broom, John Dickinson, George Read
Georgia	Abraham Baldwin, William Few, William Houstoun, William Pierce
Maryland	Daniel Carroll, Luther Martin, James McHenry, John F. Mercer, Daniel of St. Thomas Jenifer
Massachusetts	Elbridge Gerry, Nathan Gorham, Rufus King, Caleb Strong
New Hampshire	Michael Gillman, John Langdon
New Jersey	David Brearley, Jonathan Dayton, William Houston, William Livingston, William Paterson
New York	Alexander Hamilton, Robert Lansing, Robert Yates
North Carolina	William Blount, William Richardson Davie, Alexander Martin, Richard Dobbs Spaight, Hugh Williamson
Pennsylvania	George Clymer, Thomas Fitzsimons, Benjamin Franklin, Jared Ingersoll, Thomas Mifflin, Gouverneur Morris, Robert Morris, James Wilson
South Carolina	Pierce Butler, Charles Cotesworth Pinckney, John Rutledge
Virginia	John Blair, James Madison, George Mason IV, James McClurg, Edmund Randolph, George Washington, George Wythe

Why did Gerry, Randolph, and Mason refuse to sign the Constitution?

Ironically, Randolph later refused to sign the Constitution at the end of the Convention. He refused to sign it in part because he believed his constituents in Virginia would disapprove of the Constitution. He argued that the people in the states, through their representatives, should have the "full opportunity" to propose amendments to the Constitution. However, during the ratification battle in his home state of Virginia, Randolph fought for its adoption.

Gerry and Mason, key contributors throughout the summer, refused to sign the Constitution in part because it lacked a Bill of Rights. Gerry said that its major

George Mason IV, shown here, wrote the Bill of Rights with James Madison. Mason had, along with Edmund Randolph and Elbridge Gerry, opposed signing the Constitution with these assured rights for citizens.

failure was in failing to provide for a bill of rights. He later wrote: "There is no security in the proferred system, either for the rights of conscience or the liberty of the Press." For his part, a few days earlier, Mason said: "I would sooner chop off my right hand than put it to the Constitution."

Mason honestly believed that the system of constitutional government would produce either a "monarchy or a corrupt oppressive aristocracy." He also felt the "Constitution has been formed without the knowledge or idea of the people." Mason believed the delegates had exceeded their authority by secretly creating a powerful national government that would take away the powers of the states.

What did the new Constitution say about slavery?

The new Constitution did not directly address the slavery problem, probably because many of the members knew other members—particularly from the more agrarian, Southern states—would not be willing to compromise on the measure. However, the vast majority of the delegates did not want to dissolve the Union over slavery.

The issue of slavery was closely tied to the question of congressional representation. The Southern states wanted to count slaves in their population numbers because they would obtain more seats in the House of Representatives. The Northern states did not want to count slaves for purposes of legislative representation, since slaves would not vote or pay taxes. The Northern states also did not want the Southern states to obtain more power than they had.

The delegates eventually agreed to tie taxation to representation and to count slaves as three-fifths of a person. Some historians contend the Convention agreed to this compromise over slavery and representation in exchange for the exclusion of slavery in the Northwest Ordinance of 1787.

The Northern and Southern delegates bargained over the issues of slavery and trade well into August. On August 24, the Committee of Eleven issued a report that contained four provisions: (1) Congress could not prohibit the exportation of slaves until 1800; (2) Congress could tax imported slaves; (3) Exports could not be taxed; and (4) Congress could pass navigation acts by simple majority. The Northern states, which depended on commerce, wanted Congress to pass laws regulating trade.

The Constitution would extend the date to allow the importation of slaves until 1808. The Constitution also contained a clause, called the Fugitive Slave Clause, which allowed Southerners to go into northern states to recover runaway slaves. Unfortunately, the fugitive slave clause enabled the capture of free blacks in northern territory by southern slaveowners.

Thus, the Constitution approved of slavery—if somewhat less than enthusiastically—by counting slaves for the population of states for representative purposes. It also protected the African slave trade for twenty years and guaranteed that masters could recover their runaway slaves. Because of its approval of slavery, famed abolitionist William Lloyd Garrison famously burned a copy of the Constitution, calling it a "covenant with death and an agreement with Hell." However, not all members of the Convention approved of slavery. Gouvernour Morris famously referred to it as "the curse of Heaven on the states" that sanction it.

James Madison spoke about the Constitution and slavery at the Virginia ratification convention. Madison said: "The southern states would not have entered into the union of America without the temporary possession of that trade." However, Madison pointed out that under the Articles of Confederation, the slave trade could have continued forever. At least under the new Constitution, the importation of slaves would end in twenty years.

Also, the Constitution never uses the words "slave" or "slavery."

RATIFYING THE CONSTITUTION

After the Constitution was signed, what happened during the ratification process?

Article VII of the Constitution provides: "The ratification of the conventions of nine states shall be sufficient for the establishment of the Constitution between the states so ratifying the same." This meant that the "real fight" did not come on the convention floor. It came in the states over whether to ratify the Constitution. Many merchants, manufacturers, and big plantation owners in the South favored the Constitution. They knew the new Constitution would help protect their business interests.

But many small farmers did not want to sacrifice their individual freedom and become dependent on businesspeople. The battle over ratification became a great issue of the day. It captured the headlines and much space in the newspapers. Pamphlets were printed on each side. In September, Congress directed the state legislatures to call rat-

What were the principal objections of the Anti-Federalists to the Constitution?

The Anti-Federalists were particularly concerned with the so-called "necessary and proper" clause of the new Constitution. Article I, Section 18 provided Congress with the power to "make all Laws which shall be necessary and proper" for executing its powers vested in the Constitution. Other Anti-Federalists were concerned with the supremacy clause in Article I. Many Anti-Federalists viewed this clause as wiping out the powers of state governments.

Many Anti-Federalists also argued that the Constitution gave too much power to the president. Some feared that the president and the Senate would unite to become similar to the King of England and the upper house of the English Parliament, the House of Lords. The King of England and the House of Lords represented aristocrats, the upper class of society, and tended to ignore the interests of regular people.

ification conventions to vote on the new document. Under the ratification process, the state legislatures would vote to call special conventions. Delegates—often the state legislators themselves—would vote at the conventions.

The ratification process was not easy. Political leaders were divided. Supporters of the new Constitution with its strong central government called themselves Federalists. Opponents of the Constitution were called Anti-Federalists. Many of them opposed the Constitution because it failed to provide for a bill of rights and gave too much power to the federal government at the expense of state governments.

What were *The Federalist Papers,* and what was their importance?

The Federalist Papers were a series of anonymous essays that galvanized much popular support for the Constitution during the ratification struggle. In the most populous states of New York and Virginia, the Anti-Federalists fought hard. After the Philadelphia Convention, James Madison co-wrote a series of articles with Alexander Hamilton and John Jay that became known as *The Federalist Papers*. These eighty-five essays—written under the pen name Publius—are still considered the definitive work on the Constitution. Thomas Jefferson once called them "the best commentary on the principles of government which ever was written."

These articles discussed the framework of the Constitution, including the principles of checks and balances and separation of powers among the three branches of government. Hamilton, Jay, and Madison sought to persuade readers that the newly designed government was the best course of action for the young country. Hamilton wrote that the nation faced a "crisis." He wrote that if the country voted against the new Constitution, that decision would "deserve to be considered as the general misfortune of mankind."

In *Federalist Paper* No. 45, Madison argued that the state governments did not have much to fear from the federal government. Madison wrote: "The powers delegated by the proposed Constitution to the federal government are few and defined. Those which are to remain in the State governments are numerous and indefinite."

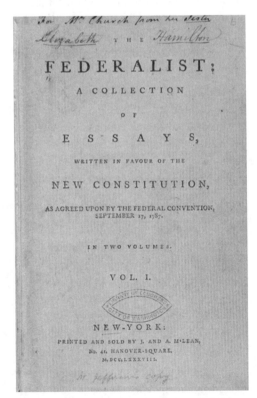

The cover of the first collection of *The Federalist Papers,* published in 1788. Written by Alexander Hamilton, John Jay, and James Madison, the essays argued for the merits of the U.S. Constitution.

Did the Anti-Federalists have their own writings?

Yes, the Anti-Federalists also relied on a series of anonymous essays. Several Anti-Federalists also wrote articles under pen names attacking various aspects of the Constitution. An Anti-Federalist who called himself the "Federal Farmer" critiqued the Constitution in a series of letters published in the Poughkeepsie (New York) Country Journal from November 1787 to January 1788. The letters also appeared in pamphlet form. For many years, it was assumed that Richard Henry Lee of Virginia was the author. Now, some historians believe the author was New York Anti-Federalist Melancton Smith.

The "Letters from the Federal Farmer" criticized the new Constitution and its proponents as showing a "strong tendency to aristocracy." The Federal Farmer argued that the Constitution concentrated too much power in the central government. The author of the Federal Farmer also made some accurate predictions about the future of our government. For example, the Federal Farmer wrote: "This system promises a large field of employment to military gentlemen and gentlemen of the law."

Robert Yates, a New York judge who served in the Convention until he left in July, wrote a series of articles under the pen name "Brutus." Brutus was the Roman republican who helped assassinate Julius Caesar to prevent Caesar from overthrowing the Roman Republic. In one of his articles he criticized the powers granted to the judicial branch. He wrote: "The supreme court under this constitution would be exalted above all other power in the government and subject to no control."

How did the battle play out between Federalists and Anti-Federalists?

The battle between Federalists and Anti-Federalists was intense. However, the Federalists possessed advantages. They enjoyed most of the media support. The large newspapers from Boston, New York, and Philadelphia took up the Federalist cause. They also seemed to have the best ammunition—the detailed document known as the Constitution. Though the Anti-Federalists made many arguments against provisions of the Constitution, they did not have their own document. The Anti-Federalists could only criticize the new document.

However, the Anti-Federalists seized upon the lack of a bill of rights as a prime weapon in the ratification battles. Delaware became the first state to ratify the Constitution, and it did so unanimously on December 7, 1787. Then an intense battle began in Pennsylvania. James Wilson took the lead in defending the Constitution in his home state.

In a well-known address delivered on October 6, 1787, Wilson argued that the inclusion of a bill of rights was "superfluous and absurd." The new Congress, Wilson argued, "possesses no influence whatsoever upon the press." Wilson pointed out that many Anti-Federalists were criticizing the new document because it provided for a standing Army. Wilson responded: "Yet I do not know a nation in the world which has not found it necessary and useful to maintain the appearance of strength in a season of the most profound tranquility."

61

In what states was the ratification debate of the Constitution closest and most intense?

Ratification was most difficult in the populous states of Massachusetts and New York. The debate in Massachusetts was particularly intense. Massachusetts voted 187–168 in favor of the Constitution on February 6, 1788, only after the Federalists agreed to recommend amending the Constitution to include protections for individual liberties.

Massachusetts became the first state officially to recommend amendments to the Constitution during the ratification process. Though the nine proposed amendments bear little resemblance to the final U.S. Bill of Rights, they were an important precursor to the Bill of Rights.

The state assembly had to vote on a state convention. Many of the Anti-Federalists in the state legislature refused to attend the assembly. They did not want the Assembly to have a quorum, or a sufficient number of members to take a valid vote. Allegedly, a mob of people broke into a local home and dragged two Anti-Federalists to the Assembly floor in order to create a quorum. The delegates voted 45–2 in favor of a ratification convention. The state convention met for five weeks. Finally, on December 12, the delegates voted for ratification by a vote of 46–23. The vote upset some citizens with Anti-Federalist sympathies. A mob of such people attacked James Wilson in Carlisle, Pennsylvania.

Pennsylvania ratified the Constitution on December 12 by a vote of 46–23. The Pennsylvania delegates also considered fifteen amendments proposed by Anti-Federalist Robert Whitehill. These proposed amendments were similar to what later became the U.S. Bill of Rights.

What happened in Virginia with respect to ratification?

Actually, New Hampshire became the required ninth state on June 21, 1788, voting 57–46 in favor of the Constitution. Although the Constitution was technically in effect after New Hampshire ratified it, the support of Virginia was essential. Virginia did not know that New Hampshire had become the necessary ninth state. Because Virginia was such a large and powerful state, her ratification of the Constitution was crucial.

Virginia was the home of James Madison, George Washington, and Thomas Jefferson, all of whom supported the Constitution. However, the state was also the home of a group of well-known Anti-Federalists, including Patrick Henry and George Mason. The battle in Virginia was particularly difficult. After one debate, Madison fell ill and was bedridden for three straight days. Some great statesmen, such as the brilliant orator from Virginia Patrick Henry, led the Anti-Federalists. During the debate on ratification in his state, Henry asked: "What right had they [the Constitution delegates] to say, 'We the People'?"

In arguing against the Constitution, Mason wrote, "It is ascertained, by history, that there never was a government over a very extensive country without destroying the liberties of the people." However, state delegate Edmund Pendleton countered in the Virginia Ratification Convention, "In reviewing the history of the world, shall we find an instance where any society retained its liberty without government?"

In June, Governor Edmund Randolph spoke in favor of the Constitution, even though he had failed to sign it the previous September. Randolph explained that he did not sign because the document did not contain necessary amendments. However, he said that because other states had proposed amendments to be passed after ratification, he would vote in favor of ratification. He also pointed out that eight other states had already ratified the Constitution.

Patrick Henry charged that Randolph had been persuaded to change positions by none other than George Washington. Though this charge cannot be proven beyond a shadow of a doubt, Washington did later name Randolph his first attorney general.

Madison managed to gather enough support for the Constitution in the Virginia state convention on June 25, 1788. The delegates narrowly approved the Constitution. Two days later, a committee at the state convention proposed a bill of rights be added to the Constitution. Virginia voted in favor of ratification by a narrow vote of 89–79. Virginia also attached proposed amendments as well, many of which would later be contained in the Bill of Rights. Some Anti-Federalists were very upset and wanted to resist the new Constitution. However, at a meeting in Richmond, Patrick Henry said that they must accept defeat: "As true and faithful republicans [honorable citizens] you had all better go home."

Many Anti-Federalists became supporters of the new government. For example, Anti-Federalist Elbridge Gerry, who refused to sign the Convention, later became James Madison's vice president.

THE BILL OF RIGHTS

Why were the first ten amendments—the Bill of Rights—added to the Constitution?

The Bill of Rights was added to the Constitution in part because many people wanted to ensure themselves protection from the new, strong federal government created by the new Constitution. The two leading political parties of the time were the Federalists and the Anti-Federalists. The Federalists generally supported a very strong central government; the Anti-Federalists showed more concern for the rights of individual state governments. The issue of the Bill of Rights was not a huge issue at the Philadelphia Convention in 1787 when the Constitution was created. Representative George Mason raised the issue, but it was quickly defeated.

However, the Bill of Rights became a huge political issue during the ratification debates in certain states. Eventually, supporters of the Constitution and ratification in a few states were able to secure ratification of the new Constitution only by promising that there would soon be the addition of a Bill of Rights.

What member of the House is sometimes called "the Father of the Bill of Rights"?

James Madison (1751–1836), fourth president of the United States, served in the U.S. House of Representatives for his home state of Virginia from 1789 until 1797. On June 8, 1789, Madison introduced in the House his proposals for amending the U.S. Constitution—creating a so-called Bill of Rights. This speech earned Madison the

James Madison, who later became the country's fourth president, was a key player in the Philadelphia Convention and in the writing of the Constitution. He is often thought of as the "Father of the Bill of Rights."

moniker "Father of the Bill of Rights." Madison sought to introduce measures which would provide a degree of individual freedom for the people from infringements by the government. Madison believed that a Bill of Rights would increase popularity for the new federal government and the U.S. Constitution. In his speech, Madison referred to the provisions in his proposed Bill of Rights as "the great rights of mankind." Madison's speech is one of the most significant in American history.

Where did Madison look for possible proposals that eventually became included in the Bill of Rights?

Madison compiled a list of various proposals from various state constitutions. Many states had a section similar to the eventual Bill of Rights. Some of these sections were called Declarations of Rights.

Isn't it true that the original Constitution (before the Bill of Rights) was already a bill of rights?

There is some credence to the argument that the Constitution as it existed before the Bill of Rights already was a type of bill of rights. For example, the Constitution prohibited Congress or state legislatures from passing bills of attainder or *ex post facto* laws. Bills of attainder are laws that target a specific group of people, while *ex post facto* laws are laws that make something a crime after the fact.

Furthermore, the Constitution prohibits Congress from suspending a writ of habeas corpus except in very limited situations, such as war. Another provision of the Constitution prohibits individuals in political office from having to take religious tests to qualify for office. All of these provisions in the body of the Constitution do provide a measure of individual freedom—similar to what the Bill of Rights does.

THE EARLY PRESIDENCY

Who were the original members of President Washington's Cabinet?

Washington sought to form a group of key advisors to assist him in leading the new federal government. He chose Alexander Hamilton as secretary of the treasury, Thomas Jefferson as secretary of state, Henry Knox as secretary of war (present-day secretary of defense), Edmund Randolph as attorney general, and Samuel Osgood as postmaster general. Congress approved of these executive branch agencies.Hamilton, Jefferson, Knox, and Randolph regularly counseled Washington on a wide range of matters. As postmaster general, Osgood did not participate in those discussions.

What two members of Washington's Cabinet disagreed mightily over many issues?

Hamilton and Jefferson disagreed mightily over many issues. Their disagreements in part contributed to the rise of the two-party political system in the United States. Hamilton was a Federalist, the party that generally favored a very strong central government and tended to ally with Great Britain. Jefferson became a Democratic-Republican, which favored a less powerful central government and tended to ally with France. Hamilton favored a strong fiscal policy, including the creation of the National Bank. Jefferson viewed the measure as an unconstitutional grab of power by the federal government. The only thing Hamilton and Jefferson seemingly could agree on was their mutual affinity for President Washington.

What did Washington think of political parties?

Washington disfavored political parties, believing they would create discord in the country. In his farewell address upon leaving office, he warned the country that political parties "are likely, in the course of time and things, to become potent engines, by which cunning, ambitious, and unprincipled men will be enabled to subvert the power of the people and to usurp for themselves the reins of government." He warned that partisan politics and different political factions could create a "frightful despotism" for the country.

How did Washington contribute to the tradition of executive privilege?

In 1796, the House of Representatives demanded to see administration documents concerning the Jay Treaty. Washington refused to hand over the documents, reasoning that only the Senate—not the House—is responsible for the ratification of treaties. Washington's act of refusing to comply with the House's demands is seen as a precursor to the concept of executive privilege.

65

What was the Jay Treaty?

The Jay Treaty was a treaty with Great Britain that the United States signed in 1794 during Washington's second term. At the time, British troops remained stationed in the American Northwest in defiance of the Treaty of Paris, the treaty that ended the Revolutionary War. Great Britain claimed the Americans had not paid back all pre-Revolutionary debts. Also, British ships were blocking American merchant vessels in the Caribbean in an attempt to stem American trade with France. Washington sent Chief Justice John Jay to negotiate a treaty with British officials. The resulting agreement was known as the Jay Treaty. The British agreed to remove their troops from the Ohio frontier. America's debts would be settled by arbitration. The British received most favored nation status for trading. Though criticized, the treaty—which was in effect for ten years—prevented an American-British conflict until the War of 1812.

EARLY UNREST IN THE COUNTRY

What was the "Whiskey Rebellion"?

The Whiskey Rebellion was an uprising among many grain farmers in western Pennsylvania. They objected to the Whiskey Act of 1791, a tax the federal government imposed on whiskey. The farmers believed the federal government overstepped its bounds by imposing too great a tax burden on farmers. The protest was seen by some as reminiscent of the colonists' protest of the British government's Stamp Act tax on the colonists.

Washington eventually considered the resistance movement serious enough that he led a formidable force of more than thirteen thousand troops to suppress the rebellion. It was the only time a sitting president actually led troops toward a battle. Washington led the troops to Carlisle, Pennsylvania, but not all the way to face the farmers who were just outside Pittsburgh. The farmers kowtowed to the federal authority, and Washington pardoned those in the uprising who swore allegiance to the federal government.

What were the controversial "Alien and Sedition Acts"?

The Alien and Sedition Acts, passed in 1798, caused great controversy. This legislation consisted of four laws: (1) the Naturalization Act, which increased the required period of residence for would-be citizens from five to fourteen years; (2) the Alien Friends Act, which gave the president the power to remove from the country outsiders he deemed "dangerous"; (3) the Alien Enemies Act, which gave the president the power to deport those aliens who were from countries at war with the United States; and (4) the Sedition Act, which made it a crime to make "false, scandalous, and malicious" writings against the government. Many—including Vice President Thomas Jefferson—opposed these laws as an invasion of state rights and a violation of individual freedoms. For example, many believed the Sedition Act of 1798 violated the First Amendment rights of freedom of speech and freedom of the press.

For the most part, the Sedition Act was used to prosecute editors of Democratic-Republican newspapers. These editors published newspapers that criticized President John Adams and his foreign policy towards France. Men such as Benjamin Franklin Bache, editor of the *General Advertiser* in Philadelphia (also known as the *Aurora*), and Anthony Haswell, editor of the *Vermont Gazette*, were arrested for their sharp criticism of Federalists. The Alien and Sedition Act was never appealed to the Supreme Court, even after judicial review was established by *Marbury v. Madison*.

What famous document did Madison draft in opposition to the Alien and Sedition Acts?

Madison—and his friend Thomas Jefferson—adamantly opposed the Alien and Sedition Acts of 1798, adopted by the Federalist-controlled Congress and signed by President John Adams. In response, Madison and Jefferson drafted the Virginia and Kentucky resolutions, documents approved by the states' respective state legislatures, declaring the new federal laws null and void. Madison drafted the Virginia Resolution, while Jefferson wrote the Kentucky Resolutions.

What was the XYZ Affair?

The XYZ Affair refers to a failed peace mission (1797–1798) between three American envoys (Charles Cotesworth Pinckney, John Marshall, and Elbridge Gerry) and three agents of the French foreign minister Charles-Maurice de Talleyrand (Jean Conrad Hottinger, Pierre Bellamy, and Lucien Hauteval). Talleyrand instructed his envoys to refuse negotiations with the American envoys unless Talleyrand received a personal payment (in actuality, a bribe) of $25,000 and a $10 million loan to France. The three Americans refused and negotiations ended, exacerbating tensions between the two countries. Adams later referred to the three French agents as X, Y, and Z.

What was the Quasi-War?

The Quasi-War was the name given to the conflict between France and the United States between 1798 and 1800. French and American vessels fought at sea for much of that time, though there never was a formal declaration of war.

THE SUPREME COURT

How was the U.S. Supreme Court created?

Article III, Section 1 of the U.S. Constitution provided that "the judicial Power of the United States shall be vested in one supreme Court, and in such inferior Courts as the Congress may from time to time ordain and establish." The Constitution was adopted in 1787 and ratified in 1788. However, the Constitution did not create the U.S. Supreme Court. Congress passed a law known as the Judiciary Act of 1789, which created the Court and established its jurisdiction. The Judiciary Act of 1789 called for six justices on the Court—a chief justice and five associate justices.

Who was the principal author of the Judiciary Act of 1789?

Oliver Ellsworth of Connecticut was the principal author of the Judiciary Act of 1789. A member of the Philadelphia Convention of 1787, Ellsworth became a U.S. senator when the Senate first convened in 1789. He was elected chair of the committee designed to follow the dictates of Article III of the new Constitution to create a federal judicial system. William Paterson from New Jersey, another member of the 1787 Convention and an original U.S. senator, also assisted in the drafting of the Judiciary Act of 1789. Both Ellsworth and Paterson later became justices on the U.S. Supreme Court. They were both classmates at the College of New Jersey (later Princeton College) before they entered politics.

Who were the first six justices on the U.S. Supreme Court?

The first six justices on the U.S. Supreme Court were John Jay (chief justice), John Rutledge, William Cushing, James Wilson, John Blair, and James Iredell. Robert H. Harrison was one of the first six justices nominated to the Court, but he declined the nomination because of poor health. In his place, President George Washington nominated Iredell of North Carolina.

John Jay was the first chief justice of the U.S. Supreme Court, serving from 1789 to 1795. He was the second governor of New York state from 1795 until 1801.

When did the U.S. Supreme Court initially meet?

The U.S. Supreme Court initially met on February 2, 1790, in the Royal Exchange Building on New York City's Broad Street. The Court met on the second floor of the building in the afternoons, as the New York state legislature met there during the morning hours. A year later, the Court convened in Philadelphia, the new national capital. The U.S. Supreme Court did not meet in Washington, D.C., until February 2, 1801.

Why is John Marshall considered the greatest of the chief justices?

In his 1996 biography of Marshall, author Jean Edward Smith referred to the chief justice as "the Definer of the Nation." Marshall's opinions gave the U.S. Supreme Court and the judicial branch the power and respect they deserved. He did this in many ways. For example, he persuaded his colleagues to drop the practice of *in seriatim* opinions, where each justice would speak and issue his own opinion. Under Marshall, the Court often spoke in one unified voice—many times through Chief Justice Marshall himself. He also established the principle of judicial review in *Marbury v. Madison* (1803), which gave the judiciary the power to review the constitutionality of legislation and executive regulations. As Supreme Court Justice Sandra Day O'Connor wrote in her book *The Majesty of the Law*: "It is no overstatement to claim that Chief Justice Marshall fulfilled the Constitution's promise of an independent federal judiciary."

Another factor of Marshall's greatness is that he was the first chief justice to serve for a significant period of time. Marshall served thirty-four years on the Court. In comparison, the first chief justice, John Jay, served only six years, and John Rutledge and Oliver Ellsworth served shorter periods of time. Justice Oliver Wendell Holmes, who served from 1902–1932, believed part of Marshall's greatness lay in his "being there" during the formative period of the nation. But Marshall was more than just an accidental force of history. He had great leadership abilities that enabled him to guide the Court during his lengthy term as the Chief.

What were the underlying facts of *Marbury v. Madison*?

Federalist President John Adams was leaving office, having suffered defeat at the hands of his vice president and political rival, Thomas Jefferson of the Democratic-Republican party. The Federalist Congress quickly passed a new judiciary act that cre-

Chief Justice John Marshall is still considered the greatest justice to lead the U.S. Supreme Court in all of American history. He served on the bench from 1801 to 1835.

69

ated many new judgeships, including forty-five justice of the peace positions. Adams's secretary of state, none other than John Marshall himself, then had to sign the commissions for these "midnight justices" for them to take office.

Unfortunately, Marshall did not have time to deliver all the commissions before the new Jefferson Administration took over the White House. Seventeen justices of the peace, including William Marbury, did not receive their commissions before Jefferson assumed office. Marbury sued Jefferson's secretary of state, James Madison (our future fourth president), asking the Court to issue a writ of mandamus forcing Madison to deliver Marbury his commission.

What did the Court rule in *Marbury v. Madison*?

Chief Justice John Marshall, who seemingly had a bit of a conflict of interest, wrote the opinion for the Court. He noted that Marbury was entitled to his commission, as he had been appointed by the president, confirmed by the Senate, and otherwise qualified for the position. The Court also determined that Madison wrongfully withheld Marbury's commission from him.

However, Marshall also ruled that Marbury's suit must fail because Section 13 of the Judiciary Act of 1789, which authorized the Court to issue writs of mandamus, was unconstitutional. Marshall reasoned that Section 13 conflicted with Article III of the U.S. Constitution, which provided that the Supreme Court had only appellate jurisdiction (not original jurisdiction) over Marbury's case. In other words, Marshall reasoned that Section 13 was unconstitutional, because it attempted to confer original jurisdiction to litigants such as Marbury, but the Constitution provided that the Court had only appellate jurisdiction, meaning the suit had to be filed in the lower courts. Marshall explained that "the jurisdiction had to be appellate, not original."

Marshall explained that the Supreme Court had the power of judicial review—the ability to determine the constitutionality or unconstitutionality of laws. He famously wrote that "it is emphatically the province and duty of the judicial department to say what the law is."

What happened to William Marbury?

Marbury never became a justice of the peace, although he did become a prominent and successful banker in Washington, D.C.

CONGRESS

When did the House of Representatives first meet?

The U.S. House of Representatives first met on March 4, 1789, but it could not perform any real work until April 1, 1789, when it achieved a quorum.

What are the exclusive powers of the House of Representatives?

The exclusive powers of the House of Representatives are to impeach public officials (they are tried in the Senate), to initiate revenue legislation, and to elect the president of the United States if there is no victor from the electoral college vote.

What are the qualifications for a person to serve in the House?

To serve in the House, a person must be at least twenty-five years of age, be a citizen of the United States for at least seven years, and reside in the state they represent at the time of the election.

What is the Speaker of the House?

The Speaker of the House is the presiding officer of the House of Representatives. The Constitution, Article I, Section 2, Clause 5 provides: "The House of Representatives shall chuse [sic] their Speaker and other Officers and shall have the sole Power of Impeachment."

The House of Representatives elects its speaker at the beginning of each Congress.

Who was the first Speaker of the House?

The first Speaker of the House was Frederick Muhlenberg (1750–1801), a member of the Federalist Party from Pennsylvania. Muhlenberg was a minister who served two terms as Speaker of the House—from 1789 to 1791 and 1793 to 1795. His brother, John Peter Gabriel Muhlenberg (1746–1807), also served in the House at the same time. John Peter served the same two terms as did Frederick, as well as an additional term from 1799–1801. John Peter also later served in the U.S. Senate in 1801.

When did the Senate first meet?

The United States Senate met for the first time in New York City on March 4, 1789. However, there was not a quorum until April.

Where did the Senate move?

The Senate moved from New York City to Philadelphia, Pennsylvania, on December 6, 1790. It remained in Philadelphia for about a decade before moving to its present location—Washington, D.C.

How are senators elected?

Senators used to be elected by state legislatures. However, in 1913 the Seventeenth Amendment became law. This constitutional amendment provided that senators

Frederick Muhlenberg was the first Speaker of the House.

would be elected directly by popular vote. It provided, in part: "The Senate of the United States shall be composed of two Senators from each State, elected by the People thereof, for six years; and each Senator shall have one vote."

What are the qualifications for a person to serve in the Senate?

A person must be at least thirty years of age, be a citizen of the United States for nine years, and reside in the state for which they are elected to serve.

What original members of the Senate later served on the U.S. Supreme Court?

Oliver Ellsworth (1745–1807) and William Paterson (1745–1806) were members of the first U.S. Senate. Ellsworth served as senator for his home state of Connecticut from 1789 until 1796, when he was nominated by President George Washington to serve as chief justice of the U.S. Supreme Court. Paterson served as senator for his home state of New Jersey. He was not a senator for very long, as he served from March 1789 until November 1790 before becoming governor of New Jersey. He later served as an associate justice on the U.S. Supreme Court, beginning in 1793.

PRE-CIVIL WAR AMERICA

PRESIDENTIAL ELECTIONS AND PRESIDENTS

What complication resulted from the election of 1800?

The problem in the election of 1800 was that Thomas Jefferson received the same number of votes as his presumed vice-presidential candidate, Aaron Burr. Both Jefferson and Burr received seventy-three votes. Because each received the same number of votes, the U.S. House of Representatives voted to determine who would serve as president. This problem led to the relatively quick passage of the Twelfth Amendment in 1804.

However, it took thirty-six ballots for the U.S. House of Representatives to break the electoral vote tie and resolve the controversy. The rules required the winner to receive an electoral margin in nine of the then existing sixteen states. In the first thirty-five ballots, Jefferson won eight states—one short of the necessary nine. Finally, on the thirty-sixth ballot, Maryland and Vermont shifted their support to Jefferson.

What was America's involvement in the Barbary War?

Thomas Jefferson became the first president to send soldiers to fight on foreign soil when he sent troops to engage Tripoli, Libya, which had declared war on the United States. In the First Barbary War (1801–1805), America faced the so-called Barbary States, which included the Sultanate of Morocco and the Regencies of Algiers, Tunis, and Tripoli. Tripoli managed to capture the USS *Philadelphia* during the conflict, but a Marine unit secured the vessel and burned it, preventing its use by the enemy. Marines later defeated Tripoli forces in the city of Derna, Libya.

Which former political foe actively lobbied for Jefferson and against Burr?

Alexander Hamilton—Jefferson's rival in President Washington's administration— was not a supporter of Thomas Jefferson. But Hamilton absolutely despised Burr. Hamilton used his considerable influence among the Federalist members of the House of Representatives to swing the election in the House to Jefferson.

One of the most famous duels in American history was between Aaron Burr and Alexander Hamilton. Hamilton died and Burr, though never found guilty of murder, saw his political career end as a result.

What happened to Aaron Burr?

Aaron Burr served as Thomas Jefferson's first vice president from 1801–1805. On July 11, 1804, he killed Alexander Hamilton in a duel in Weehawken, New Jersey. When Burr learned that he would not be Jefferson's vice president for Jefferson's second term, Burr decided to run for the governorship of New York. Hamilton vigorously opposed Burr, whom he had also opposed in the presidential election of 1800. At the duel, Hamilton fired first, but missed. Some historians have questioned whether Hamilton actually intended to hit Burr. Whatever the case, Burr hit Hamilton in the abdomen with his shot.

Burr faced indictments in both New Jersey and New York but was never brought to trial. He moved out west, seeking to acquire land in present-day Texas. Burr was suspected of plotting to form an independent nation in the southwest part of the country. Jefferson had his former vice president arrested and charged with treason in 1807. He faced trial in Richmond, Virginia, but was acquitted of all charges. Burr left the country, traveling to England and then France. He returned to the United States and practiced law in New York until his death in 1836.

What famous land expedition did Jefferson order?

Jefferson ordered Meriwether Lewis and William Clark to explore the western part of North America. This famous trip became known as the Lewis and Clark Expedition. Like Jefferson, Meriwether Lewis was born in Albemarle County in Virginia and served as Jefferson's trusted White House secretary. When Jefferson discussed the idea of a western expedition, Lewis agreed to take the lead in the matter. Lewis asked Clark, a man he met while defending federal interests during the Whiskey Rebellion, to accompany him on the trip.

What was the Monroe Doctrine?

The Monroe Doctrine was a foreign policy statement announced by President James Monroe (1758–1831; fifth president, 1817–1825) during his seventh annual address to Congress delivered in December 1823. The doctrine established that the United States would not interfere with developments on the European continent but that the United States would oppose vigorously any attempt by European countries with suspicion and

What was the Panic of 1819?

The Panic of 1819 was a major financial crisis marked by mortgage foreclosures, inflation, and banks recalling loans. The federal government and Monroe responded with the Land Act of 1820, which helped alleviate some of the financial pressure.

"as dangerous to our peace and safety." Historians have lauded the doctrine as one of the most significant statements in the history of American foreign policy.

What was the Era of Good Feelings?

The Era of Good Feelings was a period from about 1816 to 1825, during which there was relative domestic and political calm. The term is often used to describe the time period of much of the Monroe presidency. Benjamin Russell, a journalist with the Boston newspaper the *Columbian Centinel*, coined the term after President Monroe visited the New England area to quell any sectional differences.

Who were the candidates in the presidential election of 1824?

The candidates included John Quincy Adams (1767–1848) from Massachusetts; Andrew Jackson (1767–1845) from Tennessee; William H. Crawford from Georgia; and Henry Clay from Kentucky. Adams and Crawford had both served in President Monroe's Cabinet—Adams as secretary of state and Crawford as secretary of the treasury. Jackson was a U.S. senator and former war hero, while Clay was Speaker of the U.S. House of Representatives.

Who won the popular vote in the presidential election of 1824?

Jackson captured the popular vote with more than 150,000 votes, while Adams captured just over 100,000. Jackson also won more electoral votes (ninety-nine) than Adams (eighty-four). However, Jackson failed to capture the required majority of 131 electoral votes—Crawford tallied forty-one electoral votes and Clay thirty-seven. When no candidate received a majority of the electoral votes, the decision fell to the House of Representatives. The representatives from each state voted for a candidate. Adams ended up capturing thirteen states (to Jackson's seven and Crawford's four). Thus, Adams became president as he captured more than a majority of the states (thirteen out of twenty-four) to win the electoral vote and the presidency.

Who was the first Speaker of the House to have significant prominence and power in the government?

Henry Clay (1777–1852) was the Speaker of the House who acquired a great deal of power in American politics. Clay served as Speaker of the House three different times:

1811–1814, 1815–1820, and 1823–1825. He also served as a U.S. senator and U.S. secretary of state in his long and illustrious political career. He is considered one of the greatest and most influential members in the history of Congress.

Clay used his considerable powers as Speaker to pass legislation he supported and thwart legislation he opposed. He also decided the presidential election of 1824, when Clay threw his support behind John Quincy Adams instead of Andrew Jackson, who actually received more electoral votes. Clay then served as Adams's secretary of state, causing Jackson's supporters to term this the "Corrupt Bargain."

What was the "Corrupt Bargain"?

The "Corrupt Bargain" referred to a claim asserted by supporters of Andrew Jackson that John Quincy Adams and Henry Clay engaged in a corrupt bargain to obtain votes for Adams. They maintained that Clay encouraged others in the House to vote for Adams because Adams agreed to name Clay as his secretary of state if he won the presidency. While Clay did encourage members of the House to vote for Adams rather than Jackson—who later became Adams's secretary of state—the two contended that there never was any corrupt bargain. Clay maintained that he thought Adams would be better equipped to handle the presidency than Jackson.

What happened in Adams's reelection attempt?

Adams could never overcome the allegations that he did not deserve to win the election of 1824, as Jackson's supporters fanned the flames of public discontent. Furthermore, many members of Congress, allied with Jackson, continually thwarted Adams's proposals. In 1828, Jackson supporters effectively convinced enough voters that he deserved the election four years earlier, winning 178 electoral votes to only eighty-three for Adams.

What was unusual about Jackson's inauguration celebration?

Jackson's inauguration in March 1829 was attended by masses of people. A virtual mob flocked to the White House to shake hands with Jackson, who was considered a president for the people, rather than an East Coast elitist. By some accounts, Jack-

Pictured here in a c. 1843 daguerrotype, John Quincy Adams was America's sixth president. He failed to gain reelection in no small part because of the "Corrupt Bargain" scandal the Jacksonians accused him of.

> ## Whom did Andrew Jackson kill in a duel years before he became president?
>
> Jackson killed a man named Charles Dickinson in May 1806, following a dispute between Jackson and Joseph Erwin over a horse race. Apparently, Erwin owed Jackson some money after losing a bet. When there was difficulty collecting the money, Jackson or one of his friends made a negative comment about Erwin.
>
> Erwin's son-in-law, Dickinson, intervened and challenged Jackson to a duel. Dickinson—apparently quite handy with a pistol—fired first, hitting Jackson. Jackson then returned fire, killing Dickinson. Jackson carried Dickinson's bullet in his body for the remainder of his life.

son was nearly trampled by the rush of people and had to retreat from the White House grounds.

What was the Nullification Crisis?

The Nullification Crisis arose around the claims by some political leaders in South Carolina—including Jackson's first vice president, John C. Calhoun (1782–1850)—that a state could nullify federal laws it found unconstitutional and not worthy of respect. South Carolina advocated the nullification doctrine after the U.S. Congress passed a tariff bill that state leaders found unwise and unfair.

Jackson and Calhoun clashed over this issue of nullification. At one political event in 1830, President Jackson was asked to give a toast. Looking at his vice president, he said loudly: "The Federal Union—It Must Be Preserved!" Allegedly, Calhoun then gave the following toast as something of a retort: "The Union: next to our Liberty the most dear: may we all remember that it can only be preserved by respecting the rights of the States and distributing equally the benefit and burden of the Union!"

Jackson removed Calhoun supporters from his Cabinet, and it was apparent that Calhoun's political fortunes were dwindling in the Jackson Administration.

What was the "Eaton Affair"?

The Eaton Affair, also known as the Petticoat Affair (1830–1831), involved how the wives of Jackson's Cabinet members treated Peggy Eaton, the wife of Secretary of War John Eaton. Many women, including Floride Calhoun—the wife of Vice President John C. Calhoun—believed Peggy Eaton did not comport herself properly and married John Eaton far too soon after the death of her first husband.

Andrew Jackson sided with Peggy Eaton, leading to great tension among his Cabinet. It led to the effective dissolution of Jackson's original Cabinet. Jackson came to rely on a group of informal advisors known as his "Kitchen Cabinet."

77

Joseph Smith

An interesting sidebar during this time in American history is the publication of the Book of Mormon and the story of Joseph Smith (1805–1844) and Brigham Young (1801–1877). Smith declared that in 1823 he had been visited by the angel Moroni, who revealed to Smith that a tribe of Israelites had escaped the Old World to settle in North America. Moroni then told Smith where to find golden plates that were buried near his home in Vermont and that revealed the history of these people and how they believed in Jesus centuries before the Savior's birth. Smith also asserted that he had visions of Jesus and God and that they had commanded him to establish the Church of Christ (now the Church of Christ of Latter-Day Saints). After publishing the Book of Mormon in 1830, Smith and his growing number of converts were soon persecuted for their beliefs (many of them controversial, such as allowing polygamy), and they fled to Ohio and then Illinois. When Smith destroyed a newspaper that had criticized him and his church, he was arrested and, in 1844, killed by an angry mob. A successor was found in Brigham Young, who led the Mormons to a new home in Salt Lake City, Utah, where they could live free of persecution.

Who comprised Jackson's unofficial "Kitchen Cabinet"?

Jackson's "Kitchen Cabinet" consisted of Martin Van Buren (1782–1862)—his former secretary of state who would become his vice president in his second term; Francis Preston Blair, the editor of the *Washington Globe;* Amos Kendall, editor of two newspapers and later Jackson's postmaster general; William B. Lewis, who formerly served as quartermaster under General Jackson; Andrew Jackson Donelson, the president's nephew; John Overton, his longtime friend and business partner; and Roger B. Taney, his attorney general whom he later nominated as chief justice of the U.S. Supreme Court.

Who tried to assassinate President Jackson?

An unemployed house painter named Richard Lawrence fired two guns at Jackson in Washington, D.C., in February 1835 as Jackson was leaving the funeral service of former U.S. Congressman Warren R. Davis. Jackson chased his assailant with his cane and made sure Lawrence was apprehended. Lawrence was a mentally ill man who sometimes believed he was the king of England. He had tried to kill his sister before and had threatened others. Lawrence was deemed insane and never brought to trial.

What was Van Buren's role in Jackson's Cabinet?

Van Buren played a key role in Jackson's Cabinet, as he and Jackson were on good terms. Van Buren was the only member of Jackson's Cabinet who was a member of Jackson's

Kitchen Cabinet. Historians believe Van Buren helped convince Jackson to eliminate his entire Cabinet, including Vice President Calhoun. Van Buren resigned his position but worked behind the scenes to help Jackson's successful reelection.

Why was James K. Polk called the "dark horse" candidate?

In 1844, President James K. Polk (1795–1849; eleventh president, 1845–1849) did not appear on the radar screen as the next president of the United States; he had just lost two consecutive bids for the governorship of Tennessee. No one thought a candidate who could not win his own state could win the presidency. Additionally, the frontrunner for the Democratic Party at the 1844 convention was former President Martin Van Buren.

However, Van Buren made a serious blunder by publicly coming out against the annexation of Texas—adding the state to the Union—as did Whig candidate Henry Clay. Perhaps Van Buren and Clay wanted to avoid the thorny slavery question that was so divisive in the country. President Andrew Jackson saw an opportunity for his protégé and with the help of other key politicians managed to move Polk onto a later ballot at the Democratic convention.

As Van Buren could not obtain the necessary majority votes, it became clear that someone else would have to emerge. It turned out to be Polk, who became the Democratic Party's nominee.

What measure led to Polk's success in lowering the tariff?

The Walker Tariff Act of 1846—named after Polk's secretary of the treasury, Robert J. Walker—achieved the president's objective in lowering the tariffs that had been passed by the Whigs in 1842. Polk faced significant opposition in Congress. Vice President George M. Dallas cast the tie-breaking vote in the Senate that led to the law's successful passage.

What was Polk's financial plan with regard to the Treasury?

Polk wanted to avoid creating a national bank, placing the government's money in private banks instead. Polk followed the example of Martin Van Buren, who had called for an independent treasury during his presidency. Unlike Van Buren, Polk managed to have his measure—which he called the Constitutional Treasury Act—passed into law. It lasted until 1913, when Congress created the Federal Reserve System.

While many Americans do not think much about James K. Polk these days, historians often hold that he was one of the country's most accomplished presidents.

Why do some historians consider James K. Polk a great president?

Many historians consider Polk a great president because he had several major accomplishments in his one term in office. In fact, Polk's Secretary of the Navy George Bancroft, an esteemed historian, said Polk articulated four major goals upon assuming office: (1) lower tariffs; (2) create an independent treasury; (3) annex Oregon to the United States; and (4) obtain California from Mexico. Polk accomplished all four of these major objectives. President Harry Truman said of Polk: "He said exactly what he was going to do, and he did it."

WAR OF 1812

What unpopular legislation did Jefferson sign to avoid entering the English–French conflict?

Jefferson signed the Embargo Act of 1807 to keep America completely out of the conflict between Great Britain and France. Each side prohibited any of its allies from trading with its enemy. Jefferson refused to become involved in the war and responded with the Embargo Act, an attempt to show the United States's neutrality in the English–French conflict. The measure prohibited foreign trade with either nation. The banning of trade with either nation was unpopular, but it did lead to the creation of more textile mills and other industries in the United States. Jefferson lifted the embargo shortly before leaving office.

Which two future presidents were war heroes during the War of 1812?

Andrew Jackson and William Henry Harrison (1773–1841), the future seventh and ninth presidents, respectively, achieved great acclaim during the War of 1812 for military successes. Jackson led a group of militia and others against British forces in the Battle of New Orleans, which took place between December 1814 and January 1815. Jackson led American forces to a stunning victory over the British.

General William Henry Harrison won the Battle of the Thames over the Shawnee Indian leader Tecumseh in 1813. Harrison originally achieved acclaim when, as gover-

What battle in the War of 1812 led to the "Star-Spangled Banner"?

A young lawyer named Francis Scott Key became inspired to write a ballad— later known as the "Star–Spangled Banner"—after seeing an American flag still flying after the British attack on Fort McHenry in the Battle of Baltimore. His initial title was the "Defense of Fort McHenry." In 1916, President Woodrow Wilson declared the "Star–Spangled Banner" the country's national anthem.

nor of the Indiana territory, he led a successful campaign against a group of Indians at the Battle of Tippecanoe.

What caused the War of 1812?

The war between the young United States and powerful Great Britain largely came about because of France. After the French Navy was crushed by the British under Admiral Horatio Nelson (1758–1805) at the Battle of Trafalgar, Napoleon turned to economic warfare in his long struggle with the British, directing all countries under French control not to trade with Great Britain. Its economy dependent on trade, Britain struck back by imposing a naval blockade on France, which soon interfered with U.S. shipping. Ever since the struggle between the two European powers began in 1793, the United States tried to remain neutral. But the interruption of shipping to and from the continent and the search and seizure of ships posed significant problems to the American export business. In 1807, Great Britain issued an Order in Council that required even neutral vessels destined for a continental port to stop first in England; Napoleon countered with the Milan Decree, stating that any neutral vessel that submitted to British search be seized.

Back in America, the people of New England, the American region most dependent on shipping, nevertheless vehemently opposed entering into war with the British. But the country's economy was depressed as a result of the interruption of exports, and the U.S. Congress declared war on June 18, 1812. In these days before telegraph and radio, the United States did not know that on June 16 Britain had withdrawn its Order in Council, lifting its policy of shipping interference— the chief reason for the war declaration. Thus the two countries engaged in fighting for the next two and a half years. On December 24, 1814, the Treaty of Ghent officially ended the war. But once again, poor communication led to fighting: Two weeks after the treaty was signed, troops in New Orleans, unaware of the treaty, fought for control over the Mississippi River in the worst battle of the entire conflict. Although both the United States and Great Britain claimed victory in the War of 1812, neither side gained anything.

Who were the War Hawks?

The War Hawks were a group of Republicans in the U.S. Congress who advocated war with Great Britain. Elected in 1810, the congressmen took office in 1811, the failure of the Erskine agreement fresh in their

Artist Edward Percy Moran's 1912 painting "By Dawn's Early Light" depicts Francis Scott Key viewing the American flag flying over Fort McHenry after a British attack.

memories. That bit of 1809 diplomacy, arranged by British minister to the United States George Erskine and the then-U.S. Secretary of State James Madison (1751–1836), would have provided for the suspension of Britain's maritime practices that interfered with U.S. shipping, but the agreement fell apart when Erskine was recalled from office. The relationship between the United States and Great Britain—tenuous since 1807 due to trade embargoes and the impressment of American sailors into British service—deteriorated. The newly elected Congressmen were tired of the failure of diplomacy to resolve maritime problems with the British. They further felt the British were challenging the young United States through their policies, which purportedly included British aid to American Indians in the Northwest. War Hawk leader Henry Clay (1777–1852) was named Speaker of the House, and Congress soon passed a series of resolutions to strengthen the Army and Navy. When President James Madison called upon Congress to declare war on the British in June 1812, the War Hawks swung the close vote. Some historians believe the true motive behind the War Hawks's actions was not resolution of the shipping problems but rather the desire to annex parts of southern Canada to the United States.

What was future president William Henry Harrison's role during the War of 1812?

Harrison was promoted to major general and given authority over all military forces in the Northwest Territory. He battled both Indian forces—including Tecumseh and Tenskwatawa—and the British. In October 1813, he won the Battle of the Thames over Indian forces. This battle increased Harrison's fame, making him a national figure even more than the Battle of Tippecanoe.

Who was Tecumseh?

Tecumseh (1768–1813) was the leader of the Shawnee, who was involved in clashes with the Americans in the Ohio Valley. He rose to prominence by 1800 and partnered with his religious leader brother, Tenskwatawa, to create a formidable confederacy of American Indian tribes. Tecumseh and his brother founded Prophetstown, Illinois, in 1808 and rebelled against the Americans in Tecumseh's War, which essentially ended with the

Who said, "We have met the enemy, and they are ours"?

Captain Oliver Hazard Perry (1785–1819) wrote the famous words in a letter to General William Henry Harrison (1773–1841) after defeating the British at the Battle of Lake Erie on September 10, 1813. An improvised U.S. squadron commanded by Captain Perry, just twenty-eight years old, achieved the victory in the War of 1812 battle. The message he sent to Harrison (later the ninth U.S. president) was: "We have met the enemy, and they are ours: two ships, two brigs, one schooner, and one sloop." Perry received a gold medal and thanks from Congress for the victory.

Shawnee loss to Harrison at the Battle of Tippecanoe in 1811. Tecumseh, however, continued his resistance against the Americans by allying with the British during the War of 1812. Tecumseh helped the British capture Fort Detroit, but in 1813 the Americans enjoyed a decisive victory at the Battle of the Thames in Canada, and Tecumseh was killed on October 5, 1813.

What was future President Zachary Taylor's role during the War of 1812?

Taylor—then a captain—successfully defended Fort Harrison with a group of fifty men from a Tecumseh-led force of more than four hundred men in the War of 1812. The event is sometimes called the "Siege of Fort Harrison." His success earned him the rank of Brevet Major, the first time this honor was ever awarded. The designation "brevet" signified that an officer displayed particular courage during military service.

What happened to the nation's capital during the War of 1812?

British forces overran Washington, D.C., burning both the White House and the U.S. Capitol. General William Winder, whom Madison had appointed as commander in charge of defending the capital, did an inadequate job in preparing the area's defenses. Madison had to flee the city after hearing from General Winder of the oncoming British invasion.

Which member of Madison's Cabinet lost his job as a result of the burning of the Capitol?

Secretary of War John Armstrong received blame for the poor defense of the Capitol during the War of 1812. Armstrong resigned under pressure in September 1814, essen-

Artist George Munger's depiction of the White House shortly after it was burned by British troops in 1814 (the S-shaped line near the corner of the roof was, historians guess, part of a lightning-protection system, though not a lightning rod).

tially as the scapegoat for the British burning of the capital city. President James Monroe served as both secretary of war and secretary of state.

In what famous battles did Andrew Jackson prevail during the War of 1812 and the Creek War?

Jackson led a successful campaign against the Creek Indians at the Battle of Horseshoe Bend in 1814 during the Creek War (sometimes considered part of the War of 1812). Most famously, Jackson led outnumbered American forces in the Battle of New Orleans in January 1815. The defeat of the British made Jackson a national hero.

What treaty ended the War of 1812?

The Treaty of Ghent effectively ended the War of 1812. The treaty was signed in the Netherlands (present-day Belgium) in December 1814, although it was not ratified until February 1815 after the intervening Battle of New Orleans. Under the treaty, which the U.S. Senate ratified unanimously, the United States received its territories near the Great Lakes and Maine but renounced the lands they had acquired in Canada.

What treaty helped soothe relations between the U.S. and Britain in President Monroe's first year of office?

The two countries signed the Rush–Bagot treaty in 1817, demilitarizing the Great Lakes area near the northern border of the U.S. This had been a hotly contested area of military conflict during the War of 1812. Under the treaty, each side would remove military posts, and a border was established between the U.S. and British territory (later Canada). The treaty was named after U.S. Secretary of State Richard Rush and British minister Sir Charles Bagot.

TERRITORIAL CONFLICT AND EXPANSION

What was the Louisiana Purchase?

President Thomas Jefferson approved and ordered the Louisiana Purchase with Napoleon Bonaparte, the emperor of France, in 1803. Jefferson desired to acquire the French colony of Louisiana mainly to acquire the port city of New Orleans for commerce and defense purposes. Jefferson allegedly said: "There is on the globe one single spot the possessor of which is our natural and habitual enemy." In other words, President Jefferson knew and appreciated the strategic importance of acquiring New Orleans and surrounding land.

James Monroe and Robert R. Livingston, the U.S. minister to France, negotiated the purchase with French authorities. The $15 million purchase included more than 800,000 square miles, roughly doubling the size of the United States. The U.S. Senate approved the purchase—completed in the form of a treaty—by a vote of 24–7. Upon the agreement, Livingston said: "From this day, the United States take their place among the powers of the first rank."

The land acquired during the Louisiana Purchase includes what is present-day Arkansas, Missouri, Iowa, Oklahoma, Kansas, and Nebraska, much of North and South Dakota, and parts of New Mexico, Texas, Wyoming, and Montana. It was one of the best and most important land deals in American history.

What state did President Monroe acquire from Spain?

Monroe obtained present-day Florida from Spain in February 1819 under the Adams–Onis Treaty. The treaty was named after U.S. Secretary of State John Quincy

What was Monroe's policy toward Native Americans?

Monroe appeared to support a policy that would protect the rights of Native Americans to land. In his first inaugural address, he said: "With the Indian tribes it is our duty to cultivate friendly relations and to act with kindness and liberality in all our transactions." He advocated giving Native Indians simple titles to land for free, but although this seems generous on the surface, in reality the result was to break up the communal living style of the tribes so that they became separate land owners. It also allowed white settlers access to former Indian land.

Furthermore, as would be true with many presidents to follow, Monroe would go back on treaties made with the tribes in earlier years, such as breaking an 1804 treaty with the Cherokee when the president asserted in 1824 the treaty had never been made.

Adams and Spanish foreign minister Luis de Onis. Under the treaty, Spain ceded Florida to the United States, and the two countries set the southern borders of the United States, establishing that U.S. territory extended to the Pacific Ocean.

What was the Indian Removal Act?

In 1830 Congress passed the Indian Removal Act, a measure that President Jackson supported and signed into law that May. It called for the creation of an Indian territory in Oklahoma. Technically, the law called for the voluntary removal of various native tribes from the southeastern part of the United States. In practice, the law led to the forced removal of the Native Americans from their lands. The most famous of these removals was by the Cherokees from Georgia to what later became Oklahoma. This arduous journey became immortalized in history as the "Trail of Tears."

What was the impact of the Trail of Tears?

The Trail of Tears devastated many Indian tribes, most notably the Cherokee. Thousands of Cherokees died from disease and starvation in the forced removal to Oklahoma. All told, nearly 50,000 American Indians were relocated. Along the way, four thousand Cherokee died.

What were the American–Indian Wars?

Historians use the term "American–Indian Wars" to discuss a long series of military conflicts between the United States and native peoples, as the European Americans slowly took over much of North America. Indeed, one could state that the wars began

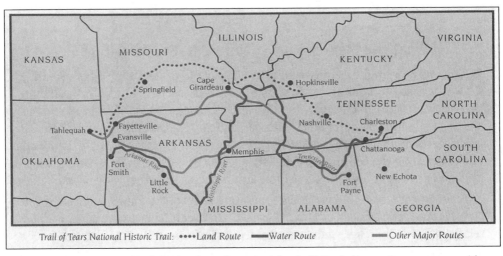

A map from the U.S. National Park Service shows the routes taken by Native Indians as they were removed from their homelands. Thousands died during the forced march.

with the 1622 Jamestown massacre and did not end until 1924, when the Apache Wars were officially declared over.

The history of the American–Indian Wars is often tragic and shameful. Much of the fighting was exacerbated by the U.S. government's penchant for breaking treaties it had signed with various American Indian tribes; the U.S. military then forcibly removed Indians from land they had been told was theirs legally, herding the tribes into smaller and smaller reservations often located on land with poor resources that the U.S. government didn't want anyway.

What diplomatic crisis arose with Canada during the Van Buren presidency?

Some Canadians began moving for independence from Great Britain. Some Americans helped the Canadians in their effort, exacerbating tensions in the U.S.–Great Britain relationship. Canadian loyalists, with support from Great Britain, then seized an American ship in 1837, the *Caroline*, containing supplies for Canadian rebels. During this seizure, American Amos Durfree was killed.

Van Buren ordered General Winfield Scott to the area to prevent further hostilities. He also issued a proclamation of neutrality, stating that the United States would remain neutral in the Canadian–British struggle.

What was the Aroostook War?

The Aroostook War was not really a war. It was a tense conflict between Maine and New Brunswick about the proper border between the United States and Canada in the area along the Aroostook River. In 1839, the Maine legislature sent militia to the river to remove what it perceived to be Canadian interlopers. The New Brunswick Lieutenant Governor Sir John Harvey issued an order to remove Americans from what he believed to be Canadian, and thus British, land. Van Buren dispatched General Scott to work out a compromise, and eventually, both countries signed the Webster–Ashburton Treaty of 1842.

What did the Webster–Ashburton Treaty accomplish?

The treaty was a significant diplomatic achievement that significantly reduced conflict between Great Britain and the United States. Signed on August 9, 1842, the main thrust of the treaty was the working out of an agreed-upon border between the state of Maine and the Canadian province of New Brunswick. The treaty was named after Secretary of State Daniel Webster and British diplomat Alexander Baring, known as Lord Ashburton.

Fortunately for the United States, Ashburton had a personal interest in bringing peace to the northeast region, as he owned a significant chunk of land in Maine and did not want to see full-blown conflict in the area.

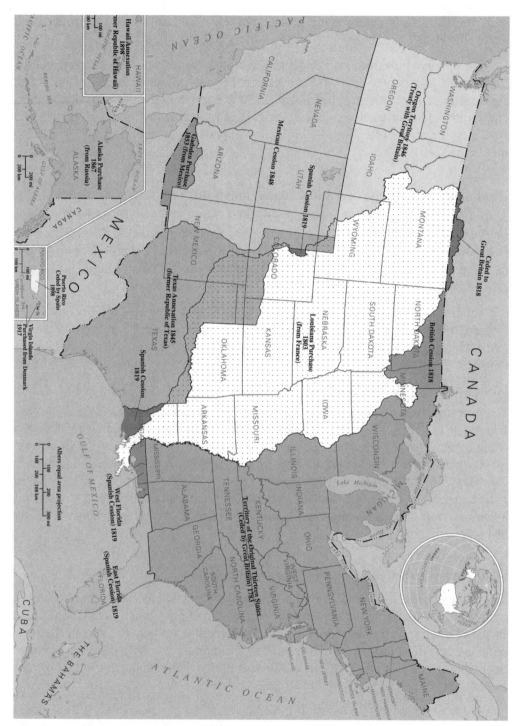

This map shows how, especially during the nineteenth century, the United States swiftly gained territory from the Atlantic to Pacific Ocean.

88

What war did President James K. Polk (1795–1849) wage that led to greater territory for the United States?

Fulfilling the Democratic phrase "manifest destiny," Polk engaged the United States in the Mexican–American War that led to the eventual annexation of California. Tensions were already hot between the two countries after the annexation of Texas, which had begun in earnest at the end of the Tyler Administration, but completed officially in Polk's term.

But Polk wanted more for the country—the provinces of New Mexico and California. Mexican troops had crossed the Rio Grande and killed American soldiers in the dispute.

Polk sent Major General Zachary Taylor (1784–1850)—his presidential successor—into the region. Taylor achieved several victories over the Mexican army at Palo Alto and Resaca de la Palma. Taylor later defeated Mexican forces at Buena Vista in 1847. American armies led by either Taylor or General Winfield Scott actually took Mexico City during the conflict.

After the United States conquered Mexico City, Mexico realized that it should sell its land in New Mexico and California and end the war. Some speculated that the United States should simply take control of all of Mexico. This was known as the "All–Mexico" campaign. Polk faced resistance to the war from many in the country and decided to obtain peace and enlarge the country with more than a half a million square miles.

How did President Polk obtain Oregon?

President James K. Polk (1795–1847) refused to back down from the British and remained steadfast in his demands that the British drop claims to the Oregon territory. Polk allegedly told at least one member of Congress, "The only way to treat John Bull [another

---

What was meant by Manifest Destiny?

The phrase Manifest Destiny was first used by American newspaper editor John O'Sullivan (1813–1895) in an article he wrote in 1845, in which he favored the annexations of Texas and Oregon. He believed that divine providence was in action and that the United States would eventually span the continent (he was right). The roots of O'Sullivan's optimistic nationalism dated back to the Puritan era and the idea that Christian settlers had a divine obligation to spread their beliefs across the continent. Religious fervor was compounded by nationalism and feelings of racial superiority over the American Indians and, later, the Mexicans in the Southwest. But it was also an economic urge to increase the territory of the United States to take advantage of natural resources, from the fur industry to timber to farm and ranch land and, in California, gold. Eventually, it spread beyond the continental United States, leading to the entry of Alaska and Hawaii as states, and even, one could argue, the space race and the moon landing.

name for Great Britain] is to look him in the eye." He acquired present-day Oregon, Washington, and part of Idaho. He obtained land up to the forty-ninth parallel, although not all the way to the 54° 40' parallel that was desired by some in the "All–Oregon" campaign.

THE MEXICAN–AMERICAN WAR

What caused the Mexican–American War?

The Mexican–American War (1846–1848) was fought over the United States's annexation of Texas. The events that led up to the conflict began in 1837 when President Jackson recognized Texas as independent (just after Texas won its war with Mexico). Republic of Texas President Sam Houston (1793–1863) felt that protection against a Mexican invasion might be necessary, so he eyed annexation to the United States. In the meantime, Mexican President Antonio Lopez de Santa Anna (1794–1876) warned that such an action on the part of the United States would be "equivalent to a declaration of war against the Mexican Republic." In June 1844, the U.S. Senate rejected a proposed annexation treaty. But later that year Democratic Party nominee Polk, an ardent expansionist, was elected president. Because the annexation of Texas had figured prominently in his campaign platform, outgoing President Tyler (1790–1862) viewed Polk's victory as a public mandate for annexation, and he recommended that Congress pass a joint resolution to invite Texas into the Union. Congress did so in February, and President Tyler signed the resolution on March 1, 1845, three days before leaving office.

Mexico responded by breaking off diplomatic relations with the United States. A border dispute made the situation increasingly tenuous: Texas claimed that its southern border was the Rio Grande River, while Mexico insisted it was the Nueces River, situated farther north. In June 1846, Polk ordered Brigadier General Zachary Taylor (1784–1850) to move his forces into the disputed area. In November, the U.S. government received word that Mexico was prepared to talk. Polk dispatched Congressman John Slidell (1793–1871) to Mexico to discuss three other outstanding issues: the purchase of California (for $25 million), the purchase of New Mexico (for $5 million), and the payment of damages to American nationals for losses incurred in Mexican revolutions. This last point was critical to the negotiations, as Polk was prepared to have the United States assume payment of damages to its own citizens in exchange for Mexico's recognition of the Rio Grande as the southern border of Texas.

But upon arrival in Mexico City, Slidell was refused the meeting—President José Joaquín Herrera (1792–1854) had bowed to pressure, opposing discussions with the United States. When Polk received news of the scuttled talks, he authorized General Taylor to advance through the disputed territory to the Rio Grande. Meanwhile, Mexico overthrew President Herrera, putting into office the fervent nationalist General Mariano Paredes y Arrillaga (1797–1849), who reaffirmed Mexico's claim to Texas and pledged to defend Mexican territory.

While Polk worked through Slidell to get an audience with the Mexican government, the attempts failed. On May 9, 1846, the Cabinet met and approved the president's recommendation to ask Congress to declare war. The next day, news arrived in Washington that on April 25, a sizeable Mexican force had crossed the Rio Grande and surrounded a smaller American reconnaissance party. Eleven Americans were killed; the rest were wounded or captured. On May 11, Polk delivered a message to Congress, concluding, "Mexico has … shed American blood upon the American soil. … War exists … by the act of Mexico herself." By the time the war was officially declared on May 13, just more than one year after Polk had been sworn into office, General Taylor had already fought and won key battles against the Mexicans and had occupied the northern Mexico city of Matamoros.

What did the United States gain from the Mexican–American War?

The Mexican–American War (1846—1848) was officially ended when the U.S. Senate ratified the Treaty of Guadalupe Hidalgo on March 10, 1848. By the treaty, Mexico relinquished roughly half its territory—New Mexico and California—to the United States. Mexico also recognized the Rio Grande as its border with Texas.

Mexico received payments in the millions from the United States, which also assumed the payment of claims of its citizens. Five years later, under the terms of the Gadsden Purchase (named after U.S. minister to Mexico, James Gadsden), the United States purchased a small portion of land from Mexico for another $10 million on June 24, 1853, which was widely regarded as further compensation for the land lost in the war. The territory the United States gained was in present-day Arizona and New Mexico, south of the Gila River.

TEXAS

Of all the states in the Union, which one was an independent republic?

Well, as you can guess from the above, Texas was an independent republic from March 2, 1836, to February 19, 1846. Before that, Texas was a part of Mexico, which gained independence from Spain in 1821. Most of the area, however, had few settlers in it. The new Mexican government was concerned about this, encouraging its citizens to settle there, but it also asked Americans to move into the territory. The Americans were told, however, that they would have to convert to Catholicism and, if they owned any slaves, they would have to give them up because slavery was illegal in Mexico. The result was a slow rise in tension between the Mexicans and the settlers from America, culminating in a revolution in which Texas declared itself an independent nation.

Who is considered the "Father of Texas"?

Stephen Austin (1793–1836), after whom the Texas capital is named, was a Virginia-born impresario who was granted the right to settle Mexican land in Texas, provided he

The Alamo remains today as a reminder of Texas' war for independence. It is one of the state's most popular tourist attractions.

bring settlers with him and have them colonize the area. Austin did so in 1823, bringing three hundred American families. By 1829 Austin had brought in a total of twelve hundred families. Initially, Austin supported the Mexican government, even helping the Mexicans to put down the Fredonian Rebellion (1826–1827), in which a number of Texans rebelled. Growing disagreements with Mexico, however, over issues such as immigration and statehood, left Austin discontented. When war officially broke out with the Battle of Gonzales on September 27, 1835, Austin supported Texas. He even commanded a force of rebels at the Siege of Béxar later that year. After the war, Austin ran unsuccessfully for president and served two months as secretary of state before his death.

What happened at the Alamo?

Four days after Texas declared its independence from Mexico, Mexico's dictator, Antonio López de Santa Anna (1794–1849), ordered the small fortification called the Alamo to be taken by force. About five thousand Mexican troops were sent, while only 187 Texans defended the fort, including the famous Jim Bowie (c. 1796–1836) and Davy Crockett (1786–1836). While they valiantly held out for thirteen days, eventually the Texans were overwhelmed, and all were killed. The slaughter became a rallying cry for Texans: "Remember the Alamo!"

Who were Jim Bowie and Davy Crockett?

In the early 1800s, when much of the land east of the Mississippi was still considered the "frontier," men like Bowie and Crockett made names for themselves as frontiersmen who gained fame in legend and even song. Bowie was perhaps the noblest of men, being involved in smuggling and the slave trade. He was primarily a land speculator, but he gained fame as the supposed inventor of the Bowie knife. Crockett was a Tennessee frontiersman who became a colonel in his state militia and later served in the U.S. Congress as a representative. His political career encountered shaky ground because of his opposition to the Indian Removal Act, and he moved to Texas in 1835.

How did the Texas Rebellion end?

On April 21, 1836, General Sam Houston (1793–1863) met General Santa Anna's forces at the Battle of San Jacinto, decisively defeating the Mexicans and chasing them back across the Rio Grande River. On May 14, Santa Anna conceded defeat, granting Texas its independence.

Who was Sam Houston?

Houston was a Virginia-born American politician who served as a U.S. senator for Tennessee, as well as its governor, during the 1820s. After leaving politics in 1829, he became caught up in a legal case in Washington, D.C., for supporting the Cherokee Nation in opposition to President Jackson's Indian Removal Act of 1830. Houston was accused of aiding the Cherokee people; the case eventually ended with Houston being charged a $500 fine. Instead of paying it, he moved to Texas. He became involved with politics there and, during the revolution, served as a general. After the war and his role in winning the Battle of San Jacinto, Houston was elected president of the Republic of Texas (David G. Burnet was Texas's first president). He served his first term from 1836–1838, and, after Mirabeau B. Lamar held the office, returned as president for a second term (1841–1844). After Texas became part of the United States, Houston went back to Washington as a senator representing his state and then was governor of Texas from 1859–1861.

How did Texas join the United States?

Fearing that Mexico might try to invade Texas, the citizens there felt their borders would be more secure if they were backed by the U.S. government. The U.S. Congress passed a bill to annex Texas on February 28, 1845; President John Tyler signed it on March 1. That October 13, the people of Texas voted to join the United States, and the state was officially annexed on December 29. However, the transfer of power from the Republic to the United States was not completed until February 19, 1846.

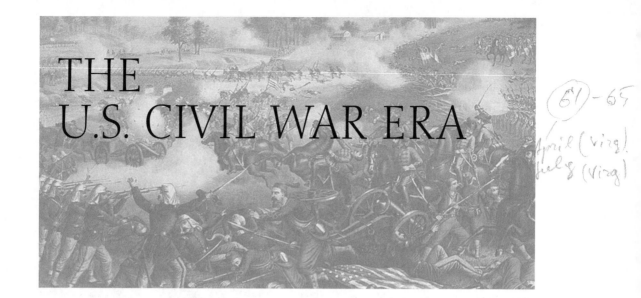

THE U.S. CIVIL WAR ERA

THE SLAVERY ISSUE

What Founding Father consistently railed against the practice of slavery?

George Mason (1725–1792) of Virginia abhorred the practice of slavery, and he was not shy about expressing his views—even at the Philadelphia Convention of 1787. At the Convention, Mason said: "Every master of slaves is born a petty tyrant." He called slavery "that slow Poison, which is daily contaminating the Minds & Morals of our People." He said the practice of slavery would "bring judgment of Heaven on the country." However, Mason himself had more than thirty slaves.

Who was Gabriel Prosser?

Gabriel Prosser (1776–1800) was a slave from Richmond, Virginia, who planned a large slave rebellion. Unfortunately for Prosser, two slaves told a prominent slaveowner, who promptly informed then-Virginia Governor James Monroe. Prosser fled from the state militia, but he was caught near Norfolk. He and several of his fellow planners were hanged. The state of Virginia (and other Southern states) began to crack down on slaves learning to read, in part because Prosser was literate.

Who was Denmark Vesey?

Denmark Vesey (1767–1822) was a former slave in South Carolina who planned a large-scale rebellion against slaveowners. Born in the Caribbean, Vesey had purchased his freedom. He rounded up other free blacks and convinced a number of slaves to participate in a planned, armed rebellion. Unfortunately—similar to the Prosser rebellion—some other slaves warned slaveowners, and Vesey and other co-conspirators were captured. Vesey and more than thirty others were hanged.

95

What slave was at least partially successful in leading an armed rebellion?

Nat Turner (1800–1831) led a rebellion in Southampton County, Virginia, that led to the deaths of more than sixty whites. Turner and his followers traveled to different farms, freeing slaves and killing their owners. Historian William J. Bennett in his excellent *America: The Last Best Hope,* Volume I, describes Turner as "a spellbinding preacher who believed he had a God-given mission to raise a band of slaves to slaughter remote farm families." Turner was captured and then executed in November 1831.

A statue in Washington Park, Ottawa, Illinois, commemorates the first Lincoln–Douglas debate in 1858.

What were the Lincoln–Douglas debates?

The Lincoln–Douglas debates were seven debates held in 1858 between Abraham Lincoln and Stephen Douglas (1813–1861) for a U.S. Senate seat in Illinois. Douglas was the Democratic candidate, while Lincoln was the Republican candidate. At that time, state legislatures selected U.S. senators. During the debates, Lincoln advocated against slavery, terming it a moral wrong. Meanwhile, Douglas said that each individual state had the right to choose on the issue of slavery. Douglas prevailed in the election because the state legislature was more Democratic. However, the debates helped transform Lincoln from an unknown regional figure into a nationally prominent politician.

What was the "Missouri Compromise"?

The Missouri Compromise of 1820 at least temporarily averted a national battle between pro-slave and anti-slave states. The controversy arose in 1819 when the territory of Missouri applied for statehood. Representative James Tallmadge, Jr. of New York introduced an amendment that would prohibit slavery in Missouri. The Missouri Compromise allowed slavery in Missouri and land south of Missouri, but prohibited slavery in lands in the northern half of the U.S., roughly the latitude of Missouri.

What was President Zachary Taylor's position on the Compromise of 1850?

The Compromise of 1850 was a federal law created largely by influential Congressman Henry Clay to address the increasingly divisive issue of slavery. Under the Compromise of 1850, California would be admitted as a free state (a state where slavery was not allowed), while other territories, such as New Mexico and Utah, could decide for themselves whether to allow slavery. The bill also contained other measures favorable to slaveowners. Taylor opposed the measure, saying that he would veto it if it came to his desk. He died before Congress passed the law. His vice president, Millard Fillmore (1800–1874), signed the measure into law.

What federal law did Senator Stephen Douglas propose that dealt with the issue of slavery?

Senator Douglas created the Kansas–Nebraska Act of 1850, which some historians consider a cause of the Civil War. Signed by President Franklin Pierce (1804–1869) in 1854, it allowed settlers in those two territories to decide for themselves whether to outlaw slavery. Many in the North opposed this law because it led to the spread of slavery. Sponsored by Senator Stephen Douglas, the bill was designed to further progress on an intercontinental railroad but devolved into a bitter dispute about the intractable slavery question. Opposition to the bill led to the creation of what became known as the Republican Party. President Pierce believed the states and territories had the right to decide for themselves whether or not to allow slavery. Because he was a Northerner who did not oppose slavery, he was sometimes pejoratively referred to as a "doughface."

The measure provided that the territories of Kansas and Nebraska could determine for themselves whether they would be slave or free territories. The measure, in effect, repealed the Missouri Compromise of 1820, which had prohibited slavery above a particular latitude and longitudinal line. The Missouri Compromise prohibited slavery in northern areas and allowed it to continue in the Southern states and territories.

What was the Underground Railroad?

The Underground Railroad was the name of the system of free houses and friendly passages for escaping slaves, fleeing from bondage in the South to free territory in the North (or to Canada). Many abolitionists, both white and black, were active in the Underground Railroad. The system began in the early part of the nineteenth century and continued to its apex in the decade before the U.S. Civil War.

Some historians estimate that as many as 100,000 slaves escaped via the Un-

Harriet Tubman was a heroine who helped slaves escape to freedom in the North via the Underground Railroad.

derground Railroad. One of the more famous activists involved in the Underground Railroad was Harriet Tubman (1820–1913), an African American woman. Tubman made at least 13 trips down South to help various slaves escape bondage.

What other causes did Harriet Tubman engage in during her long life?

Tubman aided abolitionist John Brown in his abortive attempt to lead an armed insurrection over federal property at Harpers Ferry, West Virginia. Tubman helped recruit some men for Brown's cause. She also served as a spy for Union forces during the war. She even helped the actual war effort by scouting for Union troops and assisting in attempts to rescue slaves. She also worked as a nurse and engaged in other humanitarian efforts during the conflict.

Tubman later became a visible proponent of the women's suffrage movement. She traveled to several major cities to speak about the importance of the cause.

Who was John Brown?

John Brown (1800–1859) was a fervent abolitionist best known for leading an armed insurrection on the federal arsenal at Harpers Ferry, West Virginia. Brown hoped to enlist an army of slaves to support his cause and overthrow pro-slavery forces. Brown had participated in several armed conflicts in the "Bleeding Kansas" conflict as pro– and anti–slavery forces clashed violently in several battles. In 1856, Brown and other abolitionist activists killed five slavery proponents at the so-called Pottawatomie Massacre of 1856.

Born in Connecticut, Brown moved with his family to Pennsylvania, where he became a businessman. There he operated a tannery and also raised cattle. The murder of abolitionist newspaper editor Elijah Lovejoy in 1837 marked a key turning point in Brown's life. Brown became a devotee of abolitionism. In the 1840s he moved to Springfield, Massachusetts, where he attended the Free Church and heard lectures from former slaves Frederick Douglass and Sojourner Truth. He became involved in the Underground Railroad.

Through the years, Brown became more radical in his beliefs and more willing to put his principles into action—even violent action. Brown opposed the Fugitive Slave Act of 1850, mandating that people return fleeing slaves to their owners in the South.

In October 1859, Brown led a band of eighteen men in an attempted armed takeover of Harpers Ferry. A group of Marines led by U.S. Army Colonel Robert E. Lee engaged Brown's band and captured or killed Brown's men. Brown was convicted and later hanged on December 2, 1859. He wrote at the end of his life: "I, John Brown, am now quite certain that the crimes of this guilty land will never be purged away but with blood. I had, as I now think, vainly flattered myself that without very much bloodshed it might be done."

The Harpers Ferry Raid in 1859 certainly was a contributing factor to the upcoming Civil War. Brown has a mixed legacy. Some view him as a martyr for the anti-slavery cause. Others view him as a mad terrorist.

Who was Sojourner Truth?

Isabella Baumfree (1797–1883) took the name Sojourner Truth on June 1, 1843. Her decision came after one of her many religious visions. She was a member of the Zion Church in New York but had a mystical personality that could not be confined by a church structure nor within a cult she joined for a brief period called the Mathias group. She set out on her own anti-slavery crusade, seeing it as "the secular counterpart of spiritual salvation."

Soujourner Truth

This was a period when many who spoke out against slavery were fine orators, such as Frederick Douglass. Yet Truth could well match his wit, wisdom, and eloquence. Like Douglass, Truth was in great demand as a suffrage speaker, attracting crowds of listeners. Her classic speech, "Ain't I a Woman?", attacked the views of men, as well as white women, for their neglect of the black woman's plight. Although illiterate, Sojourner Truth captivated audiences with storytelling, singing of spirituals, and her remarkable knowledge of the Bible.

What was the Fugitive Slave Act?

That is actually a two-part question. As noted above, John Brown opposed the Fugitive Slave Act of 1850, but there was also a Fugitive Slave Act of 1793, which required people to return black slaves who had run away from their owners in the South. However, there were some weaknesses in the earlier law that allowed people to ignore it without much in the way of consequences. Therefore, the U.S. Congress passed the Act of 1850, beefing up the earlier act by adding stiff penalties, both to officials who didn't arrest the escaped slave and to anyone aiding and abetting them. A $1,000.00 fine (in 1850 money) and prison time were possible. In addition, law enforcement personnel could get bonuses and promotions for capturing slaves.

What was the Crittenden Compromise?

The Crittenden Compromise, named after Kentucky politician John J. Crittenden (1787–1863), referred to a legislative attempt to avoid war and establish some sort of resolution with regard to slavery. The Compromise would have allowed slavery below the Missouri Compromise line and disallowed it above the line. Crittenden told his fellow members of the U.S. Senate: "I am for the Union; but, my friends, I must also be for the equal rights of my State under the great Constitution and in this great Union." The Crittenden Compromise was popular among some Southern politicians, but Crittenden—who served as U.S. Attorney for two different presidents—could not gain a majority. President James Buchanan (1791–1868), the fifteenth president, supported the Crittenden Compromise.

Why was the novel *Uncle Tom's Cabin* so important?

Uncle Tom's Cabin by Harriet Beecher Stowe (1811–1896) had a major impact on the country before the U.S. Civil War. Published in 1852, it depicted the harsh realities of slavery and the power of Christianity. It inspired the abolitionist movement and became the second best-selling book of the nineteenth century behind only the Bible.

The book centered on Tom—a slave—and his vicious plantation owner and master Simon Legree. The book's overarching theme is that slavery is a dehumanizing, evil practice.

In what infamous decision did the Supreme Court regard black persons as mere slaves?

The U.S. Supreme Court regarded black persons as inferior persons in its *Scott v. Sandford* decision (1857). The Court ruled that former slave Dred Scott was not free even when he was residing in free territory. Chief Justice Roger B. Taney, who wrote the majority opinion, referred to black persons as "that unfortunate race" who were "so far inferior that they had no rights which the white man was bound to respect." Some historians have even cited the decision as one of the catalysts for the horrific U.S. Civil War.

Who was Dred Scott?

Dred Scott was a slave owned by Peter Blow in Alabama. Scott moved with Blow to Missouri, another state that authorized slavery. After Blow died, his executor sold Scott to Dr. John Emerson, a St. Louis-based Army doctor. Emerson then moved his family and Scott back to Illinois, a free state. Emerson eventually moved back to St. Louis and died. Dred Scott and his wife Harriet filed a lawsuit in Missouri courts, arguing that they were freed when Dr. Emerson moved to Illinois. Emerson's widow and her brother, John Sanford (court records misspelled his name as Sandford), contested Scott's suit, leading to the *Scott v. Sandford* litigation.

Why did many believe Dred Scott had a valid claim?

Scott believed he had a valid claim because some courts had adhered to the doctrine of "once free, always free." This doctrine meant that if a slave reached free territory legally, then he or she was free because slavery was outlawed in those jurisdictions. However, the Missouri courts and the U.S. Supreme Court did not accept that argument.

How did Chief Justice Taney reject the Declaration of Independence's "All men are created equal" principle for Scott?

Taney reasoned that it was clear that the Founders did not believe this applied to members of the African race when they wrote the Declaration of Independence. He wrote

that "it is too clear for dispute that the enslaved African race were not intended to be
included and formed no part of the people
who framed and adopted this declaration."

Which two justices dissented in the Dred Scott case?

Justices John McLean (1785–1861) and
Benjamin Curtis (1809–1874) were the
Court's only two dissenters. Both men believed the majority ignored the reality that
African Americans were free men in many
states of the Union and that Dred Scott was
free after living in Illinois for years. Curtis
was so upset by the Court's decision that
he resigned from the bench shortly thereafter. The *Scott* decision was issued on
March 6, 1857; Curtis left the bench on
September 30.

Dred Scott unsuccessfully argued for his freedom
before the U.S. Supreme Court, which ruled,
significantly, as a result that the Missouri Compromise
passed by Congress was unconstitutional.

OTHER ISSUES PRECEDING THE CIVIL WAR

What were the causes of the Civil War?

There were several causes of the Civil War. One was slavery. The issue of slavery deeply
divided the Northern and Southern states. Slavery was intertwined with the social and
economic divisions between the North and the South. The South's agrarian economy
was based in large part on slave labor. Cotton served as the principal crop, and it required painstaking manual labor, even with Eli Whitney's invention of the cotton gin.
More abolitionists lived in the North and opposed the horrible institution of slavery.

The economic differences between the North and South contributed to the friction.
The North was predominantly an industrial economy; the South was an agrarian economy. Political attitudes differed significantly in the two regions: The North focused more
on federal rights, while in the South "states' rights" was more than a simple rallying cry.
Many Southern politicians believed in the theory of nullification—that a state could
nullify or ignore federal law that conflicted with its interests.

The election of Abraham Lincoln (1809–1865), the nation's sixteenth president, may
also have contributed to the Civil War. Many Southern politicians viewed Lincoln as a
pure pro-North, anti-slavery president. Seven states had seceded from the Union before

Lincoln was elected. His election hastened the number of seceding states, and conflict ensued.

However, the U.S. Supreme Court ruled in the *Slaughter-House Cases* (1872): "This constituted the war of the rebellion, and whatever auxiliary causes may have contributed to bring about this war, undoubtedly the overshadowing and efficient cause was African slavery."

What economic problem surfaced during the Buchanan Administration?

The Panic of 1857 that began before President James Buchanan (1791–1868; fifteenth president, 1857–1861) assumed office plagued him and the American economy throughout his tenure. The panic began in part after the collapse of the New York branch of the Ohio Life Insurance Company, a major force in the American economy. Thousands of American businesses and numerous banks collapsed during this economic depression. The country did not recover until after the Civil War.

Which states seceded from the Union to form the Confederacy?

Eleven states ultimately seceded from the United States. They included South Carolina, Mississippi, Florida, Alabama, Georgia, Texas, Virginia, Arkansas, Tennessee, Louisiana, and North Carolina. South Carolina seceded first in February 1861.

What were "fire-eaters"?

Fire–eaters refers to a group of ardent, pro-secessionists who pushed for secession from the Union. Some politicians from the South pushed for secession in 1850, causing some in the North to dub them by their nickname. Later, "fire-eaters" began to be a term used to describe more than politicians but anyone who actively supported secession, most notably those who were actively opposed and even supported military opposition to the federal government.

Who was Edmund Ruffin?

Edmund Ruffin (1794–1865) was a wealthy plantation owner from Virginia (and later South Carolina) who was one of the leading fire-eaters. He did make some contributions to farming, serving as the editor of the *Farmers' Register* and proposing some

Plantation owner Edmund Ruffin was a staunch fire-eater who was so upset when General Lee surrendered that he killed himself.

ways to increase the fertilization of tobacco crops. Ruffin committed suicide shortly after the Confederacy lost the Civil War. He decided to end his life after Robert E. Lee surrendered at Appomattox Courthouse.

Who was Jefferson Davis?

Jefferson Davis (1808–1889) was the president of the Confederate States of America from 1861 until 1865. Davis fought for his country in the Mexican–American War, and served as U.S. secretary of war for President Pierce. He also served as a U.S. senator for Mississippi.

In February 1861, Davis resigned from the U.S. Senate and was elected president of the Confederacy. After the end of the war, Davis faced treason charges. He never faced trial on these charges, but was pro-

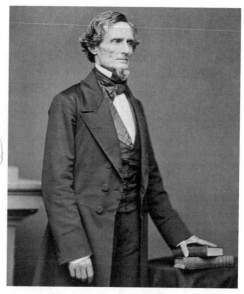

Jefferson Davis was the first and only president of the Confederate States of America.

hibited from holding public office. He served two years in prison before being released. He later became president of a college in Texas—present-day Texas A&M University. In 1881, he published a book known as *The Rise and Fall of the Confederate Government*.

Who were Copperheads?

Copperheads referred to those Northern members of the Democratic Party who opposed the Civil War. They were sometimes referred to as the Peace Democrats. They were given the pejorative nickname "Copperheads" because those who believed in the war effort viewed the Peace Democrats as venomous snakes. A prominent Copperhead was Clement Vallandigham (1820–1871), a member of the U.S. House of Representatives from Ohio. Copperheads sometimes gave active aid to the Confederate cause. Others were simply vocal critics of President Abraham Lincoln and the war effort in general.

What happened to Clement Vallandigham?

Vallandigham was arrested and charged with violating a military order that made it a crime to criticize the Union war effort. Issued by General Ambrose Burnside, the order read in part: "That hereafter all persons found within our lines who commit acts for the benefit of the enemies of our country will be tried as spies or traitors, and, if convicted, will suffer death." Burnside arrested Vallandigham in May 1863, after he gave a speech that criticized the war effort and talked about "sacrificing the liberty of all Americans to King Lincoln." He also termed the Civil War as "wicked, cruel and unnecessary."

At his military trial, he was convicted and sentenced to confinement at a military prison for the duration of the war. President Lincoln later ordered him exiled to the

Confederacy. Instead of remaining in Confederate territory, Vallandigham fled to Canada and from there campaigned for governor of Ohio. He later returned to Ohio. After the war, he unsuccessfully ran for public office. He practiced law after he did not win election. He died in 1871, accidentally shooting himself with a pistol.

THE CIVIL WAR BREAKS OUT

What was the first battle of the Civil War?

The Civil War began with the Battle of Fort Sumter in April 1861. Confederate forces fired on Fort Sumter in Charleston, South Carolina. Union forces surrendered, causing President Lincoln to call for volunteers to the Union Army. South Carolina called for the surrender of Fort Sumter earlier in December 1860, when South Carolina officially seceded from the Union. President Buchanan attempted to fortify Fort Sumter. However, Confederate forces led by General P.G.T. Beauregard aggressively pressed forward to prevent the retrenchment of Union forces.

What was the Emancipation Proclamation?

The Emancipation Proclamation was an executive order initially issued by President Abraham Lincoln in September 1862 that freed the slaves in Confederate territory. Lincoln issued the order during the height of the U.S. Civil War. Lincoln issued the order under his authority as commander in chief of the Armed Forces—a power delegated to the president in the U.S. Constitution. It provided in part:

> And by virtue of the power, and for the purpose aforesaid, I do order and declare that all persons held as slaves within said designated States, and parts of States, are, and henceforward shall be free; and that the Executive government of the United States, including the military and naval authorities thereof, will recognize and maintain the freedom of said persons.

> And I hereby enjoin upon the people so declared to be free to abstain from all violence, unless in necessary self-defence [sic]; and I recommend to them that, in all cases when allowed, they labor faithfully for reasonable wages.

And I further declare and make known, that such persons of suitable condition, will be received into the armed service of the United States to garrison forts, positions, stations, and other places, and to man vessels of all sorts in said service.

And upon this act, sincerely believed to be an act of justice, warranted by the Constitution, upon military necessity, I invoke the considerate judgment of mankind, and the gracious favor of Almighty God.

The Proclamation went into effect on January 1, 1863. The Emancipation Proclamation had a positive political impact, causing several foreign countries to shift their support to the North.

Did blacks fight in the Civil War?

Yes, blacks fought in the Civil War—the vast, vast majority on the Union side. Many Confederate politicians and military leaders opposed arming slaves. However, some realized that arming slaves was a necessity, given the superior numbers of the Union Army. Black soldiers made significant contributions to the Union War effort. Prominent among these efforts was the 54th Massachusetts Volunteer Infantry, a regiment of black soldiers who left Boston to train in South Carolina, and later saw combat action at the Second Battle of Fort Wagner in July 1863. In May 1863, black soldiers fought for the Union at the Battle of Port Hudson in Louisiana.

Who was P.G.T. Beauregard?

P.G.T. Beauregard (1818–1893) was the first major Confederate general during the U.S. Civil War. Born Pierre Gustave Toutant-Beauregard, he was born in Louisiana. He graduated from the U.S. Military Academy and served in the Mexican–American War. He later became the first Confederate brigadier general. He achieved fame with his victory at the First Battle of Bull Run in Manassas, Virginia. He later defended the city of St. Petersburg, Virginia, from attacks by larger Union forces. After the war, Beauregard returned to Louisiana, where he prospered working for the railroads and managing the Louisiana lottery.

What was the first major land battle of the Civil War?

The first major land battle of the Civil War was the First Battle of Bull Run near Manassas, Virginia, on July 21, 1861. Union forces led by General Irwin McDowell attacked Confederate forces led by General Beauregard. Union forces had some initial success, but the tide of the battle changed when Confederate reinforcements led by General Joseph E. Johnston joined the fray. Union forces ended up retreating after suffering nearly five hundred deaths and a total of nearly three thousand casualties (including those wounded and captured).

Lincoln signed a bill that called for the enlistment of nearly half a million soldiers over the next several years. The Union had expected to win the battle easily. The battle showed both sides that the war would be a more protracted affair than originally expected.

The First Battle of Bull Run near Manassas, Virginia, was the first major meeting of North versus South in the Civil War.

What was the Union's naval strategy to defeat the South?

Lincoln knew that blocking seaport trade would be a key to bringing the Confederacy to its knees, so he began to build up the rather small U.S. Navy and use its ships to form blockades of major southern ports.

What was the "Trent Affair"?

Although the British were officially neutral concerning the American Civil War, they traded with both the Union and the Confederacy. On November 8, 1861, the USS *San Jacinto* intercepted the RMS *Trent*, which was on its way to England with two Confederate diplomats, James Mason and John Slidell. The diplomats were taken prisoner, and the *Trent* was seized. England was outraged, and for a time it looked as if war could break out between Britain and the United States, which would have served the Confederacy well. President Lincoln, however, eventually agreed to release the prisoners. Mason and Slidell continued on to England and France, but their mission to form diplomatic relations with the two European powers failed.

What were the *Merrimack* and the *Monitor*?

The Confederate ship *Merrimack* and the Union ship *Monitor* were ironclad battleships that engaged in a famous battle in the Civil War against each other. The two ironclads met in a harbor at the Battle of Hampton Roads in March 1862. The two ships engaged in naval combat for nearly two hours that ended in a stalemate. Rather than see it fall into enemy hands, the Confederates destroyed the *Merrimack* in May 1862. The *Monitor* was lost in stormy waters in December 1862. The wreck of the *Monitor* was not discovered until August 1973.

What other significant Civil War battle was fought in Murfreesboro, Tennessee?

The other significant battle in Murfreesboro, Tennessee, was the Battle of Stones River—one of the bloodiest battles in the entire war. According to historians, it had the highest casualty rate of any of the major battles of the Civil War. Union general William Rosecrans battled against Confederate forces led by General Braxton Bragg. The battle was fought over a three-day period from December 31, 1862, through January 2, 1863. The Union suffered more than 12,000 casualties, while the Confederates suffered more than 11,600 casualties. Confederate General Bragg ended up retreating south after the battle, which explains why the battle is usually listed as a Union victory.

Who led Union forces at the Battle of Shiloh?

Major General Ulysses S. Grant—the future leader of the entire U.S. Army and future president of the United States—led Union forces to victory at the Battle of Shiloh in Hardin County, Tennessee, in April 1862. Confederate forces did well the first day of battle, with a surprise attack engineered by Generals Albert Sidney Johnson and P.G.T. Beauregard.

However, Grant and his Union forces recovered, defeating the Confederate forces during the second day of battle. Confederate forces had to retreat and could not stop Union forces from entering into Mississippi.

ALL–OUT WAR

When did the Union capture New Orleans?

The capture of New Orleans on May 1, 1862, was a huge turning point in the Civil War, essentially giving Louisiana back to the North. The battle began on April 18, when a fleet commanded by Commodore David G. Farragut (1801–1870) came within striking distance of the Confederate forts near the city. An unceasing bombardment commenced from the west side of the river, with much of the fire directed at Fort Jackson and Fort St. Philip. Farragut plowed through the Confederate fleet, managing to get thirteen ships upriver to capture the city. A period of chaos ensued until Farragut gained control on May 1.

For many Confederates, the loss of New Orleans was the most poignant, even searing, event of the year 1862. First had come the terrible news of Forts Henry and Donelson, then the near-victory at Shiloh that cost so many lives. Then came the news that the Federals had penetrated the inner part of Cape Hatteras, followed by the surrender of New Orleans. No less a fire-eater than Edmund Ruffin, the man who claimed to have fired the first cannon shot against Fort Sumter, expressed consternation and dismay at the loss of New Orleans. And yet, with all this bad news, the Confederacy was actually menaced even more spectacularly, right at its heart.

When did Robert E. Lee take command of the Confederate troops?

Confederate President Jefferson Davis placed Robert E. Lee (1807–1870) in charge of the Army of Northern Virginia on June 3, 1862. The Army of Northern Virginia was the primary military force of the South, which made Lee, in effect, the head commander of the Confederate forces.

General Robert E. Lee took charge of the Army of Northern Virginia in June of 1862.

When did the Seven Days Battles begin?

It began on June 26, 1862. Robert E. Lee, naturally, did not expect that this would be a set of battles lasting for seven days. He planned to attack Major General George B. Mc-Clellan's (1826–1885) exposed right flank, which "hung" to the north, and to drive him away from Richmond. The Battle of Mechanicsville, the first of the Seven Days Battles, began poorly for the Confederates because Stonewall Jackson did not get into position to attack until almost 1 P.M. (a 7 A.M. start had been anticipated). This failure of alacrity was so atypical of Jackson that many historians have given him a pass for his performance that day. What can be said is that Jackson, who had marched and ridden with great speed from the Shenandoah Valley, was exhausted. The battle began late but went on with fury into the early evening. The Confederates suffered 6,134 men killed, wounded, or missing; the Union suffered 5,031.

What was the Second Battle of Bull Run?

The Second Battle of Bull Run took place on August 28–30, 1862, near Manassas, Virginia. Like the First Battle of Bull Run, the Confederate forces prevailed in a conflict with Union forces. Confederate General Robert E. Lee inflicted great damage on Union forces led by Major General John Pope. Union forces suffered ten thousand casualties. Even though Union forces outnumbered Confederate soldiers by more than 12,000 troops, Union forces had to retreat. Confederate success is often attributed to the superior leadership of Lee and Major General Thomas "Stonewall" Jackson.

What happened at Harpers Ferry?

The garrison, under the command of Colonel John White Geary, held out longer than anticipated, but by the evening of September 14, 1862, Stonewall Jackson had twice as many men—as well as enough guns—to commence a fierce artillery bombardment. Had the Federals managed to secure the nearby hills, they might have been able to hold out. Lacking this, they readied themselves to surrender. The cavalry section of the garrison refused to yield, making a daring escape from Harpers Ferry that night. Their courage prevented the Confederates from gaining over a thousand horses and saddles, both of which were badly needed. Even so, Stonewall Jackson recorded an impressive victory. Over 11,000 Union men laid down their arms and were soon set free on parole with the understanding that they would not serve again in the war. Almost as soon as he succeeded in reducing Harpers Ferry, Stonewall Jackson redirected his men, saying they had to assist General Lee.

What happened at Antietam?

The Battle of Antietam occurred on September 17, 1862, near Sharpsburg, Maryland, and Antietam Creek. Major General George B. McClellan faced General Lee, who had set up his troops in a defensive position on the other side of the creek. Union General Joseph Hooker (1814–1879) had his men in position by 5 A.M., and the attack was made at first light. The ensuing battle was one of the bloodiest in U.S. history. The total casualties on the Union side came to 2,010 killed, 9,416 wounded, and 1,043 missing. Confederate losses are harder to be counted with certainty, partly because there had been so many desertions, but it was at least equal to the Northern loss. Therefore, we can say, with little hesitation, that roughly 25,000 Americans were killed, wounded, or went missing in one day's battle.

While McClellan failed to destroy the Confederate forces, even allowing them to withdraw south to Maryland without pursuit, Antietam is technically considered a Union victory.

What was the next major battle in 1862?

The Battle of Fredericksburg (December 11–15, 1862) was the next important battle in the Civil War and is credited as a huge victory for the South. This time, Lee was defending his troops against a frontal attack by Major General Ambrose Burnside (1824–1881). As with the hesitant McClellan, Burnside was not the best man for this job. He was unfortunate both in the weather and in his own uncertain command. An excellent commander of men, able to inspire, as well as confide, he had many fine qualities but was not the right person to command so large a force. Where McClellan erred on the side of caution, Burnside tended to err on the side of desperate action. Another trouble Burnside faced was that he had absolutely no benefit of surprise. The Confederates, from their side, could detect every move the Northern men made, and it was plainly obvious they meant to cross the river. A slaughter ensued, with Union casualties being twice that of Confederates.

Was the Battle of Chancellorsville also a Confederate victory?

Yes. Fought between April 30 and May 6, 1863, in Spotsylvania County, Virginia, it pitted Lee against the Army of the Potomac, led by Major General Joseph Hooker. Although the Union had superior numbers, Lee prooved the better strategist in this case, despite being in terrain that limited his ability to maneuver troops. The Confederates were dealt an early harsh blow when General Stonewall Jackson was severely wounded (and died several days later from those wounds). Nevertheless, the Southerners were in a fighting mood. Lee took the risky tactic of splitting his army in two, leaving enough troops to hold back the advance of Union Major General John Sedgwick so he could then deploy about eighty percent of his forces against Hooker's men. The strategy worked, but it was a hard win.

All told, the North suffered slightly more than 18,000 men killed, wounded, or missing, while the South lost in excess of 12,500. Though Lee was the clear winner of the Battle of Chancellorsville, he was not satisfied. In letters to Confederate President Davis and others, he confided that he had hoped to inflict far greater losses on the Union. And though no one wanted to say it, the South could not afford 12,500 casualties, while the North could—in strict numerical terms—afford to lose 18,000. The single greatest loss was that of Stonewall Jackson.

THE WAR TURNS SOUR FOR THE SOUTH

What two battles are considered to mark the reversal of fortunes for the South?

The Battle of Vicksburg and the Battle of Gettysburg marked a turning point in the Civil War in which the Confederacy lost its initial momentum, and the Union started to gain the upper hand.

What happened at Vicksburg?

The Battle (or Siege) of Vicksburg lasted from May 18 to July 4, 1863. Union forces led by Ulysses S. Grant backed the Confederates into a defensive position in the city of Vicksburg, Mississippi. A long siege ensued that the Union won, largely by virtue of the Southerners running out of food and other supplies. Taking the city was a major step in the Union's gaining control of the Mississippi River.

What was significant about the Battle of Gettysburg?

The Battle of Gettysburg is often considered a key turning point in the U.S. Civil War. Both the Union and the Confederacy suffered casualties in excess of 20,000 troops. The brutal three-day battle took place July 1–3, 1863. The Confederate forces were led by General Lee, while Union General George G. Meade led the Union forces.

At the end of the battle, Lee's forces retreated to Virginia. For the remainder of the war, Lee's Confederate forces were on the defensive, reacting to the advances by Union

French artist Paul Philippoteaux's painting showing "Pickett's Charge" at Cemetery Ridge on the third day of the Battle of Gettysburg, July 3, 1863. The charge was infamous for the loss of Confederate lives, and it marked the farthest advance north that the South would manage during the war.

armies. Some historians view the battle as a key strategic victory for the Union forces, although the casualties were about even during the bloody conflict.

What was the Gettysburg Address?

The Gettysburg Address was a speech delivered by President Abraham Lincoln on November 19, 1863, at the Soldiers National Cemetery in Gettysburg, Pennsylvania. Lincoln talked about the importance of preserving the union, upholding principles of equality found in the Declaration of Independence, and warning against the evils of secession.

The speech provided:

Four score and seven years ago our fathers brought forth on this continent, a new nation, conceived in Liberty, and dedicated to the proposition that all men are created equal.

Now we are engaged in a great civil war, testing whether that nation, or any nation so conceived and dedicated, can long endure. We are met on a great battle-field of that war. We have come to dedicate a portion of that field, as a final resting place for those who here gave their lives that that nation might live. It is altogether fitting and proper that we should do this.

But, in a larger sense, we can not dedicate—we can not consecrate—we can not hallow—this ground. The brave men, living and dead, who struggled here,

111

have consecrated it, far above our poor power to add or detract. The world will little note, nor long remember what we say here, but it can never forget what they did here. It is for us the living, rather, to be dedicated here to the unfinished work which they who fought here have thus far so nobly advanced. It is rather for us to be here dedicated to the great task remaining before us—that from these honored dead we take increased devotion to that cause for which they gave the last full measure of devotion—that we here highly resolve that these dead shall not have died in vain—that this nation, under God, shall have a new birth of freedom—and that government of the people, by the people, for the people, shall not perish from the earth.

Who was George G. Meade?

George G. Meade (1815–1872) was a Union general in the Civil War best known for defeating Confederate General Robert E. Lee at the Battle of Gettysburg. Meade had served in the Second Seminole War and the Mexican–American War. Born in Cadiz, Spain, where his father served as a naval agent for the U.S. government, Meade entered the United States Military Academy in 1831, graduating in 1835. He served with distinctions in several wars and achieved acclaim for his leadership during the U.S. Civil War.

Generally, Meade performed well as a military commander during the Civil War. He received some criticism for not aggressively pursuing the retreated Confederate forces at the end of the Battle of Gettysburg. But Meade led his troops to several successful battles during the Civil War. His legacy lives on to this day with Fort George G. Meade in Maryland, and a World War II warship was named in his honor.

How did Richmond, Virginia, fall?

Richmond, Virginia, served as the capital of the Confederacy and was where President Jefferson Davis governed. On the morning of April 2, 1865, hundreds of well-to-do Richmonders were worshipping at St. Paul's Church when a telegraph messenger entered. He went straight to Jefferson Davis, who rose from his pew and—with an ashen face—walked briskly out of the church and to the Confederate White House. Though he said

What was Sherman's March to the Sea?

After the Union enjoyed victories in Tennessee, Major General William Tecumseh Sherman (1820–1891) next took the city of Atlanta, Georgia, in July 1864. He then marched from Atlanta to Savannah, Georgia, using slash-and-burn tactics to destroy everything in his path, leaving the Confederates with no resources whatsoever. Sherman captured Savannah in December 1864, leaving behind a path of utter destruction that crippled the South's military and industry.

nothing, the people at St. Paul's guessed the worst: Lee's lines around St. Petersburg had been broken by the Union forces. The telegraph was from Lee, informing the president that Richmond would soon fall. Davis and his family escaped Richmond a few hours before the end, but most civilians were not so lucky. They heard the cannon fire from the south, then from the west, and guessed—correctly—that Grant and the Union forces had finally completed their death grip on the Confederate capital. By nightfall, Jefferson Davis, most of the Cabinet, and most of the higher levels of the Confederate government had escaped—but, as many Richmonders asked, where could they go? Richmond was the heart and soul of the Confederacy.

By April 1, 1865, the Union siege lines ran thirty-seven miles in a nearly complete circle of Richmond and St. Petersburg. The Confederates, too, had fought heroically, but the game was clearly up. Lee did not reveal all his decision-making, but he let Jefferson Davis know that the capital could be held no longer. Throughout the beginning of April, Lee and the Army of Northern Virginia made good their escape, heading due west. What little hope remained was that Lee would effect a meeting with Johnston and that their combined forces would somehow overcome Sherman's army. Even the most die-hard Confederate knew this was a forlorn hope, but in desperate times people often cling to what has been and will make all sorts of sacrifices to attempt to maintain it.

END OF THE CIVIL WAR

Where did General Lee surrender to Union forces?

General Lee surrendered to Union general Ulysses S. Grant at the Appomattox Court House on April 9, 1865. Lee's forces were surrounded, and the able general realized the end was in sight.

What significant battle in Texas was fought after Lee's surrender?

The Battle of Palmito Ranch took place on May 12–13, 1865, more than a month after General Lee's surrender. The battle occurred about a dozen miles from Brownsville, Texas. Technically, Confederate forces led by John "Rip" Ford defeated Union forces led by Theodore Barrett. However, later that month Texas surrendered to Union forces.

Who killed President Lincoln?

John Wilkes Booth (1838–1865), an actor, assassinated President Lincoln at Ford's Theatre in Washington, D.C. On April 14, 1865, Lincoln was at the theatre with his wife Mary Todd Lincoln to watch the play *Our American Cousin*. Booth was not starring in the play but managed to place his name in eternal infamy by shooting the president from behind in the president's box. Booth allegedly yelled, "Sic semper tyrannis" (Latin for "Thus ever for tyrants"), shot the president and then dramatically leaped from the box onto the stage. Lincoln died the next day. Booth escaped but was tracked down twelve days later in a barn in Fredericksburg, Virginia. Booth was shot and killed by Sergeant Boston Corbett. Lincoln's vice president, Andrew Johnson (1808–1875), was sworn in on April 15.

How did President Andrew Johnson spar with Congress during his presidency?

Johnson (1808–1875) and the thirty-ninth Congress—composed of the so-called "Radical Republicans"—sparred mightily over the period of Reconstruction—the period of time given to rebuilding the Union after the Civil War. Johnson favored a quick process by which the former Confederate states would be readmitted to the Union. Johnson also did not support some of the civil rights measures passed by Congress that were designed to ensure a measure of equality to the recently freed slaves.

Lincoln's murderer, John Wilkes Booth, was a famous actor, so he raised no suspicions as he entered the theater to kill the president. Afterwards, Booth was hunted down and and killed by Sergeant Boston Corbett.

Johnson vetoed the renewing of the Freedmen's Bureau, an agency that provided federal assistance to recently freed individuals. Johnson felt that this measure—like other federal civil rights legislation—invaded the sovereignty, or power, of state governments.

Johnson also sought to block passage of the Civil Rights Act of 1866 and later the Fourteenth Amendment to the U.S. Constitution. Once again, Johnson believed that the federal Congress was exceeding its powers, invading the states' sphere.

Why was Johnson impeached?

The U.S. House of Representatives vehemently felt that President Johnson was not doing his job properly. They initially attempted to impeach him in November 1867 for a variety of reasons, but the vote failed 57–108. However, the House found a new reason to impeach President Johnson after he removed Secretary of War Edwin Stanton from office in violation of a newly enacted federal law known as the Tenure of Office Act.

The Tenure of Office Act prohibited the president from discharging members of his Cabinet until a successor had received official Senate approval. Congress had passed the law in large measure to protect Stanton, whom Johnson wanted out of office. Johnson ignored the Tenure of Office Act and had Stanton—who had barricaded himself in his office—removed.

A few days later, the House impeached President Johnson. Under the Constitution, the House can impeach a president (and other federal officials), but the Senate has the power to try and convict the president. The Senate has to vote by a two-thirds margin to remove a president from office via impeachment. The Senate voted 35–19 that Johnson was guilty and should be impeached. This was one vote shy of the necessary two-thirds majority. Thus, Johnson survived the impeachment process and remained in office.

MAJOR FIGURES IN THE CIVIL WAR

How did General Thomas Jackson earn the nickname "Stonewall"?

Jackson (1824–1863) earned his nickname at the First Battle of Bull Run in July 1861. A fellow officer allegedly exclaimed, "Look, men, there is Jackson standing like a stone wall." Jackson was born in Virginia and attended West Point. After graduation, he fought in the Mexican–American War. Jackson was considered a superior military tactician and was responsible for several major Confederate victories. Tragically for him, he was killed by one of his own soldiers—"friendly fire"—at the Battle of Chancellorsville in May 1863. He actually appeared to be healing from a severe wound but died eight days later from pneumonia at age thirty-nine.

What Confederate military leader later led the Ku Klux Klan?

Nathan Bedford Forrest (1821–1877) served as a lieutenant general for the Confederacy in the U.S. Civil War. He led Confederate forces to victory at the First Battle of Murfreesboro (Tennessee) on July 13, 1862, over Union forces led by Thomas L. Crittenden. Forrest surprised Union forces at just after 4:00 A.M., inflicting casualties of nearly nine hundred. He earned acclaim for his leadership at the Battle at Brice's Crossroads in Lee County, Mississippi, on June 10, 1864. Forrest successfully led Confederate forces against a Union force that was double its size. Union General William T. Sherman referred to him as "that Devil" because of his military prowess. On the infamous side, Forrest led Confederate forces at the Battle of Fort Pillow, which featured the slaughter of many black Union soldiers.

What Confederate officer was executed for atrocities committed at the prison he commanded?

Henry Wirz (1823–1865) was a Confederate officer in charge of Andersonville Prison, also known as Camp Sumter, in Georgia. Born in Switzerland, he emigrated to the United States in 1849. Wirz's leadership over the prison was controversial, as many Union prisoners died from poor sanitation, overcrowding, or outright mistreatment. He imposed cruel punishment on prisoners. After the war, he was court-martialed for killing Union prisoners. It was alleged that he personally shot several prisoners with his revolver. He was the only person executed after the war for behavior committed during the war.

What other Civil War battles did Forrest win?

Forrest commanded Confederate forces to victories in several Civil War battles, including the Battle of Brentwood, the Battle of Fort Pillow, and the Battle of Chickamauga.

What was especially tragic about the Battle of Fort Pillow?

The Battle of Fort Pillow occurred on April 12, 1864, in Henning, Tennessee. It featured the slaughter of numerous black Union soldiers. Customary rules of engagement provided that captured soldiers were not killed by the other side. But Confederate forces under Major General Forrest slaughtered many black troops. One historian referred to the events as an "orgy of death." For this reason, the Battle of Fort Pillow is often called the Fort Pillow Massacre.

After whom was Fort Pillow named?

Fort Pillow was named after the general who oversaw its construction—Confederate Brigadier General Gideon Johnson Pillow (1806–1878). Born in Tennessee, Pillow attended school and later practiced law with future President Polk. He fought in the Mexican–American War, rising to the rank of brigadier general.

Pillow ran into trouble in the war, as he allegedly falsely took credit for two victories actually earned by General Winfield Scott. Facing court-martial, Pillow was rescued by his former law partner, then-President Polk. Scott arrested Pillow, but he escaped punishment. He had to resign from the U.S. Army after the trial.

Pillow later became a Confederate general. He is best known for losing the Battle of Fort Donelson against Union General U.S. Grant (1822–1885). Pillow made some significant advances with his troops and then inexplicably retrenched without pressing his advantage. After the war, he prospered as an attorney in Memphis, Tennessee.

What Civil War nurse later founded the American Red Cross?

Clara Barton (1821–1912) founded the American Red Cross in 1881. During the Civil War, she treated countless soldiers from both North and South. She began her humanitarian war efforts after the First Battle of Bull Run.

What former U.S. vice president later became a Confederate general?

John C. Breckenridge (1821–1875) served as vice president under President James

Clara Barton, who treated soldiers on both sides of the Civil War, founded the American Red Cross.

What Confederate general committed suicide?

Philip St. George Cooke (1809–1861) served as a Confederate brigadier general during the first year of the Civil War. He fought at the First Battle of Bull Run and also commanded troops at the Battle of Blackburn's Ford. He suffered from depression and killed himself in December 1861.

Buchanan. Breckenridge then served as a senator for the state of Kentucky. At the outbreak of the Civil War, he joined the Confederacy and was expelled from his Senate seat.

He served as a general for the Confederacy in the Civil War and later became secretary of war for the Confederacy. After the war, he fled to Cuba and later Canada. He returned to his home state of Kentucky after President Andrew Johnson pardoned former Confederates. He never returned to politics.

What military leader fought on both sides of the Civil War?

Frank Crawford Armstrong (1835–1909) fought on both sides of the Civil War. He served with the Union Army at the First Battle of Bull Run. He resigned his commission in August 1861, joining the Confederacy. He fought for the Confederacy until his capture at the Battle of Selma on April 2, 1865. Many years later, he served as United States Indian Inspector and Assistant Commissioner of Indian Affairs. He had been born on Indian territory, where his father was stationed.

Who was the longest-living Confederate general?

Simon Bolivar Buckner (1823–1914) lived until age ninety-one, outliving all other major Confederate generals in the Civil War. Born in 1823 in Hart County, Kentucky, Buckner served in both the Mexican–American War and the U.S. Civil War. He lost the Battle of Fort Donelson to Union General U.S. Grant. Afer the war, Buckner had a successful career. He became editor of the *Louisville Courier* and later served as governor of Kentucky from 1887 to 1891.

What Confederate general was the son of a Union general?

John Rogers Cooke (1833–1891) served as a Confederate general. He is best known for the sheer number of times he was wounded in battle—seven. His father, Philip St. George Cooke, served as a Union general. The younger Cooke had studied at Harvard and later served in the U.S. Army in 1855. When Virginia seceded from the Union, he joined the Confederacy. After the war, he and his father mended their differences.

What Union general was known as the "Father of the U.S. Cavalry"?

Philip St. George Cooke (1809–1895) was known as the Father of the U.S. Cavalry in part because he authored an influential Army cavalry manual. He fought at the Black Hawk War, the Mexican–American War, and the U.S. Civil War.

What two brothers were on opposite sides of the Civil War?

George B. Crittenden (1812–1880) served as a Confederate general; his brother Thomas L. Crittenden (1819–1893), served as a Union general. Their father, John J. Crittenden, was a prominent politician from Kentucky, who was a governor of Kentucky, member of the House of Representatives and Senate, and who twice served as U.S. attorney general. He introduced the failed Crittenden Compromise.

George fought in the Black Hawk War, the Mexican–American War, and the Civil War. Crittenden's military career in the Civil War was marred by a charge of drunkenness, which led to his demotion to colonel in 1862. Thomas fought in the Mexican–American War and the Civil War, serving until his resignation in 1864.

What former Confederate general later became a minister and prolific author?

Clement A. Evans (1833–1911) had a successful postwar career as a Methodist minister and prolific author. Born in Stewart County, Georgia, Evans became a lawyer at age eighteen, a judge at twenty-one, and state senator at age twenty-five. He later fought in the Civil War, rising to the rank of brigadier general. He fought in numerous battles, including Antietam, Gettysburg, Fredericksburg, and the Second Battle of Bull Run.

After the war, he became an influential minister, sometimes pastoring churches of more than a thousand members. He also wrote extensively, including the *Confederate Military History*—a twelve-volume set he coauthored.

What Confederate general later became a New York judge?

Roger Atkinson Pryor (1828–1919) served as a brigadier general during the Civil War. Born in Petersburg, Virginia, Pryor graduated college from Hampden-Sydney (Virginia) and then law school from the University of Virginia in 1848. He left law for journalism, working for the *Washington Union* and the *Richmond Daily Enquirer*. He fought at the Seven Days Battle and the more significant Battle of Antietam.

After the war, he moved to New York and practiced law with Benjamin F. Butler, a lawyer from Boston. He later served as a judge on the New York Court of Common Pleas and then the New York Supreme Court.

What Confederate general later became head of the Southern Historical Society?

Jubal A. Early (1816–1894) was a Confederate general who served under both Generals Lee and Jackson. Known as "Old Jubal" or the "Bad Old Man," Early practiced law before the war. He fought aggressively during the war, including in the summer of 1864, when he led the so-called Washington raid, causing panic in the Potomac area. After the war, he went to Mexico and Canada. He returned to Virginia in 1869 and resumed the practice of law. He then became president of the Southern Historical Society.

What Union general later became U.S. president?

Ulysses S. Grant became the eighteenth president of the United States, largely as a result of the popularity he acquired as the major war commander of Union forces during the second half of the Civil War. Grant defeated Confederate General Robert E. Lee and accepted Lee's surrender at Appomattox Courthouse in 1865, effectively ending the war.

Grant rose through the ranks, distinguishing himself by capturing the Confederate stronghold at Vicksburg, Mississippi. After he won the Battle of Chattanooga in late 1863, Lincoln elevated him to commander of all the Union Army. Grant engaged in a series of battles with famed Confederate General Robert E. Lee. After the Union prevailed, Grant was celebrated as a war hero. He was promoted to general of the Army of the United States in 1866. Grant emerged as a political force and won the presidential election of 1868. He served two terms as president.

Ulysses S. Grant led the Union forces in the second half of the Civil War. After the war, from 1869 to 1877, he served as his country's eighteenth president.

What Union general had great success in military campaigns in Georgia and South Carolina?

Union General William Tecumseh Sherman (1820–1891) compiled an impressive military record during the Civil War, defeating numerous Confederate generals and forces. He was an able commander, known for his complete and total victories. He was known for utilizing "scorched earth" policies in his destruction of Confederate forces in his way. He won battles in Vicksburg, Mississippi; Chattanooga, Tennessee; Atlanta, Georgia; and other Southern cities. He led his forces on the so-called "March to the Sea"— the name given to Sherman's march through Georgia to Savannah.

Sherman and his troops burned crops, torched buildings, and killed livestock of Confederate forces or supporters. Sherman successfully marched through Georgia and later sent President Lincoln a telegraph, offering the City of Savannah as a Christmas gift.

When Grant became president, he promoted Sherman to commanding general of the United States Army. He focused on protecting railroads from Indian attacks. Sherman died in 1891. Ironically, one of the pallbearers at Sherman's funeral was his former military foe—Confederate General Joseph Johnston.

What Union general began emancipating slaves during the war without authorization from the president?

General David Hunter (1802–1886), sometimes known by the moniker "Black Dave," fought in the Second Seminole War, the Mexican–American War, and the Civil War. During the Civil War, he enlisted black men to fight as soldiers for the Union cause. In 1862, he created controversy when he began freeing slaves in the states of Georgia, South Carolina, and Florida. Hunter issued an order in May 1862, declaring that the three states were placed under martial law and that persons in those areas who were slaves are now free. Lincoln reprimanded Hunter, as the president favored a process of gradual emancipation.

Hunter continued to enlist black soldiers for the war effort in South Carolina. Harper was an effective military commander during the War, defeating Confederate forces at the Battle of Piedmont in June 1864.

What Union general later served as secretary of war and in other prominent positions?

Russell A. Alger (1836–1907) enlisted as a private for the Union forces in 1861. He served with distinction, capturing Confederate forces at the Battle of Trevillian Station. He later earned the awards of brevet brigadier general and brevet major general for his bravery and success during the war.

After the war, Alger ran a successful lumber company before entering politics. He served as governor of Michigan from 1885–1887, U.S. secretary of war under President William McKinley from 1897–1899 and then as a senator from Michigan from 1902–1907.

What Union general later served as U.S. surgeon general of the army?

Dr. Joseph K. Barnes (1817–1883) served as a medical inspector with the rank of lieutenant colonel in the U.S. Civil War. He received a promotion to brigadier general with

---

What Union general was related to two U.S. presidents?

Charles Francis Adams, Jr. (1835–1915) served as a colonel and then brigadier general in the Union Army during the Civil War. He was the grandson of the sixth president, John Quincy Adams, and the great-grandson of the second president, John Adams.

Born in 1835 in Boston, Massachusetts, Charles Francis Adams, Jr. graduated from Harvard in 1856. He then served in the Civil War, earning commendations for his bravery during the Gettysburg War. He actually served as a colonel during the war but was awarded the honorary title of brevet brigadier general because of his bravery. He later achieved success in the railroad business.

the rank of U.S. surgeon general. He served as the twelfth U.S. surgeon general of the U.S. Army from 1864–1882. He was at the deathbeds of two presidents—Abraham Lincoln and James A. Garfield.

What Union general was known as the "Rock of Chickamauga"?

George Henry Thomas (1816–1870) was a Union general known for his brave performance at the Battle of Chickamauga in northern Georgia in April 1863. Confederate forces under General Braxton Bragg overran much of the Union forces under General William Rosecrans. However, Thomas managed to hold his Union line, averting a complete defeat for the Union Army. For this performance, he was dubbed the "Rock of Chickamauga." He later routed Confederate forces at the Battle of Nashville in December 1864. During this conflict, the Confederates suffered nearly six thousand casualties.

RECONSTRUCTION

What was Reconstruction?

Reconstruction refers to the period of time after the U.S. Civil War during which the United States freed the slaves took steps to provide freedom to the formerly enslaved and reconstructed society by providing for a process by which the former Confederate States could be readmitted into the Union. The United States under President Lincoln set about to create reconstructed governments in the seceded states.

Reconstruction was led by members in the thirty-ninth Congress, known as the "Radical Republicans." These members sought to impose sharp controls over the former Confederate states and passed much legislation to try to provide protection for the civil rights of former slaves.

What is Juneteenth?

Juneteenth refers to June 19, 1865, when slavery was abolished in Texas. It marks the official end of slavery in the United States. It also is called Freedom Day or Emancipation Day. It is still celebrated in the United States. More than forty states recognized Juneteenth as a holiday.

On June 18, 1865, Union forces led by General Gordon Granger marched into Galveston, Texas, seizing control. The next day Granger announced an official order of the U.S. government. It read:

> The people of Texas are informed that, in accordance with a proclamation from the Executive of the United States, all slaves are free. This involves an absolute equality of personal rights and rights of property between former masters and slaves, and the connection heretofore existing between them becomes that between employer and hired labor.

What three constitutional amendments were highlights of the Reconstruction era?

The three Reconstruction amendments were the Thirteenth Amendment, ratified in 1865; the Fourteenth Amendment, ratified in 1868; and the Fifteenth Amendment, ratified in 1870. The Thirteenth Amendment outlawed slavery and involuntary servitude. The Fourteenth Amendment made the recently freed slaves citizens of the United States and provided key protections, such as due process and equal protection. The Fifteenth Amendment protected the right to vote.

What does the Thirteenth Amendment say?

The Thirteenth Amendment provides:

> Section 1: Neither slavery nor involuntary servitude, except as a punishment for crime whereof the party shall have been duly convicted, shall exist within the United States, or any place subject to their jurisdiction.

> Section 2. Congress shall have power to enforce this article by appropriate legislation.

During Reconstruction, what former slave became the first African American member of the House?

Joseph Rainey (1832–1887), a former slave, became the first African American member of the U.S. House of Representatives in 1870 from South Carolina. Rainey served in the House during Reconstruction from 1870 until 1879. He lost his seat in an election against John Smythe Richardson (1828–1894). During his tenure in the House, he served as speaker pro tempore beginning in 1874.

Who were carpetbaggers?

Carpetbaggers was a pejorative term used by Southerners used to describe Northerners who moved to the South during the period of Reconstruction. Carpetbaggers allegedly came to the South to exploit economic opportunities and advantage themselves over many native-born Southerners. Today the term is used to describe a politician who moves to another area and runs for office.

Who were scalawags?

Scalawags was another negative term used to describe those Southerners who supported Reconstruction and the Northern policies of racial integration and some measure of equality for blacks. Scalawag originally referred to low-grade farm animals. Some Southern newspaper writers used the term to apply to those who supported the Union or Union policies after the Civil War.

What is the history of the Ku Klux Klan?

The Ku Klux Klan (KKK) is a white supremacist group originally formed in 1865 in Pulaski, Tennessee, when Confederate Army veterans formed what they called a "social club." The first leader (called the "grand wizard") was Nathan Bedford Forrest.

Members of the KKK hold a march in Washington, D.C., on August 8, 1925. The KKK has had periods of resurgence in American history whenever racial strife has increased, such as after the Civil War and during the Civil Rights movement.

As the unofficial arm of resistance against Republican efforts to restore the nation and make full citizens of its black (formerly slave) population, the Ku Klux Klan waged a campaign of terror against blacks in the South during Reconstruction (1865–1877). Klan members, cloaked in robes and hoods to disguise their identity, threatened, beat, and killed numerous blacks. While the group deprived its victims of their rights as citizens, their intent was also to intimidate the entire black population and keep them out of politics. White people who supported the federal government's measures to extend rights to all black citizens also became the victims of the fearsome Klan. Membership in the group grew quickly, and the Ku Klux Klan soon had a presence throughout the South.

In 1871 the U.S. Congress passed the Force Bill, giving President Ulysses S. Grant (1822–1885) authority to direct federal troops against the Klan. The action was successful, causing the group to disappear—but only for a time. In 1915 the society was newly organized at Stone Mountain, Georgia, as a Protestant fraternal organization (called "The Invisible Empire, Knights of the Ku Klux Klan, Inc."), this time widening its focus of persecution to include Roman Catholics, immigrants, and Jews, as well as blacks. Members of all of these groups became the target of KKK harassment, which included torture, whippings, and public lynchings. The group, which proclaimed its mission of "racial purity," grew in number and became national, electing its own to public

123

office in many states, not just the South. But the society's acts of violence raised the public ire. By the 1940s, America's attention focused on World War II (1939–1945), and the Klan died out or went completely underground. The group had another resurgence during the 1950s and into the early 1970s as the nation struggled through the era of civil rights. The Klan still exists today, fostering the extremist views of its membership and staging marches to demonstrate its presence on the American landscape. Such demonstrations are often attended by protestors.

Who were the Radical Republicans?

The Radical Republicans were a segment of the Republican Party from the 1850s to the 1870s who strenuously opposed slavery, passed laws to protect those recently freed from slavery, and imposed stringent requirements on former Confederate states before they could be readmitted into the Union. They were instrumental in passing the Reconstruction Amendments, impeaching President Andrew Johnson, and limiting the voting (and other) rights of former Confederates. The Radical Republicans achieved their greatest influence in the thirty-ninth Congress, which began in May 1865. The thirty-ninth Congress passed much Reconstruction-era legislation. For example, this Congress passed the Civil Rights Act of 1866; passed the Freedmen's Bureau Bill of 1866; ratified the Thirteenth Amendment, which ended slavery; and passed the Fourteenth Amendment. Both houses of Congress during the thirty-ninth Congress were dominated by the Republican Party. For example, at the end of the thirty-ninth Congress, there were nine Democrats and forty-one Republicans in the Senate.

Some of the more instrumental Radical Republicans were Thaddeus Stevens (1792–1868) from Pennsylvania, Charles Sumner (1811–1874) from Massachusetts, and John Bingham (1815–1900) from Ohio. Stevens opposed slavery, actively supported and participated in the Underground Railroad, opposed harsh treatment of Native Americans, and even ordered that he be buried in a black cemetery. Sumner helped form the Freedman's Bureau, supported suffrage for blacks, and introduced numerous pieces of civil rights legislation. Bingham was the principal architect of Section 1 of the Fourteenth Amendment, which contained the Privileges and Immunities, Due Process, and Equal Protection clauses.

What member of the Radical Republicans was known as the "Father of Reconstruction"?

Thaddeus Stevens was a member of the U.S. House of Representatives from Pennsylvania from the 1840s until his death in 1868. He was the leader of the Radical Republicans and known as "the Father of Reconstruction." Born with a club foot, Stevens overcame his physical disadvantage and became a leading attorney, winning numerous cases before the U.S. Supreme Court. During his legal career, he represented many types of people who faced discrimination, including African Americans, American Indians, Seventh-Day Adventists, Mormons, Jews, and Chinese.

Stevens was an ardent abolitionist, who virulently opposed slavery. He once said: "I wish I were the owner of every Southern slave so that I might cast off the shackles from their limbs and witness the rapture which would excite them in the first dance of freedom." When Stevens died, he was buried—as he had requested while alive—at an African American cemetery.

Who was John Bingham?

John Bingham (1815–1900) was a member of the U.S. House of Representatives from the state of Ohio, best known for drafting a good portion of the Fourteenth Amendment. Bingham was reared in the city of Cadiz, Ohio, where he was exposed to abolitionist beliefs. He attended college at Franklin College (Indiana), where his opposition to slavery developed even more. Bingham served in the House from 1855 until 1863 and then again from 1865 until 1873. He later served as U.S. ambassador to Japan. U.S. Supreme Court Justice Hugo Black once referred to Bingham as the "Madison of the Fourteenth Amendment."

Who were the Redeemers?

The Redeemers were a group of Southern Democrats who gradually asserted more power, seeking to wrest political control away from the Radical Republicans, Carpetbaggers, and others who sought to ensure a greater measure of equality in the South. The Redeemers often wanted to return to the older system in the South, fearing any system that would give blacks any real measure of political or social equality. The Redeemers supported the removal of federal troops from the Southern states. This process of wrestling control back to the Southern Democrats is sometimes referred to as Redemption.

What was "Seward's Folly"?

William Seward

Seward's Folly refers to the purchase of Alaska from the Russians in an 1867 treaty. The name refers to William Seward (1801–1872), U.S. secretary of state from 1861 to 1869, who brokered the deal. As a U.S. senator representing New York from 1849 to 1861, Seward was interested in the whaling business. Alaska had an active whaling population, but at the time was owned by the Russians. Russia, though, wished to sell the territory by the 1860s because, during its involvement in the Crimean War, it saw Alaska as vulnerable to the British. Seward took advantage of this and bought what would become America's forty-ninth state for $7.2 million. At the time, most Americans felt the far-northern lands were not worth anything and hence deemed the purchase "folly." Today, historians consider the purchase to be Seward's greatest contribution to the nation.

What did the 1875 Civil Rights Act prohibit?

The 1875 Civil Rights Act prohibited unlawful discrimination in places of public accommodation, including inns, hotels, railroads, and theaters. Section 1 of the law provided: "That all persons within the jurisdiction of the United States shall be entitled to the full and equal enjoyment of the accommodations, advantages, facilities, and privileges of inns, public conveyances on land or water, theatres, and other places of public amusement; subject only to the conditions and limitations established by law, and applicable alike to citizens of every race and color, regardless of any previous condition of servitude."

The thirty-ninth Congress, led by the so-called "Radical Republicans," justified the passage of the Civil Rights Act of 1875 as a necessary law to stamp out the incidents and badges of slavery and involuntary servitude imposed upon African Americans. Congress believed the law would help enforce two recently enacted constitutional amendments—the Thirteenth Amendment, which outlawed slavery, and the Fourteenth Amendment, which attempted to give recently freed slaves the same general rights as white citizens.

Why did the Court strike down the Civil Rights Act of 1875?

The Court invalidated the Civil Rights Act of 1875 because it determined the law reached beyond Congress's power under the Thirteenth and Fourteenth Amendments. The majority believed Congress did not have the power to prohibit simple private wrongs, as opposed to wrongs committed by government officials.

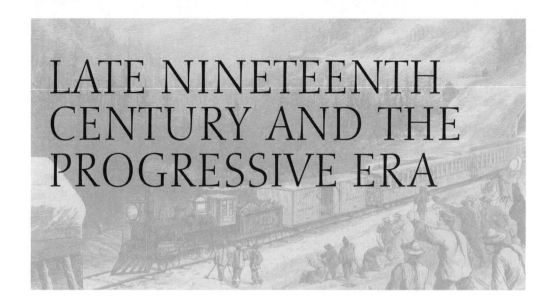

LATE NINETEENTH CENTURY AND THE PROGRESSIVE ERA

THE GRANT ADMINISTRATION

How did Ulysses S. Grant become president?

Grant was a war hero of the highest order. The Republicans heralded him as their next nominee. In Chicago, at the 1868 Republican convention, the party nominated him on the first ballot as its candidate. He ran against New York Democrat Horatio Seymour. Grant handily defeated Seymour by a 214–80 electoral vote margin.

What financial crisis occurred during Grant's first term?

Black Friday happened on September 24, 1869, in Grant's first term as president. It occurred when two Wall Street speculators, Jay Gould and Jim Fisk, attempted to buy all the gold at the financial markets. Their attempts to corner the market led to a financial panic that forced the closing of the stock market. Unfortunately, Gould and Fisk were friends with Grant's brother-in-law Abel Rathbone Corbin, husband to Grant's sister Virginia.

What other financial crisis occurred during Grant's time as president?

The Panic of 1873, a worldwide economic depression, occurred during President Grant's tenure. Eighteen thousand businesses failed, including a quarter of the nation's railroads. The panic began in the United States with the failure of Jay Cooke & Company, a major bank. Unemployment reached a high of nearly fifteen percent. This panic lasted until 1879.

What were some of the other scandals that rocked the Grant Administration?

In 1875, Secretary of the Treasury Benjamin Bristow exposed the Whiskey Ring Scandal, involving officials and businessmen supposedly pocketing millions of dollars in liquor taxes. Many officials allegedly bribed Internal Revenue Service agents and oth-

ers, including IRS supervisor John McDonald and Grant's private secretary, Orville E. Babcock.

The Indian Trading Scandal also rocked the Grant Administration, and impeachment charges were brought against Secretary of War William W. Belknap for allegedly accepting a bribe over an Indian trading post position. He became the first member of a presidential Cabinet to be impeached. Although he resigned immediately, the House nevertheless impeached him. The Senate acquitted him because he had already resigned.

The Delano Affair also rocked the Grant Administration. Secretary of the Interior Columbus Delano allegedly took bribes for fraudulent land grants. He resigned from office in October 1875.

What efforts at helping African Americans occurred during Grant's first term?

Grant issued a proclamation that celebrated the Fifteenth Amendment, which had ensured recently freed slaves the right to vote. He also approved of the passage by Congress of a civil rights law known as the Ku Klux Klan Act of 1871, which sought to reduce violence against blacks.

What was unusual and controversial about the election of 1876?

The election of 1876 was unusual because Democrat Samuel Tilden won the popular vote by nearly three hundred thousand votes over Republican Rutherford B. Hayes (1822–1893) but ended up one electoral vote shy of winning the election. On the night of the election, Tilden had clearly captured the popular vote and was only one electoral vote short of winning the election. However, the states of Florida, South Carolina, Oregon, and Louisiana could go to Hayes, which would give him 185 electoral votes.

Democrats charged that fraud in the vote counting occurred in several of the Southern states. They pointed out that in several Southern states, there were Republican-con-

128

Initial settlers to the territory of Oregon began making their way there in the early nineteenth century, and the Treaty of 1818 established joint occupation of the region by both Americans and British. In 1846, the two nations signed the Oregon Treaty, giving the United States full claim to Oregon.

The trail that settlers followed was first established by fur traders and was little more than a path through grasslands and forests. The first migrant trains started in Independence, Missouri, in the 1830s, and settlers followed a route that took them about twenty-two hundred miles across the Great Plains along the Platte River Valley, through the South Pass of the Rocky Mountains in what is now Wyoming, then following the Columbia River to the rich farmlands of western Oregon. From the 1830s to the late 1860s, about 400,000 people traveled the route, many succumbing to sickness, starvation, and Indian attacks. The wagon train era largely ended with the completion of the Transcontinental Railroad in 1869.

What were some other important trails?

The Oregon Trail was not the only route, of course. Others included the Bozeman Trail, connecting Montana to Oregon; the California Trail, which diverted from the Oregon Trail at Fort Hall Idaho, then went south through Nevada and split into several trails entering the northern part of California; and the Mormon Trail, which went to Salt Lake City after going through the South Pass.

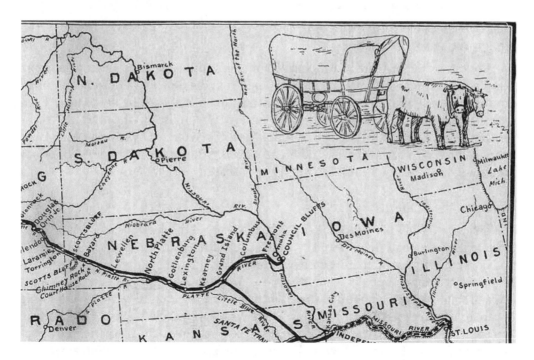

Did the Donner Party really resort to cannibalism?

The story of the Donner Party is one of the most tragic in American history. Jacob (c. 1781–1846) and George Donner (1784–1847) led a group of eighty-nine emigrants from Springfield, Illinois, in 1846. Their goal was to reach California, following the California Trail. However, in an effort to save time, they diverted from the established trail to pursue what they believed to be a shorter route through the Sierra Nevadas. Following the advice of a trail guide named Lansford Hastings, they came to regret this choice, as Hastings's advice resulted in a number of delays that cost them precious weeks. The final blow came when Hastings, who had been scouting several days ahead of the main party, left behind a note that said the pass he thought they could take was not a viable route. He told the party to take another path, which led them into trouble when an October snow storm blocked their way, and they became hopelessly stuck in the mountains. One member of the party, James Reed, managed to reach Sutter's Fort, where he asked Sutter to send a rescue mission. Several unsuccessful attempts were made. As supplies ran out, many party members perished; in the end, only forty-five people survived. A number of the survivors later stated that in order to survive, they had to cook and eat human flesh, although some later retracted their statements.

What is a Conestoga wagon?

The Conestoga wagon was a large, horse- (or oxen-) drawn wagon used to transport heavy loads over long distances. Its name comes from the Conestoga River of Lancaster County, Pennsylvania, where they were manufactured. It should be noted that "Conestoga wagon" is not a synonym for just any covered wagon used in the nineteenth century but rather refers to the specific style of wagon characterized by curved floors, large hoops to hold up a canvas cover, and broad wheels. When caulked properly, the Conestoga wagon could also be used as a temporary boat to cross wide rivers.

What was the Gold Rush?

The California Gold Rush was sparked by the discovery of the precious metal in 1848 by James Wilson Marshall (1810–1885) in the American River, near the town of Coloma. He was working at a sawmill there owned by John Sutter, the same Sutter who had tried to help the lost Donner party by sending supplies. Word got out quickly about the discovery, and soon people from around the country and the world were racing to California to pan for gold and make their fortunes. These people were called "49ers," and many of them entered the state by way of the port city of San Francisco, which experienced a population boom. Gold–mining towns also sprang up everywhere. Law enforcement became problematic, and such towns became havens for prostitution and violent crimes.

The boom started by the Gold Rush became a bust pretty quickly. By the end of the 1850s, all the most easily obtainable gold (that is, gold found without deep mining) had been taken. It was a formidable take, however. About 750,000 pounds had been scooped up, which would be worth over $15 billion at 2015's market rate. Even as the lust for gold gradually subsided, the state of California had been forever changed. San Francisco had grown into a major port city, and the population of the state rose to over 350,000 (from about 100,000 before the Gold Rush). Most importantly, the Gold Rush accelerated the admission of California as a state in the Union, which occurred in 1850.

What was the Oklahoma Land Rush?

In 1889, President Benjamin Harrison (1833–1901) declared that the "Unassigned Lands" in what is now Oklahoma would be opened up to settlers on a first come, first served basis. In accordance with the Homestead Act, anyone who could stake a claim in the territory would be granted a 160-acre plot. The gimmick was that everyone would be lined up at the border of the area, and at noon on April 22, 1889, they would all race to grab what land they could. The result was quite a sight to see! People on horseback or in wagons tore out into the dusty region to get their—virtually—free land. About fifty thousand people, called "boomers," participated, and the Land Rush quickly established the Oklahoma Territory (what had once been Indian land), which led to Oklahoma's statehood in 1907. There were several other land runs (or rushes) after 1889, including in 1891, 1892, and 1895.

THE "WILD" WEST

Has the "Wild West" been romanticized in America?

Hollywood movies featuring heroic stars ranging from Tom Mix (1880–1940) to John Wayne (1907–1979) have certainly portrayed this period of American history in roman-

How did the nickname "Sooner" get associated with Oklahomans?

A "Sooner" was someone who broke the rules established by the Oklahoma Land Rush by sneaking into the territory before April 22, 1889. Many of these people were railroad employees, prospectors, and federal employees who had excuses to be on the land for other reasons than staking claims. They were there "sooner" than they should have been under the rules but managed to cheat the system in many cases. Although a Sooner was really someone who broke the rules, the connotation later became more positive: a person who was progressive, ambitious, prosperous. The nickname was later applied to the University of Oklahoma's students and teams, as well as to the state in general.

tic terms, as did Western novels by writers such as Owen Wister (1860–1938) and Zane Grey (1872–1939) and the paintings and sculptures of Frederic Remington (1861– 1909). The settling of the final American frontier stretches roughly from the time immediately following the Civil War and into the early few years of the twentieth century. The life of the farmer, rancher, or miner was anything but glamorous. Many people died young from disease, the hardship of the work (imagine no modern plumbing, electricity, or machinery), or were killed by American Indians or criminal gangs.

When did the first battles between the Far Western tribes and the United States take place?

In 1853, a small incident outside of Fort Laramie (in present-day Wyoming)—having to do with ownership of a single cow—led to a confrontation between Native Americans and whites. A veteran of the Mexican–American War and the War of 1812, Commodore Matthew Perry is credited with opening the trade door between Japan and the United States.

What was so different about the horse warriors of the Great Plains?

Many tribal peoples showed that their courage and willpower equaled that of the imperialist invaders. However, the horse peoples of the Great Plains had something most of the others did not: namely, horses. Runaway horses from Spanish Mexico reached the Great Plains by about 1700, radically transforming the lives of the native peoples. Previously, their hunting range had been in the neighborhood of fifty square miles; the appearance of the horse increased that by a factor of almost ten. Of course, there were some negatives involved. Numerous Great Plains peoples who had previously lived in peace with each other—thanks to distance—now went to war. Two wars—between the Cheyenne and the Crow and the Cheyenne and the Pawnee—are among the best known. But when white Americans encroached upon territory west of the Mississippi, they found many well-mounted peoples who quickly obtained muskets and rifles. As a result, the Indian Wars of the Trans-Mississippi West had a different character than East Coast battles.

What was "Custer's Last Stand"?

More formally known as the Battle of Little Big Horn, on June 25, 1876, Lieutenant Colonel George Armstrong Custer (1838–1876) took on a band of Lakota Sioux (led by Chief Sitting Bull) and Northern Cheyenne Indians at the mouth of Little Big Horn River in South Dakota. The American troops were there because the land had become desirable for its gold, but it was sitting on land in the Black Hills considered sacred by the American Indians (the Americans were, once again, ignoring a treaty with the native tribes). Custer, commanding the Seventh Calvary, had been ordered to await reinforcements but decided to attack anyway. Sitting Bull was ready for Custer, however; he repelled attacks by Custer's subordinates and then surrounded Custer and 265 troops, slaughtering them all in a battle that lasted about an hour. When the American reinforcements arrived, most of the Indians surrendered, but Sitting Bull escaped to Canada.

"The Custer Fight" by Charles Marion Russel (1903) dramatically depicts the hopeless odds Lieutenant Colonel Custer faced against the Cheyenne.

What happened to Crazy Horse and Sitting Bull?

Chief Crazy Horse was captured by the whites and killed in a scuffle. Whether this was premeditated or not is unknowable. Chief Sitting Bull, the best known of the medicine men of the Sioux tribe, crossed into Canada, seeking refuge and protection from the British government. When he returned a year later, he, too, was taken into custody. As important as these men were, their military accomplishments pale in comparison to those of Chief Joseph of the Nez Perce.

How did the Nez Perce hold out for so long?

They were a tribal people, living in what is now central Washington State, when the U.S. government decided to move them to a location unfamiliar to them. Although Chief Joseph was an admirer of General Nelson Miles, the American military commander, he decided to escape with his people to Canada. The great trek of the Nez Perce began in 1877 and lasted four months.

The Nez Perce always fought defensively, attempting to increase the distance between themselves and their pursuers. They inflicted several defeats on the pursuing American forces, however, and admiration for their determination began to grow, even among white Americans. In September 1877, the Nez Perce reached the rolling lands just shy of the Canadian border. They settled down for a night of good rest that proved fatal; the Americans, who had pursued them from three different directions, opened fire the next morning.

135

Could the Nez Perce have escaped?

Not this time. Almost two thousand bluecoats surrounded them, and the Indians were down to their last one-hundred-odd warriors. On the morning of October 3, 1877, Chief Joseph emerged from his hiding place, presented himself to the white soldiers, and declared: "Tell General Miles that I know his heart. … From where the sun now stands, I shall fight no more forever." Most American schoolchildren learn these famous words and admire both Chief Joseph and the men who captured him. The sad part of the story—and less known—is that Joseph and his remaining Nez Perce band were eventually sent to a remote section of Idaho, as unfamiliar and distasteful to them as the earlier reservation had been.

Was that the end of fighting for American Indians?

Not quite. The Cheyenne, who were divided into northern and southern groups, fought on for several more years. The Apaches fought both the Mexican military and the U.S. Army until the capture of their chief, Geronimo. But none of these Indian groups really had a chance: they were all ground down, eventually, by the enormous power of the U.S. military.

The final indignity for the Western tribes took place in the winter of 1890 at Wounded Knee, South Dakota. Native Americans from several different tribes had been influenced by the so-called "Ghost Dance" which harkened to earlier times, claiming that the whites would eventually be extinguished. Given the relative strength of the two peoples, this assertion seems ridiculous, but just enough men in the U.S. military took it seriously to bring about a bloodbath. The Battle of Wounded Knee, on December 23, 1890, was the last stand by the Plains tribes. From that point on, they either assimilated into Anglo-American culture or lived separate lives from it; in neither case did they threaten it. Although they did not know it, the Native Americans had a parallel—at the same time they resisted the U.S. cavalry, a major native tribe fought Queen Victoria's soldiers in South Africa.

Who were some famous Wild West gunslingers?

The list of Western gunslingers and tales of their lethal deeds can and has filled many books, but a selection of a few of the more famous is listed below:

1. Billy the Kid (1859–1881): Born William H. McCarty, he was orphaned at a young age and put into foster care. Entering a life of small crimes at a very young age, he is said to have killed his first man at age twelve because he was being teased. As a teenager, he became involved in the infamous Lincoln County War in New Mexico Territory—basically a war against two factions battling over the local dry goods trade. In 1878, during this war, he killed Sheriff William Brady and Deputy George Hindman. By age eighteen, he supposedly had killed seventeen people. On the run, he later agreed to offer testimony in court about the ranch wars in New Mexico in exchange for his freedom. While in prison, he had second thoughts, broke out,

killed two guards, and was on the run again. However, Sheriff Pat Garrett caught up with him and shot him dead on July 14, 1881. Although only four of his murders are definitely confirmed, Billy the Kid is said to have killed twenty-one men during his short life.

2. Jesse James (1847–1882): One of the leaders of the James–Younger Gang, after fighting with guerilla tactics for the Confederacy during the Civil War, James pursued an active career of train, stagecoach, and bank robbing. Although criminals, the gang developed a devoted following of people who saw them as modern-day Robin Hoods, even though there is no record that they ever shared the money they stole. James died when a member of his own gang, Robert Ford, shot him in the back in hopes of getting the reward money for James's life.

3. John Wesley Hardin, Sr. (1853–1895): The son of a Methodist preacher and descendant of Revolutionary War hero Colonel Joseph Hardin, it might be surprising that Hardin's life veered toward crime. It started when he was still in school; an argument with a fellow student ended with Hardin stabbing his peer with a knife, nearly killing him. Next, at age fifteen, Hardin killed a former slave who had, he said, attacked him. His father felt that Texas State Police (many of whom were former slaves) would not believe the story and ordered Hardin to go into hiding. Instead, Hardin stayed. When the police came to arrest him, he shot three of them dead and then fled to Kansas. There, he infamously shot a man dead because he was snoring. Eventually he was arrested, spending seventeen years in prison. While incarcerated, he studied law and became an attorney. Not long after his release, he was shot in the back of the head during a dice game.

4. Butch Cassidy (1866–c. 1908) and the Sundance Kid (1867–c. 1908): Their real names were Robert LeRoy Parker and Harry Longabaugh, respectively. Cassidy, who took his name from a boyhood mentor who taught him how to use a gun, led the Wild Bunch gang. Butch, Sundance, and their followers perpetrated a string of bank and train robberies but were forced to flee to South America when pressure from law enforcement became too intense. While in Bolivia,

A mug shot of Butch Cassidy, dated 1894. Bandits and gunslingers like Cassidy have been romanticized in books and films about the Old West, but outlaw men (and women) were truly dangerous people, not Robin Hoods.

the Bolivian army allegedly surrounded and killed them. However, family members later claimed they snuck back into the United States and lived quietly into old age.

5. Belle Starr (1848–1889): Born Myra Maybelle Shirley, she was a friend of the James–Younger Gang. She took up a life of crime with them and became nicknamed the "Bandit Queen," often offering her home in Missouri to the gang to hide out when things got hot. She took the name "Starr" from a Cherokee family involved in horse stealing with whom her husband, James Reed, associated. After her husband was killed by law enforcement, she married Sam Starr in 1880 and went to prison for a year for stealing horses. After she got out, she was murdered by an unidentified assailant.

6. Wild Bill Hickok (1837–1876): James Butler Hickok had a varied career that included fighting for the Union Army during the Civil War, working as a stagecoach driver, gambling, scouting, gunfighting and working as a lawman. He also was an actor and, in a manner reminiscent of a Davy Crockett exploit, wrestled with and killed a bear, suffering multiple injuries but recuperating after four months. Hickok's reputation as a gunfighter began in 1861 after killing a man over a property payment dispute; he was acquitted but four years later found himself tried for another shootout. On July 21, 1865, he and Davis Tutt had the first recorded "quick-draw" gunfight in Springfield, Missouri. This kind of fight was made famous in Western movies but rarely occurred in real life. Both men faced each other, drew their pistols, and shot. Hickok was acquitted in this case, too; then, after coolly killing three other armed men, he was the subject of a *Harper's New Monthly Magazine* story that greatly exaggerated his exploits. After the Civil War, Hickok worked as a deputy marshal in Kansas and was briefly an actor in Niagara Falls, performing in *The Daring Buffalo Chasers of the Plains* in 1867. While in Kansas, he briefly worked in law enforcement with Buffalo Bill Cody. In the late 1860s, Hickok also was a scout for the Tenth Cavalry and Custer's Seventh Cavalry. In 1869, he became a city marshal in Hays, Kansas, and sheriff of the county; in 1871, he was made a marshal in Abilene, Texas (during this time he met and befriended John Wesley Hardin, although he didn't know Hardin was an outlaw). In 1873, he worked with Cody on a play called *Scouts of the Plains*. Hickok's eyesight began to fail him, and his gun–slinging days were over by this time. He then married Agnes Thatcher Lake and worked on a wagon train. He died in Deadwood, South Dakota, shot in the back of the head while playing cards. The killer, Jack McCall, later testified that Hickok had murdered his brother.

What really happened at the O.K. Corral?

Probably the most famous of all gunfights during the "Wild West" chapter of American history—the gunfight at the O.K. Corral in Tombstone, Arizona, as it has come to be known—has been the subject of books and movies over the years. In films such as director John Ford's *My Darling Clementine* (1946), the gun battle goes on for several minutes. In reality, it took about thirty seconds. Not only that, but it actually didn't occur at the O.K. Corral (to answer the question above, nothing happened there), but, rather, near Fly's Photographic Studios, several doors down.

The fight was between the Clanton cowboys, consisting of brothers Ike (1847–1887) and Billy Clanton (1862–1881), Tom (1853–1881) and Frank McLaury (1849–1881), and Billy Claiborne (1860–1982). On the other side was Marshal Virgil Earp (1843–1905), Deputy Marshal Wyatt Earp (1848–1929), Assistant Marshal Morgan Earp (1851–1882), and Deputy Marshal John Henry "Doc" Holliday (1851–1887; "Doc" had a D.D.S.). The Clantons and their followers were considered "cowboys," which at the time meant they were outlaws, not ranchers. An embellished "fact" about the gunfight was the supposedly central role of Wyatt Earp in the conflict; this was largely the result of a 1931 book by Stuart N. Lake, *Wyatt Earp: Frontier Marshal*, that portrayed the man with fictionalized flair.

None of these men had a sterling reputation: Doc Holliday had been a gambler; Wyatt Earp had been involved with brothels, misappropriation of funds, and even horse theft. Most of the bad blood between the two sides was the result of petty insults and disagreements. The Earps used the excuse of a local ordinance against carrying guns to put pressure on the Clantons and McLaurys not long before the gun battle.

While some say that Ike Clanton provoked the battle by bragging the night before how he was going to kill the Earps, when the fight occurred on October 26, 1881, Virgil Earp shot first. Virgil killed Billy Clanton, shooting him in the chest; Doc Holliday killed Tom McLaury; Wyatt shot Frank McLaury in the stomach. Before dying, however,

An 1890 photo of Buffalo Bill and Native American members of his Wild West Show company.

Frank and Billy managed to return fire, wounding Doc, Virgil, and Morgan. Meanwhile, Ike and Billy Claiborne ran for their lives, later testifying they were unarmed at the time.

The Earps were charged with murder, but a local judge declared their actions justified. A lot of sentiment in the town of Tombstone, however, leaned toward the cowboys, and the Earps and Holliday were never welcomed there again.

What was the most famous Wild West show?

As the West began to be tamed, the phenomenon of Wild West shows began to appear in the 1870s. The most famous of these was "Buffalo Bill's Wild West," produced by William Frederick "Buffalo Bill" Cody (1846–1917). As a young man, Cody worked for the Pony Express and as a bison hunter. He served in the Union Army during the Civil War and was an army scout during the Indian Wars, earning a Medal of Honor in 1872. The next year, he traveled to Chicago and partnered with Texas Jack Omohundro (1846–1880) to create the "Scouts of the Plains" show in which Wild Bill Hickok also appeared. In 1883, Cody founded his iconic Wild West show, a kind of combination between circus and Vaudeville. The shows included displays of marksmanship, horse riding, animal acts, mock battles with Indians, and so on. It made stars out of performers such as Pawnee Bill (Gordon William Lillie, 1860–1942) and Annie Oakley (1860–1926) and featured some people who already had reputations, such as Chief Joseph, Geronimo, and Calamity Jane. The shows were expensive to produce, however, and with the rise of sports such as baseball and rodeos, Wild West shows faltered. Buffalo Bill went bankrupt in 1913.

TRAINS AND COMMUNICATIONS

What was the Pony Express?

While the Pony Express has become a fixed, romantic image of the American West, it only operated for eighteen months. The idea was to create a quicker way to deliver mail from the East to California. Although it achieved statehood in 1850, it was largely cut off from the rest of the nation. Mail at the time was delivered by ship. It took several months, since the vessels carrying mail had to travel all the way down to Cape Horn and then back up the Pacific coastline. By setting up about 150 stops along the way, where riders and/or horses could be changed, the Pony Express became a relay system that delivered letters in just over a week. Privately owned, the Pony Express was eventually intended to be sold to the government and operated by the Postal Service; however, with the advent of the transcontinental telegraph in 1861, the idea died—and so did the Pony Express.

After the Pony Express, what was the next communication achievement in America?

Taking the federal government up on its offer to provide a yearly subsidy to the first company that built a transcontinental telegraph line, the Western Union Telegraph Company completed the line on October 24, 1861, connecting eastern and western lines at Salt Lake City, Utah, and making nearly instant communication popular from the East Coast to San Francisco.

How did the Transcontinental Railroad come about?

The idea was initially proposed by businessman Asa Whitney, who asked Congress in 1845 to pass a resolution to fund a railroad that would stretch to the West Coast. Nothing came of the idea until the Gold Rush of 1849 dramatically increased immigration westward. Proposals and surveys continued for several years, as people tried to determine the best route. Ultimately—perhaps ironically—the route chosen through the Sierra Nevada Mountains went through Donner Pass.

President Lincoln signed the Pacific Railroad Act in 1862, but the Civil War stalled the project. Finally, in 1865, work began. Two companies were formed: the Central Pacific Railroad Company and the Union Pacific Railroad Company. The former started construction in Sacramento,

A poster advertising the mail services of the Pony Express.

California, the latter in Omaha, Nebraska. The race was on, and the stakes were high: each company was granted thousands of acres of land and $48,000 in government bonds for every mile of track built. The Central Pacific had the more daunting task, because much of its route had to go through mountains. When the two tracks finally met at Promontory Point, Utah (territory), Central Pacific had completed 690 miles of track to Union Pacific's 1,086.

The completion of the Transcontinental Railroad on May 10, 1869, had a dramatic effect on the country. The technology made wagon trains obsolete. Travel to California became much less expensive, and shipment of goods (including mail) also became more practical. The construction of the railroad itself also encouraged immigration into the country, with some fifty thousand Chinese immigrants being employed by Central Pacific, while Union Pacific employed Irish immigrants, as well as many Civil War veterans. Along the route of the railroad, numerous towns sprang up. As with the Gold Rush days of San Francisco, these places were often lawless homes for violent crime and prostitution.

What law did President Grover Cleveland (1837–1908) sign that regulated railway rates?

Cleveland signed into law the Interstate Commerce Act of 1887, creating the federal Interstate Commerce Commission (ICC) that monitored railway rates. The law was designed to ensure that such rates would be "reasonable and just."

Who was Eugene Debs?

Debs (1855–1926) was a radical labor leader who in 1893 founded the American Railway Union (ARU), an industrial union for all railroad workers. Debs was a charismatic speaker, but he was also a controversial figure in American life around the turn of the twentieth century. He vigorously dissented and protested U.S. involvement in World War I and was put in prison under the 1918 Sedition Act. President Warren G. Harding (1865–1923) later ordered Debs freed for time served but did not grant him an official pardon.

What was the Pullman strike?

In 1894, workers at the Pullman Palace Car Company, which manufactured railcars in Pullman, Illinois (near Chicago), went on strike to protest a significant reduction in their wages. Pullman was a model "company town," where the railcar manufacturer—founded by American inventor George W. Pullman (1831–1897) in 1867—owned all the land and buildings and ran the school, bank, and utilities. In 1893, in order to maintain profits following declining revenues, the Pullman Company cut workers' wages by 25 to 40 percent but did not adjust rent and prices in the town, forcing many employees and their families into deprivation. In May 1894, a labor committee approached Pullman Company management to resolve the situation. The company, which had always refused to negotiate with employees, responded by firing the labor committee members. The firings incited a strike of all thirty-three hundred Pullman workers.

In support of the labor effort, Eugene Debs assumed leadership of the strike (some Pullman employees had joined the ARU in 1894) and directed all ARU members not to haul any Pullman cars. A general rail strike that paralyzed transportation across the country followed. In response to what was now being called "Debs's Rebellion," a July 2, 1894, federal court order demanded all workers to return to the job, but the ARU refused to comply. President Cleveland ordered federal troops to break the strike, citing it inter-

Strikers face the Illinois National Guard at Chicago's Arcade Building during the 1894 Pullman Railroad Strike.

fered with mail delivery. The intervention turned violent. Despite public protest, Debs, who was tried for contempt of court and for conspiracy, was imprisoned in 1895 for having violated the court order. Debs later proclaimed himself a socialist and became leader of the American Left, running unsuccessfully for president as the Socialist Party candidate in 1900, 1904, 1908, 1912, and 1920. He actively supported the causes of the International Workers of the World (IWW), a radical labor organization founded in 1905.

What major law signed by President William Howard Taft (1857–1930) gave the federal government greater control over railroad rates?

President Taft signed into law the Mann–Elkins Act of 1910, giving the ICC more authority over railroad rates. It also gave the ICC control over the telephone and telegraph industries. Congress abolished this agency in 1995.

THE PROGRESSIVE ERA

What was the Progressive Era?

The Progressive Era was a period of American history from the late 1880s to the 1920s marked by increasing governmental regulation of business, social reform, and prohibition of exploitative labor practices. The administrations of numerous presidents—most notably Theodore Roosevelt (1858–1919) and Woodrow Wilson (1856–1924)—featured elements of Progressivism. The Progressive Era was not confined to a single political party, as segments of both of the two major political parties—the Democrats and the Republicans—embraced Progressive causes.

The Progressive Era saw an expansion of governmental power, an increase in suffrage for women, anti-trust legislation, a push for modernization, the support of Prohibition, an increase in educational opportunities, and a greater emphasis placed on science and medicine.

What was the Progressive Party?

The Progressive Party was created in 1912 to serve as a separate third party to compete with the more traditional Republican and Democratic Parties. The party was formed largely to support the presidential ambitions of former Republican President Theodore Roosevelt, who had left office in 1909. Roosevelt's successor was his former secretary of war, William Howard Taft (1857–1930), who later became U.S. Supreme Court chief justice. Roosevelt and Taft split politically, as Roosevelt believed Taft had become too conservative and abandoned Roosevelt's more progressive causes.

Roosevelt then formed the Progressive Party to run in the 1912 presidential election. The Progressive Party was also known as the Bull Moose Party. Roosevelt and Taft split the Republican vote, leading to a landslide election victory for the Democratic candidate, Woodrow Wilson (1856–1924). The Progressive Party continued for a few years but never gained respect equal to that of the two major parties. It gradually disappeared from the political scene.

What Progressive Party candidate became governor of California?

Hiram Johnson (1866–1945) served as governor of California from 1911–1917 and later served as a U.S. senator for nearly thirty years. Johnson was a member of the Progressive Party and, in fact, served as Theodore Roosevelt's running mate in the 1912 presidential election. However, Johnson ran as a Republican during the presidential election of 1920, losing the nomination to eventual future President Harding.

Who were the robber barons?

"Robber barons" was a pejorative term applied to wealthy businessmen of the late nineteenth and early twentieth centuries. They amassed immense wealth in part due to exploitative labor practices. They often paid low wages and provided their workers with miserable working conditions during the age of the Industrial Revolution. During this time period, factories were built to house new machines, causing a population shift from rural to developing urban areas by the mid–1800s, as people went where the work was. Factory owners turned to child labor and, in the United States, to the steady influx of immigrants to run the machinery in their plants. As industry grew, it required financial institutions that could provide money for expansion, thus giving birth to a new breed of wealthy business leaders whom critics called "robber barons." These industrial and financial tycoons included Jay Gould (1836–1892), James J. Hill (1838–1916), and James B. Duke (1856–1925).

But as industry evolved, government and policy changes did not keep pace: Serious social, political, and economic problems resulted, including poor and often dangerous working conditions, exploitation of workers (including child laborers), overcrowded housing, pollution, corruption, industry monopolies, and a widening gap between the rich and the poor. Change was slow to come, but social activism and government reforms in the late 1800s and during the Progressive Era of the early 1900s—much of which centered around trade unions—alleviated some of these problems. The rapid development of industry caused sweeping social changes: The Western world, which had long been agriculturally based, became an industrial society where providing goods and services became the primary focus.

What was the Sherman Anti-Trust Act?

Passed by Congress in 1890, the Sherman Anti-Trust Act was an attempt to break up corporate trusts (combinations of firms or corporations formed to limit competition and monopolize a market). The legislation stated that "every contract, combination in the form of trust or otherwise, or conspiracy in the restraint of trade" is illegal. While the Act made clear that anyone found to be in violation of restraining trade would face fines, jail terms, and the payment of damages, the language lacked clear definitions of what exactly constituted restraint of trade. The nation's courts were left with the responsibility to interpret the Sherman Anti-Trust Act, and the justices proved as reluctant to take on big business as Congress had been.

The legislation was introduced in Congress by Ohio Senator John Sherman (1823–1900) in response to increasing outcry from state governments and the public to pass national anti-trust laws. Many states had passed their own anti-trust bills or had made constitutional provisions prohibiting trusts, but the statutes proved difficult to enforce, and big businesses found ways around them. When the legislation proposed by Sherman reached the Senate, conservative congressmen rewrote it; many charged the senators made it deliberately vague. In the decade after its passage, the federal government prosecuted only eighteen anti-trust cases, and court decisions did little to break up monopolies.

But after the turn of the twentieth century, a progressive spirit in the nation grew; among progressive reformers' demands was that government regulate business better. In 1911, the U.S. Justice Department won key victories against monopolies, breaking up John D. Rockefeller's (1839–1937) Standard Oil Company of New Jersey and James B. Duke's (1856–1925) American Tobacco Company. The decisions set a precedent for how the Sherman Anti-Trust Act would be enforced and demonstrated a national intolerance toward monopolistic trade practices.

What was the Panic of 1893?

The failure of the Philadelphia and Reading Railroad brought about the Panic of 1893. After the major railroad collapsed, numerous banks followed suit. It was considered the country's worst economic depression until the Great Depression in 1929.

What was the Clayton Anti-Trust Act?

In 1914 national anti-trust legislation was strengthened by the passage of the Clayton Anti-Trust Act, which outlawed price fixing (the practice of pricing below cost to eliminate a competitive product), made it illegal for the same executives to manage two or more competing companies (a practice called interlocking directorates), and prohibited any corporation from owning stock in a competing corporation. The creation of the Federal Trade Commission (FTC) that same year provided further insurance that the government would investigate U.S. corporations engaging in unfair practices.

Between 1880 and the early 1900s, corporate trusts proliferated in the United States, becoming powerful business forces. The vague language of the Sherman Anti-Trust legislation and the courts' reluctance to prosecute big businesses based on that Act did little to break up the monopolistic giants. The tide turned against corporate trusts when Theodore Roosevelt (1858–1919) became president in September 1901 after President William McKinley's (1843–1901) assassination. Roosevelt launched a "trust-busting" campaign, initiating, through the Attorney General's office, some forty lawsuits against American corporations such as American Tobacco Company, Standard Oil Company, and American Telephone and Telegraph (AT&T). Government efforts to break up the monopolies were strengthened in 1914, during the Wilson presidency, when Congress passed the Clayton Anti-Trust legislation and created the Federal Trade Commission (FTC), which is responsible for keeping business competition free and fair.

RACE RELATIONS

What measure did President Chester A. Arthur (1829–1886) sign with regard to Chinese immigration?

Arthur reluctantly signed the Chinese Exclusion Act of 1882, suspending or banning further Chinese immigration to the United States for ten years. Arthur opposed the measure but signed it for pragmatic reasons.

What did President Rutherford B. Hayes do with respect to Chinese immigration?

More and more Chinese immigrated to the United States in the 1860s and 1870s. Much of the workforce in California consisted of Chinese laborers. When the Chinese began

Chinese immigrants came to the United States by the thousands in the later part of the nineteenth century, many to work on the railroad boom of the time.

competing for jobs with others, pressure built to curb the level of immigration. Congress passed a law that abrogated a treaty the U.S. signed with China that specifically allowed Chinese immigration.

President Hayes vetoed this measure and authorized Secretary of State William Evarts and a commission headed by James B. Angell to negotiate a new treaty with China. The Treaty of 1880 allowed the government to limit immigration from China but also provided for the protection of rights for Chinese already in the United States.

What law passed in Grover Cleveland's first term as president sought to assimilate Native Americans?

Congress passed—and Cleveland signed into law—the Dawes Act of 1887, seeking to assimilate Native Americans into American life. Under the measure, many reservation lands were divided into separate plots. Native Americans who renounced their tribal allegiances were then granted these parcels of land.

What ignominious Supreme Court decision upheld segregation ("Jim Crow") laws?

The U.S. Supreme Court upheld a Louisiana segregation law by a 7–1 vote in *Plessy v. Ferguson* (1896). The case involved a constitutional challenge to a Louisiana law that mandated separate railway accommodations for whites and blacks. Rodolphe Desdunes

147

(1849–1928), the leader of New Orleans' American Citizens' Equal Rights Association, had recruited his friend Homer Plessy to challenge the law.

Plessy was considered an ideal test plaintiff, as he was seven-eighths white and one-eighth black—a so-called "octoroon." In this time period, one drop of black blood meant a person was considered black. Sure enough, officials arrested Plessy for sitting in the whites-only section of a train car. The case proceeded to the U.S. Supreme Court, which upheld the law based on the "separate but equal" doctrine—that separate facilities based on race did not violate the Equal Protection Clause, as long as each race was afforded roughly the same facilities.

For the majority, Justice Henry Billings Brown (1836–1913) wrote: "We consider the underlying fallacy of the plaintiff's argument to consist in the assumption that the enforced separation of the two races stamps the colored race with a badge of inferiority. ... If the two races are to meet upon terms of social equality, it must be the result of each other's merits and a voluntary consent of individuals. ... If one race be inferior to the other socially, the Constitution of the United States cannot put them on the same plane."

However, Justice John Marshall Harlan (1833–1911) filed a solitary dissent that has proved to be one of the great opinions of American constitutional law. Harlan famously wrote:

"But in view of the Constitution, in the eye of the law, there is in this country no superior, dominant ruling class of citizens. There is no caste here. Our Constitution is color-blind and neither knows nor tolerates classes among citizens. In respect of civil rights, all citizens are equal before the law. The humblest is the peer of the most powerful. The law regards man as man and takes no account of his surroundings or of his color when his civil rights as guaranteed by the supreme law of the law are involved." Harlan warned his colleagues that their decision in *Plessy v. Ferguson* would be as "pernicious as the decision" in *Dred Scott v. Sandford* (1857)—the decision that had upheld slavery.

What event led to the formation of the NAACP?

In 1908, an angry white mob destroyed black homes and businesses in the so-called Springfield (Illinois) Race Riot. The mob was incensed over two alleged crimes committed by black men—the killing of a white homeowner by Joe James, a young black man, and the alleged rape of white woman Mabel Hallam by black man George Richardson. The white mob moved to the local jail, only to learn that the Sheriff Charles Werner had moved the men out of town to another jail. The National Guard had to be called in to quell the rioting. Later, Hallam admitted that her rape accusation against Richardson was false. James was executed for the murder of the white homeowner.

The Springfield Race Riot caused many concerned white and black citizens to meet in New York City to discuss how to deal with racial friction and discrimination. A result of that meeting was the formation of the National Association for the Advancement of Colored People (NAACP). The stated purpose of the NAACP is "to ensure the political, educational, social, and economic equality of rights of all persons and to eliminate racial hatred and racial discrimination."

Who was W.E.B. Du Bois?

William Edward Burghardt Du Bois (1868–1963) was a leading American intellectual who helped cofound the NAACP. Du Bois attended Harvard University, becoming the first African American to earn a doctorate there. Du Bois also was a noted author, writing such works as *The Souls of Black Folks*, *Black Reconstruction in America*, *The Negro*, and *Color and Democracy*. He was an avowed antiwar activist and promoter of equality around the world for colored persons. He traveled around the world and spent the last few years of his life in Ghana.

What black political leader did Du Bois oppose?

Du Bois opposed the more conservative approach of the other leading black political leader of the time, Booker T. Washington (1856–1915). Born a slave in Virginia, Washington attended Hampton University and became a leading spokesman for the black community. He urged blacks to improve their lot through education and to avoid directly challenging Jim Crow laws. He was the leader of Tuskegee Normal and Industrial Institute. His prominence as the leading black intellectual force earned him access to the leading white politicians of the day. President Theodore Roosevelt invited Washington to have dinner with him at the White House in October 1901. Both Roosevelt and

The founder of the NAACP, W. E. B. Du Bois (left) and Booker T. Washington (right) both fought for black rights and freedoms, though Du Bois objected to Washington's more conservative approach to race relations.

Washington received death threats for the dinner. Washington authored numerous books in his life, most notably his autobiography, *Up from Slavery* (1901).

What terrorist group revived itself in 1915?

The Ku Klux Klan returned to existence in 1915, as William J. Simmons (1880–1945) reformed the group in Stone Mountain, Georgia. The original KKK was formed in 1865 in Pulaski, Tennessee, but was essentially disbanded during Reconstruction. The Klan owed its revival largely to the popularity of a movie called *The Birth of a Nation,* produced by D.W. Griffith (1875–1948). *The Birth of a Nation* depicted the Klan as a patriotic organization and portrayed blacks unfavorably. The silent movie was based on Thomas Dixon's book *The Clansman*.

This second KKK was marked by virulent strains of anti-Catholicism and appealed predominantly to white Protestant men in the South and Midwest. In the 1920s, the Klan claimed four to five million members. One of its members was future U.S. Supreme Court Justice Hugo Black (1886–1971), who claimed he joined the Klan in his home state of Alabama for political reasons. Black later renounced the Klan and became a Supreme Court justice known for protecting civil rights.

What awful form of punishment did the Klan sometimes inflict on blacks?

Some Klan members resorted to the awful extrajudicial form of punishment known as lynching to kill blacks and others who ran afoul of the group's beliefs. Lynching was not something new to the early twentieth century, as lynchings had occurred with frequency in the late 1800s as well. But the 1910s and 1920s witnessed an alarming number of lynchings—many by the Klan. The Tuskegee Institute estimates that there were more than thirty-two hundred lynchings of blacks from the 1880s to 1950s. Blacks were not the only victims of lynching; nearly thirteen hundred whites were lynched during that time period as well.

The problem was so severe that U.S. Congressman Leonidas C. Dyer (1871–1957) introduced the so-called Dyer Anti-Lynching Bill in 1918 in Congress. The measure did not pass then, but Dyer reintroduced the measure, and it passed the House in 1922. However, a Senate filibuster prevented the measure from passing Congress and becoming law. Dyer continued in his crusade to pass a federal anti-lynching law but was unsuccessful. Dyer had become convinced that such a law was necessary after the horror of the St. Louis riots of 1917, where an angry white mob attacked black workers.

TWO PRESIDENTS MURDERED

Who was the second U.S. president to be assassinated?

Charles Julius Guiteau (1841–1882) ended James Garfield's (1831–1881) presidency by shooting him in Elberton, New Jersey, on July 2, 1881. Guiteau, a member of the Stal-

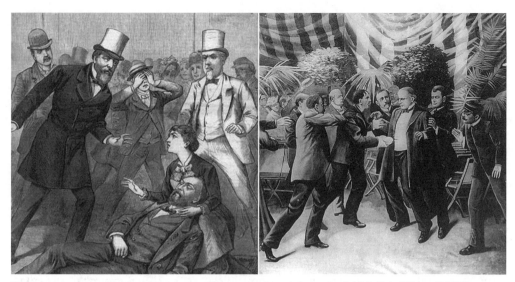

Within twenty years, Americans saw two presidents assassinated: James Garfield (left) in 1881 and William McKinley in 1901.

wart wing of the Republican Party, had supported Garfield during the presidential election. He somehow thought that his support merited him an appointment as an ambassador. The administration politely rejected Guiteau, sending him into a rage. He began stalking the president for a couple of months and finally got the nerve to follow through with his murderous intentions. Guiteau claimed he had killed Garfield to "unite the Republican Party and save the Republic." Garfield did not die immediately, but he never recovered. Although surgeons removed the bullets from his body, he was bedridden until his death on September 19, 1881.

Who killed President William McKinley?

Leon F. Czolgosz shot President McKinley (1843–1901) on September 6, 1901, in Buffalo, New York, at a concert hall named The Temple of Music. McKinley was attending the Pan-American Conference there. Czolgosz was a self-avowed anarchist who believed that McKinley represented an oppressive government that exploited the working class. McKinley died on September 14, 1901.

Czolgosz was not a formal member of the Anarchist Party but attended several lectures and speeches by the group. He particularly enjoyed a speech by noted anarchist Emma Goldman. Historians believe that Czolgosz was inspired by the assassination of King Umberto I of Italy by Gaetano Bresci.

Czolgosz stood trial later that month. A jury convicted him and recommended a sentence of death. He was executed on October 29, 1901. His last words reportedly were: "I killed the president because he was the enemy of the good people—the good working people. I am not sorry for my crime."

151

TEDDY ROOSEVELT

How did Teddy Roosevelt become president?

Vice President Theodore Roosevelt (1858–1919) became president after Leon Czolgosz assassinated President McKinley. He followed in the footsteps of John Tyler, Millard Fillmore, Andrew Johnson, and Chester A. Arthur as vice presidents who became president following the untimely death of the sitting president. At age forty-two, Theodore Roosevelt became the youngest person to become president.

What major trust did Roosevelt break up during his first couple years in office?

Roosevelt instructed his attorney general, Philander C. Knox, to investigate the Northern Securities Trust, a conglomeration of James J. Hill's Great Northern Railroad, E. H. Harriman's Union Pacific Railroad, and J. P. Morgan's Northern Pacific Railroad. Northern Securities Trust served as a holding company for their collective earnings. Roosevelt earned his reputation as a trust-buster extraordinaire, as the U.S. Supreme Court ruled in 1904 that the company did violate the Sherman Anti-Trust Act.

Before he was president, Theodore Roosevelt organized the first voluntary calvary in the Spanish–American War, the Rough Riders. They famously seized San Juan Ridge (and San Juan Hill) in 1898.

What major disaster struck San Francisco in 1906?

The Quake of 1906 struck at 5:12 A.M. on April 18 and registered 8.3 on the Richter scale. Twenty seconds of trembling were followed by forty-five to sixty seconds of shocks. The quake cracked water and gas mains, which resulted in a fire that lasted three days and destroyed two-thirds of the city. The destruction and loss of lives were great: As many as three thousand (of San Francisco's 400,000 people) were killed; the entire business district was demolished; three out of five homes either crumbled or burned; 250,000 to 300,000 people were left homeless; and 490 city blocks were destroyed.

The quake was a milestone for American journalism: The offices of the city's newspapers the *Examiner* (owned by William Randolph Hearst; 1863–1951), the *Call*, and the *Chronicle* all burned. But the first day after the disaster, the three papers joined forces across the bay in Oakland to print a combined edition, the *California Chronicle-Examiner*. Across the country, Will Irwin (1873–1948) of the *New York Sun*, who had been a reporter and editor at the *Chronicle* from 1900 to 1904, wrote a story, "The City That Was," which he completed from memory alone. It was picked up by papers around the country and became a journalism classic. The San Francisco tragedy demonstrated the newfound ability of the American press to create an instant national story from a local event.

The Bay Area was hit again by a sizeable quake in 1989. As millions tuned in to watch the World Series at Candlestick Park outside San Francisco, the TV cameras began to shake. Because of media coverage of the baseball game, the earthquake had literally been broadcast live around the world. Once again, fires resulted from broken gas mains, and the damage was extensive. The so-called Loma Prieta quake registered 7.1 on the Richter scale, claimed sixty-seven lives, and damaged $15 billion worth of property. San Francisco's Marina District was particularly hard hit—at least in part due to the fact that the area was built largely on landfill, including debris from the 1906 quake. The San Francisco earthquake of 1906 remains the worst to ever hit an American city.

What other labor crisis did President Teddy Roosevelt resolve in his first term?

Roosevelt intervened in the United Mine Workers' strike in eastern Pennsylvania. The United Mine Workers' union found it difficult to bargain with the mine operators. After coal prices skyrocketed, Roosevelt threatened to take over the mines as a federal receivership unless the two sides could reach a bargain. The operators agreed to binding arbitration; the net result was that the workers received a ten percent wage raise, and the operators received a ten percent price increase for coal.

What famous canal was built in the early part of the twentieth century?

The Panama Canal was built by the United States beginning in 1904 and ending in 1914. The Canal is a key bridgeway between the Atlantic and Pacific Oceans. France had worked on building such a canal in the 1880s but never completed the project. Colombia used to control the land known as Panama, but a new country emerged in 1903 with assistance from the United States under the leadership of President Roosevelt. In 1904, the U.S. government purchased not only the French excavating equipment but also paid the country of Panama a hefty sum for the canal. The Panamanian government acquired the canal in 1999. The Panama Canal remains vital to world trade, as tens of thousands of large cargo ships pass through the waters on the Isthmus of Panama.

Why was Roosevelt called "The Great Conservationist"?

Roosevelt actively promoted the goal of conserving the country's natural resources. He supported a federal law providing for the construction of dams and aqueducts in the west. He supported the first Federal Bird Reservation at Pelican Island. He expanded the National Forestry Service and set aside 230 million acres for preserves, parks, and refuges.

Who tried to assassinate Theodore Roosevelt when he ran for president again in 1912?

John Flammang Schrank, a thirty-six-year-old man, shot Roosevelt outside a hotel in Milwaukee, Wisconsin. Fortunately, the bullet hit his breast pocket, which contained his metal eyeglass case. While bleeding, Roosevelt still managed to deliver his speech (nearly an hour long). He reportedly said: "It takes more than one bullet to kill a Bull Moose." Schrank believed the ghost of William McKinley appeared to him in a dream and instructed him to kill Roosevelt. He spent the rest of his life in mental hospitals.

PRESIDENT WILLIAM HOWARD TAFT

What was "Dollar Diplomacy"?

Dollar Diplomacy referred to the U.S. policy toward gaining economic footholds in countries in Central and South America. Taft and Knox formulated a plan that would use U.S. strength to set up favorable economic positions for U.S. business interests. The term is used pejoratively by some who criticized the United States for overreaching and exploiting foreign countries for economic gain.

What did Taft do with respect to trusts?

Taft pursued the goal of breaking up large trusts as much as Roosevelt did. The difference was that Taft pursued the goal just as much as—if not more than—Roosevelt but did not make big pronouncements like

William Howard Taft, the twenty-seventh president of the United States, also served as chief justice of the U.S. Supreme Court from 1921 to 1930.

his predecessor. The federal government filed ninety anti-trust suits during Taft's tenure—more than those filed during the Roosevelt Administration. His administration won victories over Standard Oil and the American Tobacco Company.

What two states were admitted to the Union during Taft's administration?

New Mexico and Arizona became the forty-seventh and forty-eighth states, respectively, while Taft was president. Thus, the Taft presidency oversaw the completion of the full continental United States. Only Alaska and Hawaii would be added to reach the current total of fifty.

What amendment was added to the Constitution during Taft's administration?

The necessary number of thirty-six states ratified the Sixteenth Amendment, and it became a part of the Constitution in February 1913, before Taft left office. The amendment provides: "The Congress shall have the power to lay and collect taxes on incomes, from whatever source derived, without apportionment among the several States, and without regard to any census or enumeration."

GROWING POWER OF JOURNALISM

Who were muckrakers?

Muckrakers referred to a group of investigative journalists who exposed various social ills during the late-nineteenth and early twentieth centuries. It was a term given to a wide variety of these investigative-style journalists who exposed corruption or wrongdoing in society during the Progressive Era. Muckrakers were responsible for exposing town-hall corruption, unsanitary food-handling practices, abuses at mental institutions, greed in the oil industry, and a variety of other problems. The term is often attributed to President Theodore Roosevelt, who talked about writers dealing "in the muck" and who held the "muck-rake." Roosevelt, however, generally supported the muckrakers in theory, saying: "I hail as a benefactor every writer or speaker, every man who, on the platform, or in book, magazine, or newspaper, with merciless severity makes such attack provided always that he in his turn remembers that the attack is of use only if it is absolutely truthful."

Who were some of the leading muckrakers?

They included Upton Sinclair (1878–1968), who wrote the book *The Jungle*, exposing horrific practices in the meatpacking industry; Nellie Bly (1864–1922), who went undercover and exposed abuses in a women's mental health institution (called a lunatic asylum); Jacob Riis (1849–1914), who wrote about poverty in his book *How the Other Half Lives: Studies among the Tenements of New York City*; Lincoln Steffens (1866–1936), who wrote about municipal corruption in his book *The Shame of the Cities*; and Ida Tarbell (1857–1944), who wrote about greed in the oil industry in her *History of the Standard Oil Company*.

These muckrakers and their work often had an indelible impact on the world they wrote. For example, Upton Sinclair's *The Jungle* was responsible in part for the enactment of the Federal Meat Inspection Act of 1906 and the Pure Food and Drug Act of 1906.

What is the *Chicago Defender*?

The *Chicago Defender* is a weekly newspaper based in Chicago that was founded in 1905 for black readers. It was perhaps the foremost paper of the so-called Negro press, sometimes called "America's Black Newspaper." Founded by Robert Sengstacke Abbott (1870–1940), a Georgia-born man who earned a law degree, the newspaper became the premier newspaper for black readers and made Mr. Abbott a millionaire. Abbott sought to combat racial prejudice and expose all aspects of discrimination in society. He also campaigned for a federal anti-lynching law. In the 1950s, the newspaper became known as the *Chicago Daily Defender* to reflect its daily—instead of weekly—distribution. In 2003, it returned to a weekly publication.

INNOVATIONS IN THE PROGRESSIVE ERA

Who invented the telephone?

While not born in America, Alexander Graham Bell (1847–1922) invented the telephone while living in Boston, Massachusetts. Born in Scotland and educated there and at London University, Bell was a speech and elocution teacher by trade who came up with the telephone while designing a means to transmit speech via wires as a way to teach the deaf. He came up with the concept to accomplish this in 1874 and two years later had the technology patented.

What American industrialist developed the first automobile that could be bought by the masses?

Henry Ford (1863–1947) was an American industrialist who did not invent the automobile but was the first to oversee the mass development of automobiles on an assembly line. An electrical mechanic in the 1890s, Ford looked to found his own company. He was unsuccessful in his first two attempts, but in 1903 he successfully began Ford Motor Company. His company focused on the mass production of an automobile known as the Model T. Ford, and

Alexander Graham Bell invented the telephone in 1874.

Besides the telephone, what were some of Alexander Graham Bell's other accomplishments?

Although much of the wealth he enjoyed during his lifetime came from inventing the telephone, Bell made many other contributions to science. For example, he developed the technology that led to the creation of the iron lung (essential for saving lives in the days before the cure for polio was discovered), created a device to detect metal in wounds, experimented with hydrofoils and airplanes (years before the Wright Brothers), and helped Thomas Edison make the phonograph commercially viable. He also founded the magazine *Science* and contributed to the creation of the National Geographic Society.

he became an immensely wealthy man as a result of the successes of his mass production and sale of automobiles. Ford paid healthy wages for the time to his workers. However, he also opposed World War I during its early years and was also known for his strident anti-Semitic views. It was reported that Ford even took a liking to German leader Adolf Hitler, who allegedly had a picture of Ford in his office.

How did the Wright Brothers invent the first airplane?

Orville (1871–1948) and Wilbur (1867–1912) Wright invented the first successful airplane in the early part of the twentieth century. In the 1890s, the Wright brothers operated a bicycle repair shop. They became fascinated with the possibility of machine-powered human flight. They traveled to Kitty Hawk, North Carolina, to conduct experiments with their gliders. On December 17, 1903, they flew their rudimentary airplane all of twelve seconds for about 120 feet. But the brief flight led to quick developments. By 1908, the Wright brothers had a plane fly for more than an hour and a half. In 1909, the United States Army gave the brothers a contract to build aircraft at $30,000 per machine.

Who was the "Wizard of Menlo Park"?

Thomas Alva Edison (1847–1931) was one of America's greatest inventors. Largely self-educated, his early interest in the telegraph combined with his entrepreneurial spirit. He set up a laboratory in Menlo Park, New Jersey, where he proceeded to invent hundreds of devices—by the end of his career, Edison held 1,093 U.S. patents. Among his inventions are the incandescent lightbulb, the phonograph, the fluoroscope, and the Kinetograph (an early motion-picture camera).

Who was Nikola Tesla?

Nikola Tesla (1856–1943) was an inventor who once worked for Thomas Edison. Born in Serbia, he moved to New York City, becoming a U.S. citizen in 1891. A mechanical and electrical engineer, he is now recognized as a brilliant inventor, possibly surpasing Edison.

Thomas Edison's (left) technical advances made him the most famous inventor of his day, but his former employee and later rival, Nikola Tesla (right), is now considered by many to have been the more brilliant inventor when it comes to lighting and other electrical devices.

His ideas conflicted with Edison's early on, and Tesla left Menlo Park. He helped develop the alternating current (AC) electrical supply system, while Edison favored DC (direct current). The AC system eventually won out. Tesla also came up with the induction motor (which ran on AC), the fluorescent lightbulb, early robotics, the laser, the radio (the U.S. Supreme Court overturned Guglielmo Marconi's 1943 patent, concluding that Tesla had invented radio as early as 1897), remote controls, and wireless communications.

FROM WORLD WAR I TO THE ROARING TWENTIES

WORLD WAR I

How did the United States enter World War I?

The United States did not want to enter World War I. The conflict arose after Austrian heir Franz Ferdinand was assassinated by Bosnian assassin Gavrilo Princip. Austria-Hungary blamed Serbia for the assassination, and soon much of the world was plunged into World War I, or the "Great War." U.S. President Woodrow Wilson desperately wanted to avoid the conflict. He successfully ran for reelection in 1916 on fulfilling his promise to keep the country out of war.

However, Germany was extremely militaristic and kept sinking ships on the high seas. In May 7, 1915, a German submarine sunk a British passenger ship called the *Lusitania*. The torpedo attack led to the deaths of nearly twelve hundred people, including 128 Americans. The sinking of the *Lusitania* was one of the prime reasons the United States seriously considered entering the war. Then, in February 1917, German forces torpedoed an American naval ship, the *Housatonic*. As a result, President Wilson severed all diplomatic ties with Germany.

On March 1, 1917, the United States learned of the "Zimmerman Telegram," allegedly sent by German Foreign Secretary Alfred Zimmerman to a Mexican ambassador. British intelligence agents intercepted the telegram and conveyed its contents to the United States. The telegram proposed a German–Mexican alliance against the United States. The Zimmerman Telegram was the straw that broke the camel's back, and President Wilson asked Congress for a declaration of war. According to President Wilson, "the world must be made safe for democracy." The United States formally entered World War I on April 6, 1917.

What role did economics play into the United States's entrance into World War I?

Economics also played a factor in the U.S. decision to assist England and France. Each of these countries had borrowed millions of dollars from the United States. If Germany defeated the Allies, then the United States and its banking industry would not receive the monies it had lent.

What U.S. politician resigned from Wilson's Cabinet over U.S. policy toward Germany?

William Jennings Bryan (1860–1925) resigned as President Wilson's secretary of state because of his feeling that the U.S. was pursuing a nonpacifist course that would embroil it into the Great War. Bryan nearly became president himself; he was

President Woodrow Wilson remained neutral on World War I until 1917, when he finally decided that the United States should declare war on Germany and its allies.

the Democratic Party's nominee in three different elections (1896, 1900, and 1908). He also served in the U.S. House of Representatives for Nebraska from 1891–1895. Bryan was a great speaker and an excellent attorney. He achieved fame for battling famous defense attorney Clarence Darrow in the famous Scopes Trial concerning the teaching of evolution in schools, which Bryan, a devout Christian, adamantly opposed. Bryan died in Dayton, Tennessee, five days after the conclusion of the Scopes Trial.

Bryan resigned as secretary of state in June 1915 because he opposed President Wilson's policy of strictly responding to any acts of aggression or infringement against the U.S. Bryan still supported President Wilson during his reelection and even asked the president to allow him to assist the U.S. military.

What U.S. senator survived expulsion proceedings after denouncing U.S. involvement in World War I?

Robert M. La Follette, Sr. (1855–1925), a United States senator from Wisconsin, faced expulsion proceedings for delivering a fervent speech that criticized U.S. entry into World War I. La Follette also advocated that American citizens should not lose their free-speech rights during times of war. The La Follette investigation dragged on for more than a year. Meanwhile, World War I ended, and La Follette's political party, the Republicans, had gained control of the Senate. In January 1919, the Senate voted 50–21 against expelling La Follette. La Follette later moved to the Progressive Party and in

1924 ran for president. He garnered seventeen percent of the popular vote during that election. He remained in the United States Senate until his death in 1925 and is considered one of the most influential senators in U.S. history.

Was America ready for war in 1917?

In technical terms, the United States was not ready. The Regular U.S. Army numbered about 140,000, and much of its equipment was outdated. There were still some Civil War cannons in its arsenal. The U.S. Navy was efficient but small.

In moral terms and sheer enthusiasm, however, America was ready for war. For three years and from a distance of three thousand miles, Americans had witnessed the death and destruction of the Great War. Many were weary of waiting and wished to play an active part. Even so, rather few suspected just how decisive President Wilson would become. After dragging his feet for three years, Wilson acted with alacrity once the war began.

When did the U.S. resort to military conscription?

To make it more palatable, Wilson's administration called it the "Selective Service." Almost immediately upon declaring war, Wilson realized more men would be needed, and the first Selective Service draft looked for 560,000 soldiers. Even that proved insufficient, however, and soon the projection was for an army of 1.3 million men. When it came to top leadership, Wilson and Secretary of War Henry Stimson had rather few choices. Most of the Spanish–American War leaders had left the service for more profitable opportunities. One leader emerged: Brigadier General John Pershing (1860–1948).

What was the Committee on Public Information?

The Committee on Public Information was a body of the U.S. government created by executive order. Wilson appointed journalist and politician George Creel (1865–1953) to head the Committee. Its purpose was to influence the public to support the war effort. The Committee instituted a propaganda campaign that pervaded all media to increase the public's support for the war. The Committee produced its own newspaper, the *Official Bulletin*.

Unfortunately, the Committee also contributed to a climate of intolerance for those who opposed the war and exhibited an alarming lack of concern for civil liberties. Wilson abolished the Committee in August 1919, also by executive order. Creel later wrote a memoir about the Committee, *How We Advertised America*.

What was the "Fourteen Points" speech, and what were the points in that speech?

The Fourteen Points refers to a speech President Wilson delivered before the U.S. Congress on January 8, 1918, that outlined the fourteen provisions a peace treaty to end World War I must contain. Those fourteen points were:

1. An open peace process free of secret diplomacy
2. Free navigation on the seas

3. Equality of trade between nations free from economic conditions

4. Reduction of national armaments

5. Review of colonial claims with consideration given to the concerned population

6. Evacuation of Russian territory by other countries

7. The removal of troops from Belgium and recognition of it again as an independent sovereign state

8. Freeing of all French territory and French acquisition of the Alsace-Lorraine territory

9. Realignment of borders of Italy

10. A chance for autonomy for the people of Austria-Hungary

11. Evacuation and restoration of Rumania, Serbia, and Montenegro

12. Sovereignty for the Turkish part of the Ottoman Empire but recognition of other nationalities under Turkish rule

13. A free Poland, and

14. A general association of all member nations

Who was John J. Pershing?

Pershing (1860–1948) was an American general and war hero best known for leading the American Expedition Forces in World War I. He helped guide American forces during the decisive Western Front. Known as "Black Jack," Pershing had earned valuable experience in battles during the Indian Wars (the Apache and Sioux) and the Spanish–American War of 1898. Pershing approved of some American forces to participate

in the Battle of Hamel on July 4, 1918, a decisive Allied victory led by Australia with assistance from the United States and Great Britain. For his successful efforts in World War I, Congress approved the promotion of Pershing to "General of the Armies of the United States." No American military general had ever received such a high honor or rank.

Who was Pershing's naval counterpart?

Rear Admiral William Sims (1858–1936) is less well known than Pershing, but he played a key role in helping the U.S. Army reach Europe. Reaching England soon after the declaration of war, Sims was appalled by the losses Britain was taking from U-Boat attacks; he accurately predicted

General John "Black Jack" Pershing led U.S. forces in Europe during World War I.

that Britain would be forced off the battlefield if something were not done. Sims established a convoy system under which U.S. warships escorted British and American merchantmen across the North Atlantic. He found the British more willing to cooperate than he expected, and Queenstown, Ireland, was soon almost an American naval base.

How eager were the Americans to get into this conflict?

They were chomping at the bit. One thing most American soldiers—or "Yanks"—shared throughout the war was an overwhelming confidence that they would win. Caution and anxiety played a role among the Americans at all levels and ranks, but there was no pessimism, no sense of impending defeat. Whether he came from Missouri, Massachusetts, or California, the typical American infantryman believed the Stars and Stripes would prevail.

What lay behind this confidence was the enormous amount of materiel the United States provided for the Allied cause. Matters in the American war industry could be, and often were, chaotic, but a lot of things got done. For example, by the end of the war, America was producing ten thousand airplanes a year.

When did the first American troops arrive in France?

Only a skeleton crew was available to move right away, but immediacy was necessary, as morale in the French army had reached a low point. On July 4, 1917, Colonel Charles Stanton stood at the grave of the Marquis de Lafayette in Paris and declared: "Lafayette, we are here." These were but the first of three million Americans who were deployed. It became obvious to the Germans, however, that they must win the war quickly to prevent the Americans from tipping the balance in the Allies's favor.

Where were the Americans most needed?

In late May 1918, the Germans broke through in the Argonne area, coming within forty miles of Paris. A division of U.S. Marines was rushed to the area called Belleau Wood, and a fierce fight developed over who would control this one-square-mile area. The Marines were fresh and inexperienced, but some of that worked in their favor; the Germans did not intimidate them. The fight went on for a full week; when it was over, Germany's General Erich Ludendorff's third sledgehammer blow had failed. Now was the time for the Germans to seek peace, but Ludendorff would not permit it. The Kaiser was on the verge of a nervous breakdown, and no one else had the authority to put Ludendorff in his place. As a result, the war continued, with ever more disastrous results.

When did the tide finally turn in the Allies's favor?

By the beginning of July, the Germans were exhausted. Even Ludendorff conceded that nothing could be gained by further assaults. The Germans, therefore, went on the defensive while the Allies made their first major attacks. Beginning on July 18, 1918, the French and Americans moved forward in the Aisne-Marne offensive. Their assault was preceded by a massive artillery barrage, and roughly four hundred tanks slowly rumbled from their positions to attack the German lines. The Germans suffered thirty thousand men killed, wounded, and missing on the first day of battle, and things only became worse from their perspective. Another joint Allied offensive began on August 8. On that single day, the Allies liberated nineteen French villages and advanced nine miles; they also captured sixteen thousand Germans. Ludendorff later referred to August 8, 1918, as the "black day of the German Army."

By this time (the summer of 1918), how many tanks were in the field?

British and French factories had labored since the spring of 1916; now, two years later, they had manufactured a total of about fifty-five hundred tanks. The best of these was the British Mark IV, but it was supplemented by the Renault-FT, made in France. By contrast, the Germans were skeptical about the importance of tanks and had deployed only about twenty of them by 1918. No less an authority than General Pershing declared that the fate of infantry battles would continue to rest with the rifle and bayonet. The German defenders ardently hoped that the Allies would not make any more tanks, because the mechanical monstrosities—as so many called them—could move into and then up out of trenches.

How did the U.S. government dramatically increase the size of the U.S. military?

The U.S. Congress passed, and President Woodrow Wilson signed into law, the Selective Service Act of 1917. This law empowered the federal government to impose a draft. At the start of World War I in 1914, the U.S. army had only 100,000 troops. The law initially required all men aged 21–30 to register for military service. The law was later amended to increase the age range from 18–45. By the end of the war, two million people had volunteered, and another 2.8 million had been drafted. The U.S. Supreme Court upheld the constitutionality of the law in 1918 in the *Selective Draft Law Cases*.

How many U.S. soldiers fought and lost their lives in World War I?

The United States armed forces consisted of nearly five million at the end of World War I. More than 110,000 Americans lost their lives during the War.

Who were Doughboys?

The Doughboys was the name given to American soldiers in World War I. The nickname originated with the Mexican–American War of 1846–1848. The origins of the term "doughboys" is less than

An American "Doughboy" receives a medal from Britain's King George V in this c. 1918 photo.

clear. Some suggest it related to the white belts worn by the soldiers in World War I. Another explanation comes from the chalky dust often found on American soldiers during the Mexican–American War.

How did World War I end?

Although the United States had been ill-prepared to enter the war, the American government mobilized quickly to rally the troops—and the citizens—behind the war effort: In April 1917, the U.S. Regular Army was comprised of just more than 100,000 men; by the end of the war, the American armed forces stood some five million strong. The arrival of the U.S. troops gave the Allies the manpower they needed to win the war. After continued fighting in the trenches of Europe, which had left almost ten million dead, in November 1918 Germany agreed to an armistice, and the Central Powers finally surrendered. In January 1919, Allied representatives gathered in Paris to draw up the peace settlement.

When did the German and Allied representatives meet?

They first met at Compiègne on November 8, 1918. The German diplomats tried to play the Bolshevik card, saying that the Allies did not realize the serious danger of communism. Field Marshal Ferdinand Foch rejected this position, saying that all armies tended to see breakdown in order at the end of a war. He demanded to know if the Germans were ready to sign an armistice and ticked off a long list of terms, all of which aimed to ensure that Germany would be completely disarmed and possibly even broken apart and no longer exist as a military power.

When did fighting cease?

The German and Allied representatives signed the armistice at 7 A.M., but the fighting was scheduled to cease at 11 A.M., meaning the eleventh hour of the eleventh day of the

Is it fair to say that America won World War I?

Ever since 1918, it has raised the ire of British and French commentators when they hear that the United States "won" the war, because to them it is apparent that their nations sacrificed far more. They are half right. Britain, France, and the other Allied nations gave and sacrificed far more of their manpower and material resources than did the United States, so in a way, *their* efforts "won" the war. However, technically speaking, especially looking at who delivered the most important punches and whose entry into the war tipped the balance in favor of the Allies, a good case can be made for the United States. And if one asks which country gained the most while expending the least, then it is a tie between the United States and Imperial Japan.

eleventh month of the year. The symbolic nature of that hour was well understood, but handfuls of men died between seven and eleven that morning, and a few others died even after the last bell (metaphorically) had been rung. Fighting did not completely cease until later that afternoon.

No one had a clue, at that moment, just how great the human and material losses were. It took years to estimate that two million Germans, three million Russians, 1.3 million French, and 900,000 British had died during the Great War. Turkish losses are more difficult to estimate. The nations that came off the lightest, by far, were Japan and the United States. America suffered roughly fifty thousand killed in battle and many others that later died of their wounds, but given the huge role the United States played in the last three months of fighting, this was not a relatively high toll. Japan, which seized several Pacific Islands from Germany, lost about 350 men in the war.

AFTER THE GREAT WAR

How was President Wilson involved in the peace process?

Wilson led the American delegation to the Paris Peace Conference in late January 1919. At this conference, the Allied countries outlined the terms of the ultimate peace agreement, including the Treaty of Versailles. This treaty signaled the end of World War I and placed blame for the war on the Germans. The Paris Peace Conference also called for a League of Nations, a precursor to the modern-day United Nations. Wilson actively promoted the idea of a League of Nations, even touring around the United States to obtain support. For his efforts, he received the Nobel Peace Prize in 1919.

What laws did President Wilson sign during the time of World War I that limited First Amendment freedoms?

President Wilson signed into law the Espionage Act of 1917 and the Sedition Act of 1918. Although parts of the Espionage Act of 1917 are still law today, some of the provisions were applied to punish antiwar, dissident political speech. Individuals faced lengthy prison terms for circulating leaflets critical of the U.S. war effort and the draft. The U.S. Supreme Court began to develop a body of law explaining the meaning of the First Amendment free-speech clause ("Congress shall make no law ... abridging the freedom of speech ...) in response to cases that involved convictions of Socialists, anarchists, and other political dissidents.

What was the League of Nations?

The League of Nations was the forerunner to the United Nations. It was an international organization established by the Treaty of Versailles at the end of World War I (1914–1918). Since the United States never ratified that treaty, it was not a member.

The League was set up to handle disputes among countries and to avoid another major conflict such as the Great War (as World War I was referred to until the outbreak of World War II). But the organization proved ineffective; it was unable to intervene in such acts of aggression as Japan's invasion of Manchuria in 1931, Italy's conquest of Ethiopia in 1935–1936, occupation of Albania in 1939, and Germany's takeover of Austria in 1938.

The League of Nations dissolved itself during World War II (1939–1945). Though unsuccessful, the organization did establish a basic model for a permanent international organization.

Why didn't the United States of America join the League of Nations?

The United States did not join the League of Nations because many members of the U.S. Senate feared it would embroil the country in world conflicts that the country was better off avoiding. Several leading Republican senators, such as Henry Cabot Lodge (1850–1924) and William Borah (1865–1940), opposed U.S. involvement in the League of Nations. These senators particularly opposed Article X of the Covenant of the League of Nations, providing that participating nations would assist any other member of the League who was subject to foreign aggression. Lodge and Borah favored a policy of isolationism and hoped to extricate the United States from most world problems.

How did the Treaty of Versailles pave the way for World War II?

In the aftermath of World War I (1914–1918), Germany was severely punished: One clause in the Treaty of Versailles even stipulated that Germany take responsibility for causing the war. In addition to its territorial losses, Germany was also made to pay for an Allied military force to occupy the west bank of the Rhine River, intended to keep Germany in check for the next fifteen years. The treaty also limited the size of Germany's military. In 1921, Germany received a bill for reparations: It owed the Allies $33 million.

While the postwar German government had been made to sign the Treaty of Versailles under the threat of more fighting from the Allies, the German people nevertheless faulted their leaders for accepting such strident terms. Not only was the German government weakened, but public resentment over the Treaty of Versailles soon developed into a strong nationalist movement—led by German chancellor and führer Adolf Hitler (1889–1945).

THE PROHIBITION ERA

What was Prohibition?

Prohibition referred to the American policy of outlawing the manufacture and distribution of alcohol. Prohibition became a staple of the temperance movement, as many people believed alcohol caused a variety of social ills. Many religious groups, including the Women's Christian Temperance Union, opposed alcohol. Another key player in the policy of Prohibition was the Anti-Saloon League, which successfully lobbied government officials for the illegalization of alcohol.

Prohibition culminated with the passage of the Eighteenth Amendment to the U.S. Constitution, which provided:

Section 1. After one year from the ratification of this article the manufacture, sale, or transportation of intoxicating liquors within, the importation thereof into, or the exportation thereof from the United States and all territory subject to the jurisdiction thereof for beverage purposes is hereby prohibited.

Section 2. The Congress and the several States shall have concurrent power to enforce this article by appropriate legislation.

Section 3. This article shall be inoperative unless it shall have been ratified as an amendment to the Constitution by the legislatures of the several States, as provided in the Constitution, within seven years from the date of the submission hereof to the States by the Congress.

Only two states—Connecticut and Rhode Island—voted against the ratification of the Eighteenth Amendment. The Federal Bureau of Investigation had the responsibility to enforce the policies of Prohibition, including the Volstead Act, which was the federal law passed to enforce the Eighteenth Amendment.

Although called "the Noble Experiment," Prohibition failed. It led to overcrowding in jails, corruption of public officials, and the growth of organized crime. During this period, many who consumed alcohol turned to other drugs, such as opiates. Public discontent over Prohibition gathered political steam, eventually leading to the adoption of the Twenty-First Amendment, which repealed the Eighteenth Amendment. It remains the only constitutional amendment to repeal a previous amendment. It also was the only constitutional amendment to be passed by state-ratifying conventions instead of state conventions.

After whom was the Volstead Act named?

The Volstead Act was named after U.S. House of Representatives member Andrew Volstead (1860–1947), who served twenty years in the House from Minnesota. A Republican, Volstead served as chair of the House Judiciary Committee from 1919 to 1923, placing him in the position of monitoring and working heavily on the National Prohibition Act, subsequently called the Volstead Act. He served ten terms in Congress but lost reelection while seeking an eleventh term. He then served as legal advisor to the chief of the National Prohibition Enforcement Bureau. After the repeal of Prohibition, he returned to the private practice of law in Minnesota.

Who was Carrie Nation?

The Kentucky-born Carrie Nation (1846–1911) became famous as a temperance agitator in the early 1900s. The saloon was illegal in her resident state of Kansas, and she felt it her divine duty to take her hatchet to ruin any place that sold intoxicants. Between

Prohibition advocate Carrie Nation (1846–1911) campaigned to make alcohol illegal even before Prohibition. Seen here in a 1902 event in Ann Arbor, Michigan, she was famous for using a hatchet to smash bottles and casks in saloons.

1899 and 1909, she went on wrecking expeditions (which she called "hatchetations") throughout the state, incurring the wrath of business owners and government officials. Though many might have favored national prohibition of alcohol, Nation's actions were extreme to say the least, causing her to be arrested, imprisoned thirty times, and even shot at. She persisted, however, buoyed by the belief that she was performing a public— and even divine—service. The propitiously named Carrie A. Nation (who tried, it seems, to carry the nation straight to the water fountain) did not live to see Prohibition become a constitutional amendment in 1919 nor to see it revoked in 1933.

What was a speakeasy?

Once alcohol became illegal, an illegal business in booze naturally arose. Alcohol was either imported or made locally in secret and then sold to underground establishments called speakeasies, which were basically bars and taverns in hidden locations. The word "speakeasy" came about to describe them because customers and bartenders would speak in hushed tones so as not to be heard outside by passing law enforcement.

What famous gangster initially prospered during the Prohibition Era?

Several gangsters profited handsomely during Prohibition by controlling the illegal flow of alcoholic beverages—the "bootlegging" trade. Perhaps none became as famous—or infamous—as Alphonse Gabriel Capone (1899–1947). Born in Brooklyn, Al Capone got into early trouble as a young teenager. He later moved to Chicago as a young man and became involved in smuggling and other criminal activity. Capone fell under the leadership of gangster Johnny Torio (1882–1957), the leader of the so-called "Chicago Outfit."

After Torio was severely injured by gunfire from rival gangsters, Torio turned the reins of power over to Capone. Capone made his mentor proud by expanding the vast criminal enterprise based on bootlegging, prostitution, gambling, and political bribery. Capone became the leading organized crime figure in the country and achieved cultlike status with some for his charitable donations to various causes.

Capone was eventually brought to trial for income tax evasion. After Chicago police had been unable to bring Capone to

The FBI's Public Enemy Number One during the 1920s, infamous gangster Al Capone was never found guilty of murder, bribery, bootlegging, or other violent crimes; instead, he finally went to prison on tax evasion charges.

justice for his criminal activities, including murder, the Federal Bureau of Investigation determined that the only way to prosecute the crime boss would be through violation of tax laws. For two and a half weeks in October 1931, the case against Capone was heard in a Chicago courtroom. He was found guilty on five counts of tax evasion, sentenced to eleven years in prison, and charged $50,000 in fines and $30,000 in court costs. While his first jail cell, in Illinois's Cook County Jail, allowed him the luxuries of a private shower, phone conversations, telegrams, and even visits by other gangsters, including Charles "Lucky" Luciano (1897–1962) and "Dutch" Schultz (1901–1935), Capone was eventually moved to Alcatraz Island in San Francisco Bay, where he received no privileges. Released in 1939, Capone lived out his remaining years with his wife and son in Miami Beach, where he was reportedly haunted by imaginary killers.

WOMEN'S SUFFRAGE

Who was Alice Paul?

Alice Paul (1885–1977) was a groundbreaking feminist before the word "feminist" came into fashion. The Mount Laurel, New Jersey, institute named in her honor describes her as "the architect of some of the most outstanding political achievements on behalf of women in the twentieth century."

Paul was born to Quaker parents who instilled in her a belief in gender equality. After completing high school at the top of her class, Paul graduated from Swarthmore College in 1905 and began work toward an advanced degree. In 1906 she traveled to England, where she continued her studies, did social work, and became actively involved in the suffrage movement. She was arrested three times for her involvement in protests.

In 1916, when the American women's suffrage movement was divided and "dead in the water," Paul founded the National Woman's Party (NWP), an organization that spearheaded the campaign for U.S. women's suffrage and that continued working for women's rights and equality into the twenty-first century. Paul's leadership of the suffrage movement was critical to pass the Nineteenth Amendment (1920), which guaranteed women the right to vote; she organized thousands of activists to put enormous pressure on the White House and Congress. Paul employed what was then considered a most unladylike strategy of "sustained, dramatic, nonviolent protest." The suffrage campaign was characterized by national speaking tours, marches, and pickets (including the first ever at the White House). When protesters were arrested, they sometimes endured brutal prison conditions and staged hunger strikes.

What was the Nineteenth Amendment?

The Nineteenth Amendment was the culmination of the women's suffrage movement, giving women the legal right to vote nationwide. It provided: "The right of citizens of the United States to vote shall not be denied or abridged by the United States or by any State on account of sex." The amendment was drafted in the nineteenth century by Susan B. Anthony (1820–1906) and Elizabeth Cady Stanton (1815–1902). The U.S. Senate rejected the amendment in 1887. The amendment did not come before the U.S. Congress in the next several decades—a period of time known in the women's movement as "the doldrums."

Suffragettes from Maryland picket the White House in this 1917 photograph.

Another attempt to pass the amendment failed to clear the U.S. House of Representatives in 1915. But in the next several years, President Woodrow Wilson publicly supported the amendment. The amendment finally cleared Congress in 1919 and then was sent to the states for ratification. Tennessee became the thirty-sixth state to vote for the amendment—the necessary number at that time for official ratification. The Nineteenth Amendment became part of the Constitution in 1920.

What was unusual about the ratification vote in Tennessee?

The vote was unusually close in the Tennessee General Assembly with regard to the Nineteenth Amendment. The official final vote tally was 49–48. The vote was 48–48, but a young state legislator named Harry T. Burn (1895–1977), who had initially opposed the measure, provided the vote necessary to approve the amendment.

The twenty-four-year-old Burn was persuaded to change his mind by his mother, Phoebe Ensminger Burn, who wrote her son to "be a good boy" and "help Mrs. Catt put the 'rat' in ratification." For this reason, Burn's mother has been called the "the mother who saved suffrage."

Who was "Mrs. Catt"?

"Mrs. Catt" was the nickname of women's suffrage leader Carrie Chapman Catt (1859–1947), who served as the president of the National American Woman Suffrage Association and founded the League of Women Voters. Catt also worked on issues of international suffrage. She later worked as an antiwar activist, decrying abuses against Jewish people in Germany.

ROARING TWENTIES

What were the "Roaring Twenties"?

The Roaring Twenties is a term used to describe the relative prosperity and cultural richness of the decade of the 1920s in the United States, particularly in larger cities. The time period was characterized by patriotism in the wake of World War I, the burgeoning of jazz music, and an embrace of new technologies. Because of the explosion of jazz music during this time period, some refer to it as the "Jazz Age." The Roaring Twenties also featured a greater American appreciate for sports heroes, such as baseball star Babe Ruth and heavyweight boxer Jack Dempsey.

What was the Teapot Dome scandal?

Teapot Dome was an oil field on public lands in Salt Creek, Wyoming, the home state of U.S. Secretary of the Interior Albert B. Fall (1861–1944). Fall leased the petroleum lands to Sinclair Oil without any competitive bidding. Fall had also leased the Elk Hills Naval Petroleum Reserve in central California to wealthy oilman Edward Doheny. During President Warren G. Harding's (1865–1923) administration, it was revealed that Doheny had given a personal loan of $100,000 to Fall. For his conduct, in 1929 a jury found Fall guilty of bribery and sentenced him to one year in prison. He became the first person from a presidential administration to serve time in prison for official political actions.

What other scandals beset President Harding's administration?

Harding had named Charles R. Forbes director of the War Insurance Risk Board, which became the Veterans Bureau. Forbes had a distinguished war record and was a friend of both President Harding and his wife, Florence. However, Forbes engaged in corruption by embezzling money from contractors, giving them low-priced bids for building veterans hospitals. He was convicted in 1925 and served more than a year in prison. Charles

Oilman Edward Doheny (second from the right at the table, he is the man with the white mustache) is shown here testifying before Congress in 1924. Doheny received financial favors from Secretary of the Interior Albert B. Fall during the Teapot Dome scandal that rocked Washington.

F. Cramer, legal advisor for the Veterans Bureau, committed suicide. Another scandal involved Harry M. Daugherty, Harding's attorney general. Daugherty allegedly accepted bribes from bootleggers. He resigned from his position in 1924 (during President Calvin Coolidge's [1872–1933] administration). Daughtery was never charged with a crime for this allegation. However, he did face other criminal charges for bribes. Two juries deadlocked, and he never was convicted of anything. It is interesting that Daugherty's assistant, Jess Smith, destroyed his personal papers and committed suicide shortly after Harding asked for his resignation. It was perhaps because of these so-called "friends"—sometimes loosely referred to as the "Ohio Gang"—that Harding lamented: "My God, this is a hell of a job. I have no trouble with my enemies. ... But my damn friends, they're the ones that keep me walking the floor at night."

What speech on civil rights by President Harding was considered controversial at the time?

Harding delivered a speech on October 26, 1921, at Capitol Park in Birmingham, Alabama. He told the Southern audience that the time had come for political equality for blacks. He told the audience, which *The New York Times* called a conservative estimate of 100,000 people, that he would speak frankly to the audience "whether you like it or not." He did say that social equality was not attainable but called for political equality for blacks. "I would say let the black man vote when he is fit to vote; prohibit the white man voting when he is unfit to vote."

What policy of peace did President Coolidge's administration successfully pursue?

Coolidge's administration—most notably his secretary of state, Frank B. Kellogg—helped pull off the Kellogg–Briand Pact. This pact—named after Kellogg and French diplomat Aristide Briand—called for countries to avoid war and try to resolve disputes through peaceful means. More than sixty countries agreed to the terms. For his efforts, Kellogg received the Nobel Peace Prize in 1929.

What tax policies did Coolidge pursue?

Coolidge signed into law two bills that reduced income taxes and eliminated the gift tax. The most significant of these laws, the Revenue Act of 1926, lowered taxes significantly across the board. He kept corporate taxes at a lower level than his predecessors. Coolidge's policies seemingly helped the economy, as unemployment dropped and businesses profited. The stock market rose during Coolidge's time in the White House.

What significant measure did Coolidge sign that benefited the aviation industry?

Coolidge signed into law the Air Commerce Act of 1926, giving the federal government power over the commercial aviation industry. The measure also created the first two

commercial air routes.

What groundbreaking feat did Charles Lindbergh accomplish?

On May 20 and 21, 1927, Charles Lindbergh (1902–1974) became the first man to fly solo nonstop across the Atlantic Ocean. He did so on a monoplane called the *Spirit of St. Louis,* flying from New York City to outside Paris, France. His achievement made him a

Aviator Charles Lindbergh poses in front of the *Spirit of St. Louis* in this 1927 photograph.

What tragedy befell the Lindberghs' first child?

On March 1, 1932, Charles Lindbergh III, the twenty-month-old son of Charles Lindbergh and his wife, Anne, disappeared from their home in Hopewell, New Jersey. A ransom note for $70,000 was sent to the Lindberghs, but after the money was left for the kidnapper, the baby was nowhere to be found until police discovered it about a mile from the Lindbergh home. Tragically, the baby was dead. Evidence led to a German immigrant named Bruno Richard Hauptmann, who was tried, found guilty, and, in 1935, executed. The sensational case led to the establishment of kidnapping as a federal crime.

hero, and the U.S. Air Force Reserve pilot was promoted to colonel. During World War II, Lindbergh flew fifty missions, and after the war, as a brigadier general, assisted in locating the best sites to establish air force bases. Toward the end of his life, he became active in promoting environmental causes.

What was the Scopes trial?

The July 1925 trial of Dayton, Tennessee, public schoolteacher John T. Scopes (1900–1970) was dubbed the "monkey trial" because at issue was Scopes's teaching of evolution in his classroom. Having yielded to religious beliefs in creationism (the story of human origins told in the Bible's book of Genesis), Tennessee state law prohibited teaching public school students about the theories of English naturalist Charles Darwin (1809–1882). Darwin's scientifically credible work *On the Origin of Species* argued that humans had descended from apelike creatures. Celebrated attorney Clarence Darrow (1857–1938) defended Scopes; lawyer and former presidential candidate William Jennings Bryan (1860–1925), known as the "Great Commoner," argued for the prosecution. For twelve days in the summer of 1925, the small town in eastern Tennessee became the site of a showdown between modern scientific thought and traditional fundamentalism, or as some observed, between cosmopolitan and rural America. Spectators crowded the courtroom, eventually forcing the proceedings to be moved to the courthouse lawn. Journalists issued daily reports that were published in newspapers across the country.

Darrow made history when he called Bryan himself to the stand; it was a daring move on the defense attorney's part. Since Bryan eagerly accepted the summons, the judge allowed the questioning. Darrow first got Bryan to agree that every word in the Bible is true; then he set in to reveal the hazards of such a literal interpretation—asking, for example, how Cain had found himself a wife if he, Abel, Adam, and Eve were the only four people on Earth at the time. Darrow succeeded in shaking the prosecutor, who finally admitted that he did not believe Earth was made in six days. Bryan retaliated by accusing Darrow of insulting the Bible, to which Darrow replied, "I am examining you on your fool ideas that no Christian on earth believes." It was drama better than any novelist could write. Darrow lost the case, which was later overturned on a technicality. Scopes had only been charged a $100 fine for violating the state law, which was repealed in 1967. But the trial, preserved in the play and film *Inherit the Wind*, is still remembered today: Scopes's crime was not sensational, his trial did not break any legal ground, and the defense had not won a brilliant victory, but the proceedings, carried out in the midsummer heat of the American South, epitomized the era and, ultimately, made a great story.

Sadly, Bryan never made it out of Dayton alive; he died five days after the trial. Many years later, in *Epperson v. Arkansas* (1968), the U.S. Supreme Court ruled that a law forbidding the teaching of evolution in public schools violated the Establishment Clause of the First Amendment, which provides for separation of church and state.

Why is the court martial of Billy Mitchell famous?

The 1925 military trial of William "Billy" Mitchell (1879–1936) made headlines because of the defendant's open and controversial criticism of the U.S. military. A U.S. general in World War I, Mitchell returned from the experience convinced that the future military strength of the country depended on air power. In fact, he had commanded the American Expeditionary Force during the war in Europe, and had even proposed to General John Pershing that troops be dropped by parachute behind German lines; Pershing dismissed the idea. The war over, in 1921 Mitchell declared that "the first battles of any future war will be air battles." But when the Navy and War Departments failed to develop an air service, Mitchell was outspoken about it, charging the military with incompetence and criminal negligence and describing the Administration as treasonable.

Those were fighting words. Charged with insubordination and "conduct of a nature to bring discredit upon the military service," Mitchell's trial began on October 28, 1925. After lengthy hearings, on December 17, 1925, Mitchell was found guilty and was suspended without pay from the military for a period of five years. Congress entered the fray, proposing a joint resolution to restore Mitchell's rank, but President Coolidge upheld the court's decision. Mitchell responded by resigning. He returned to civilian life but continued to write and speak about his belief in an air force. He died in 1936, about five years too soon to see his predictions come true: In surprise air raids on December 7, 1941, the Japanese attacked U.S. military installations in the Philippines and Hawaii. Although the U.S. military rose to the occasion, entering World War II and building an impressive and mighty air fleet, many observers felt the military could have been better prepared to stage that monumental effort had Mitchell's advice been heeded years earlier.

THE GREAT DEPRESSION, WORLD WAR II, AND ITS AFTERMATH

THE GREAT DEPRESSION

What was the "Great Depression"?

The defining moment of Herbert Hoover's (1874–1964) presidency was the Great Depression. The Great Depression was a severe economic depression that impacted not only the United States but much of the world from 1930 to the early 1940s. Unemployment rose to nearly twenty-five percent during the height of the Great Depression in the United States. Numerous banks collapsed, and the Federal Reserve arguably did not respond adequately. Farmers were devastated by the economic downturn, as crops dropped in price by as much as sixty percent. The Depression began with the precipitous decline of the U.S. stock market on October 29, 1929—a day known as Black Tuesday. Some historians blame the wide, unequal disparity of wealth in the country for causing the Great Depression. Many historians believe that the Great Depression began to dissipate when the U.S. government began spending more and more money on the war effort for World War II, overcoming the nation's serious unemployment problem.

If the Depression began with Black Tuesday, then what was Black Thursday?

While most people think of October 29, 1929, as the fateful day when the stock market crashed, five days before that—on Black Thursday, October 24, 1929—was actually the first sign of disaster. On that day, 12.9 million shares were traded, and panic began to sweep Wall Street. Even with this mess, many economists and businesses continued to keep their heads firmly embedded in the sand. The day ended in a rally that briefly caused the market to recover, but the worst was yet to come when Black Tuesday saw stock values plummet by $30 billion.

Much of the farmland in the American heartland turned to uncultivatible sand during the terrifying years of the Dust Bowl. The environmental disaster was the result of improper farming techniques and resulted in mass migrations of many families to California and other points west.

What was a "Hooverville"?

During the Great Depression, throngs of the unemployed began constructing ramshackle homes in destitute communities that became known as "Hoovervilles." This unflattering name stemmed from hatred for a president who people felt was failing to help them. "Hooverville" was first coined in a 1930 newspaper article, and it was first used to describe a town outside the Chicago area.

What was the Dust Bowl?

America was hit in the 1930s not only by the Depression but also by an environmental disaster that devastated the farming heartland of the country. Poor farming practices were a significant factor in causing the Dust Bowl. Since grain prices at the time were skyrocketing, farmers plowed over natural grasslands to plant wheat. Instead of rotating crops to create healthier soil, they planted wheat repeatedly, depleting soil integrity and leaving no substantial root systems to hold soil in place. When a long drought hit the region from 1934 to 1937, plants were swept away and huge dust storms ensued, covering a 150,000-square-mile swath of Kansas, Oklahoma, Texas, Colorado, and New Mexico. It was so bad that many people had to abandon their homes, and a population migration ensued (John Steinbeck's great American novel *The Grapes of Wrath* follows a fictional family representing the hard times faced by so many Americans because of the Dust Bowl).

The federal government created the Soil Conservation Service (part of the New Deal, see below) in 1935 to teach farmers how to rehabilitate and conserve farmland. The program worked, and much of the area that had suffered revived by 1941. But farmers repeated the mistake of poor cultivation and harvesting during World War II, until the government once again had to step in to subsidize farmers who, in exchange, agreed to convert farmland back to natural grassland.

What significant labor legislation was signed by President Hoover?

President Hoover signed into law without comment the Norris–LaGuardia Act of 1932, named after Senator George Norris of Nebraska and Representative Fiorello LaGuardia of New York. This law prohibited judges from issuing injunctions, or court orders, limiting peaceful labor striking.

What was the New Deal?

The New Deal is the name given to a series of economic programs initiated by President Franklin D. Roosevelt ("FDR") (1882–1945) and his administration to improve the American economy that continued to be mired in the Great Depression. In his inaugural address, President Roosevelt promised a "new deal" for the "forgotten people."

The New Deal focused on the three Rs: relief, recovery, and reform. It consisted of the creation of the Social Security system, the Federal Deposit Insurance Corporation, and the Civilian Conservation Corps, which gave jobs to many unemployed young men. Another law that passed as part of the New Deal was the Fair Labor Standards Act of 1938, which provided better working conditions for laborers. Another important aspect of New Deal legislation concerned the creation of the Securities and Exchange Commission.

Roosevelt garnered popular support for many of his New Deal programs through a series of speeches to the American public known as "fireside chats." Roosevelt gave thirty fireside chats during 1933 and 1934. They contributed greatly to the popularity of the president as a leader for the people.

What was the Works Progress Administration?

In 1935, President Roosevelt issued an executive order establishing the Works Progress Administration (WPA). Essentially, this released massive amounts of federal money to build bridges, roads, airports, and buildings. In addition, funds were provided for the Federal Art Project and Federal Writers' Project to help artists, not just laborers. Young people were also helped with part-time work through the National Youth Administration that was part of the WPA. While it existed, the WPA employed 8.5 million people, building 116,000 buildings, seventy-eight thousand bridges, and over 650,000 miles of road. With the entrance of the United States into World War II, many of those jobs were turned toward military projects, and the WPA was discontinued in 1943.

How did the CCC differ from the WPA?

Like the WPA, the Civilian Conservation Corps (CCC) was designed to employ the many people who had lost work because of the Great Depression. The CCC's focus, however, was on young people working in the outdoors to help protect and develop the country's natural resources; that is, it promoted environmental projects such as national parks. It provided not only jobs but also training that might be transferred outside the CCC. As with the WPA, the CCC ended with the onset of World War II.

How else did Roosevelt's New Deal affect labor in America?

Unions got a much-needed boost in the late 1930s because one of the provisions of the New Deal was to grant collective bargaining powers to what were then called trade or craft unions. With collective bargaining protected, workers in a variety of industries now had the power to negotiate better wages and working conditions from companies, especially in the industrial sector. This gave rise to powerful organizations such as the United Auto Workers and the Congress of Industrial Organizations (CIO), which later merged with the AFL (American Federation of Labor) to form the AFL-CIO. By the end of World War II, about twelve million American workers belonged to unions, dramatically changing the economic landscape of the country.

Why was Social Security started in the United States?

Another part of President Franklin Roosevelt's New Deal was the passage of the Social Security Act of 1935, which FDR signed into law on August 14 of that year. The purpose of the act was to help prevent senior citizens from falling into poverty after they retired. It was also designed to help people with disabilities and to assist mothers and their children who were struggling financially.

Who were the "Four Horsemen"?

The "Four Horsemen" were a group of conservative justices on the U.S. Supreme Court in the 1930s, who invalidated many of President Roosevelt's New Deal programs. The "Four Horsemen" were Justices Pierce Butler (1866–1939), Willis Van Devanter (1859–1941), George Sutherland (1862–1942), and James McReynolds (1862–1946). These justices believed that the federal government was overreaching in its attempt to invoke its Commerce Clause powers over local matters.

Who tried to kill President Roosevelt before he was officially sworn in as president?

Giuseppe Zangara, a thirty-two-year-old, Italian-born bricklayer, tried to assassinate President–Elect Roosevelt in Miami, Florida. Apparently, he had also thought about killing President Hoover. Zangara was motivated in his violent actions by the belief that the president was responsible not only for massive unemployment but for his own physical ailments. Zangara missed Roosevelt but did kill Chicago's Mayor Anton Cermak and

What was the story behind the famous outlaws Bonnie and Clyde?

Bonnie and Clyde

Bonnie Parker (1910–1934) and Clyde Barrow (1909–1934) were the most glamorous thieves and killers of the 1930s. Married when just teenagers, they started their lives of crime quite young. Barrow was imprisoned for robbery at a young age, but after he was paroled in 1932, the couple went on a crime spree, creating a gang that included Clyde's brother Buck, Buck's wife, Blanche, and Barrow's boyhood friend Raymond Hamilton, as well as others. They traveled the country, robbing banks in Texas, Oklahoma, New Mexico, Louisiana, and Missouri. Along the way, according to reports, they killed nineteen people, mostly police officers. Because they were young, married, and daring, Bonnie and Clyde developed a reputation as glamorous as Robin Hood and his merry men or the earlier Jesse James gang. They often paused on their travels to pose for photos, sporting their weaponry and smiling for the camera. On May 23, 1934, the couple was shot to death near Sailes, Louisiana, gunned down by a combined force of Texas and Louisiana state police. Famous in their own time, their names were celebrated and romanticized again in the 1967 film *Bonnie and Clyde.*

wounded several others. Cermak allegedly told FDR on the way to the hospital: "I'm glad it was me and not you, Mr. President."

What constitutional amendment was passed during Roosevelt's tenure?

The Twenty-First Amendment was ratified in 1933, the first year of Roosevelt's presidency. The Twenty-First Amendment repealed the Eighteenth Amendment, which had established Prohibition. Upon signing the measure, Roosevelt said in part: "I trust in the good sense of the American people that they will not bring upon themselves the curse of the excessive use of intoxicating liquors to the detriment of health, morals, and social integrity."

What was the Court Packing Plan?

Roosevelt became very angry when the Supreme Court struck down many of his New Deal laws. He supported a measure that would allow the president to appoint a new justice every time an existing justice reached seventy years of age, with a maximum of six additional justices. This plan did not get very far because it was met with widespread opposition. However, some speculate that pressure from Roosevelt caused at least some members of the Court to look with a bit more favor on some New Deal measures. Whatever the case, the Court's number remained the same at nine and has stayed constant.

Where was the 1939 World's Fair held?

The 1939 World's Fair was held in New York City. More than forty-four million people attended this fair, the second largest ever on American soil. It focused much energy on the technologies of the future. Its slogan was "Dawn of a New Day." RCA introduced the television to the American public at this World's Fair. Shortly after World War II, television became a mainstream medium of communication and has remained such in the world ever since.

Which justice switched his vote in two minimum wage cases?

Justice Owen Roberts (1875–1955) switched his vote from striking down a minimum wage law in *Morehead v. New York ex. rel. Tipaldo* (1936) to upholding such a law in *West Coast Hotel Co. v. Parrish* (1937). It was said that Robert's change of mind was the "switch in time that saved nine," a reference to President Roosevelt's sharp criticism of the Court and his proposal in 1937 to "pack" the Court with additional justices. In reality, Roberts had indicated his support for the minimum wage law in a Court conference in December 1936, before President Roosevelt's court-packing plan was announced.

Why is Franklin Delano Roosevelt considered one of the country's greatest presidents?

Roosevelt is considered near the top of the list because of his leadership during the travails of the Great Depression and World War II. He connected to the people with his fireside chats and economic legislation designed to bring relief and recovery to many of those who were suffering. His leadership with Winston Churchill (1874–1965) proved vital to the free world in ensuring victory in World War II against the dangerous threat posed by Nazi Germany and Japan.

WORLD WAR II

What was Roosevelt's position on the war?

Roosevelt saw the threat that Hitler's Germany presented to the Western world. While maintaining a position of official neutrality, he reached an understanding with British Prime Minister Winston Churchill that Germany must be stopped. They issued the Atlantic Charter, which sought to ensure that democracy would flourish and triumph over totalitarian regimes. His leadership—along with that of Churchill and, to a lesser extent, Joseph Stalin of Russia—helped lead to a victory for the Allied forces over Germany, Japan, and the other war enemies.

When Japan attacked the United States at Pearl Harbor on December 7, 1941, Roosevelt showed forceful leadership and resolve in the face of a direct threat to national security and existence. He wrote in his memorably evocative phrase to Congress, asking for a declaration of war: "Yesterday, Dec. 7, 1941—a date which will live in infamy—the United States of America was suddenly and viciously attacked by naval and air forces of the Empire of Japan."

What happened at Pearl Harbor?

On the night before the attack, the Japanese moved a fleet of thirty-three ships to within two hundred miles of the Hawaiian island of Oahu, where Pearl Harbor is situated. More than three hundred planes took off from the Japanese carriers, dropping the first bombs on Pearl Harbor just before 8:00 A.M. on December 7, 1941. There were eight American battleships and more than ninety naval vessels in the harbor at the time. Twenty-one of these were destroyed or damaged, as were three hundred planes. The biggest single loss of the day was the sinking of the battleship USS *Arizona*, which went down in less than nine minutes.

More than half the fatalities at Pearl Harbor that infamous December day were due to the sinking of the *Arizona*. By the end of the raid, more than twenty-three hundred people had been killed, and about the same number were wounded.

Two ships, the USS *West Virginia* and the *Arizona,* are engulfed in flames as they sink in Pearl Harbor during the Japanese attack of December 7, 1941.

Pearl Harbor forever changed the United States and its role in the world. When President Roosevelt addressed Congress the next day, he called December 7 "a date which will live in infamy." The United States declared war against Japan, and on December 11, 1941, Germany and Italy—Japan's "Axis" allies—declared war on the United States. The events of December 7 had brought America into the war, a conflict from which it would emerge as leader of the free world.

When did the first U.S. troops begin fighting in World War II?

Late in 1942, the United States sent its first troops across the Atlantic, making amphibious landings in North Africa, followed by Sicily and the Italian peninsula. The first allied landings were in Morocco (Casablanca) and Algeria (Oran and Algiers) on November 8. (Algiers became the Allied headquarters in North Africa for the duration of the war.) The combined forces of the initial landing included more than 100,000 troops, launching the American military effort in the Atlantic theater of conflict. One American newspaper headline announced: "Yanks Invade Africa."

Was the U.S. mainland attacked during World War II?

Yes, the continental United States was hit twice during the war, but with no casualties and only minimal damage. The first attack occurred at approximately 7:00 P.M. on February 23, 1942, when a Japanese submarine shelled an oil storage field about twelve miles north of Santa Barbara, California. The Japanese were trying to hit oil tanks there, evidently with the intent of producing a spectacular explosion. But after firing a reported sixteen or seventeen rounds, they had struck only one pier. Most of the shells fell into the sea, well short of their targets. U.S. planes gave chase, but the submarine

What were the Zoot Suit Riots?

As if the country were not going through enough with World War II, there was violence at home, too, when in 1943 riots broke out in Los Angeles between Mexican Americans and white military men, as well as some other minority groups. The violence is today often linked to the death one year earlier of José Gallardo Diaz. Although what caused his death was never discovered, the police arrested seventeen Mexican Americans, nine of whom were convicted and sent to San Quentin Prison. The rioting also spread from L.A. to San Diego, Oakland, and Beaumont, California, as well as New York City; Detroit, Michigan; Philadelphia, Pennsylvania; and Chicago, Illinois.

The name for the riots comes from the fact that Mexican Americans found zoot suits to be fashionable (Italians and African Americans did, too). The suits were characterized by baggy pants with tight cuffs and jackets with padded shoulders and wide lapels.

got away. There were no injuries and only minimal damage, but the event put the nation on heightened alert to the possibility of more attacks.

The February 23 attack took place shortly after President Roosevelt had begun his fireside chat, addressing the nation over the radio. He talked about how this war was different, since it was being waged on "every continent, every island, every sea, every airlane in the world." He also said, "The broad oceans which have been heralded in the past as our protection from attack have become endless battlefields on which we are constantly being challenged by our enemies." The unsuccessful assault at Ellwood was the first attack on mainland U.S. soil since the War of 1812 (1812–1814). The event stirred fears of conspiracy and rattled nerves up and down the West Coast.

There was one other strike on mainland soil during World War II: At Fort Stevens, Oregon, at the mouth of the Columbia River. On the evening of June 21, 1942, a Japanese submarine fired some seventeen rounds of shells at the coastal military installation but caused no damage.

What controversial executive order did Roosevelt sign that interned Japanese Americans?

On February 19, 1942, President Roosevelt signed Executive Order 9066, which provided in part:

> I hereby authorize and direct the Secretary of War, and the Military Commanders whom he may from time to time designate, whenever he or any designated Commander deems such action necessary or desirable, to prescribe military areas in such places and of such extent as he or the appropriate Military Commander may determine, from which any or all persons may be excluded, and with respect to which, the right of any person to enter, remain in, or leave shall be subject to whatever restrictions the Secretary of War or the appropriate Military Commander may impose in his discretion.

While the law did not specifically mention the Japanese, military commanders used this executive order to intern more than 110,000 Japanese Americans for the duration of the war. First Lady Eleanor Roosevelt opposed the measure. Even FBI director J. Edgar Hoover opposed the measure, believing the Japanese spies had been caught shortly after the attack on Pearl Harbor.

What was D-Day?

The military uses the term "D-Day" to designate when an initiative is set to begin, counting all events out from that date for planning. For example, "D-Day minus two" would be a plan for what needs to happen two days before the beginning of the military operation. While the military planned and executed many D-Days during World War II—most of them landings on enemy-held coasts—it was the June 6, 1944, invasion of Normandy that went down in history as *the* D-Day.

A truly awe-inspiring display of military might, the D-Day invasion of the coast of Nazi-occupied France represented the largest all-out offensive in world history. Although the loss of life on the Allies' part was massive, there was no way the Germans could have repelled such a relentless assault.

What happened at Normandy?

Normandy, a region in northwestern France that lies along the English Channel, is known for the June 6, 1944, arrival of Allied troops that proved to be a turning point in World War II. Officially called Operation Overlord (but known historically as D-Day) and headed by U.S. General Dwight D. Eisenhower (1890–1969), the initiative had been in the planning since 1943, and it constituted the largest seaborne invasion in history. After several delays due to poor weather, the Allied troops crossed the English Channel and arrived on the beaches of Normandy on the morning of June 6.

Brutal fighting ensued that day, with heavy losses on both sides. At the end of the day, the Allied troops had taken hold of the beaches—a firm foothold that would allow them to march inland against the Nazis, eventually pushing them back to Germany. While it was a critical Allied victory (which history has treated as the beginning of the end for German chancellor and führer Adolf Hitler), the invasion at Normandy was still to be followed by eleven more months of bloody conflict; Germany would not surrender until May 7, 1945.

Who was George Marshall, and what was his plan?

George Marshall (1880–1959) was the leading American military leader during World War II. Marshall served as Chief of Staff of the Army and oversaw the U.S. war plans with its Allies. He served as President Franklin D. Roosevelt's chief military advisor during the war. British Prime Minister Winston Churchill once referred to Marshall as the "organizer of victory."

Marshall did not lead troops into battle, but he had a key role in the overarching plans and strategic thinking. He also handpicked or recommended many of the top American generals, including Eisenhower and George S. Patton (1885–1945). Marshall later served as both as secretary of state and then secretary of defense under President Harry S. Truman (1884–1972). Marshall earned the Nobel Peace Prize for his role in constructing the so-called "Marshall Plan," designed to provide economic relief to struggling European countries in the post-World War II world. Later, President Truman once said of Marshall: "I don't think in this age in which I have lived that there has been a man who has been a greater administrator, a man with a knowledge of military affairs equal to General Marshall."

What was the Bataan Death March?

The Bataan Death March was one of the most brutal chapters of World War II. On April 9, 1942, American forces on the Bataan Peninsula of the Philippines surrendered to the Japanese. More than seventy-five thousand American and Filipino troops became prisoners of war (POWs). On April 10, they were forced to begin a sixty-five-mile march to a POW camp. Conditions were torturous—high temperatures, meager provisions, and gross maltreatment. The troops were denied food and water for days at a time; they were not allowed to rest in the shade; they were indiscriminately beaten; those who fell behind were killed. On stretches where some troops were transported by train, the boxcars were packed so tightly that many POWs died of suffocation. The forced march lasted more than a week. Twenty thousand men died along the way.

But the end of the march was not the end of the horrors for the surviving POWs. About fifty-six thousand men were held until the end of the war. They endured starvation, torture, and horrific cruelties; some were forced to work as slave laborers in Japanese industrial plants, and some became subjects of medical experiments. In August 1945 their POW camp was liberated by the Allied forces, and the surviving troops were put on U.S. Navy vessels for the trip home. As part of the United States's 1951 peace treaty with Japan, surviving POWs were barred from seeking reparations from Japanese firms that had benefited from their slave labor. This injustice continued to be the subject of proposed Congressional legislation into the early 2000s, with no positive outcome for the veterans as of 2005.

Why was the Battle of Midway important in World War II?

It was the turning point for the Allied forces fighting the Japanese in the Pacific. The battle for Midway Island (actually two small islands situated about thirteen hundred miles west-northwest of Honolulu, Hawaii) began on June 4, 1942. The Japanese aimed to control Midway as a position from which its air force could launch further attacks on

Hawaii. As the Japanese fleet approached the islands, which were home to a U.S. Navy base (established in 1941), U.S. forces attacked. Fighting continued until June 6. The Japanese were decisively defeated, losing four aircraft carriers; the United States lost one. The victory proved that Allied naval might could overcome Japan's.

In what World War II battle did aircraft carriers engage?

Aircraft carriers from the United States and Japan first squared off in the Battle of the Coral Sea (near Australia and the Solomon Islands), fought in May 1942. The battle was important because it repre-sented the first time Allied forces had

The USS *Yorktown* is shown here as it is hit by a Japanese torpedo during the Battle of Midway. The *Yorktown* would sink, but the Americans won this decisive battle in the Pacific theater.

thwarted Japanese expansionism. Each side claimed victory after the conflict. Histori-ans view the battle as significant in that it represented a new type of naval warfare.

What was decided at the Yalta Conference?

In February 1945, President Roosevelt met with Soviet Premier Joseph Stalin and British Prime Minister Winston Churchill in the Crimean town of Yalta. At this point of the war, Roosevelt knew Germany would soon be defeated, but victory in the Pacific was somewhat less certain. So he made an agreement with the Soviet Union that if they agreed to de-clare war on Japan and help with the effort to conclude that chapter of the conflict, the United States would grant a number of concessions in Europe. In essence, the conference set up what would become the Eastern Bloc of European nations that would come under the influence of Soviet Russia (Eastern Europe would become Communist). In addition, the Russians would be allowed to have influence over Manchuria in Asia. Initially, the Yalta Conference was considered a success, but it wouldn't be too long before politicians and historians would conclude that the Soviets were given far too much power.

What happened on Iwo Jima?

During February 1945, Allied forces and the Japanese fought for control of Iwo Jima, a small island in the northwest Pacific Ocean, 759 miles south of Tokyo. Japan was using Iwo Jima as a base from which to launch air attacks on U.S. bombers in the Pacific. Cap-turing the island from the Japanese became a key objective for the United States. On Feb-ruary 19, 1945, the Fourth and Fifth U.S. Marine Divisions invaded the island.

Fighting over the next several days claimed more than six thousand U.S. troops. On the morning of February 23, after a rigorous climb to the top of Mount Suribachi (Iwo

Jima's 550-foot inactive volcano), U.S. Marines planted an American flag. Although small, it was visible from around the island. Later that day, a larger flag was raised atop Mount Suribachi by five Marines and a navy hospital corpsman. The moment was captured by American news photographer Joe Rosenthal. His famous photo became the inspiration for the U.S. Marine Corps Memorial (dedicated November 10, 1954) in Arlington, Virginia.

What top American flying ace died after a plane malfunction?

Richard Bong (1920–1945) was the top American flying ace during World War II in terms of number of enemy aircraft shot down. During World War II engagements, Bong shot down forty enemy planes. A fighter pilot in the Air Force, he earned the Medal of Honor, the Silver Star, and other military honors for his accomplishments. Born in Wisconsin, Bong joined the Army Air Corps Aviation Cadet Program. One of his instructors there was future U.S. Senator and U.S. presidential candidate Barry Goldwater (1909–1998). Bong engaged in numerous combat missions against the Japanese in and around the Philippines. He flew two hundred combat missions during World War II, earning the moniker "Ace of Aces." Sadly, he died in August 1945 while working as a test pilot for Lockheed. He was inducted in the National Aviation Hall of Fame. His former mentor George C. Kenney (1889–1977) wrote a book appropriately entitled *Ace of Aces: The Dick Bong Story*.

What ultimate weapon did President Truman sanction in order to end World War II?

Truman ordered the use of the atomic bomb on Japan, who would not surrender. He reasoned that the dropping of the bomb would save American lives, as it was estimated that half a million American troops or Allied forces would die if an invasion took place in

Who were the Code Talkers?

Code Talkers were Navajo Indians who provided secure communications for the U.S. military's Pacific operations during World War II. Serving in the Marines, the Navajo servicemen were recruited because of their language, which is unwritten and extremely complex. Military officials believed the Japanese would not be able to decipher intercepted communiqués transmitted in Navajo.

The first Navajo recruits attended boot camp in May 1942 and developed and memorized a dictionary of military terms to use in encrypting messages. The trained code talkers were deployed with Marine units throughout the Pacific theater. They worked around the clock, with tremendous speed and accuracy, to transmit vital information about military tactics, battle orders, and troop movements. Their messages were sent over telephone and radio; because of the complexity of the language, the Japanese military was never able to break the code. About four hundred Navajos served as Code Talkers during the war, contributing mightily to the success of U.S. military assaults at Guadalcanal, Iwo Jima, and other Pacific venues.

Japan. The first bomb was dropped on Hiroshima on August 6, 1945. When Japan refused to surrender, he ordered the military to drop another atomic bomb on Nagasaki on August 9, 1945. Japan asked for peace the very next day and surrendered soon after that.

While the loss of lives was horrific, some historians contend that without dropping the bombs, Japan may not have surrendered, and more lives would have been lost. The United States surely would have had to lose many more troops if it invaded Japan.

What was the *Enola Gay*?

The *Enola Gay* was the name of the American B–29 bomber that dropped the first atomic bomb ever used in warfare. On August 6, 1945, the *Enola Gay* flew over Hiroshima to drop an A-bomb over the city. The explosion killed an estimated eighty thousand people, and leveled an area of about five square miles in Hiroshima, an important manufacturing and military center. Thousands more died later from radiation exposure.

What are "V-E Day" and "V-J Day"?

"V-E Day" stands for Victory in Europe Day, and "V-J Day" stands for Victory over Japan Day. After the German surrender was signed in Reims, France (the headquarters of General Eisenhower), in the wee hours of May 7, 1945, U.S. President Harry S. Truman declared May 8 "V-E Day"—the end of the World War II fighting in Europe.

But it was not until the Japanese agreed to surrender on August 14, 1945, that World War II ended. September 2, 1945, was declared the official "V-J Day," since that was when Japan signed the terms of surrender on the USS *Missouri* anchored in Tokyo Bay.

The *Enola Gay,* which dropped the atomic bomb on Hiroshima, can be viewed at the Steven F. Udvary-Hazy Center at the National Air and Space Museum in Washington, D.C.

Why did Einstein write to President Roosevelt urging U.S. development of the atomic bomb?

Albert Einstein (1879–1955), born in Germany and educated in Switzerland (where he also became a naturalized citizen), was an ardent pacifist. But, being a brilliant observer, he quickly perceived the threat posed by Nazi Germany. Einstein was visiting England in 1933 when the Nazis confiscated his property in Berlin and deprived him of his German citizenship. Some might call it lucky that the Nobel Prize-winning (1921) scientist was out of the country when this happened—in the coming years, other Jews certainly suffered worse fates, as Nazi Germany under despotic ruler Adolf Hitler (1889–1945) persecuted and killed more than six million Jews.

Einstein moved to the United States, where he took a position at the Institute for Advanced Study in Princeton, New Jersey. There he settled and later became an American citizen (1940). In August 1939, just before Hitler's troops invaded Poland and began World War II, Einstein wrote a letter to President Roosevelt, urging him to launch a government program to study nuclear energy. He further advocated that the United States build an atomic bomb, cautioning that such an effort might already be underway in Germany.

The United States did in fact begin developing the atomic bomb, which releases nuclear energy by splitting heavy atomic particles. The program was called the Manhattan Project, and it was centered at Oak Ridge, Tennessee, and Hanford, Washington, where scientists worked to obtain sufficient amounts of plutonium and uranium to make the bombs. The bombs themselves were developed in a laboratory in Los Alamos, New Mexico. The project was funded by the government to the tune of $2 billion. The first atomic device (made of plutonium) was tested in Alamogordo, New Mexico, on July 16, 1945. Less than a month later, the United States dropped atomic bombs on Hiroshima and Nagasaki.

After the war, Einstein—who was always interested in world and human affairs and regretted the death and destruction in Japan—advocated a system of world law that he believed could prevent war in the atomic (or nuclear) age. A Zionist Jew, in 1952 he was offered the presidency of the relatively new state of Israel (founded in 1948), but he declined the honor. He died in New Jersey in 1955.

What American scientist is often called the "Father of the Atomic Bomb"?

Julius Robert Oppenheimer (1904–1967) is often called the "Father of the Atomic Bomb." A physics professor at the University of California, Berkeley, Oppenheimer was the head of the Manhattan Project. Oppenheimer worked with a group of leading scientists, including the Italian–born Enrico Fermi (1901–1954), and under the direction of Lieutenant General Leslie Groves (1896–1970).

Following World War II, Oppenheimer—seeing the devastating and awesome power of the atomic bomb his laboratory had created—became a vocal advocate of international control of atomic energy. When the United States began developing the hydrogen bomb (also called a "thermonuclear bomb" because of the high temperatures it requires in order to create a reaction), Oppenheimer objected on both moral and technical grounds: The hydrogen bomb was a far more destructive weapon than the atomic bomb.

In 1953, Oppenheimer was suspended from the U.S. Atomic Energy Commission (AEC) because he was believed to pose a threat to national security. Hearings were held, but the New York-born scientist was cleared of charges of disloyalty. A decade later, in 1963, the organization gave Oppenheimer its highest honor, the Enrico Fermi Award, for his contributions to theoretical physics. Indeed, Oppenheimer had done much to further the science during his lifetime: At the University of California, Berkeley ("UC Berkeley"), he established a center for research in theoretical physics; taught at the California Institute of Technology; and served as director of the Institute for Advanced Study from 1947–1966. There he met Einstein, who worked at the institute from 1933 until his death in 1955.

What occurred at the Potsdam Conference?

The Potsdam Conference (in Potsdam, Germany) was the follow-up to Yalta, where the leaders of the Soviet Union, Britain, France, and the United States met before the end of the war, agreeing to meet after Germany's surrender to decide such issues as the determination of new national borders. Winston Churchill was replaced by Prime Minister Clement Atlee, and President Truman took the place of the deceased President Roosevelt. The Allied Control Commission was set up, in which Britain, the United

President Harry S. Truman (seated center) is flanked by Soviet leader Joseph Stalin (right) and British Prime Minister Clement Attlee at the 1945 Potsdam Conference.

States, the Soviet Union, and France would divide Germany into four occupation zones until a new German government could be established. Terms for reparations were also established, in which Germany would pay these countries for the costs of the war. Unlike Roosevelt, President Truman was more suspicious of Stalin and the Russians, and he also wanted to be somewhat less harsh on the Germans when it came to reparations (many believed that extremely harsh penalties against Germany after World War I had contributed to the rise of the Nazis).

Other major effects of Potsdam included the establishment of a new Poland, in which that country received large areas of what had been Germany, and also deported most Germans from that land. A Council of Foreign Ministers was created to negotiate terms between Germany's former allies and the United States, Soviet Union, Britain, and China.

The conference lasted from July 17 to August 2, 1945 (before Japan surrendered). A formal statement was issued by the Allies to Japan that it must surrender unconditionally and immediately or face utter destruction. It was during this time, too, that President Truman told Stalin that the Americans had successfully tested the first nuclear bomb.

POSTWAR PERIOD

What U.S. senator in 1945 delivered a "speech heard 'round the world"?

Arthur Vandenberg (1884–1951) delivered his "speech heard 'round the world" in January 1945. A Republican from Michigan, Vandenberg served in the Senate from 1928 until his death in 1951. In his most famous speech, Vandenberg announced that he now supported a general foreign policy of working with other Allied countries instead of pursuing a policy of isolationism. He also emphasized his willingness to put aside political differences with the Democratic president to further the best interests of the country. In the following passage, Vandenberg emphasized the need to move beyond complete self-interest:

> The next thing we need to do, Mr. President, if I may be so bold, in this spirit of honest candor, is to appeal to our Allies, in the name of reason, to frankly face the postwar alternatives which are available to them, and to us, as a means to preserve tomorrow's peace for them and for us.
>
> There are two ways to do it. One way is by exclusive individual action in which each of us tries to look out for himself. The other way is by joint action in which each of us undertake to look out for each other.
>
> The first way is the old way that has twice taken us to Europe's interminable battlefields within a quarter century. The second way is the new way in which our present fraternity of war becomes a new fraternity of peace. I do not believe that either we or our Allies can have it both ways. They serve to cancel out each other. We cannot tolerate unilateral privilege in a multilateral peace. Yet that

seems to be the fatalistic trend today. I think we must make our choice. I think we need to make it wholly plain to our major Allies that they, too, must make their choice.

I hasten to make my own personal viewpoint clear. I have always been frankly one of those who has believed in our own self-reliance. I still believe that we can never again—regardless of collaborations—allow our national defense to deteriorate to anything like a point of impotence. But I do not believe that any nation hereafter can immunize itself by its own exclusive action.

Vandenberg is considered one of the greatest senators in American history. He is one of only nine U.S. senators to have his portrait displayed in the Senate Reception Room. The other eight are Daniel Webster, John C. Calhoun, Henry Clay, Robert La Follette, Robert Taft, Oliver Ellsworth, Thomas Hart Benton, and John F. Wagner.

What constitutional amendment was passed in response to FDR's long tenure as president?

The Twenty-Second Amendment—sometimes dubbed the "FDR amendment"—prohibits anyone from serving as president for more than two full terms. Ratified in 1951, the measure provides:

> No person shall be elected to the office of the president more than twice, and no person who has held the office of president, or acted as president, for more than two years of a term to which some other person was elected president shall be elected to the office of the president more than once. But this Article shall not apply to any person holding the office of president, when this Article was proposed by the Congress, and shall not prevent any person who may be holding the office of president, or acting as president, during the term within which this Article becomes operative from holding the office of president or acting as president during the remainder of such term.

What other significant act was passed after World War II that affected American leadership?

The Presidential Succession Act of 1947 was signed by President Truman to supersede changes made in 1886. In the original Presidential Succession Act of 1792, if the president died or was otherwise unable to perform his duties, he would be succeeded by the

What famous saying was on President Truman's desk?

Truman had a sign on his desk that read, "The Buck Stops Here." It became a mantra associated with Truman, who recognized that he had to make tough decisions as the country's commander in chief.

vice president, followed by the president pro tempore of the Senate and then the Speaker of the House of Representatives. When businessmen such as the Carnegies and Rockefellers started to become so wealthy in the 1880s that they were influencing politics, the Presidential Succession Act of 1886 was passed, replacing the president pro tempore and Speaker with a series of Cabinet secretaries (career politicians being replaced in power with secretaries often coming from the business world). The 1947 Act signed by Truman reversed that again, making the line of succession as follows: vice president, speaker of the House, president pro tempore of the Senate, secretary of state, secretary of the treasury, secretary of defense, and attorney general, etc.

What was the Fair Deal?

President Harry S. Truman's "Fair Deal" was the name given to his policies for improving the lives of average Americans. His domestic "Fair Deal" program included federal funding for housing, increases in the minimum wage, improved civil rights, and increased Social Security benefits.

What was the Truman Doctrine?

The Truman Doctrine was a foreign policy that stressed that the United States must help other countries to contain and prevent the spread of communism. Truman said in a 1947 speech: "I believe it must be the policy of the United States to support free peoples who are resisting attempted subjugation by armed minorities or by outside pressures." He said this to justify U.S. aid to Greece and Turkey to counter the threat of Soviet influence.

The Truman Doctrine helped lead to active U.S. involvement in the North Atlantic Treaty Organization—a military agreement between various European countries.

What is NATO?

NATO stands for the North Atlantic Treaty Organization, a military alliance formed on April 4, 1949, when twelve countries (Belgium, Canada, Denmark, France, Iceland, Italy, Luxembourg, the Netherlands, Norway, Portugal, the United Kingdom, and the United States) signed the North Atlantic Treaty in Washington, D.C. Each member nation agreed to treat attacks on any other member nation as if it were an attack on itself. In other words, any aggressor would have to face the entire alliance. This was NATO's policy of deterrence, a way of discouraging any attacks by the Soviet Union or other Eastern Bloc countries. The organization had the

Seated left to right at a table during a NATO summit in Newport, Wales, are France's President François Hollande, Ukraine's President Petro Poroshenko, U.S. President Barack Obama, British Prime Minister David Cameron, German Chancellor Angela Merkel, and Italy's Prime Minister Matteo Renzi.

further benefit of discouraging fighting among the member countries. In 1952, the alliance was joined by Greece and Turkey.

What executive order did Truman issue that changed the composition of the military?

Truman issued Executive Order 9981 on July 26, 1948, which called for "equality of treatment and opportunity for all persons in the armed forces without regard to race, color, religion or national origin." This led to the desegregation of the American military and is considered a milestone in the quest for civil rights in the United States.

Who tried to assassinate President Truman?

On November 1, 1950, Griselio Torresola and Oscar Collazo, Puerto Rican nationalists, shot at guards outside Blair House—the house in Washington, D.C., where President Truman lived while the White House was being renovated. The two men wanted to draw worldwide attention to the cause of independence for Puerto Rico. One guard and Torresola were killed during the gunfire. Collazo and two guards were injured. Collazo was convicted and sentenced to death. Truman, who did not believe in capital punishment, commuted his sentence to life in prison. He became eligible for parole in 1966 but remained in prison until President Jimmy Carter granted him clemency; he was released for time served.

THE KOREAN WAR

What other war with U.S. involvement occurred while Truman was president?

The Korean War took place from 1950–1953. At the end of World War II, Korea—which had been conquered by Japan—was divided into North and South Korea. North Korea was a Communist country, while South Korea was a democratic country. When North Korea invaded South Korea, Truman believed military action was necessary to stop the spread of communism.

How was the Thirty-Eighth Parallel established as a border between North and South Korea?

Japan had occupied the Korean Peninsula as part of its empire from 1910 until the end of World War II, when the United States and the Soviet Union agreed to divide it into North and South, with the border being the Thirty-Eighth Parallel. The Soviets put the North into trusteeship, and the Americans did the same with the South.

How did the United States get involved in the Korean War?

Because the United States did not emphasize the importance of the Korean peninsula as part of its foreign policy, the leader of North Korea, Kim Il-Sung, saw this as a sign that South Korea would not get support from the Americans if needed. Therefore, the North Koreans decided to invade South Korea in an attempt to reunify the country. The United States, it turned out, would not put up with this and, enlisting the backing of the United Nations, aided the South. The situation worsened considerably when China sent troops to back the North in 1950, and a protracted war was the result. In 1953, the two sides called a truce, but, technically, North and South Korea are still at war to this day.

With what famous general did Truman clash with and later relieve of duty?

Truman clashed with General Douglas MacArthur over the Korean War. MacArthur's soldiers and UN troops had pushed North Korean forces past the Thirty-Eighth Parallel. However, when MacArthur pushed into North Korea, China sent thousands of troops into North Korea, forcing a retreat by UN forces.

MacArthur urged President Truman to approve of military action against China. Truman, fearing the development of World War III, declined. This led to the Korean War's ending in a stalemate rather than a clear victory. MacArthur publicly challenged Truman's authority, declaring "there is no substitute for victory." Truman fired MacArthur for challenging his authority as commander in chief.

SOCIAL CONFLICT AND CHANGE: 1950s–1970s

THE BEAT GENERATION, HIPPIES, AND FLOWER POWER

What was the Beat Generation?

After World War II, and even before the Baby Boomer generation of the 1960s, a countercultural movement was beginning in the United States that questioned earlier generations' standards concerning money, work, sexuality, and religion. The term, coined by author Jack Kerouac, has been interpreted multiple ways: "beat," meaning tired, then later possibly referring to "beatific" in a spiritual way. The Beats wished to shrug off the dreary conventions of working to earn money and conforming to social norms by liberating the spirit through drugs, sex, jazz music, and Eastern spiritual practices, especially Zen Buddhism.

Who coined the word "Beatniks"?

Beatniks were social radicals who dressed shabbily or in dark clothes, spoke the language of jazz musicians (even if they were not themselves musicians), were interested in poetry and spirituality, and rejected what they viewed to be a materialistic culture. The word, obviously derived from Beat, was coined by San Francisco journalist Herb Caen in 1958. In the media, such as television and movies, Beatniks were usually portrayed as negative characters—violent, shiftless, and lazy.

Which literary figures influenced the Beat Generation in America?

A number of authors heavily influenced and inspired the Beat movement. Most prominent among them were Jack Kerouac (1922–1969), whose 1957 novel *On the Road* was based on his travels across America; poet Allen Ginsberg (1927–1996), the author of

Howl (1955), an epic poem lamenting the loss of America's youth; and William S. Burroughs (1914–1997), the author of the mind-bending novel *Naked Lunch* (1959). Poets Gregory Corso (1930–2001), Lawrence Ferlinghetti (1919–), and Gary Snyder (1930–) were others.

What was meant by "Flower Power"?

Coined by Allen Ginsberg in 1965, Flower Power referred to the concept of passive resistance against military and police force. "Flower Children" who followed this concept also vehemently opposed the Vietnam War and supported rights for women, homosexuals, and other minorities. They also tended to be environmentalists and concerned about animal welfare.

Who were the hippies?

Most hippies of the 1960s and 1970s were young (fifteen to twenty-five years old), white, and from middle-class families. The counterculture (antiestablishment) movement advocated peace, love, and beauty. Having dropped out (of modern society) and tuned in (to their own feelings), these Flower Children were as well known for their political and social beliefs as they were for their controversial lifestyle: They opposed American involvement in the Vietnam War, rejecting an industrialized society that seemed to care only about money; they favored personal simplicity, sometimes living in small communes where possessions and work were shared, or living an itinerant lifestyle, in which day-to-day responsibilities were few, if any; they wore tattered jeans and bright clothing, usually of natural fabrics, grew their hair, braided beads into their locks, walked around barefoot or in sandals, and listened to a new generation of artists, including the Beatles, the Grateful Dead, Jefferson Airplane, Bob Dylan, and Joan Baez. Some hippies were also known for their drug use: Experimenting with marijuana and LSD, some hoped to gain profound insights or even achieve salvation through the drug experience—something hippie guru Timothy Leary told them was possible. New York City's East Village and San Francisco's Haight-Ashbury neighborhood became countercultural havens. The movement began on American soil but was soon embraced elsewhere as well—principally Canada and Great Britain.

Why does Woodstock remain such an iconic image of the 1960s counterculture?

Considered one of the most pivotal events in modern American music history, the Woodstock Music and Art Fair was held from August 15–18, 1969, in upstate New York. During the event, some of the most

Cars like the VW bug and this VW bus became symbols of the hippie generation. Hippies often hand-painted the cars and traveled the country, sleeping in their vehicles or camping as part of their free-spirited lifestyle.

famous musicians of the time performed (many before they were famous), including Jimi Hendrix, The Who, Jefferson Airplane, Ravi Shankar, Janis Joplin, Joe Cocker, Joan Baez, Santana, the Grateful Dead, Creedence Clearwater Revival, and Crosby, Stills, Nash & Young. The event became a free-for-all, especially when the false rumor was spread that the concert was free (the organizers had wanted to make money from the concert, but it got out of hand). As a result, 400,000 people showed up. There were no facilities to support them all, and things like potable water and toilet facilities became scarce. Rain turned the open field into a muddy slip-and-slide; many in the audience took drugs and sometimes went naked. The entire intense event became a symbol of the mantra "Sex, Drugs, and Rock 'n' Roll."

What was "psychedelic music" and culture?

Psychedelic music, art, and culture in general attempted to capture the experience of drug use and mind-freeing philosophies. Artists used bright colors and blended images to try to emulate hallucinogenic experiences (tie-dyed shirts also reflected the style, as did lava lamps and the use of black lighting). Psychedelic music could refer to many genres, including everything from soul, folk, and rock to Indian sitar and other non-Western music.

What American psychologist, professor, and Harvard researcher had a tremendous influence on the 1960s counterculture?

Dr. Timothy Leary (1920–1996) graduated from UC Berkeley, teaching there and later at Harvard. From 1959–1963, while at Harvard, he was also a researcher and became interested in the possibilities of hallucinogenic drugs to treat psychological disorders. The one he felt showed promise

Dr. Timothy Leary is seen here giving a lecture at the State University of New York at Buffalo in 1969. Leary advocated the use of LSD, under the supervision of a psychologist, as a way of treating alcoholism and certain psychological disorders.

203

was lysergic acid diethylamide (LSD). Leary organized experiments on prisoners and then students, having them take the then-legal drug and recording their reactions.

Leary traveled the country, lecturing about the benefits of LSD, but only under the supervision of a trained psychologist. He felt it was useful in helping to reform criminals and in treating alcoholism. His research, showing that many subjects in his experiments reported enlightening spiritual experiences, appealed to young people at the time, and LSD became a favorite experimental drug. The federal government made LSD possession illegal in 1968; however, it was still used to treat some cancer patients until 1980. Today, research into possible benefits of the drug has resumed around the world.

What happened at Kent State University (Ohio) in May 1970?

In May 1970, protests occurred on the Kent State campus in reaction to President Nixon's announcement regarding an invasion of Cambodia and an escalation of the Vietnam War. There were protests on college campuses nationwide; Kent State was no exception. On May 2, 1970, with tensions running high, the Ohio National Guard was called in to help restore order. The guards carried M–1 rifles. A wooden ROTC building was set on fire and burned to the ground.

A rally was scheduled for noon on May 4. However, a large throng of demonstrators was present on campus, and tensions rose even higher than before. The head of the Ohio National Guard, Robert Canterbury, issued an order to disperse the crowd of demonstrators.

Rocks were thrown at the Guardsmen. Some guards may have felt they were in dire danger, and they fired in self-defense. Others view it as an unjustified action. For whatever reason, many Guardsmen fired their guns into the air. However, a few Guardsmen fired into the crowd. Four students (Jeffrey Miller, Allison Beth Krause, William Knox Schroeder, and Sandra Lee Scheuer) were killed; nine more were injured.

A grand jury indicted eight members of the Ohio National Guard. However, a federal district court judge dismissed the criminal charges. Civil actions were brought against the Guardsmen, the state of Ohio, and Kent State. A federal civil jury ruled in favor of the defendants. However, the plaintiffs appealed to the Sixth U.S. Circuit Court of Appeals, which reversed. After this reversal, the parties reached a settlement. The signed statement by the defendants stated:

> In retrospect, the tragedy of May 4, 1970, should not have occurred. The students may have believed that they were right in continuing their mass protest in response to the Cambodian invasion, even though this protest followed the posting and reading by the university of an order to ban rallies and an order to disperse. These orders have since been determined by the Sixth Circuit Court of Appeals to have been lawful.

> Some of the Guardsmen on Blanket Hill, fearful and anxious from prior events, may have believed in their own minds that their lives were in danger. Hindsight suggests that another method would have resolved the confrontation. Better ways must be found to deal with such a confrontation.

We devoutly wish that a means had been found to avoid the May 4th events culminating in the Guard shootings and the irreversible deaths and injuries. We deeply regret those events and are profoundly saddened by the deaths of four students and the wounding of nine others which resulted. We hope that the agreement to end the litigation will help to assuage the tragic memories regarding that sad day.

What Pulitzer Prize-winning photograph occurred in the aftermath of the shooting?

John Paul Filo (1948–), a photojournalism student at Kent State, took a photograph of fourteen-year-old Mary Ann Vecchio standing over a slain Jeffrey Miller. The photograph was published by the *Valley Daily News*, a satellite of the *Pittsburgh Tribune-Review*, where Filo worked as a staffer. It remains a stark and searing reminder of the violence and horror that occurred at Kent State that day.

OTHER STRUGGLES IN HUMAN RIGHTS

What were the "Stonewall Riots"?

The Stonewall Riots were a series of spontaneous demonstrations by gays and lesbians in Greenwich Village in New York City in late June 1969. The riots were a direct response to allegedly repressive police conduct at a gay club in the Village known as the Stonewall Inn. The police allegedly targeted the club because it was operating without a liquor license, in violation of the law. However, many believed the police action was simply an overreaction and another example of police-targeted activity at gay bars. The protest turned violent, as angry demonstrators hurled bottles and other objects at police officers. The demonstrations were quelled only after the New York City Riot Police Squad was deployed.

The Stonewall Riots are seen as a key moment in the history of the gay rights movement. In fact, the Stonewall Riots are often seen as the beginning of the LGBT movement (despite two prior decades of organizing in the U.S. and earlier efforts in Europe). Within two years of the riots, several major gay rights groups emerged. Just one year later, the first Gay Liberation Day March was held in New York City.

Who was Harvey Milk?

Harvey Milk (1930–1978) was the first openly gay politician elected in the state of California. He won election to the San Francisco Board of Supervisors in 1977. He was instrumental in helping to pass a gay rights ordinance for the city. He also urged gays and lesbians to be open about their sexuality and advocate for their rights. In November 1978, Milk was assassinated by former San Francisco Board of Supervisors member Dan White. Milk became a martyr for the gay rights movement in the United States. In 2008, a film about his life—appropriately titled *Milk*—won eight Academy Awards, including

Best Picture and Best Actor for Sean Penn (1960–), who played the leading role.

What is feminism?

Feminism is the belief that there should be equality between the sexes and that political and social activism is needed to achieve this equality.

What was the ERA?

ERA stands for the Equal Rights Amendment, a constitutional amendment proposed by Congress in 1972. It stated that "equality of rights under the law shall not be denied or abridged by the United States or any state on account of sex." In proposing the amendment, Congress gave the states ten years in which to ratify it. But by 1982, only thirty-five of the necessary thirty-eight states approved the amendment. The failure to ratify the ERA was the result of disagreement over how the language would be interpreted. Supporters believed the amendment would guarantee women equal treatment under the law; opponents feared the amendment might require women to forfeit the financial support of their husbands and require them to serve in the military.

Harvey Milk is seen in this 1973 photo with his sister-in-law, Audrey Milk, during a campaign in the Castro District of San Francisco. Although Milk served less than a year as a San Francisco city supervisor, his work for gay rights and his 1978 assassination set him up as a martyr in the gay community.

What did the U.S. Supreme Court decide in *Roe v. Wade*?

The Court, under Chief Justice Warren Burger, ruled 7–2 in *Roe v. Wade* that the "Fourteenth Amendment's concept of personal liberty ... is broad enough to encompass a woman's decision whether or not to terminate her pregnancy." The Court determined that the Fourteenth Amendment's due process clause and its liberty interest included a woman's right of personal privacy to have an abortion. The Court did not rule that women have an unfettered constitutional right to decide whether to have an abortion. Rather, Justice Harry Blackmun's opinion balanced a woman's interest in personal privacy against the state's interest in protecting future life. Blackmun's opinion divided the pregnancy term into three periods, or trimesters. During the first trimester, a woman has an unqualified right to have an abortion. During the second trimester, the state can regulate abortions "in ways that are reasonably related to maternal health." During the last trimester—when the fetus becomes viable, or able to live outside the mother's womb—the state can regulate and even prohibit abortions. The Court also determined that a fetus was not a person within the meaning of the Fourteenth Amendment.

The Court's decision invalidated a Texas law that criminalized abortions except when the abortion was necessary to save the life of the mother.

Who is Gloria Steinem?

A journalist and founder of *Ms.* magazine, Gloria Steinem (1934–) was a leader of the feminist movement, most visibly in the 1960s and 1970s. She campaigned for the Equal Rights Amendment and, in 1971, helped found the National Women's Political Caucus.

Who was Betty Friedan?

Betty Friedan (1921–2006) authored the 1963 book *The Feminine Mystique,* which many credit with sparking the feminist movement of the 1960s. She was also the founder and first president of the National Organization for Women. Friedan also founded the National Association for the Repeal of Abortion Laws (now the NARAL Pro-Choice America). Although, of course, strongly for women's rights, in her later life she often criticized more extreme feminists.

Ms. magazine founder Gloria Steinem was a leader in the feminist movement.

Who was César Chávez?

Mexican American farm worker César Chávez (1927–1993) was a labor union organizer and spokesperson for the poor. Born in Arizona, his family lost their farm when he was just ten years old; they became migrant workers in California, where farm production—particularly of grape crops—depended on the temporary laborers. Chávez knew the migrant worker's life intimately, and as a young man he began working to improve conditions for his people. In 1962 he organized California grape pickers into the National Farm Workers Association. Four years later, this union merged with another to form the United Farm Workers Organizing Committee, or UFWOC (the name was changed to the United Farm Workers of America, or UFW, in 1973). An impassioned speaker known for crushing bunches of grapes in his hands as he delivered his messages, Chávez went on to lead a nationwide boycott of table grapes, since growers refused to accept the collective bargaining efforts of the UFWOC. By the end of the 1970s, California growers of all crops had accepted the migrant workers' union. Like Martin Luther King, Jr., Chávez maintained that nonviolent protest was the key to achieving change.

When did the modern environmental movement start?

The first Earth Day (April 22, 1970) is often used as a marker for the beginning of modern environmentalism in America. The 1960s and 1970s saw increasing concern about pollution, especially air and water pollution. Another spark in the movement was the 1962 bestselling book by Rachel Carson, *Silent Spring,* which forecast a world in which wildlife was devastated and the world severely polluted by industry run amok without government regulations.

The movement built upon student antiwar sentiments, but the actual idea for Earth Day came from U.S. Senator and Governor Gaylord Nelson (1916–2005) of Wisconsin, who was very active in environmental conservation. Today, the movement, while still concerned with pollution, has been focusing on the issue of climate change.

THE CIVIL RIGHTS MOVEMENT

What impact did World War II have on civil rights?

World War II played a major impact on the burgeoning concept of civil rights for African Americans. Numerous African Americans joined the war effort, many to escape numbing poverty. While the armed forces were segregated, the war effort brought at least some mingling of the races. Many African Americans fought bravely in the war, earning the respect of many of their white colleagues. Some thoughtful Americans of all races also noticed the dissonance between the United States of America in combating and opposing the racial hatred espoused by Nazi Germany and Führer Adolf Hitler, but then practicing discrimination and segregation at home. Furthermore, many African American soldiers noticed less discrimination in countries such as France and became less satisfied with the negative conditions in the United States. This provided an opportunity for many to question segregation more forcefully and persistently.

When did racial segregation end in the Armed Forces?

In 1947, civil rights leader A. Philip Randolph (1889–1979) helped form the Committee Against Jim Crow in Military Service. It ended on July 26, 1948, when President Truman signed Executive Order 9981, which stated: "It is hereby declared to be the policy of the president that there shall be equality of treatment and opportunity for all persons in the armed services without regard to race, color, religion, or national origin."

What Supreme Court decision inspired the civil rights movement?

The U.S. Supreme Court's decision in *Brown v. Board of Education of Topeka, Kansas* (1954) invaliding segregated public education inspired the civil rights movement. The Supreme Court ruled that segregation in public education violated the Equal Protection Clause of the Fourteenth Amendment. The decision inspired countless people who believed that the promise of civil rights and equality could become reality. The decision in *Brown* led to a series of lawsuits that challenged segregation in nearly all aspects of public life.

What was the Montgomery Bus Boycott?

The Montgomery (Alabama) Bus Boycott was a seminal point in the American Civil Rights Movement that occurred in 1955 and 1956 to protest segregation in Montgomery's transit system. Under the city's policy (and that of many others in the southeastern United States), black passengers had to sit in the back rows of the bus, while white passengers sat in the front. The boycott was inspired after the arrest of African American Rosa Parks (1913–2005), arrested after she refused to give her seat to a white passenger.

The African American community rallied to the cause and refused to use city buses. Many traveled together in carpools, rode in black-owned taxis, or walked to their jobs. Many suffered for their resistance. Parks lost her job as a seamstress as a result of her pivotal role in the protest.

In June 1956, a panel of three federal district judges ruled 2–1 in *Browder v. Gayle* that the segregated system was unconstitutional. The majority reasoned the segregation policy violated both due process and equal protection rights. The majority concluded: "We hold that the statutes and ordinances requiring segregation of the white and colored races on the motor buses of a common carrier of passengers in the City of Montgomery and its police jurisdiction violate the due process and equal protection of the law clauses of the Fourteenth Amendment to the Constitution of the United States."

Rosa Parks (seen here with Martin Luther King Jr. in the background) was key in launching the Montgomery Bus Boycott when on December 1, 1955, after a long day at her job as a seamstress, she refused to give up her seat to a white person after a bus driver told her to.

Who were some key leaders of the Montgomery Bus Boycott?

Some key leaders of the Montgomery Bus Boycott included E.D. Nixon (1899–1997), who had worked with Rosa Parks at the

NAACP; Ralph Abernathy (1926–1990), minister at the First Baptist Church; and a young minister from Dexter Avenue Baptist Church named Martin Luther King, Jr. (1929–1968). King became president of the Montgomery Improvement Association and later became the most visible leader of the civil rights movement.

What was Dr. King's background before he became involved in the civil rights movement?

Martin Luther King, Jr. was born in 1929 in Atlanta, Georgia. He was named Michael King at birth but his father, the Reverend Martin Luther King, Sr. (1899–1984), changed the boy's first name to Martin. (His father actually changed both their first names from "Michael" to "Martin" after a trip to Germany in 1934 in admiration for the great religious reformer Martin Luther [1483–1546].) King was a precocious student who skipped two grades in high school and entered Morehouse College at age fifteen. He earned a B.S. in sociology and then attended Crozer Theological Seminary near Chester, Pennsylvania, where he graduated in 1951. He then earned his doctorate degree from Boston University. King followed in his father's footsteps, agreeing to pastor Dexter Avenue Baptist Church in the mid–1950s. It was from this position that Dr. King found himself in the middle of civil rights activities.

Who were the Little Rock Nine?

The Little Rock Nine were nine African American students who integrated Little Rock Central High in 1957. Arkansas Governor Orval Faubus (1910–1994) called out the Arkansas National Guard to prevent the Little Rock Nine from entering the all-white school in September 1957. President Dwight D. Eisenhower called on a segment of the U.S. Army, ordering the National Guard to obey Army troops rather than the commands of Governor Faubus. Eisenhower believed that no state should defy rulings of the U.S. Supreme Court and the federal government: "Under the leadership of demagogic extremists, disorderly mobs have deliberately prevented the carrying out of proper orders from a federal court."

The Little Rock Nine members were Ernest Green, Elizabeth Eckford, Jefferson Thomas, Terrence Roberts, Carlotta Walls LaNier, Minnijean Brown, Gloria Ray Karl-

What was the anthem of the Civil Rights movement?

The spiritual "We Shall Overcome" was the anthem of the civil rights movement. Folk singer Pete Seeger (1919–2014) and others affiliated with People's Songs produced the song in 1947. Many other popular artists—including Joan Baez (1941–)—sang the song during the early 1960s. The music director at the Highlander Folk School, Zilphia Horton (1910–1956), is credited with creating the song with other musicians at the school in 1947. Many believe a basis for the song is Dr. Charles Tindley's (1851–1933) "I'll Overcome Someday."

mark, Thelma Mothershed, and Melba Patillo Beals. President Bill Clinton, himself a former governor of Arkansas, presented the group with Congressional gold medals in 1999.

What was the nonviolence movement?

Rev. King was committed to bringing about change by staging peaceful protests. He had carefully studied the works of Mohandas K. ("Mahatma") Gandhi (1869–1948) and was impressed by the Indian man's commitment against official authority. King led a campaign of nonviolence as part of the civil rights movement.

The most prominent hero of the 1960s Civil Rights Movement was Dr. Martin Luther King Jr.

What were the civil rights activities of Dr. Martin Luther King, Jr.?

Dr. King became the national symbol for civil rights and the pre-eminent leader of the civil rights movement. He first entered prominence as a twenty-six-year-old pastor of the Dexter Avenue Baptist Church during the Montgomery Bus Boycott. He later served as president of the Southern Christian Leadership Conference (SCLC). He helped lead civil rights protests in St. Augustine, Florida; Selma and Birmingham, Alabama; and Albany, Georgia.

He entered national consciousness when he delivered his famous "I Have A Dream" speech at the March on Washington in August 1963. He won the Nobel Peace Prize in 1964 for his nonviolent attempts to fight for racial equality. In his later years, Dr. King focused on poverty. He was assassinated on April 4, 1968, in Memphis, Tennessee.

What was the "Letter from a Birmingham Jail"?

"The Letter from a Birmingham Jail" was an open letter written by Dr. King to eight white ministers in Birmingham. King wrote the letter in response to a published letter by the eight white ministers called a "Call to Unity." The white ministers supported racial equality but disagreed with direct, nonviolent action. The ministers urged protestors not to engage in unlawful action but contended that protestors should use more patience and rely on court decisions to slowly move the country in a positive direction. They wrote: "We further strongly urge our own Negro community to withdraw support from these demonstrations and to unite locally in working peacefully for a better Birmingham. When rights are consistently denied, a cause should be pressed in the courts and in negotiations among local leaders and not in the streets. We appeal to both our white and Negro citizenry to observe the principles of law and order and common sense."

King disagreed with this more passive strategy. He said that civil rights activists must continue their push for a more just society. He famously wrote, "Injustice anywhere is an injustice everywhere." The white ministers in Birmingham had questioned the pace of the civil rights movement and the breaking of laws as a form of protest. In his letter, Dr. King emphasized that there was a difference between just laws and unjust laws. "I would agree with St. Augustine that "an unjust law is no law at all." He explained: "I submit that an individual who breaks a law that conscience tells him is unjust and willingly accepts the penalty by staying in jail to arouse the conscience of the community over its injustice is in reality expressing the very highest respect for law."

Who was Fred Shuttlesworth?

Fred Shuttlesworth (1922–2011) was a civil rights leader from Alabama during the Civil Rights Movement. He cofounded the Southern Christian Leadership Conference and the Alabama Christian Movement for Human Rights. A reverend of a Baptist Church, Shuttlesworth challenged segregation in Birmingham—often at great personal risk. Shuttlesworth's courage was legendary. Dr. King referred to him as "one of the nation's most courageous freedom fighters." Some even referred to him as the "Wild Man from Birmingham." He was nearly beaten to death by a white mob after he tried to enroll his children in a nearby all-white school. When a doctor treated him and amazingly found no concussion, he famously replied: "Doctor, the Lord knew I lived in a hard town, so he gave me a hard head."

His house and church were bombed. But Shuttlesworth survived and remained a fearless civil rights leader. He often directly challenged police commissioner Eugene "Bull" Connor (1897–1973) and other civil rights leaders. He suffered chest injuries from the spray of fire hoses on Connor's orders. Shuttlesworth later moved to Cincinnati, where he pastored a church. He moved back to Birmingham in 2008 after suffering a stroke. In 2008, the airport in Birmingham was renamed the Birmingham–Shuttlesworth International Airport.

What was the most notorious bombing during the civil rights era?

The most notorious bombing in Birmingham, Alabama, and of the entire Civil Rights Movement was the Sixteenth Street Baptist Church Bombing, an act of terrorism that

Why was Birmingham called "Bombingham"?

The city of Birmingham, Alabama, was called "Bombingham" by some because of the sheer number of bombings in black neighborhoods in the city, including at least eighteen unsolved bombings in its black neighborhoods. Dr. King called Birmingham "the most thoroughly segregated big city in the United States." He added that "[t]here have been more unsolved bombings of Negro homes and churches in Birmingham than any city in this nation."

occurred on September 15, 1963. The blast on Sunday morning killed four young, black girls: Addie Mae Collins, Cynthia Wesley, Carole Robertson, and Denise McNair. More than twenty other people were injured in the blast.

The church had been a focal point for civil rights leaders in Birmingham. Leaders such as Dr. Martin Luther King, Jr., Fred Shuttlesworth, and others used the church for meetings. Decades later, three members of the Ku Klux Klan were tried and convicted: Robert Chambliss, Thomas E. Blanton, Jr., and Bobby Frank Cherry.

What was the Children's Crusade?

The Children's Crusade was a key part of the civil rights movement in Birmingham when thousands of black students participated in what civil rights leaders referred to as "D-Day." The students skipped school and marched in the streets to protest segregation and injustice. More than six hundred students were arrested. Some of the students were even subjected to fire hoses by law enforcement officials—a fact that turned public opinion more strongly in the movement's favor. Some, including President John Fitzgerald Kennedy ("JFK") (1917–1963) and Malcolm X, condemned the use of children in this manner in the civil rights movement. Many parents also were worried about their children being so directly involved in the movement. But Dr. King told the worried parents: "Don't worry about your children; they are going to be all right. Don't hold them back if they want to go to jail, for they are not only doing a job for themselves, but for all of America and for all of mankind." But the Crusade received front-page coverage by national media outlets and effectively showed the brutality and unfairness of those enforcing segregation laws.

What was Bloody Sunday?

Bloody Sunday refers to the tragic events around a civil rights march on March 7, 1965, from Selma to Montgomery, Alabama. The march was designed to draw attention to voting rights abuses and the killing of a young civil rights protestor in Marion, Alabama. State and local police used their billy clubs to repress and abuse the more than six hundred civil rights protestors who marched across the Edmund Pettis Bridge, risking their personal safety. Civil rights leaders John Lewis (1940–) and Hosea Williams (1926–2000) led the march. Bloody Sunday was televised across the world.

Whose death inspired the Selma march?

Jimmie Lee Jackson (1938–1965), a protestor and deacon in a local church, was shot to death behind Zion Methodist Church in Marion, Alabama, by Alabama state trooper James Bonard Fowler. Jackson and others were marching to the Perry County jail to protest the imprisonment of civil rights worker James Orange. Jackson was unarmed. Fowler claimed that he acted in self-defense, as Jackson allegedly made a move for Fowler's holster to grab his gun. A grand jury declined to indict Fowler in September 1965.

In May 2007, Fowler was indicted for Jackson's murder. He pled guilty to manslaughter and was released from prison after serving only five months.

Marchers, led by Dr. Martin Luther King Jr., walked for five days from Selma to Montgomery, Alabama, in March 1965 to protest unfair voting laws and segregation in the South.

Who was Malcolm X?

Malcolm X (1925–1965) was an influential civil rights leader known for his activism and advocacy on behalf of civil rights. Born Malcolm Little in Omaha, Nebraska, he went to prison for robbery at age twenty. In prison, Little converted to the Nation of Islam. He later became a key follower of Elijah Muhammad, the leader of the Black Muslims. For a time, Malcolm X was Muhammad's most eloquent and powerful spokesman, but he began to have differences with his older mentor. Eventually, Malcolm X left the Nation of Islam in March 1964. He disavowed the Nation of Islam's hard-line stance on segregation and agreed to work with other civil rights leaders. This apparently displeased a segment of the Nation of Islam, as three members of the group assassinated Malcolm X in New York in February 1965. These three members were convicted, although they continued to maintain their innocence even decades later.

What does the letter "X" in Malcolm X's name stand for?

The influential but controversial African American leader was a staunch defendant of black rights. He took the surname "X" in 1952 upon his release from prison. He explained that the letter stood for the unknown African name of his ancestors. Malcolm X's family's name, Little, was that given to his slave ancestors by their owner. By adopting X as his surname, it was both a bitter reminder of his family's slavery and an affirmation of his (unknown) African roots.

214

What was "CORE"?

CORE is the acronym for the civil rights group Congress for Racial Equality. Founded in 1942 by James L. Farmer, Jr. and several others, it played a significant role in the American civil rights movement. CORE focused on exposing the evils of segregation and discrimination through various acts of nonviolent, direct action. CORE did not just engage in activism in the southern U.S. CORE attacked employment discrimination, voting rights abuses, and other modes of discrimination in society. Many of its activities occurred in Chicago, Illinois.

CORE also was active in Freedom Summer—a campaign of civil rights in Mississippi during the summer of 1964. CORE proposed the creation of Freedom Schools and trained young civil rights activists. Three members of CORE—James Chaney, Michael Schwerner, and Andrew Goodman—were brutally murdered near Philadelphia, Mississippi, that summer.

Malcolm X was a civil rights leader who was assassinated after leaving the Nation of Islam and embracing a more nonviolent approach to racial justice.

What was Freedom Summer?

Freedom Summer, or the Mississippi Summer Project, was a project in the summer of 1964 to combat voting discrimination and to campaign for voting rights in Mississippi, a state with stark civil rights abuses. Members of CORE and other civil rights groups set up Freedom Schools, Freedom House, and other havens to help those who faced discrimination and repression.

Who was Medgar Evers?

Medgar Evers (1925–1963) was a civil rights leader and field secretary for the NAACP in Mississippi. He became a martyr for the movement after his assassination in June 1963 by a white supremacist named Byron de la Beckwith. A veteran of World War II, Evers helped lead the fight to integrate the University of Mississippi by James Meredith. Meredith also applied for admission to the University of Mississippi's law school, but his application was denied.

What was the White Citizens Council?

The White Citizens Council was a group of white citizens adamantly opposed to desegregating public schools and to the advancement of civil rights for African Americans. It was formed in either Greenwood or Indianola, Mississippi. Local chapters sprouted up all across the South. The group was not a violent white supremacist group like the Ku Klux Klan but instead preferred to use economic and political retaliation as weapons against civil rights activists.

What was "SNCC"?

SNCC was the Student Nonviolent Coordinating Committee, a major player in the American civil rights movement. Founded in 1960 at Shaw University in Raleigh, North Carolina, it played a significant role in the sit-ins, freedom rides, and other forms of nonviolent, direct action during the movement. SNCC also played a major role in organizing and getting greater participation for the March on Washington.

What are "sit-ins"?

Sit-ins are a form of nonviolent, direct action in which a protestor occupies a particular place by sitting down and expressing his opposition to a policy or course of action. The most famous types of sit-ins occurred during the civil rights movements in the 1950s and 1960s, when young students and other activists challenged segregation policies. For example, many activists conducted sit-ins at lunch counters, restaurants, libraries, and other public facilities.

These forms of mass disobedience often led to violent responses from those who supported segregation. They were a very effective tool to show the righteousness and dedication of the civil rights activists and the negativity of those opposed to such action.

What were the most famous sit-ins of the civil rights movement?

The sit-ins that had the widest impact were conducted in Greensboro, North Carolina. These actions attracted national and even international attention and dramatized the evils of segregation in stark terms for much of the rest of the country. In February 1960, four students at North Carolina Agricultual and Technical State University (Greensboro) conducted a sit-in at the lunch counter of the Woolworth's store in Greensboro. The four students were Joseph McNeil, Franklin McCain, Ezell Blair, Jr., and David Richmond. The four were members of the NAACP's Youth Council.

Who were the Freedom Riders?

The Freedom Riders were a group of civil rights activists who rode interstate buses into states that practiced segregation. The activists visibly challenged the policies of segregation on buses. They sought to draw larger public attention to the civil rights cause. The riders would have a black person and a white person sit together. They also would have several black riders ride in the first few rows of the bus. Both of these practices violated custom and tradition in some Southern states. The first Freedom Ride began in May 1961 from Washington, D.C. Some Freedom Riders endured frightful beatings, particularly in Alabama. Ku Klux Klan members attacked Freedom Riders in the Alabama cities of Anniston, Birmingham, and Montgomery.

Who was A. Philip Randolph?

Asa (A.) Philip Randolph (1889–1979) was a famous civil rights leader who led the first black labor union and planned the influential March on Washington that took place in August 1963. He organized the Brotherhood of Sleeping Car Porters, the first labor union composed predominantly of blacks. Randolph was instrumental in convincing Presidents Franklin D. Roosevelt and Harry Truman to issue executive orders banning discrimination in the defense industries and the desegregation of the armed forces. In 1941, Randolph said that "a wave of bitter resentment, disillusionment, and desperation was sweeping over the Negro masses."

What was the March on Washington?

The March on Washington was a famous civil rights gathering and political rally of more than 250,000 people conducted in Washington, D.C., on August 28, 1963. The purpose of the march was to galvanize public support for the civil rights movement and to bring greater public awareness to the cause of civil rights. The march is considered perhaps the most influential single event during the Movement. Many consider it an important catalyst in the eventual passage of federal legislation designed to bring equal justice in the country.

Hundreds of thousands of people swarmed around the Washington Monument and Reflecting Pool during the 1963 March on Washington, where Dr. Martin Luther King Jr. would also give his famous "I Have a Dream" speech.

Numerous civil rights leaders gave speeches, including NAACP President Roy Wilkins, Whitney Young, Jr. of the Urban League, John Lewis, A. Philip Randolph, and others.

What was the most famous speech given during the March on Washington?

The most famous speech delivered at the March on Washington was the "I Have a Dream" speech delivered by Dr. Martin Luther King, Jr. It is considered one of the greatest speeches in world history. King famously aspired that his children be judged "not by the color of their skin but by the content of their character." His refrains of "I Have a Dream" and "Let Freedom Ring" reverberated through much of the nation's collective conscience. Historian William Bennett in *America: The Last Best Hope (Vol. II)* wrote of King's speech: "[It] changed things. It changes things still."

What were the Watts Riots?

The Watts riots occurred from August 11–17, 1965, in the Watts section of Los Angeles. The six-day tragedy resulted in thirty-four deaths and more than a thousand people injured. The uprising began after a young black man named Marquette Frye was arrested by a white police officer. Several officers allegedly used excessive force in arresting Frye. They also later arrested his mother and brother. Many individuals in the community protested what they perceived to be unfair treatment at the hands of law enforcement. This incident incited more large-scale protests that degenerated into the burning and looting of businesses. A 1965 report, "Violence in the City: An End or a Beginning?" identified poverty, lack of educational opportunities, and a precipitous relationship between blacks and the Los Angeles Police Department as components of the problem. The report recommended the creation of a City Human Rights Commission and called on society to help provide greater opportunities for blacks.

How did Dr. King die?

Dr. King was assassinated while standing outside the second-floor balcony of the Lorraine Motel in Memphis, Tennessee, on April 4, 1968. James Earl Ray (1928–1998), a career criminal, was arrested and charged with assassinating Dr. King. Ray confessed and pled guilty to avoid the death penalty. However, he later recanted his confession, and for the rest of his life maintained his innocence. Some believe he may not have been involved in the killing of Dr. King or that at least there were many others involved in the assassination of the leading civil rights leader.

What was the Black Panther Party?

The Black Panther Party was a political organization known for its advocacy of radical socialism and black nationalistic pride. The Black Panthers rejected the nonviolent teachings of Dr. Martin Luther King, Jr. and adopted a more confrontational stance toward white America. They particularly preached against police brutality and urged con-

What was Black Power?

The Black Power Movement focused on black pride and a more aggressive stance toward a racist white establishment. The movement is generally traced to 1966, when some leaders of SNCC, tired of the violent response with which peaceful protesters were often met, urged activists to adopt a more decisive and aggressive stance and began promoting the slogan "Black Power." A key leader of this movement was Stokely Carmichael (1941–1998), who began using the slogan "Black Power" in speeches. For example, he said: "It is a call for black people in this country to unite, to recognize their heritage, to build a sense of community. It is a call for black people to define their own goals, to lead their own organizations."

frontation at times with white police officers. The leaders of the Black Panther Party included Huey Newton (1942–1989) and Bobby Seale (1936–). Newton and Seale co-founded the party in 1966, calling it the Black Panther Party for Self Defense.

Who were the Chicago Eight?

The Chicago Eight were a group of defendants charged with inciting rioting at the 1968 Democratic National Convention in Chicago, Illinois. The defendants were Abbie Hoffman, Jerry Rubin, David Dellinger, Tom Hayden, Rennie Davis, John Froines, Lee Weiner, and Bobby Seale. The eight were prosecuted in a federal courtroom on charges of conspiracy and inciting a riot. The presiding judge was Federal District Court Judge Julius Hoffman, who showed evident bias against the defendants. He ordered Seale bound and gagged in the courtroom for his repeated outbursts and eventually had his case severed from the other seven defendants. For this reason, the remaining defendants are often known as the Chicago Seven.

A jury acquitted the defendants of conspiracy charges but found five of the defendants (all except Froines and Weiner) guilty of inciting a riot. They were sentenced to five years in prison. However, a federal appeals court reversed the convictions in part because of Judge Hoffman's evident bias. The U.S. Department of Justice opted not to seek a second trial against the defendants.

In what case did the Burger Court first consider the constitutionality of Affirmative Action?

The Burger Court considered the constitutionality of an affirmative action program in *Regents of the University of California v. Bakke* (1978). The case concerned the admissions policy at the medical school of the University of California, Davis. The UC Davis Medical School had a policy that reserved sixteen of its hundred seats for minority applicants. Allan Bakke, a white male rejected by the school in 1973 and 1974, sued the school, claiming that the school violated his rights under Title VI of the Civil Rights Act of 1964 and the Equal Protection Clause of the Fourteenth Amendment. Bakke's grade point average and MCAT scores were significantly higher than many minority candidates. The U.S. Supreme Court ruled 5–4 that the school's policy amounted to a quota. The Court determined that the school could not carry its burden of proving that Bakke would have been denied entrance without its "unlawful special admissions program."

Did the Court rule that an educational institution could not consider race in its admissions policy?

No, the U.S. Supreme Court also ruled 5–4 that a university has a compelling interest in achieving a diverse class and that race can be an important factor in that calculus. Justice Lewis Powell wrote that diversity "clearly is a constitutionally permissible goal for an institution of higher learning." He explained that a university constitutionally can institute an admissions policy where "race or ethnic background is simply one element in the selection process."

POLITICAL CONFLICT AND CHANGE: 1950s TO THE 1970s

Who was U.S. president during much of the 1950s era?

President Dwight D. Eisenhower was the nation's leader from 1953–1961, a key period in the Cold War era. A five-star general during World War II, he oversaw an age of economic prosperity in the United States.

What was the importance of the Federal-Aid Highway Revenue Act of 1956?

One of Eisenhower's major accomplishments during this period was signing the Federal-Aid Highway Revenue Act of 1956, which provided federal funds to states for constructing interstate highways. Eisenhower supported such highways because they would be useful to move troops and equipment across the country during a war, but the effects on American society were even greater. Americans became a nation of travelers, not only for vacations, but also to commute to work, which in turn encouraged the rise of suburbs around cities. National parks also became more accessible, which led to the ability of more Americans to experience the nation's natural beauty.

What other important project was begun during the Eisenhower Administration?

While Eisenhower was president, the United States launched its space program and conceived plans for Project Apollo, which would later be adjusted under President Kennedy to have the goal of landing men on the moon.

THE RED SCARE

When did the Cold War begin?

In the years after World War II, the nations of Western Europe and the United States became alarmed by Soviet advances into Eastern Europe, and many Europeans and Amer-

What U.S. state was formerly its own kingdom?

Hawaii, America's fiftieth state, was an independent kingdom from 1795 until 1893. It had previously been a collection of independent peoples led by chiefs, who were then unified under Kamehameha the Great (c. 1758–1819) with the help of European weapons and military advice. In 1893, it became a republic led by Sanford B. Dole (1844–1926), and in 1900 it became a territory of the United States. Hawaii officially became America's fiftieth state on August 21, 1959.

icans voiced concerns that Communists, led by the Soviet Union, were plotting to take over the world. Political leaders in England, the United States, and elsewhere referred to this new menace in grim terms. In March 1946, former British prime minister Winston Churchill (1874–1965) warned of an "Iron Curtain" of Soviet totalitarianism that had divided the European continent; in 1947, President Truman announced a policy of containment of communist incursion into other countries. This policy came to be known as the Truman Doctrine, and it remained an integral part of American foreign policy for the next forty years, ultimately leading to the nation's involvement in the Korean War and the Vietnam War.

The eroding relationship between the Western powers and the Soviet-led countries of Eastern Europe was largely brought on by disagreements over Germany. At the close of World War II, marked differences of opinion on what to do with Germany had resulted in a plan for joint government of the nation by the Allies—the Soviet Union, the United States, Britain, and France. But the arrangement quickly proved unworkable. By 1948, Germany was in serious economic straits, and the United States, Britain, and France began to discuss uniting their zones. The Soviets responded by ordering a blockade of land and water traffic into Berlin, control of which had been divided between the Allies after the war (the Soviets controlled East Berlin, while the other Allies controlled West Berlin).

To counter the blockade, Great Britain and the United States ordered an airlift operation to provide food and other supplies to the people of West Berlin, alleviating the effects of the eleven-month Soviet blockade. In 1949, the East-West differences resulted in the formal division of Germany into two countries: West Germany—formed by the zones occupied by the United States, Great Britain, and France—was allowed to form a democratic government, and it became officially known as the Federal Republic of Germany. The same year, East Germany (also known as the German Democratic Republic) was formed out of the Soviet zones and was folded into the "Eastern Bloc" countries.

By 1949, the year that the Soviet Union exploded its first nuclear bomb, the world had been roughly divided into two camps: The United States and its democratic allies (including the nations of Western Europe and other anti-Communist governments) and

and the Eastern Bloc (the Soviet Union and its satellite countries). These camps were soon girded by formal political alliances. In 1949, a military alliance known as the North Atlantic Treaty Organization (NATO) was formed by twelve nations (the United States, Great Britain, France, Italy, Norway, Portugal, Iceland, Denmark, Canada, Belgium, Luxembourg, and the Netherlands).

By 1955, three more countries—Greece, Turkey, and West Germany—joined the alliance. The Soviet Union responded by creating the Council for Mutual Economic Assistance (COMECON) in 1949 and the Warsaw Pact in 1955. COMECON was an effort to coordinate economic and industrial activities among Communist nations, while the Warsaw Pact was a military agreement between the Soviets and the Communist governments of Eastern Europe.

The Cold War deepened during the course of the 1950s, as distrust on both sides was increased by the shadow of possible nuclear destruction. Both the United States and the Soviet Union funneled vast resources into the development of weapons systems, as each side believed deterrence would determine the victor in the Cold War: It would be won by the nation able to create weapons so powerful that the other nation would be deterred from attacking. The military buildup became an all-out arms race.

Competition between the Eastern Bloc and the West spilled over into athletics, the arts, and the sciences. In 1957, the Soviets beat the West into space when it launched the first artificial satellite, Sputnik, which they followed in 1961 by completing the first successful manned space launch. The United States responded by stepping up its space program and vowing to put a man on the moon.

What was the "Domino Principle"?

The "Domino Principle" was a term used by President Eisenhower to explain the threat of Communist expansion. He explained that the spread of communism would have severe ramifications: "You have a row of dominoes set up, you knock over the first one, and what will happen to the last one is the certainty that it will go over very quickly."

What was McCarthyism?

At home, the hysteria of the Cold War era reached its height with the so-called McCarthyism of the 1950s; historian Doris Kearns Goodwin described it as "one of the most destructive chapters in American political history." In early 1950, Republican Senator Joseph McCarthy (1908–1957) of Wisconsin claimed to possess a list of more than two hundred known Communists in the U.S. State Department. The startling accusation launched congressional inquiries conducted by the Senator's Subcommittee and the House Committee to Investigate Un-American Activities (HUAC). Suspicions of Communist subversion ran high—even in Hollywood, where a "blacklist" named those who were believed to have been involved in the Communist Party. McCarthy never produced his laundry list of offenders in the State Department, and the sorry chapter was closed when, on live television, the senator's bitter attacks went too far: In televised hearings in

1954, the senator took on the U.S. Army, determined to ferret out what he believed was a conspiracy to cover up a known Communist in the ranks. Faced with McCarthy's slanderous line of questioning, Army counsel Joseph Welch (1890–1960) delivered a reply that finally disarmed McCarthy, saying, "Have you no sense of decency, sir? If there is a God in heaven, your attacks will do neither you nor your cause any good." The retort was met with applause in the courtroom, heralding the end of the Communist-in-our-midst hysteria.

Senator Joseph McCarthy led a witch hunt against supposed Communist Americans as head of the House Committee to Investigate Un-American Activities.

What U.S. senator earned acclaim for her "Declaration of Conscience" speech against McCarthyism?

Margaret Chase Smith (1897–1995) was the first female to serve in both the U.S. House and Senate. She served in the House from 1940 to1949 and in the Senate from 1949–1973, representing Maine. Smith sought the Republican nomination for president in 1964 but failed to win the nomination. She lost her Senate seat in the 1972 election.

On June 1, 1950, she delivered her famous "Declaration of Conscience" speech, deploring the inquisitorial actions of fellow Senator Joseph McCarthy (1908–1957). She did not refer to Senator McCarthy by name, but it was obvious to whom she was referring. Her speech is considered one of the greatest in American political history.

Smith eloquently said on the Senate floor:

I speak as a Republican, I speak as a woman. I speak as a United States Senator. I speak as an American.

The United States Senate has long enjoyed worldwide respect as the greatest deliberative body in the world. But recently that deliberative character has too often been debased to the level of a forum of hate and character assassination sheltered by the shield of congressional immunity. ...

It is strange that we can verbally attack anyone else without restraint and with full protection and yet we hold ourselves above the same type of criticism here on the Senate Floor. Surely the United States Senate is big enough to take self-criticism and self-appraisal. Surely we should be able to take the same kind of character attacks that we dish out to outsiders.

I think that it is high time for the United States Senate and its members to do some soul searching—for us to weigh our consciences—on the manner in which we are performing our duty to the people of America—on the manner in which we are using or abusing our individual powers and privileges.

I think that it is high time that we remembered that we have sworn to uphold and defend the Constitution. I think that it is high time that we remembered; that the Constitution, as amended, speaks not only of the freedom of speech but also of trial by jury instead of trial by accusation. ...

Yet to displace it with a Republican regime embracing a philosophy that lacks political integrity or intellectual honesty would prove equally disastrous to this nation. The nation sorely needs a Republican victory. But I don't want to see the Republican Party ride to political victory on the Four Horsemen of Calumny— Fear, Ignorance, Bigotry and Smear. ...

I don't like the way the Senate has been made a rendezvous for vilification, for selfish political gain at the sacrifice of individual reputations and national unity. I am not proud of the way we smear outsiders from the Floor of the Senate and hide behind the cloak of congressional immunity and still place ourselves beyond criticism on the Floor of the Senate.

As an American, I am shocked at the way Republicans and Democrats alike are playing directly into the Communist design of "confuse, divide and conquer." As an American, I don't want a Democratic Administration "white wash" or "cover up" any more than I want a Republican smear or witch hunt.

As an American, I condemn a Republican "Fascist" just as much as I condemn a Democrat "Communist." I condemn a Democrat "fascist" just as much as I condemn a Republican "Communist." They are equally dangerous to you and me and to your country. As an American, I want to see our nation recapture the strength and unity it once had when we fought the enemy instead of ourselves.

It is with these thoughts I have drafted what I call a "Declaration of Conscience." I am gratified that Senator Tobey, Senator Aiken, Senator Morse, Senator Ives, Senator Thye and Senator Hendrickson, have concurred in that declaration and have authorized me to announce their concurrence.

For his part, McCarthy referred to Smith and the other senators who signed her "Declaration of Conscience" as "Snow White and the Six Dwarves."

Who were the Rosenbergs?

Husband and wife Julius (1918–1953) and Ethel Rosenberg (1915–1953) were tried for conspiracy to commit wartime espionage. Arrested in 1950, the Rosenbergs were charged with passing nuclear weapons data to the Soviets, enabling the Communists to develop and explode their own atomic bomb—an event that had been announced to the American public by President Truman on September 23, 1949. As the realization set in that the United States could now be the victim of an atomic attack, the anxieties of the

Cold War heightened. Citizens were encouraged to build bomb shelters, school children participated in air-raid drills, civil-defense films (such as *How Can I Stay Alive in an Atom Bomb Blast?*) were screened, and entire towns conducted tests of how residents would respond in the event of an "A-bomb."

Meanwhile, the leak of top-secret information from the Manhattan Project at Los Alamos, New Mexico, was traced to New York City machine-shop owner Julius Rosenberg, his wife Ethel, and her brother, David Greenglass. Historian Doris Kearns Goodwin writes that the "short, plump Mrs. Rosenberg looked more like one of my friends' mothers than an international

Ethel and Julius Rosenberg are shown here after being found guily of espionage, the first time American citizens were ever so charged.

spy." Indeed, the case marked the first time American civilians were charged with espionage, and the trial made international headlines. Though the Rosenbergs were only two of many involved in the conspiracy, theirs was the heaviest of the punishments handed down in the cases against the spy ring. For their betrayal and their refusal to talk, the Rosenbergs were sentenced to death; in issuing the sentence, Judge Irving Kaufman accused the couple of having "altered the course of history." The penalty rocked the world: As Supreme Court Justice Felix Frankfurter put it, they "were tried for conspiracy and sentenced for treason." They were electrocuted on the evening of June 19, 1953, as New York's Union Square filled with an estimated ten thousand protesters.

What was the U-2 incident?

The U-2 incident was a diplomatic crisis that occurred in May 1960, when the Soviet Union shot down an American U–2 spy plane piloted by Central Intelligence Agency ("CIA") agent Francis Gary Powers (1929–1977). A few weeks before an international summit, Powers flew the U-2 plane over the Soviet Union in attempts to gather photographic evidence of Soviet military and missile capabilities. The Soviets shot down the plane.

The United States and President Eisenhower claimed that the plane was not a spy plane but a weather forecasting plane that had unintentionally flown off course. Soviet premier Nikita Khrushchev announced that Powers was captured as a prisoner. The incident proved a great embarrassment to the United States and Eisenhower, as the administration was caught in a lie.

What happened to Francis Gary Powers?

Powers was sentenced to three years in prison, followed by seven years of hard labor by Soviet authorities. In February 1962, the United States and the Soviet Union exchanged prisoners. The United States turned over Soviet spy Rudolf Abel—who was really KGB Colonel Vilyam Fisher—for Powers and American student Frederic Pryor.

Powers later worked for Lockheed Martin as a test pilot from 1963–1970. He had to leave Lockheed Martin after his memoir *Operation Overflight: A Memoir of the U–2 Incident* (1970) was published.

THE SPACE RACE

What was the "Space Race"?

"The Space Race" refers to the intense competition between the United States and the Soviet Union over exploratory successes in space. Both countries were spurred by an obsessive desire to better the other country in the midst of the Cold War. The Soviet Union beat the United States into space with the launch of Sputnik, which they followed in 1961 by completing the first successful manned space launch. The United States responded by stepping up its space program and vowing to put a man on the moon.

When was NASA created?

The National Aeronautics and Space Administration was founded on July 29, 1958, as a direct reaction to the Soviets' launching of Sputnik.

What was the first U.S. space program?

After NASA was founded, Project Mercury was almost immediately established with the goal of launching a manned space flight. Seven men—the Mercury Seven—were chosen for the program: Alan Shepard, Jr. (1923–1998), Virgil "Gus" Grissom (1926–1967), John Glenn, Jr. (1921–), Scott Carpenter (1925–2003), Wally Schirra, Jr. (1923–2007), Gordon Cooper, Jr. (1927–2004), and Deke Slayton (1924–1993). Six manned flights were achieved between 1961 and 1963.

Who was the first American in space?

John Glenn became the first American to go into space on February 20, 1962, when he rode aboard the *Friendship 7,* completing four orbits of the Earth in just under five hours.

Who was the first person to go into space?

The first person in space was not an American but a Russian cosmonaut named Yuri Gagarin (1934–1968). A colonel in the Soviet Air Force, he piloted a Vostok spacecraft around the planet on April 12, 1961. This, along with the success of Sputnik, helped to panic the Americans into the space race.

American astronaut John Glenn is shown here aboard the *Friendship 7* in 1962.

What program followed Project Mercury?

After Project Mercury, the next phase of the U.S. space program was Project Gemini, which ran from 1961 to 1967. The goal of the project was to prepare for the eventual Moon landing by running flights long enough to equal the time astronauts would have to survive in space if they were traveling to the Moon and back. Gemini capsules held two astronauts, and ten manned, low-Earth-orbit exercises were completed between 1965 and 1966. The program ran concurrently with Project Apollo, developing techniques for space flight that assisted the astronauts on the Moon missions.

Did the Apollo Program always intend to send a man to the Moon?

Originally, the Apollo Program merely aimed to launch three men into space, and this was seen as the logical progression from the two-man flights of Gemini. President John F. Kennedy changed the plan to include Moon landings. Six missions—from *Apollo 11* to *Apollo 17* (excluding 13)—landed on the Moon between 1969 and 1972, and twelve astronauts walked on the lunar surface.

What space setback did the U.S. suffer in January 1967?

On January 27, 1967, a fire broke out in the *Apollo I* spacecraft during ground testing at Cape Kennedy. Three astronauts were killed. They were Gus Grissom, Edward White,

Why didn't *Apollo 13* land on the Moon?

Two days after its launch on April 11, 1970, an oxygen tank aboard the craft exploded, damaging the Service Module, which made it unsafe for landing. What followed were several days of tense navigation, during which it was uncertain whether the three men aboard—James A. Lovell, Jack Swigert, and Fred W. Haise—would even make it back to Earth alive. The explosion caused the ship to lose power, water, and air, and the astronauts had to retreat into the Landing Module, which then served as a kind of lifeboat. Because of the loss of power, it was decided to use the Moon's gravity to swing the ship around and back to Earth; also unprecedented was the fact that the crew had to power up the Command Module from a complete shut-off as it approached Earth. The combined skill of the crew and the command center on the ground managed to return all three astronauts to Earth safely nearly four days after the malfunction.

and Roger Chaffee. An extensive April 1967 report revealed that a defective electrical wire caused the tragic fire. The tragedy and subsequent report led to many safety modifications and a significant improvement in the space program.

Who were the first men to walk on the moon?

The first men to walk on the moon were American astronauts Neil Armstrong (1930–2012) and Edwin "Buzz" Aldrin, Jr. (1930–), who were aboard the *Apollo 11* spacecraft. On July 20, 1969, Armstrong stepped out of the lunar module from *Apollo 11* and walked on the moon. He uttered the famous words, "That's one small step for a man, one giant leap for mankind." (The live voice transmission had dropped the "a" before "man," but it was added in later.)

Apollo 11's successful trip to the moon vindicated the policy of President John F. Kennedy, who in 1961 had ordered a dramatic escalation in the U.S. space program—in part to compete against and beat the Soviet Union's space program. On May 25, 1961, President Kennedy said that "this nation should commit itself to achieving the goal, before the decade is out, of landing a man on the moon and returning him safely to the earth."

When did the space shuttle program begin?

NASA's space shuttle program launched a new era for space exploration and discovery. Unlike the vehicles used in earlier programs, the shuttles were reusable. The system included a planelike orbiter in which the astronauts rode and which had a large payload bay, a large external tank, and two smaller rocket boosters positioned on either side of the main tank. As the shuttle escaped the earth's atmosphere, the booster rockets were jettisoned; upon returning to Earth, the orbiter would glide down and land on an airstrip just like an airplane.

One of the most historical moments in not just American but world history was the moment when Neil Armstrong first set foot on the Moon on July 20, 1969.

There were six shuttles in the fleet: *Enterprise*, which was never flown, *Columbia*, *Challenger*, *Discovery*, *Endeavor*, and *Atlantis*. Together, they carried 777 astronauts into space. The ships, though, never voyaged to the Moon or another planet; they were designed to orbit Earth and were used to do research experiments, carry cargo (such as satellites and supplies) to the International Space Station, and to service equipment in space, such as the Hubble Space Telescope.

The program lasted from 1981–2011, at which point the shuttles were decommissioned.

What impact did the *Challenger* disaster have on the U.S. space program?

On January 28, 1986, the space shuttle *Challenger* burst into flames a mere seventy-three seconds into its takeoff. All seven members of the crew perished in the explosion. The immediate effect was that all scheduled launches were scratched, pending the outcome of the government investigation into the disaster. President Ronald Reagan (1911–2004) acted quickly to establish a Presidential Commission to look into the accident, appointing former Secretary of State William P. Rogers (1913–2001) as its chair. Rogers conducted a thorough investigation involving public and private hearings, more than six thousand people, fifteen thousand pages of testimony, 170,000 pages of documents, hundreds of photographs, and reports of independent technical studies. Additionally, the Commission reviewed flight records, film evidence, and the recovered debris.

On June 6, 1986, the Commission released its report, citing the cause of the disaster as the failure of the O-ring seals "that are intended to prevent hot gases from leaking through the joint during the propellant burn." The Commission had learned that although both NASA and the O-ring manufacturer Morton Thiokol were concerned about the seals (which had also been used on other shuttles), they had come to regard them as an acceptable risk. The Commission went on to say that "the decision to launch the Challenger was flawed." The U.S. House of Representatives' Committee on Science and Technology, which spent two months conducting its own hearings, also concluded that the disaster could have been prevented, citing that "meeting flight schedules and cutting costs were given a higher priority than flight safety."

With the blame for the disaster placed on NASA's doorstep, public confidence in the agency plummeted, and NASA's own astronauts became concerned that their lives had been unnecessarily put at risk. However, the Commission also made nine recommendations to NASA, including redesigning the solid rocket booster joints, giving astronauts and engineers a greater role in approving launches, reviewing the astronaut escape systems, regulating the rate of shuttle flights to maximize safety, and reforming the shuttle program's management structure.

What space shuttle tragedy occurred in the early twenty-first century?

The U.S. space shuttle *Columbia* was lost upon its reentry into Earth's atmosphere on the morning of February 1, 2003. All seven crew members died.

The *Columbia* was in the skies over Texas about fifteen minutes before its scheduled landing at Florida's Kennedy Space Center when, shortly before 9:00 A.M. (EST), ground controllers lost data from temperature controllers on the spacecraft. Over the next sev-

The space shuttle *Columbia* is shown here during a successful landing. One of the greatest tragedies of the American space program was when the shuttle blew up while reentering the atmosphere over Texas on February 1, 2003.

eral minutes, NASA ground control lost all flight data. At about the same time, witnesses in Texas reported the sound of rolling thunder and debris falling from the sky. Heat-detecting weather radar showed a bright red streak moving across the Texas sky. The shuttle was forty miles above Earth and traveling at eighteen times the speed of sound when it disintegrated, leaving a trail of debris from eastern Texas to western Louisiana. The investigation later revealed that damage to the spacecraft had gone unseen during the mission, causing the Columbia to break apart upon reentry.

The shuttle was commanded by Rick Husband and piloted by William McCool. The mission specialists were Michael Anderson, Kalpana Chawla, David Brown, and Laurel Clark. The payload specialist was Israeli astronaut Ilan Ramon. In President George W. Bush's (1946–) remarks to the nation that day, he said, "These men and women assumed great risk in the service to all humanity. In an age when space flight has come to seem almost routine, it is easy to overlook the dangers of travel by rocket. … These astronauts knew the dangers and faced them willingly."

The *Columbia* tragedy occurred within a week of the anniversaries of two other deadly NASA disasters: the *Challenger* explosion on January 28, 1986, and the launch-pad fire that killed three Apollo astronauts on January 27, 1967. After investigating the cause of the *Columbia* disaster, NASA focused on implementing a new system of sensors to detect potentially fatal damage to spacecraft while in orbit. NASA relaunched its space shuttle program in late July 2005 with the *Discovery*.

JFK

What made President Kennedy so popular?

John F. Kennedy, a Democrat, inspired many Americans during his brief time in the Oval Office. He narrowly defeated Republican candidate Richard Nixon by a vote of 313–219 in the electoral vote, but he captured the popular vote only by 49.7% to 49.5%. He famously told Americans during his inaugural address on January 20, 1961: "And so, my fellow Americans: Ask not what your country can do for you—ask what you can do for your country."

Some were inspired by Kennedy's military service. He had served in the U.S. Navy from 1941 to 1945, rising to the rank of lieutenant. His patrol torpedo ("PT") boat was attacked by a Japanese destroyer in August 1943. He managed to swim to safety, saving the life of a fellow soldier in the process. He won a Purple Heart and the Navy and Marine Corps Medal. Kennedy also earned acclaim for his book *Profiles in Courage* (1956), which won a Pulitzer Prize in 1957. The book examined eight U.S. senators who showed courage in taking unpopular stands.

Others were inspired by his relative youth, his beautiful wife, Jacqueline (1929–1994), and their young family. The Kennedy White House became sort of the American version of the royal family. The media loved the Kennedy family. The Kennedy White House was sometimes called "Camelot"—a term first used by the First Lady in reference to her husband's love of King Arthur stories and of the play by the same name.

Kennedy also earned the support of many for his eventual strong support on behalf of civil rights for African Americans. His brother, Robert F. Kennedy (1925–1968), served as his attorney general and also increased the popularity of his brother. Many viewed Robert Kennedy as an excellent leader due to his stance against organized crime and his support of civil rights.

Another source of Kennedy's popularity came after his assassination. A nation mourned its young leader. It was a national day of mourning. Grown adults wept openly. People alive during that dreadful day still recall it quite vividly. Many believe President Kennedy would have become one of the nation's greatest presidents, as many predicted he would be re-elected and serve a second term.

What was the Bay of Pigs invasion?

This was a failed plan begun in the Eisenhower Administration but approved by President Kennedy. After Communist leader Fidel Castro (1926–) came to power in Cuba in 1959, the U.S. government viewed him as a threat. The Central Intelligence Agency (CIA) trained thousands of Cuban nationals, who were to be brought back to Cuba to lead an uprising. The nationals were to land on a beach in the Bay of Pigs. The U.S. government would provide air support once the Cuban nationals initiated an uprising. The plan failed miserably, as the CIA-trained nationals were overwhelmed by Castro's forces. The U.S. did not provide air support. Kennedy accepted responsibility for the failure.

What was the Cuban Missile Crisis?

The Cuban Missile Crisis referred to a tense situation that some feared would lead to a nuclear war between the United States and the Soviet Union. President Kennedy learned that there was a missile base being constructed in Cuba using Soviet materials. The world tensed as Soviet ships headed toward Cuba. Kennedy forcefully declared that the United States would search all Soviet ships heading towards Cuba. The Soviet ships turned away and sailed back home. Kennedy's Secretary of State Dean Rusk (1909–1994) said: "We're eyeball to eyeball and I think the other fellow just blinked."

What well-known volunteer program did President Kennedy establish?

Kennedy established the Peace Corps by executive order in March 1961. Its stated purpose was "to promote world peace and friendship through a Peace Corps, which shall make available to interested countries and areas men and women of the United States qualified for service abroad and willing to serve, under conditions of hardship if necessary, to help the peoples of such countries and areas in meeting their needs for trained manpower." Kennedy named his brother-in-law, Robert Sargent Shriver, Jr. (1915–2011), as the first director of the Peace Corps.

When was President Kennedy assassinated?

Kennedy was killed on November 22, 1963, in Dallas, Texas, while riding in an open motorcade. A number of shots rang out from the Texas School Book Depository. Two bullets struck the president, hitting him in the neck and head. Rushed to a local hospital, he was pronounced dead almost immediately. The accused assassin was Lee Harvey Oswald (1939–1963), a Communist sympathizer who worked at the book depository. Two days later, Jack Ruby (1911–1967), a Dallas nightclub owner, shot Oswald as police were transporting him to a local jail. Ruby was convicted and sentenced to death. He gained a new trial but died in prison of lung cancer while awaiting the new trial date.

Who was behind the Kennedy assassination?

That question may never be answered. President Lyndon B. Johnson (1908–1973) ("LBJ"), who assumed the position after Kennedy's death, appointed a commission to examine the circumstances of the assassination. Chaired by U.S. Supreme Court Justice Earl Warren, the Warren Commission concluded: "The shots which killed President Kennedy and wounded [Texas] Governor [John] Connally were fired by Lee Harvey Oswald." A U.S. House of Representatives committee in 1979 concluded that there probably was a conspiracy behind the Kennedy assassination but was "unable to identify the other gunman or the extent of the conspiracy."

This official White House photo shows John F. Kennedy and First Lady Jacqueline Kennedy arriving in Dallas on November 22, 1963, just hours before the assassination.

Numerous theories have abounded over the years, including some that maintain that the Mafia, the CIA, Fidel Castro, or anti-Vietnamese groups were involved in the plot to kill President Kennedy. Many still don't believe that Lee Harvey Oswald acted alone.

LBJ

What was "The Great Society"?

"The Great Society" was LBJ's term—similar to President Franklin D. Roosevelt's "New Deal"—for a fairer, inclusive society free from racism and poverty. Johnson told a crowd in 1964: "In your time, we have the opportunity to move not only toward the rich society and the powerful society but upward to the Great Society. The Great Society rests on an abundance and liberty for all. It demands an end to poverty, and racial injustice, to which we are totally committed in our time."

The Great Society covered various areas of life, including education, health, civil rights, internal improvements, labor, and culture. Johnson's plan included the Medicare and Medicaid programs, which provided health care for the elderly and the poor. It also included the creation of the Job Corps, which provided educational and occupational opportunities for troubled youth. One famous recipient of the Job Corps program was a young man from Texas named George Foreman, who later became a two-time world heavyweight boxing champion. With respect to culture, the National Foundation for the Arts and Humanities was created, and the Corporation for Public Broadcasting was formed.

What historic appointment did President Johnson make to the U.S. Supreme Court in 1967?

President Johnson appointed Thurgood Marshall (1908–1993) to the U.S. Supreme Court in 1967, the first African American to serve on the U.S. Supreme Court. Marshall had won great recognition as an attorney in numerous civil rights cases filed on behalf of the NAACP, including *Brown v. Board of Education*. In 1961, President Kennedy appointed him to the U.S. Court of Appeals for the Second Circuit. Johnson made history when he chose Marshall to be the first African American solicitor general in 1965, then appointed him to the U.S. Supreme Court in 1967, where he served until 1991. Marshall was known for his opposition to the death penalty, opinions protective of freedom of speech, and for his unwavering commitment to principles of equality.

THE VIETNAM WAR

What caused the Vietnam War?

In the simplest terms, the long conflict in Southeast Asia was fought over the unification of Communist North Vietnam and non-Communist South Vietnam. The two countries had been set up in 1954. Prior to that, all of Vietnam was part of the French colony of Indochina. But in 1946, the Vietnamese fought the French to control their own country. The United States provided financial support to France, but the French were ultimately defeated in 1954. Once France withdrew its troops, an international conference was convened in Geneva to decide what should be done with Vietnam. The country was divided into two partitions along the seventeenth parallel. This division of land was not intended to be permanent, but the elections that were supposed to reunite the partitions were never held. Vietnamese president Ho Chi Minh (1892–1969) took power in the north, while Emperor Bao Dai (1913–1997)—for a while—ruled the south.

But the Communist government opposed the non-Communist government of South Vietnam and believed the country should remain united. The North Vietnamese supported antigovernment groups in the south and, over time, stepped up aid to those groups. These Communist-trained South Vietnamese were known as the Viet Cong. Between 1957 and 1965, the Viet Cong struggled against the South Vietnamese government. But in the mid–1960s, North Vietnam initiated a large-scale troop infiltration into South Vietnam, and the fighting became a full-fledged war.

China and the Soviet Union provided the North Vietnamese with military equipment but not manpower. The United States provided both equipment and troops to non-Communist South Vietnam in its struggle against the Viet Cong and North Vietnam. By 1969 there were more than half a million American troops in South Vietnam. This policy was controversial in America, where protests to involvement in the Vietnam War continued until the last U.S. troops were brought home in 1973. In January of that year, the two sides agreed to a cease-fire, but fighting broke out again after the American ground troops left. On April 30, 1975, South Vietnam surrendered to North Vietnam, and the war, which had lasted nearly two decades, ended. North Vietnam unified the countries as the Socialist Republic of Vietnam.

For its part, the North Vietnamese called the conflict a "war of national liberation"; they viewed the long struggle as an extension of the earlier struggle with France. They also perceived the war to be another attempt by a foreign power (this time the United States) to rule Vietnam.

Why did the United States get involved in Vietnam?

The policy of involvement in the Vietnam conflict began in the mid–1950s, when President Truman provided U.S. support to the French in their struggle to retain control of Vietnam. In the Cold War era (1947–1989), government leaders believed the United States must come to the assistance of any country threatened by communism. Truman's successors in the White House—Presidents Eisenhower, Kennedy, and Johnson—also followed this school of thought, fearing a "domino effect" among neighboring nations.

What was the Tet Offensive?

The Tet Offensive was a turning point in the Vietnam War (1954–1975). The assault began during Tet, a festival of the lunar new year, on January 30, 1968. Although a truce had been called for the holiday, North Vietnam and the Viet Cong issued a series of attacks on dozens of South Vietnamese cities, including the capital of Saigon, as well as military and air installations. American troops and the South Vietnamese struggled to regain control of the cities, in one case destroying a village (Ben Tre) in order to "save it" from the enemy. Fighting continued into February. Although the Communist North ultimately failed in its objective to hold any of the cities, the offensive was critical in the outcome of the war: As images of the fighting and destruction filled print and television media, Americans saw that the war was far from over, despite pre-Tet reports of progress in Vietnam. The Tet Offensive strengthened the public opinion that the war could not be won. It altered the course of the American war effort, with President Johnson scaling back the U.S. commitment to defend South Vietnam.

What was the My Lai Massacre?

My Lai was a horrific chapter in American military history, during which U.S. troops fighting in South Vietnam took the small village on March 16, 1968. The incident did not come to light until more than a year later, after which time it became clear that the unit of 105 soldiers who entered My Lai that morning had faced no opposition from the villagers. Even so, at the end of the day as many as five hundred civilians—including women and children—lay dead. Although charges were brought against some of the men, only the commander of the company, Lt. William Calley, was convicted. His sentence of life imprisonment for the murder of at least twenty-two people was later reduced to twenty years, and he was released on full parole in November 1974.

Social protest against the Vietnam War was widespread not only in America but other countries as well. In this photo, young protesters march in Washington, D.C., in 1971.

Why did so many Americans protest U.S. involvement in the Vietnam War?

The Vietnam War divided the American public: The antiwar movement maintained that the conflict in Southeast Asia did not pose a risk to U.S. security (contrary to the "domino effect" that Washington, D.C., foresaw), and in the absence of a threat to national security, protesters wondered, "What are we fighting for?" Meanwhile, President Johnson slowly stepped up the number of troops sent to Vietnam. Many never came home, and those who did came home changed. Mass protests were held, including the hallmark of the era, the sit-in. Protesters accused the U.S. government of not only involving Americans in a conflict in which the country had no part but of supporting a corrupt, unpopular—and undemocratic—government in South Vietnam.

Those Americans who supported the nation's fight against communism eventually became frustrated by the United States' inability to achieve a decisive victory in Vietnam. Even for so-called "hawks," who supported the war, the mounting costs of the war hit home when President Johnson requested new taxes. As the casualty count soared, public approval of U.S. participation in Vietnam dropped. By the end of the 1960s, under increasing public pressure, the government began to withdraw American troops from Vietnam. The evacuation of American ground troops was not complete until 1973. But even then, soldiers who were missing in action (MIAs) and prisoners of war (POWs) were left behind.

What were the "Pentagon Papers"?

"The Pentagon Papers" refers to a seven thousand-page study commissioned by Secretary of Defense Robert S. McNamara. McNamara ordered a study that traced the history of U.S. involvement in the Vietnam conflict. Only fifteen copies of this classified study existed.

What did the U.S. Supreme Court rule in the "Pentagon Papers" case?

The Court ruled 6–3 in *New York Times Co. v. United States* (1971) that the *New York Times* and the *Washington Post* could publish a classified study of U.S. involvement in the Vietnam War. The newspapers contended that allowing the government to halt the publication on matters of urgent public interest would constitute an invalid prior restraint on free expression. The government contended further publication of the study would compromise U.S. intelligence and endanger U.S. troops. The six justices in the majority wrote a three–paragraph *per curiam* opinion that noted that prior restraints are presumptively invalid and that the government failed to carry its burden that such a prior restraint was justified in this case. Three justices dissented, emphasizing that more time was needed to carefully evaluate the thousands of pages in the Pentagon Papers to determine if the government's national security interests were compelling. Each justice wrote a separate opinion.

How did the newspapers acquire copies of the Pentagon Papers?

Daniel Ellsberg (1931–), one of the authors of the study, made a copy of the Pentagon Papers to Neil Sheehan, a reporter with the *New York Times*. Ellsberg, a former Marine and consultant to the Department of Defense and the State Department, believed the study needed to be released to expose government duplicity. Ellsberg had access to the study because he worked for the Rand Corporation. He also gave copies of parts of the story to other newspapers, including the *Washington Post*.

What happened to Daniel Ellsberg?

Ellsberg was first indicted on theft of government property charges on June 29, 1971 (the day before the U.S. Supreme Court decision in the *New York Times Co. v. United States* decision). He faced a second indictment in Los Angeles in December 1971 on thirteen counts, ranging from conspiracy to espionage to theft of government property. Ellsberg and codefendant Anthony Russo faced a trial beginning in January 1973. The trial lasted eighty-nine days. U.S. District Court Judge William Matthew Byrne, Jr. dismissed the charges after a series of disclosures, including the revelation that White House operatives had engineered a burglary of Ellsberg's psychiatrist to obtain his file. The FBI had intercepted Ellsberg's phone conversations and, apparently, President Richard M. Nixon (1913–1994) spoke to Judge Byrne about him becoming the new FBI director. The judge determined: "The bizarre events have incurably infected the prosecution of this case ... the only remedy available that would assure due process and a fair administration of justice is that this trial be terminated and the defendants' motion for dismissal be granted and the jury discharged." Ellsberg continues in his role as a lecturer, writer, and activist, campaigning against government corruption and nuclear weapons. He recently published a book about the Pentagon Papers entitled *Secrets: A Memoir of Vietnam and the Pentagon Papers*.

NIXON

What foreign policy successes did President Nixon have during his administration?

President Nixon had many accomplishments in the foreign policy arena. He opened a new era in the relationship between the United States and China. Nixon was the first president to visit China, a country with which the U.S. had no diplomatic relations. Nixon and Chinese leader Mao Tse-tung (1893–1976) appeared together in public, a sight many would never have predicted given the hostilities between the two nations. The breakthrough in U.S.–China relations arguably forced the Soviet Union to come to the table with the United States because it feared a better relationship between its two rivals. This culminated in President Nixon and Soviet leader Leonid Brezhnev signing the Strategic Arms Limitations Talks (SALT). Under this agreement, the superpowers agreed to curtail missile development and slow the arms race that seemingly threatened world peace.

What was ping-pong diplomacy?

Ping-pong diplomacy is the term given to the agreement between the United States and the People's Republic of China to allow the exchange of table tennis players to each other's countries. The U.S. table tennis team was competing in March 1971 in the World Table Tennis Championships in Japan. They received an invitation from Chinese government officials to enter and tour parts of the country. The U.S. table tennis team and a few accompanying journalists visited Beijing in April 1971—the first time China had allowed official U.S. visitors since 1949. The next year, the Chinese national table tennis team visited the United States. The diplomatic successes of the U.S. and Chinese table tennis teams helped facilitate President Nixon's historic trip to China to meet with Chinese leader Mao.

President Richard Nixon made great strides in foreign relations, most significantly, perhaps, with China. But, because of the Watergate scandal, he was also the first president to resign from office.

Who played the key role in Nixon's foreign policy successes?

Henry Kissinger (1923–) played a key role in the administration's foreign policy from Vietnam to China to the Soviet Union and elsewhere around the world. He served first as Nixon's national security advisor, and then in 1973 became Nixon's secretary of state. He helped negotiate the Paris Peace Accords, which effectively ended U.S. involvement in Vietnam. For this, he won the 1973 Nobel Peace Prize along with North Vietnamese leader Le Duc Tho, who refused the award. Kissinger also crafted the policy of détente (the easing of strained relations) with the Soviet Union and prepared the way for Nixon's historic visit and agreement with China. Kissinger stayed on as President Gerald R. Ford's (1913–2006) secretary of state. Kissinger practiced diplomacy in the spirit of Realpolitik, viewing the process of diplomacy through a pragmatic rather than an ideological lens.

How did Nixon reshape the U.S. Supreme Court?

Nixon reshaped the U.S. Supreme Court by appointing four men to the U.S. Supreme Court who generally were more conservative than their predecessors. In 1969, he appointed D.C. Circuit Court of Appeals judge Warren E. Burger (1907–1995) chief justice to replace Earl Warren. Burger served until his retirement in 1986. He crafted many important First Amendment decisions, including the Court's decisions in *Lemon v. Kurtzman* (1971) and *Miller v. California* (1973). Burger also sought to reign in what he perceived to be some of the criminal justice, pro-defendant rulings of the Warren Court.

Nixon appointed Harry Blackmun (1908–1999), a close friend of Burger's, as a justice in 1970, a position in which he served until 1994. Burger and Blackmun originally were known as the "Minnesota Twins" because they were both from the Gopher State and often voted the same way in many cases. Over time, Blackmun—who had been a judge on the U.S. Court of Appeals for the Eighth Circuit—moved to the left in his judicial philosophy. He later renounced capital punishment in 1994, his last year on the Court, when he proclaimed: "I shall no longer tinker with the machinery of death."

Nixon also appointed Lewis F. Powell, Jr. (1907–1998) to the Court, where he served from 1972–1987. Powell was a distinguished attorney who had been a former president of the American Bar Association. He tended to vote as a moderate on the Court and was the key swing vote in many cases. A famous editorial cartoon once had the caption: "Lewis, tell us what the law is."

Nixon's last appointment was Arizona-based William H. Rehnquist (1924–2005), who had never been a judge before his Supreme Court appointment. Rehnquist worked in the Justice Department as assistant attorney general to the Office of Legal Counsel. He came to the Court in 1972 and did not leave until his death. Rehnquist was the most conservative justice on the Burger Court. He filed solitary dissents so often in cases that his law clerks dubbed him "the Lone Ranger." In 1986, President Ronald Reagan elevated him to chief justice as Burger's replacement, in which position he served until his death.

What was Watergate?

Watergate refers to a series of events in President Nixon's administration that culminated in his ignominious resignation. It began when five members of the President's Committee to Re-elect the President (CREEP) broke into the Democratic National Committee headquarters at the Watergate Hotel in Washington, D.C.

Washington Post reporters Carl Bernstein and Bob Woodward uncovered a massive plan by the Nixon Administration of spying and sabotage conducted in support of the president's reelection campaign. Twenty-five of Nixon's aides served prison sentences as a result of their participation in the Watergate cover-up. Watergate eventually led to Nixon's resigning the presidency after the House Judiciary Committee began impeachment hearings.

What was the Saturday Night Massacre?

The Saturday Night Massacre was the October 20, 1973, controversy involving President Nixon, the Justice Department, and the Special Prosecutor. Nixon had hired Archibald Cox (1912–2004) to serve as the special prosecutor to look into Watergate. Cox, who had served as U.S. solicitor general under President Kennedy, asked Nixon for tapes in the White House. Nixon refused but said he would turn over edited transcripts. When Cox balked, Nixon wanted him fired.

Nixon ordered U.S. Attorney General Elliot Richardson (1920–1999) to fire Cox, but Richardson refused and resigned. Nixon then ordered Assistant U.S. Attorney General

William Ruckelshaus (1932–) to fire Cox, but he also refused (and had resigned earlier). Ultimately, Solicitor General Robert Bork (1927–2012) fired Cox. Richardson and Ruckelshaus held a press conference, decrying the actions. Richardson declared: "At stake, in the final analysis, is the very integrity of the government processes I came to the Department of Justice to help restore."

When did Nixon resign?

The House of Representatives initiated impeachment proceedings against Nixon in May 1974, voting to impeach 27–11 on a charge of obstruction of justice. He then lost the U.S. Supreme Court case in July 1974. Facing full impeachment in the Senate, Nixon resigned on August 9, 1974. Nixon told the American public: "I have concluded that because of the Watergate matter I might not have the support of Congress that I would consider necessary to back the very difficult decisions and carry out the duties of this office in the way I believe the interests of this nation require." He added that "the nation needs a full-time president."

Did Nixon face jail time?

President Nixon never served any jail time. Instead, his successor, President Gerald Ford, Nixon's vice president, gave his former boss a "full, free, and complete pardon" on September 8, 1974. Ford stated: "After years of bitter controversy and divisive national debate, I have been advised, and I am compelled to conclude, that many months and perhaps more years will have to pass before Richard Nixon could obtain a fair trial by jury in any jurisdiction of the United States under governing decisions of the Supreme Court." He concluded:

> Now, therefore, I, Gerald R. Ford, president of the United States, pursuant to the pardon power conferred upon me by Article II, Section 2, of the Constitution, have granted and by these presents do grant a full, free, and absolute pardon unto Richard Nixon for all offenses against the United States which he, Richard Nixon, has committed or may have committed or taken part in during the period from January 20, 1969 through August 9, 1974.

Historians now say Ford was right to do so for a couple of reasons: 1) by accepting the pardon, Nixon had to admit his guilt for the record, and 2) as part of the deal, all records from the White House regarding Watergate were preserved.

On September 8, 1974, President Gerald R. Ford officially pardoned President Richard Nixon of any wrongdoing during the Watergate scandal.

PRESIDENTS FORD AND CARTER

What was unique about President Ford with respect to his tenure as vice president and president?

Gerald R. Ford is the only person in American history to be vice president and president without being elected to either office. He was appointed vice president after Spiro Agnew resigned, and he was appointed president after Richard Nixon resigned.

What was the Helsinki Agreement?

The Helsinki Agreement, or Helsinki Accords, was an international agreement signed in 1975 by more than thirty-five countries, including the Soviet Union. The United States, under the leadership of President Ford, and other Western countries agreed to recognize the territorial boundaries created by the Soviet Union in the wake of World War II. In exchange, the Soviet Union and other Eastern countries agreed to observe human rights principles. The act's ten major principles included recognizing territorial boundaries, preserving peace, equal rights, and self-determination for people, and refraining from the use of force.

What two women tried to assassinate President Ford?

In two different instances, women shot at President Ford in September 1975. On September 5, Lynette "Squeaky" Fromme, a follower of imprisoned cult leader Charles Manson, pointed her gun at Ford in Sacramento, California, but Secret Service agent Larry Buendorf quickly intervened. Fromme was given a life sentence for her attempted assassination of Ford. She finally received parole in August 2009.

On September 22, Sara Jane Moore fired a shot at President Ford that missed. As she was about to take a second shot, ex-Marine Oliver Sipple heroically dived toward her and knocked her arm. Moore was a left-wing sympathizer and former FBI informant who hoped to gain acceptance in radical revolutionary circles. She was given a life sentence but was paroled in 2007, after President Ford died.

What economic condition plagued President Jimmy Carter's (1924–) years in the White House?

Inflation peaked during the Carter years, creating an unstable economic environment. Carter had been a harsh critic of Ford's economic policies, but the economy worsened during his presidency. Both inflation and unemployment rose in Carter's tenure because of the lessening value of the U.S. dollar, caused in part by greater dependence on foreign oil.

What did Carter do when the Soviet Union invaded Afghanistan?

He protested the invasion and attempted to enlist support from other countries to condemn the Soviet action. He also boycotted the 1980 Olympic Games held in Moscow. That led to the Soviets boycotting the 1984 Olympic Games in Los Angeles, California.

What was the Carter Doctrine?

The Carter Doctrine was President Carter's declaration that the United States would not tolerate Soviet attempts to gain control of the Persian Gulf region. Carter proclaimed in his January 1980 State of the Union address: "Let our position be absolutely clear: An attempt by any outside force to gain control of the Persian Gulf region will be regarded as an assault on the vital interests of the United States of America, and such an assault will be repelled by any means necessary, including military force."

Why did the United States give up control of the Panama Canal?

President Carter signed two treaties that relinquished American control over the Panama Canal to Panama. Carter said his objective was "fairness, not force" in turning over the canal to Panama. The U.S. Senate passed the treaties by a vote of 68–32.

What were the Camp David Accords?

The Camp David Accords were a series of agreements between Egypt's President Anwar El Sadat (1918–1981) and Israeli Prime Minister Menachem Begin (1913–1992), with the assistance of President Carter. Carter brought the two leaders together from the hostile countries to Camp David, the name for the country retreat of U.S. presidents. The three leaders crafted the so-called Camp David Accords, named after the location where the three met in secret over a twelve-day period in September 1978.

President Jimmy Carter (center) shakes hands with Egyptian President Anwar Sadat (left) and Israeli Prime Minister Menachem Begin at the conclusion of the Camp David Accords in 1978.

> ## Which of Carter's Cabinet appointees became the country's first African American female to serve in that office?
>
> Carter appointed Patricia Roberts Harris as Secretary of Housing and Urban Development in 1977. She left that position to become Carter's Secretary of Health, Education, and Welfare in 1979. Previously, she had served as U.S. ambassador to Luxembourg during the Johnson Administration and as dean of Howard Law School. She later unsuccessfully challenged Marion Barry for mayor in the District of Columbia.

The Camp David Accords consisted of two agreements: (1) *A Framework for Peace in the Middle East* and (2) *A Framework for the Conclusion of a Peace Treaty between Egypt and Israel*. They later led to the formal peace agreement, the Israel–Egypt Peace Treaty, signed in March 1979. For their efforts, Sadat and Begin received the Nobel Peace Prize. The Camp David Accords were probably the high point of Carter's presidency.

What was the Iran hostage crisis?

The Iran hostage crisis was a diplomatic nightmare for the United States and President Carter. It occurred in November 1979, when Iranian students—who called themselves the Muslim Student Followers of the Imam's Line—under the sway of religious leader Ayatollah Ruhollah Khomeini (1902–1989) ordered the storming of the American embassy and took more than sixty Americans hostage. Earlier that year, the Shah of Iran had lost power, and Muslim extremists took control of the country. Khomeini, who had been banished from Iran for more than fifteen years by the Shah, returned, imbuing the country with fervent anti-American hostility. Khomeini called the United States "the Great Satan."

The Iran hostage crisis doomed Carter's presidency, as he was unsuccessful in negotiating with the Ayatollah, and ordered an ultimately failed rescue attempt. The rescue operation—known as Operation Eagle Claw—resulted in the death of eight U.S. servicemen. Fifty-two of the hostages were not released until President Reagan took office in January 1981.

What was SALT II?

In June 1979, U.S. President Jimmy Carter and Soviet Union premier Leonid Brezhnev (1906–1982) signed the SALT II Treaty, which sought to reduce the dangerous arms race between the world's two nuclear superpowers. Many members of the Senate believed the treaty was too favorable to the Soviets. Also, the Soviet Union invaded Afghanistan, leading to even greater strain between the two countries. Because of this, the Senate never formally ratified the treaty. However, the two countries acted as if the treaty went into effect. In 1986, President Reagan withdrew the United States from the SALT II treaty, alleging that the Soviets were violating the agreement.

TECHNOLOGY

Who invented the first personal computer?

Development of the personal computer (PC), a microcomputer designed to be used by one person, was first developed for business use in the early 1970s. Digital Equipment Corporation developed the PDP–8, predominantly used in scientific laboratories. The credit for developing a computer for home use goes to Steve Wozniak (1950–) and Steve Jobs (1955–2011), college dropouts who founded Apple Computer in 1976. They spent six months working out of a garage, developing the crude prototype for Apple I, which was bought by some six hundred hobbyists—who had to know how to wire, program, and set up the machine. Its successor, Apple II, was introduced in 1977 as the first fully assembled, programmable microcomputer, but it still required customers to use their televisions as screens and to use audio cassettes for data storage. It retailed for just under $1,300. That same year, Commodore and Tandy introduced affordable personal computers. In 1984 Apple Computer introduced the Macintosh (Mac), the first widely used computer with a graphical user interface (GUI). By this time, International Business Machines (IBM) had introduced its PC (1981), which quickly overtook the Mac, despite the fact that IBM was behind in developing a user-friendly graphical interface.

When was email invented?

Short for "electronic mail," email was invented in 1971 by computer engineer Ray Tomlinson (1941–), who developed a communications program for computer users at the Advanced Research Projects Agency (ARPA). The result was ARPAnet, a program that allowed text messages to be sent to any other computer on the local network. ARPAnet is now hailed as the Model T of the Information Superhighway. The technology expanded in the 1970s with the use of modems, which connect computers via telephone lines. Within a decade of its introduction, email had become widely used as a communications mode in the workplace. In the 1990s, usage expanded rapidly to Internet users at home, school, and elsewhere. Some technology analysts call email the "killer app" (application) of the Internet, the most powerful tool on the worldwide computer network.

TRANSITION TO A NEW CENTURY: 1980s TO 2014

THE REAGAN ERA

Why was President Reagan called "The Great Communicator"?

Reagan was called the Great Communicator because he was a powerful speaker who had the ability to charm his viewing and listening audiences.

What was "Reaganomics"?

Reaganomics is the name given to Ronald Reagan's economic policies, which included broad tax cuts, cuts in social programs, and increases in defense spending. Reagan came into office with the mantra: "government isn't the solution to our problems, government is the problem." He believed in supply-side economics, reducing government taxes on business to allow the private sector to grow the economy. Critics charged that Reaganomics favored the rich to the detriment of the poor and constituted a form of "trickle-down" economics.

What was the S&L crisis?

The financial debacle known as the savings and loan crisis was the worst national economic problem since the Great Depression. It had its roots in the late 1970s under the Carter Administration but came to a head in the 1980s when rising interest rates made many savings and loan institutions insolvent. On top of that, the Federal Savings and Loan Insurance Corporation (FSLIC) that insured the S&Ls went bankrupt. The result was that, since the bad loans made on real estate and junk bonds were insured by the federal government, taxpayers ended up picking up the tab to the tune of $124 billion. How exactly this all happened is rather complicated and actually can be traced back to regulations passed as far as the 1930s. The simple explanation is that deregulation al-

Who were the Keating Five?

During the S&L Crisis, five U.S. senators—Alan Cranston (D-CA), John Glenn (D-OH), Dennis DeConcini (D-AZ), John McCain (R-AZ), and Donald W. Riegle (D-MI)—were approached by Charles Keating, Jr., who was chair of the Lincoln Savings and Loan Association. The entity was in trouble because of the S&L crisis, and Keating gave the senators a total of $1.3 million in campaign contributions; in return, the politicians met with federal banking regulators on Keating's behalf. Lincoln Savings and Loan went under anyway, costing taxpayers about $3 billion. The Keating Five were all subjected to Ethics Committee investigations. Cranston was censured; the other four were reprimanded by Congress.

lowed for S&Ls to behave more like corporate banks and make loans and investments that were not secure; greed set in, and when interest rates rose, the S&Ls didn't have enough money to cover called-in loans. Almost 750 savings and loans closed their doors, and the healthier S&Ls that remained open had to pay additional taxes amounting to about $30 billion in costs. Court cases are still proceeding to this day, costing businesses an estimated additional $10 billion in legal fees.

What was the War on Drugs?

The War on Drugs was the catchphrase used by the Reagan Administration to define its efforts to combat what many saw as a crack cocaine epidemic in the country—a drug that particularly devastated many urban communities. In 1986, Reagan signed a criminal law that imposed mandatory minimum sentences and created greater sentences for drug traffickers. First Lady Nancy Reagan participated actively in the fight against drugs with her national campaign, "Just Say No."

Who shot President Reagan?

On March 30, 1981, John Hinckley, Jr. shot President Reagan at the Washington, D.C., Hilton Hotel. Reagan—who had been in office only a short time—suffered only an injured arm and a punctured lung. Hinckley shot White House Press Secretary James Brady (1940–2014) in the head, leaving him disabled. He also shot Secret Service Agent Timothy McCarthy and D.C. Metropolitan police officer Tom Delahanty.

Hinckley, who came from a wealthy family, allegedly acted irrationally out of an obsession for actress Jodie Foster, who had starred in the film *Taxi Driver* as a child prostitute. Hinckley identified with the protagonist in the movie, Travis Bickle, who tries to assassinate a United States senator; Bickle is convinced that violence is the answer to the social ills he feels have caused the downfall of Foster's character. A jury found Hinckley not guilty by reason of insanity, and he remains confined in a mental hospital to this day.

A photographer snapped this photo of President Reagan just before Reagan was shot by John Hinckley Jr. at the Washington Hilton Hotel on March 30, 1981. Immediately behind and to the president's left is White House Press Secretary James Brady, who received severe head injuries. Brady later became a staunch advocate for gun-control laws. Also shown are Tom Delahanty (policeman on far right) and Secret Serviceman Timothy McCarthy (far right, light suit).

What small military action did the United States win in 1983?

Reagan ordered the deployment of American troops to the island of Grenada. Reagan deployed more than seven thousand troops to support the government from a left wing military coup by a Cuban-supported regime. It was the United States's first major military operation since Vietnam and led to an easy American victory. President Reagan kept his promise to remove American troops by the end of the year.

Why did the United States try to kill Libyan leader Muammar al-Gaddafi?

Reagan targeted Libyan leader Muammar al-Gaddafi for his sponsorship of terrorists who attacked the United States. Reagan referred to Gaddafi, who became the leader of Libya in 1969, as the "mad dog of the Middle East." U.S. air forces targeted several areas near Tripoli (Libya's capital) on April 15, 1986. Reagan justified the attack after learning that Gaddafi was responsible for the bombing of a West Berlin disco that left two Americans dead. Reagan also believed that Gaddafi had sponsored attacks on the airports in Rome, Italy, and Vienna, Austria, in 1985.

How did President Reagan become associated with "Star Wars"?

Although it was a clever name that reminded people of the science-fiction blockbuster movie, "Star Wars" actually referred to the serious military strategy called the Strategic

Defense Initiative (SDI). The concept was that the United States could create a kind of shield in space consisting of satellites that would be able to shoot down any long-range nuclear missiles from countries such as the Soviet Union. Reagan unveiled the idea on March 23, 1983, and hoped that scientific advancements could make nuclear weapons obsolete. SDI outraged Soviet leader Mikhail Gorbachev, who reasoned that if the United States were invulnerable to nuclear attack, what was there to prevent the Americans from attacking the Soviet Union? Reagan and Gorbachev would later discuss SDI at their meetings, including the 1986 Reykjavic, Iceland summit, without reaching a compromise.

SDI was eventually declared technologically impossible, and the concept of missile defense eventually morphed under President Bill Clinton's administration (1946–) to become the Ballistic Missile Defense Organization in 1993. The BMDO has a much more modest goal of regional missile defense concepts defending troops against localized attacks.

What was the Iran–Contra affair?

It was a series of actions on the part of U.S. federal government officials, which came to light in November 1986. The discoveries had the immediate effect of hurting President Reagan, whose policy of antiterrorism had been undermined by activities initiated from his own executive office. Following in-depth hearings and investigations into "who knew what and when," special prosecutor Lawrence Walsh (1912–2014) submitted his report on January 18, 1994, stating that the dealings with Iran and with the Contra rebels in Nicaragua had "violated United States policy and law."

The tangled string of events involved Reagan's National Security Advisers Robert McFarlane (1937–) and Admiral John Poindexter (1936–), Lieutenant Colonel Oliver North (1943–), Poindexter's military aide, the Iranian government, and Nicaraguan rebels.

The U.S. officials evidently had begun their dealings with both the Iranian government and the Nicaraguan rebels with the goal of freeing seven Americans, who were held hostage by Iranian-backed rebels in Lebanon. President Reagan had met with the families of the captives and was naturally concerned about the hostage situation. Under pressure to work to free the hostages, McFarlane, Poindexter, and North arranged to sell an estimated $30 million in spare parts and antiaircraft missiles to Iran (then at war

---

What did President Reagan famously say in Berlin in 1987?

One of the phrases most often quoted to come out of Reagan's mouth was "Mr. Gorbachev, tear down this wall." The day was June 12, 1987, and Reagan was giving a speech at the Brandenberg Gate in Berlin, Germany, which had long been divided by the Berlin Wall that continued to stand as a symbol of the Cold War. The wall *did* came down two years later, on November 9, 1989, signaling the end of the Cold War; Germany reunited in 1990 and the following year saw the collapse of the Soviet Union into independent republics.

During a speech next to Berlin's Brandenberg Gate on June 12, 1987, President Ronald Reagan famously challenged Soviet union leader Mikhail Gorbachev to tear down the Berlin Wall and end the division of East and West Germany.

with neighboring Iraq). In return, the Iranian government would put pressure on the terrorist groups to release the Americans.

Profits from the arms sale to Iran were then diverted by Lieutenant North to the Contras in Central America, who were fighting the dictatorial Nicaraguan government. Congress had already passed laws that prohibited U.S. government aid to the Nicaraguan rebels; the diversion of funds certainly appeared to violate those laws.

The Iran–Contra affair led to North's dismissal and to Poindexter's resignation. Both men were prosecuted. Though the hostages were freed, Reagan's public image was seriously damaged by how the release had been achieved.

During the Iran–Contra hearings in 1987, National Security Commission officials revealed that they had been willing to take the risk of providing arms to Iran in exchange for the safe release of the hostages because they all remembered the U.S. government's failed attempt in 1980 to rescue hostages held at the American Embassy in Tehran, Iran.

Nevertheless, the deal with Iran had supplied a hostile country with American arms that could then be used against the United States. In 1987, Iran launched an offensive when it attacked Kuwaiti oil tankers that were registered as American and laid mines in the Persian Gulf. The United States responded by sending in the navy which attacked Iranian patrol boats. During this military initiative, the U.S. Navy accidentally shot down a civilian passenger jet, killing everyone on board.

What major law signed by President George H. W. Bush (1924–) has had a significant impact for those with disabilities?

On July 26, 1990, President George H. W. Bush signed into law the Americans with Disabilities Act (ADA). This law prohibits public or private employers with fifteen or more employees from discriminating against qualified individuals with disabilities. The law generally requires employers to provide reasonable accommodations for such employees, rather than just terminating or otherwise discriminating against such employees.

A qualified person with a disability refers to an employee who can—with or without a reasonable accommodation—perform the essential functions of a job. A disability under the law is defined as a mental or physical impairment that significantly impairs someone's life activities; someone with a record of such an impairment; or someone who is regarded as having such an impairment.

The law overwhelmingly passed both the House and Senate with overwhelming bipartisan support. The ADA not only impacts employment practices. It also prevents disability discrimination in areas of public accommodation. This means that businesses often must provide proper access to those with disabilities. President Bush was effusive in his praise of the law and its potential impact on signing the law. He stated:

> This act is powerful in its simplicity. It will ensure that people with disabilities are given the basic guarantees for which they have worked so long and so hard: independence, freedom of choice, control of their lives, the opportunity to blend fully and equally into the rich mosaic of the American mainstream. Legally, it will provide our disabled community with a powerful expansion of protections and then basic civil rights. It will guarantee fair and just access to the fruits of American life which we all must be able to enjoy. And then, specifically, first the ADA ensures that employers covered by the act cannot discriminate against qualified individuals with disabilities. Second, the ADA ensures access to public accommodations such as restaurants, hotels, shopping centers, and offices. And third, the ADA ensures expanded access to transportation services. And fourth, the ADA ensures equivalent telephone services for people with speech or hearing impediments.

What treaty did President Bush sign with Soviet President Mikhail Gorbachev?

Presidents Bush and Gorbachev (1931–) signed the 1991 Strategic Arms Reduction Treaty, in which both countries pledged to reduce their nuclear arms. Bush called the treaty a "significant step forward in dispelling half a century of mistrust." It was these two leaders—Bush and Gorbachev—who played a key role in the historic ending of the Cold War, a truly remarkable accomplishment between the two superpowers.

President George H. W. Bush signed the Americans with Disabilities Act in 1990.

Who was Manuel Noriega?

U.S. forces invaded Panama and removed dictator Manuel Noriega from power. Noriega had defied the results of a democratic election in his country in which he had been ousted. The U.S. faced charges of "American imperialism" for its intervention. Bush referred to the U.S. deployment of more than twenty thousand troops as "Operation Just Cause."

What fellow member of the Reagan Administration did Bush pardon?

Bush pardoned Reagan's Secretary of Defense Caspar Weinberger, who faced criminal charges arising out of the Iran–Contra scandal. Bush called Weinberger a "true American patriot."

What was the "North American Free Trade Agreement"?

Bush signed the North American Free Trade Agreement (NAFTA) with the leaders of Canada and Mexico. This measure greatly reduced tariffs on the countries' goods, and many believed it had a positive impact on the economy.

What "not guilty" verdict led to significant rioting in Los Angeles?

On April 29, 1992, a jury in Simi Valley, California, rendered a "not guilty" verdict in the trial of four white Los Angeles police officers for assaulting a black motorist named Rodney King (1965–2012). The jury also found three of the four officers not guilty of using excessive force.

This verdict outraged many residents of South Central Los Angeles, who for years complained about police brutality. The verdict outraged many, because there was a videotape that showed the officers beating King. King, who had a criminal record, had led the officers on a high-speed car chase, exceeding more than one hundred miles per hour. Eventually, the officers used a taser on King and appeared to beat him for a significant period of time. King suffered a broken cheekbone, a skull fracture, and other injuries.

A local resident named George Holliday caught the beating on videotape. The nine-minute videotape was key in leading to charges against four of the five officers in state court. On the day the verdict was announced, rioting began in South Central Los Angeles. The rioting lasted five days, leading to more than fifty deaths and two thousand injuries. Order was not restored until the California Army National Guard and U.S. Marines from a nearby base were deployed. The riots are known under several names, including the Rodney King Riots, the L.A. Riots, or the South Central Riots.

Later, the four officers—Stacey Koon, Laurence Powell, Timothy Wind, and Theodore Briseno—were charged in federal court with civil rights violations. A federal jury found Koon and Powell guilty and sentenced them to more than two years in prison.

What happened to Rodney King?

Rodney King was never charged with a crime, even though he was driving under the influence and fleeing from the police at speeds exceeding 100 m.p.h. Instead, because of the excessive force used by the police, the city of Los Angeles awarded King nearly $4 million in damages after a civil suit. King continued to have trouble with the law in subsequent years, including driving under the influence and domestic violence problems. He later wrote a book and appeared on the television show "Celebrity Rehab." He was found dead in his swimming pool in 2012. He was forever linked with the 1992 L.A. Riots, but also for the statement: "Why Can't We All Just Get Along."

What charges of sexual harassment nearly derailed a Supreme Court nominee?

Justice Clarence Thomas (1948–) narrowly survived contentious confirmation hearings to earn Senate confirmation by a narrow vote of 52–48. The hearings arose because of sexual harassment charges against Thomas by law professor Anita Hill (1956–), who used to work under Thomas at the U.S. Department of Education and the Equal Employment Opportunity Commission. The allegations were controversial, in part, because Hill initiated the charges years after the fact, on the eve of Thomas's confirmation. Thomas vehemently denied the allegations and declared in his testimony:

> This is not an opportunity to talk about difficult matters privately or in a closed environment. This is a circus. It's a national disgrace. And from my standpoint, as a black American, it is a high-tech lynching for uppity blacks who in any way deign to think for themselves, to do for themselves, to have different ideas, and

it is a message that unless you kowtow to an old order, this is what will happen to you. You will be lynched, destroyed, caricatured by a committee of the U.S. Senate rather than hung from a tree.

The televised hearings were watched by millions of Americans—with many divided along political party lines.

THE FIRST PERSIAN GULF WAR

What brought about the first Persian Gulf War?

American planners, especially those who concentrated on the geopolitics of oil, had been jittery for more than a decade, but the situation seemed fairly calm in the midsummer of 1990. Then, on August 2, 1990, three divisions of the Iraqi Army crossed the border into Kuwait.

Saddam Hussein and his government claimed Kuwait on historical, geographical terms, saying it had once belonged to Iraq. Beyond that, however, it was obvious that he desired the oil revenues of Kuwait, which he needed after spending so much money fighting Iran (the Iran–Iraq War lasted from 1980–1988, and Iraq was the loser; interestingly, the United States had supported Hussein in the conflict). In 1990, Kuwait produced 1.7 million barrels of oil per day, not far behind Iraq's 2.6 million. By adding Kuwait's oil to his own, Hussein would become the second–largest producer of petroleum in the entire world after Saudi Arabia (which then produced 5.3 million barrels per day). Saudi Arabia was very much on the minds of American strategists, because it was possible that the Iraqi Army would continue to move south.

When and how did the war begin?

On January 17, 1991, two days after the UN resolution deadline expired, coalition forces began a massive, dramatic aerial bombardment of the Iraqi positions in Kuwait. Roughly twenty-eight hundred aerial sorties were made that day, and this remained the average for the next thirty-seven days of the bombardment. No one could say for certain how much damage was done, but Americans who watched CNN (Cable Network News) were treated, each night, to a series of photographs that suggested the bombs were indeed falling on their targets. The Bush Administration rightly feared that hundreds of thousands of protesters would turn out in the United States, but the protests of 1991 were tame compared to those of 1967 and 1968. Many people who had been young protesters in 1968 were now college administrators and high-level business people, and the Bush Administration proved adept at "managing" the dissent. It must be said, too, that the protesters made a clear division—as they had not in 1967 and 1968—of excoriating the policy while supporting the soldiers in the field.

255

How did Americans feel as armed conflict neared?

A good deal of apprehension existed. Those who examined the military situation on its own merits concluded that America and its allies would prevail, while those who harkened back to Vietnam believed that Iraq might prove yet another quagmire. President Bush, so articulate and even charming when speaking to international leaders, proved the opposite when speaking to his own countrymen; a World War II bomber pilot, he kept his cards close to the chest.

By January 1991, the size of the coalition buildup was startling. Over 630,000 troops were in Saudi Arabia, about 470,000 of them American. The coalition forces had 3,449 tanks, of which nineteen hundred were American. Numbers do not tell the whole story, however. The U.S. forces employed the M1 Tank, far superior to the T–72s used by the Iraqi military. Then, too, the coalition forces had a great advantage in aircraft, as well as materiel on the ground. One of the "smallest" yet most important articles were the night glasses employed by many U.S. soldiers; these gave them a distinct advantage in what followed.

When did the ground war begin?

On February 24, 1991, hundreds of thousands of coalition soldiers went into action. Their tactics were described as those of "distraction and outflanking," but in truth little disguise was necessary. The Iraqi soldiers who were still alive put up a fight until the coalition forces rained artillery on them; from that moment forward, they began to surrender. One of the most surprising photographs was of an Iraqi soldier captured by U.S. Marines; upon realizing that he would not only be spared but would actually be fed, he kissed the hands of the Marines who captured him.

How long did it take to liberate Kuwait City?

That was the question posed by *Time* magazine, which highlighted the success of Operation Desert Storm with a cover photograph of U.S. soldiers in Kuwait City. The photograph revealed both the joy felt by the liberated and the panorama of U.S. soldiers who took part in the operation. Of the ten U.S. soldiers shown, five were African American, and one looked Asian. This revealed a startling change in the racial and ethnic demographics of the U.S. Armed Forces. What the photograph did not reveal—and what became apparent only later—is that seven percent of the U.S. forces in the Persian Gulf were female. A major social and gender revolution was happening quietly behind the scenes and would become much more evident during the Second Gulf War.

Who made the decision to call the war at "one hundred hours"?

The ground war began on February 24 and ended on February 28. Because of the different time zones, reporters used slightly different "numbers," but most accounts concur that the war lasted approximately one hundred hours. The decision to end the war came from President Bush.

After being overrun by Iraq in January 1991, Kuwait City was liberated by the Americans by the end of February.

Almost at the very hour the war officially ended, some American servicemen reported seeing strange, dark clouds; when it rained that night, some personnel went out to get a nice soaking. Instead of refreshing rain, they encountered a heavy mist that they later learned was residue from oil refineries which Hussein's men had set afire. The Persian Gulf War was over, but the conflict with Saddam Hussein festered a very long time.

Why did President Bush and the other coalition leaders not push on to Baghdad?

President Bush was criticized for this on many occasions, but it must be remembered that the UN resolution did not call for Hussein's overthrow, just the liberation of Kuwait. President Bush and his top advisers also feared that advancing further might result in chaos that would be even worse than what Iraq currently experienced. On balance, most thoughtful analyses came to the same conclusion: It was wise for the coalition to liberate Kuwait, but *not* to push on to Baghdad.

Anyone looking from an airplane or at aerial reconnaissance photos would have concluded that Hussein's end was near. He had lost perhaps 100,000 men in the war, and those who survived looked shell-shocked and dismayed. The Road of Death, as it was called, ran nearly one hundred miles from Kuwait City to the north, and it was littered with destroyed cars, tanks, and personnel carriers. No one knows how many people perished on that terrible highway, but it was surely the single greatest infliction of punishment from the air ever seen in war. About the only means of revenge Hussein could employ was to set the oil refineries ablaze.

What were the terms of the truce?

Hussein's regime had to disavow any claims to Kuwait. More important, it had to agree to a series of "no-fly" zones, over which only coalition airplanes could fly. This was meant, quite intentionally, to prevent Hussein from punishing anyone who rose in revolt against him, and many coalition leaders believed that the Shiite minority in southern Iraq—as well as the Kurdish minority in northern Iraq—would rise very shortly. They did, but with disastrous consequences.

The truce also stipulated that Hussein had to allow UN weapons inspectors into Iraq and that they were to be given free access to all his major munitions plants in order to determine whether Iraq was stockpiling chemical weapons: nerve gas was especially feared. Saddam Hussein agreed to all these terms.

PRESIDENT CLINTON: A BRIEF RETURN TO PROSPERITY

What was the Family and Medical Leave Act?

President Bill Clinton signed into law the Family and Medical Leave Act of 1993, which provided that employees working for employers with fifty or more employees could take a three-month period of paid or unpaid leave (at the employer's discretion) for pregnancy or a serious medical condition.

What is the Line Item Veto Act of 1996?

President Clinton signed into law the Line Item Veto Act of 1996, giving the president the power to veto specific budgetary provisions of a bill without impacting the rest of the legislation. The measure had been introduced by Senator Robert Dole. The U.S. Supreme Court invalidated the measure in *Clinton v. City of New York* (1998) by a 6–3 vote. Writing for the majority, Justice John Paul Stevens wrote: "This Act gives the president the unilateral power to change the text of duly enacted statutes." He concluded, "If there is to be a new procedure in which the president will play a different role in determining the final text of what may 'become a law,' such change must come not by legislation but through the amendment procedures set forth in Article V of the Constitution."

CONTROVERSIES, DISASTER, AND TERROR

What controversial military policy regarding gay service members began in 1993?

"Don't Ask, Don't Tell" was a policy that prevented the military from discriminating against gays, as long as they did not publicly announce that they were gay. However, if a military person publicly announced he or she was gay, then the armed services could discharge that person. The policy proclaimed that a person who engaged in active homosexual conduct could be dismissed from the armed services because his or her presence could undermine morale and discipline in the Armed Forces.

President Barack Obama (1961–) formally certified the end of the policy in July 2011, stating:

> Today, the discriminatory law known as "Don't Ask, Don't Tell" is finally and formally repealed. As of today, patriotic Americans in uniform will no longer have to lie about who they are in order to serve the country they love. As of today, our armed forces will no longer lose the extraordinary skills and combat experience of so many gay and lesbian service members. And today, as Commander in Chief, I want those who were discharged under this law to know that your country deeply values your service. …

> For more than two centuries, we have worked to extend America's promise to all our citizens. Our armed forces have been both a mirror and a catalyst of that progress, and our troops, including gays and lesbians, have given their lives to defend the freedoms and liberties that we cherish as Americans. Today, every American can be proud that we have taken another great step toward keeping our military the finest in the world and toward fulfilling our nation's founding ideals.

What major terrorist attacks occurred on U.S. soil in the 1990s?

In February 1993, a bomb in a car in the bottom parking lot of the North Tower of the World Trade Center in New York City exploded, killing six people and injuring more than a thousand. Ramzi Yousef (1967–)—who had received some training from the terrorist group al-Qaeda—and several others planned and implemented the attack. In February 1995, Pakistani authorities captured Yousef, who received a life sentence from a federal judge in New York. He later exclaimed in federal court: "Yes, I am a terrorist, and proud of it as long as it is against the U.S. government and against Israel, because you are more than terrorists; you are the one who invented terrorism and using it every day. You are butchers, liars and hypocrites."

In April 1995, former U.S. military members Timothy McVeigh (1968–2001) and Terry Nichols (1955–) carried out the Oklahoma City bombing, destroying a federal building that caused the death of 168 people and injured more than six hundred . It was the worst act of terrorism on U.S. soil until the September 11, 2001, attack in New York

What did the United States do regarding the Rwandan genocide?

The Clinton administration failed to act quickly in Rwanda. Because of that inaction, the Rwanda genocide occurred, in which Hutu militants—including some in the government—slaughtered more than 800,000 Tutsis and many moderate Hutus. Many believe that if the United Nations and the United States had intervened more quickly, the bloodshed would have been much less. To his credit, during a 1998 visit to Rwanda, Clinton apologized for not acting sooner.

City. McVeigh and Nichols had been upset over the U.S. invasion at the Branch David-ian compound in Waco, Texas, in 1993 and the U.S. actions in Ruby Ridge, Idaho, where FBI snipers killed some of the children of alleged white separatist Randy Weaver (1948–). In fact, McVeigh planned to carry out the attack on April 19, 1995, two years to the day after the Waco invasion. McVeigh was convicted and later executed in June 2001, the first execution of a federal prisoner in thirty-eight years. Nichols was sentenced to multiple life sentences and will remain incarcerated for the rest of his life.

What was Whitewater?

Whitewater refers to a failed land deal by Jim and Susan McDougal and Bill and Hillary Clinton. The McDougals convinced the Clintons to invest money in a land development project. The four agreed to buy more than 230 acres of land in the Ozark Mountains in Arkansas, which they hoped they would sell for a handsome profit. Pursuant to that plan, the four formed the Whitewater Development Corporation. The Clintons claimed that Jim McDougal was the active partner and that they were passive, silent partners. Jim and Susan McDougal faced criminal charges, but the Clintons were never charged with a crime. Jim McDougal faced many criminal charges for fraud for allegedly using pro-ceeds from federally insured savings and loans to pay for the land.

Who is Monica Lewinsky?

Monica Lewinsky (1973–) was a twenty-two-year-old White House intern who had a sexual affair with President Clinton. Extramarital affair allegations had dogged Clinton for years,

but this one was more problematic. Clinton testified under oath in a deposition that he never had sex with Lewinsky in a suit brought by Paula Jones (1966–), a woman who sued Clinton for sexual harassment for conduct while he was governor of Arkansas.

Independent Counsel Ken Starr (1946–)—who was investigating Clinton for other White House scandals—cited the Lewinsky matter in detail in his re-port. The alleged lies in Clinton's testi-mony in the Paula Jones case led to impeachment charges for perjury and ob-struction of justice.

What happened during President Clinton's impeachment process?

The Republican-controlled House voted to impeach Clinton on perjury and obstruc-

White House intern Monica Lewinsky's affair with President Bill Clinton led to the president being impeached in 1998. Clinton was never convicted of any crime, however.

tion of justice in December 1998. However, in a twenty-one-day trial presided over by U.S. Supreme Court Justice William Rehnquist, the U.S. Senate acquitted Clinton on both counts. The Senate voted 50–50 and 45–55 on the two counts, far short of the necessary sixty-seven votes needed for conviction.

What blogger made headlines with his reporting on the Clinton–Lewinsky controversy?

Matt Drudge (1966–) blogged about the Monica Lewinsky–Bill Clinton controversy before it hit the traditional mainstream media. Drudge blogged about the events in his news aggregation site, *The Drudge Report*. Drudge also was the first to report that Jack Kemp would be Republican presidential nominee Bob Dole's running mate. Drudge's reporting inspired a legion of other online bloggers who in some ways changed the face of modern journalism and news reporting.

Why is President Clinton looked on favorably by many, despite such controversies as Whitewater and Monica Lewinsky?

Under President Clinton, the United States enjoyed one of its most economically prosperous periods. Certainly not the least of these accomplishments was that Clinton oversaw the longest period of economic expansion in American history: One hundred fifteen months of growth, averaging about four percent a year for the gross domestic product. Twenty-two million jobs were created, and unemployment dropped from seven to four percent. Welfare rolls were cut in half, and median family income rose over $6,000 from 1993 to 2000 (in contrast, during the Bush era, it had been shrinking by $2,000 per year). Finally, home ownership for families increased from about 64 percent to nearly 68 percent, a record under any U.S. president. On a national level, the government paid off $360 billion in debt—when Clinton left office, the country was actually had a $237 billion surplus.

In addition to economic accomplishments, what else did President Clinton achieve?

Clinton championed education. He created HOPE scholarships for college students and Lifetime Learning tax credits through which taxpayers could deduct bills used toward their education. President Clinton also increased Pell Grants and the Federal Work-Study Program. Along with his vice president, Al Gore, Clinton spearheaded the way to connect more schools than ever to the Internet (ninety-five percent by the time he left office).

Regarding law and order, President Clinton put 100,000 more police on the streets, funded programs to help prevent crime, and signed the Brady Bill in 1993, preventing tens of thousands of potential criminals from buying guns. During his eight years in office, crime rates dropped every year. He not only made the streets safer at home, but Clinton worked with Russian President Boris Yeltsin to obtain and dismantle 1,700 former Soviet nuclear warheads.

President Bill Clinton and Al Gore on the campaign trail in 1992. Clinton served two terms and oversaw the greatest economic expansion in U.S. history.

PRESIDENT GEORGE W. BUSH AND THE BEGINNING OF THE WAR ON TERROR

Whom did Bush defeat to win the presidency in 2000?

Republican Bush defeated Democrat Al Gore, vice president for Bill Clinton, in arguably the most controversial election in American history. Gore won the popular vote, and some media outlets actually proclaimed Gore the winner. However, Bush ended up capturing the Electoral College—and the presidency—by a vote of 271–266. Gore had served in the U.S. House of Representatives and the U.S. Senate for Tennessee before serving two terms as Clinton's vice president.

What made the election so controversial?

The election was controversial due to the awarding of Florida's twenty-five electoral votes to Bush—a decision ultimately made by the U.S. Supreme Court. Gore was initially predicted president by some media outlets as a result of exit polling, but that was retracted when poll results showed Bush pulling ahead.

The media then declared Bush the winner, but vote results were still coming from three Florida counties—Miami-Dade, Broward, and Palm Beach—that were expected to vote in favor of Gore. The gap shrunk to just two thousand votes statewide—enough to force a recount. Gore asked for manual hand recounts in four counties—the three mentioned earlier and Volusia County.

Florida's secretary of state, Republican Katherine Harris, certified the results on November 14, 2000, declaring Bush the winner. Lawsuits erupted over the recounting; Gore wanted the recounting process continued and the deadline extended, and Bush wanted the result declared official.

The Florida Supreme Court ruled in favor of Gore, saying that the recount process deadline should be extended. However, the U.S. Supreme Court effectively decided the election in *Bush v. Gore* (2000), ruling that Florida's system of counting votes differently in different counties violated the Equal Protection Clause. The result was deemed largely political, as it was decided by a 5–4 vote: The five more conservative justices—Chief Justice William Rehnquist, Antonin Scalia, Anthony Kennedy, Sandra Day O'Connor, and Clarence Thomas—voted for Bush. The four more liberal justices—John Paul Stevens, Ruth Bader Ginsburg, Stephen Breyer, and David Souter—voted for Gore.

What was the Moscow Treaty?

President Bush and Russian President Vladimir Putin signed the Moscow Treaty—also known as the Strategic Offensive Reductions Treaty (SORT)—on May 24, 2002, in Moscow. Under the measure, each country agreed to keep its level of operational nuclear warheads between seventeen hundred and twenty-two hundred. SORT is an extension of earlier treaties between the two countries such as SALT I and II and START I, II, and III.

What is "No Child Left Behind"?

On January 8, 2002, President Bush effected No Child Left Behind (NCLB). Bush had sought to improve education as Texas governor, and called for national educational reform during his presidential campaign. NCLB requires school districts to meet specific state standards and testing to ensure that children are learning. The federal law does not set national standards but allows states to set their own standards to measure student

President George W. Bush named the first two African Americans to serve as secretaries of state. Who were they?

President Bush's secretaries of state were Colin Powell (1937–) and Condoleezza Rice (1954–). Powell, a four-star general, had been national security advisor to President Reagan and chair of the Joint Chief of staffs under President Bush. He served as Bush's secretary of state from 2001–2005.

Rice was Bush's national security advisor from 2001–2005. Previously, she had been provost at Stanford University, her alma mater, and served as a key member of President Bush's national security team.

competency. NCLB also led to increased funding for education in the country. But NCLB's critics charge that it has distorted education by focusing too much on standardized tests and does not teach enough about civic education and other subjects.

What awful terrorist strike occurred that defined the early years of the Bush administration?

On September 11, 2001, nineteen Islamic radicals conducted the worst terrorist strike on American soil (9/11). They hijacked four commercial airliner jets and crashed two airplanes into the Twin Towers of the World Trade Center in New York City, killing more than three thousand people. They crashed another plane into the Pentagon, killing nearly two hundred people. A fourth plane was grounded in Pennsylvania, due to the heroic efforts of the passengers who stormed the attackers, saving countless lives but losing their own.

The hijackers were all members of the terrorist group al-Qaeda led by Osama bin Laden (1957–2011). The United States and other countries responded with a global War on Terror and sought to cripple al-Qaeda.

What did Bush say in his speech to the country after 9/11?

President Bush gave an inspired speech to the American public following 9/11. His remarks included:

As with the North Tower of the World Trade Center, the destruction of the South Tower was complete. Many who witnessed the 9/11 attacks in New York were stunned that the landmark towers had completely collapsed.

Terrorist attacks can shake the foundations of our biggest buildings, but they cannot touch the foundation of America. These acts shatter steel, but they cannot dent the steel of American resolve.

The search is underway for those who are behind these evil acts. I've directed the full resources for our intelligence and law enforcement communities to find those responsible and bring them to justice. We will make no distinction between the terrorists who committed these acts and those who harbor them.

None of us will ever forget this day, yet we go forward to defend freedom and all that is good and just in our world.

What is "al-Qaeda"?

Al-Qaeda (an Arabic phrase meaning "the base") is a global network of terrorists who banded together during the 1990s and proclaimed to carry out a holy war on non-Islamic nations. While the group knows no national boundaries, certain nations—including Afghanistan—were known to be al-Qaeda strongholds.

Led by the elusive Osama bin Laden, a wealthy exiled Saudi, the group conducted terrorist training programs in several Muslim (mostly Middle Eastern) countries and was funded by loyalists around the world. One of the United States' first actions following the 9/11 attacks (which were later confirmed to have been carried out by al-Qaeda operatives) was to freeze bank accounts of persons and organizations with suspected ties to the terrorist group.

The roots of al-Qaeda can be traced to the Soviet invasion of Afghanistan in 1979, when thousands of Muslims, including bin Laden, joined the Afghan resistance. The ten-year conflict was a rallying point for Islamic extremists. Bin Laden returned home to Saudi Arabia in 1989, determined to perpetuate a holy war (jihad) by maintaining the funding, organization, and training that had made the Afghan resistance victorious against the Soviets. By the early 1990s, he emerged as a leader in the Muslim world, proclaiming his goal to reinstate the Caliphate (a unified Muslim state). He also proclaimed the United States to be an enemy of Islam; he considered the nation responsible for all conflicts involving Muslims. The Saudi government rescinded his passport in 1994, and bin Laden fled his homeland. He eventually found safe harbor in Taliban-ruled Afghanistan. According to the report issued by the 9/11 Commission, bin Laden's declaration of war came in February 1998, when he and fugitive Egyptian physician Ayman al-Zawahiri "arranged from their Afghanistan headquarters for an Arabic newspaper in London to publish a *fatwa* issued in the name of a World Islamic Front." The statement claimed that America had declared war against God and his messenger, and they called for retaliation.

Under bin Laden's direction, al-Qaeda carried out several attacks on American targets, including the August 7, 1998, bombings of U.S. embassies in Kenya and Tanzania—killing 258 and injuring five thousand—and the 9/11 attacks, killing nearly three thousand people. After the Global Coalition Against Terrorism, led by U.S. forces, launched its attack on Afghanistan in October 2001, bin Laden was believed to have fled for Pakistan. Capturing him and other al-Qaeda leaders and operatives was the key objective of the United States in its efforts to dismantle the terrorist network.

What federal law did Congress pass—and President Bush sign—shortly after 9/11?

In October 2001, Congress passed a law known as Providing Appropriate Tools Required to Intercept and Obstruct Terrorism, better known by its acronym—the PATRIOT Act. President Bush signed the measure into law on October 26, 2001. The law served as a lightning rod for controversy and sparked debate over the proper balance between national security and civil liberties. Supporters contend that the Patriot Act was necessary to protect the country from future terrorist attacks to help prevent another 9/11 attack; critics charged that the Patriot Act violated constitutional rights and gave government too much power.

Part of the problem when discussing the Patriot Act is confusion over the vast number of provisions in the law. It consisted of more than three hundred pages, and amended more than fifteen different federal laws. The law permitted roving wiretaps, sneak-and-peek warrants, and national security letters and sought to bridge the gap between U.S. foreign and domestic intelligence.

Some provisions of the law arguably were necessary to bring surveillance laws up to speed in the technological age. Other provisions seemed to encroach unnecessarily upon the Constitution's Fourth Amendment right to be free from unreasonable searches and seizures.

President Bush adamantly believed the Patriot Act was necessary to fight the War on Terror and to prevent future terrorist attacks on American soil. Supporters contend that the Patriot Act helped American law enforcement break up terror cells and prevented another 9/11 for the remainder of Bush's presidency.

What country and regime did Bush order attacked after 9/11?

President Bush, with Congressional approval, authorized an attack on Afghanistan, which began on October 7, 2001. The so-called "Operation Enduring Freedom" sought to crush the Taliban government in Afghanistan that had given safe haven to the al-Qaeda regime. The war in Afghanistan initially was successful, in the sense that the Taliban regime was toppled and some members of al-Qaeda captured. However, the war has dragged on, and its popularity has waned as U.S. casualties have risen.

President George W. Bush signed the Patriot Act on October 26, 2001. The controversial law spawned many protests among American citizens who feared it gave the federal government unprecedented powers to invade people's privacy.

What is the Taliban?

The Taliban was the ultraconservative faction that ruled Afghanistan from late 1996 until December 2001, when its government crumbled following a U.S.-led military campaign. The Persian word "taleban" means "students"; the group was made up of Afghan refugees who, during the Soviet invasion (1979–1989), had fled their country for Pakistan, where they attended conservative Islamic religious schools. After the Soviet withdrawal from Afghanistan and amidst the unrest that ensued, the Taliban rose to prominence. They gained control of Afghanistan region by region, eventually taking the capital of Kabul in 1996.

While in power, the group put into force strict laws based on a fundamental interpretation of Islam. The Taliban excluded women from Afghan society, and it allowed the nation to become a training ground for Islamic terror groups such as al-Qaeda. Very few nations recognized the Taliban government. Its human rights abuses—principally the complete disenfranchisement of women and girls—were decried by the international community. But the breaking point came after 9/11: When the American government requested that the suspected 9/11 mastermind be extradited from Afghanistan to the United States, the Taliban refused. The group was forcibly ousted in the brief military campaign that followed. In December 2001, the UN convened a conference in Bonn, Germany, where leaders of anti-Taliban ethnic factions decided on a post-Taliban transitional government, led by Pashtun leader Hamid Karzai. (The Pashtuns are the dominant group in Afghanistan, representing about 42 percent of the population. The next largest group is the Tajik, which represents about 27 percent of the population in the highly fragmented nation of 28.5 million people.) Attendees also agreed to a UN-led peacekeeping operation. Though ethnic rivalries and sporadic conflicts continued under the transitional government, Afghanistan made strides in building a stable, democratic government.

What are WMDs?

WMDs are Weapons of Mass Destruction: nuclear, biological, or chemical weapons that can cause extensive casualties. The term emerged during World War II; the abbreviated

---

What was the Second Persian Gulf War?

Also known as the Iraq War, it was a short-lived invasion of Iraq by a U.S.–British coalition during March and April 2003. Bush and British Prime Minister Tony Blair (1953–) decided to attack Iraq again after the Iraqi goverment failed to permit UN inspectors to check on their weapons capabilities, as per the terms of the 1991 cease-fire agreement. The biggest sticking point of the argument to once again bomb Iraq had to do with "weapons of mass destruction," which the Americans insisted Hussein was hiding somewhere in secret storage areas.

"WMD" became part of everyday language in the late 1990s and early 2000s, as the world's superpowers and the United Nations turned their attention to serious threats posed by rogue states and terrorists in a post-Cold War society.

Following the launch of the 2003 Iraq War, WMDs were regularly in the news. The Bush Administration and its chief ally, Tony Blair, faced sharp public criticism when no weapons of mass destruction were found in Iraq. The presence of WMDs in that rogue state had been the justification for the controversial invasion. In 2004, President Bush appointed a bipartisan commission to look into why U.S. intelligence agencies had concluded that Iraq possessed WMDs. In late March 2005, the commission released to the public an unclassified version of its report. The report concluded that intelligence errors had overstated Iraq's WMD capabilities. It stated, "The daily intelligence briefings ... before the Iraq war were flawed. ... This was a major intelligence error." The commission outlined seventy-four recommendations to improve intelligence gathering among the United States' fifteen spy agencies. The classified version of the report contained information on the intelligence community's assessments of the nuclear programs of many of the "world's most dangerous actors." It also provided more details on intelligence concerning the al-Qaeda terrorist network.

In Britain, the intelligence failures concerning Iraq spurred a years-long controversy, damaging Blair's approval ratings and posing tragic consequences. In addition to the loss of life in Iraq, British weapons inspector David Kelly took his own life after publicly accusing the government of overstating the need for war. As in the United States, Britain took steps to tighten controls on its intelligence gathering to prevent errors in judgment.

Despite the fact that no WMDs were found in Iraq, the White House stood firm on the decision to invade Iraq. On September 11, 2004, the Office of the Press Secretary released a fact sheet, "Three Years of Progress in the War on Terror." The document stated in part, "We were right to go into Iraq. We removed a declared enemy of America, who had defied the international community for twelve years and who had the capability of producing weapons of mass murder and could have passed that capability to the terrorists bent on acquiring them. Although we have not found stockpiles of weapons of mass destruction, in the world after September 11, that was a risk we could not afford to take."

What dictator met the end of his power during the Bush presidency?

President Bush called for the invasion of Iraq in 2003, which he called a necessary extension of the War on Terror. Bush believed that Iraqi dictator Saddam Hussein (1937–2006) was harboring and creating WMDs and was not adhering to UN sanctions with regard to weapons and testing of facilities. The invasion, which included U.S. and multinational forces, began in March 2003 and led to the fall of Baghdad and Hussein's regime. The U.S. military led a bombing campaign called "Shock and Awe." The attack ended Hussein's twenty-four-year stranglehold of control in Iraq.

What happened to Saddam Hussein?

U.S. forces captured Hussein on December 13, 2003. The U.S. turned him over to the new Iraqi government, which tried Hussein for various crimes in November 2006. He was found guilty and was executed in December 2006.

What was the controversy about Guantanamo Bay?

After 9/11, the U.S. military began holding terror suspects at a detention center at the naval base at Guantanamo Bay, Cuba. The U.S. Navy has occupied Guantanamo since the Spanish–American War in 1898, paying an annual lease to Cuba. The White House labeled the detainees "enemy combatants"; the controversy came when they were not charged with any crimes, yet they continued to be held.

The first detainees were transported to Guantanamo, or "Camp Gitmo," in January 2002 after being captured in Afghanistan. But no charges were made against any detainees until more than two years later, in February 2004. American lawyers challenged the Bush administration policy at Guantanamo, saying it was a violation of the due process clause of the U.S. Constitution. In January 2005, one district court judge agreed with the prosecution, saying that the Constitution applied to the prisoners: they could not be deprived of their liberty without due process of law. The Bush administration immediately moved to appeal the ruling. Some in the international community also

Guantanamo Bay is a U.S. military base on the island nation of Cuba. Originally occupied by the United States after the Spanish–American War in 1898, in recent years it has served as a prison for suspected terrorists.

strongly criticized the U.S. government for holding the suspects. One of Britain's most senior judges called the policy a "monstrous failure of justice." The U.S. Supreme Court has ruled that the detainees at Guantanamo have the legal right to petition the courts and challenge their confinements.

In response to the widespread criticism, the U.S. Defense Department considered making major changes to the tribunals set up to prosecute terror suspects at Guantanamo. The changes were to bring the tribunals in line with the judicial standards of U.S. court-martials.

But questions also arose about the treatment of the detainees and the methods used to interrogate them. Human rights groups charged abuses. In the spring of 2005, UN officials working in the area of war crimes were awaiting a visit to Guantanamo; the holdup was that they requested full access to the facilities and the prison population, conditions the government was reluctant to allow.

President Barack Obama had said in his campaigning for president that he would close Guantanamo Bay, referring to it as a "sad chapter in American history." However, Guantanamo Bay still holds more than 160 detainees as of the end of 2014.

What was the worst hurricane in U.S. history?

Hurricane Katrina, which hit the Gulf Coast in late August 2005, was not only the most disastrous hurricane in U.S. history, but it was also the nation's worst single weather disaster. Although not the strongest possible hurricane when it made landfall (Katrina had weakened from "category 5" to "category 4" just before it struck the Gulf Coast), Katrina was a monster: The storm stretched about two hundred miles in diameter, packed winds up to 145 miles per hour, produced torrential rain and huge waves, spawned twisters throughout the region, and pushed up a twenty-eight-foot storm surge—a surge usually found only in category 5 hurricanes.

Katrina moved ashore on the Gulf Coast on Monday, August 29, 2005. In anticipation of the hurricane, New Orleans, which sits below sea level, had been evacuated. But tens of thousands stayed—out of necessity (such as law enforcement and health care workers), because they were unable to evacuate, or because they chose not to leave. Some twenty-three thousand of those who stayed holed up in the aging Superdome sports arena, set up as an emergency shelter. The structure barely withstood the lashing winds of Katrina, which blew off portions of the dome. On Tuesday morning, after Katrina ravaged Louisiana, Mississippi, and Alabama before weakening as it moved inland, officials and news reporters generally agreed that there was unbelievable damage all along the coast, but New Orleans had "dodged a bullet": The Big Easy had not taken the worst of it. (Gulfport and Biloxi, Mississippi, appeared the hardest hit; the devastation there was astonishing.) As reports of damage surfaced, it became clear that about 90 percent of the structures along the Gulf Coast were destroyed and hundreds of thousands of people were displaced by Katrina. The death toll was not known, and officials conceded it would take time to determine. The storm had been so ruinous—of biblical proportions, some said—

that rescue and recovery would take weeks and months. Later, when the full extent of damage began to be discovered, the recovery estimates were revised to years.

On Tuesday, August 30, New Orleans' fate changed: levees that protected the city could not hold back a swollen Lake Pontchartrain; 80 percent of the city filled with water twenty-five feet deep. Officials and volunteers could not get flood victims out fast enough, often plucking them from rooftops or finding them in attics, where survivors sought refuge as waters rose. The city descended into chaos and lawlessness. Heart-wrenching images of human despair filled the media, touching people around the nation. Americans responded by donating money, goods, and time. The American Red Cross launched the largest mobilization effort in its history. The Federal Emergency Management Agency (FEMA, a part of the Department of Homeland Security [DHS]), the Coast Guard (also part of the DHS), and the U.S. military struggled to keep pace with Katrina's aftermath all along the coast.

For all the effort, it was widely acknowledged that the government's response to the disaster was inadequate and late. On Friday, September 2, President Bush said that the results had been unacceptable; he further promised to "make it right." While politicians and the people spoke out on the subject, some experts said the catastrophe had simply overwhelmed the system: Emergency programs across the nation had been set up to rely on local and state response first, backed by the federal government. In Katrina's case, the devastation was so great that localities and states were either unable to respond at all or could not respond with enough help; federal intervention had been needed sooner and in greater measure to alleviate human suffering and protect lives. However, government officials all seemed of one accord: Fact-finding could wait; victims could not. Cities and states across the nation sent resources to the Gulf Coast and set up emergency centers to receive storm refugees, whose needs were both immediate (water, food, clothing, shelter, medicine, health care, and counseling) and long term (jobs, schools, and permanent housing).

On Wednesday, September 7, nine days after Katrina struck, the situation continued to unfold. New Orleans ordered a forced evacuation of the holdouts; the city remained flooded with toxic floodwaters as repairs were made in the levees and the hazardous water began to be pumped out. Efforts to reunite families, separated in the chaos, were ongoing. For many days, rescue workers all along the Gulf Coast moved from house to house to find survivors; at this juncture, they needed to identify and count the dead. The death toll was expected to be in the thousands. The affected area was ninety thousand square miles—about the size of Minnesota. Property damage was projected to be at least $26 billion in insured losses and perhaps twice that amount in uninsured losses. (Katrina had also caused damages as it struck Florida as a category 1 hurricane on August 26; it later moved into the warm waters of the Gulf of Mexico and strengthened before striking the Gulf Coast.)

Katrina's aftermath was felt in every state of the union: volunteers shored up efforts to assist survivors who were being relocated in an effort to ease the burden on the afflicted region; schools across the nation opened doors to displaced students; fuel prices skyrocketed, and natural gas and heating oil prices promised to follow, as offshore rigs and Gulf Coast refineries suffered; and most Americans worried about the government's response to the catastrophe. The disaster made an impact around the world as well, with some ninety-five countries offering assistance.

BARACK OBAMA AND HIS PRESIDENCY

What was the first measure that Barack Obama signed into law?

The first bill Obama signed into law was the Lilly Ledbetter Fair Pay Act, which extends the time period an individual has to file a suit under the Equal Pay Act. Congress had passed the law in response to the U.S. Supreme Court's decision in *Ledbetter v. Goodyear Tire & Rubber Co.* (2007), when the Court ruled that Lilly Ledbetter did not file her Equal Pay Act lawsuit in a timely matter. The Court had reasoned that the limitations period began when the pay agreement was made, not with each new paycheck.

With Ms. Ledbetter present, Obama signed the measure, stating, "It is fitting that with the very first bill I sign—the Lilly Ledbetter Fair Pay Restoration Act—we are upholding one of this nation's first principles: that we are all created equal and each deserve a chance to pursue our own version of happiness."

What was the Great Recession?

In what some call the worst economic downturn in the U.S. economy since the Great Depression, the Great Recession began in 2007 as a result of poor financial regulation that, in turn, led to banks issuing dubious home mortgages to citizens who did not have good credit or financial histories. In addition, the U.S. Financial Crisis Inquiry Commission concluded that banks and other financial firms were taking too many risks, speculating with billions of dollars on investments that were not solid. The recklessness was encouraged by what was, until 2007, a seemingly strong economy and unrealistic escalation of home values. When the housing bubble inevitably burst, financial institutions found themselves with hundreds of billions of dollars in bad loans. Homes were

President Barack Obama, the United States's first black president, faced challenges such as the Great Recession and several wars overseas during his presidency.

foreclosed, people were evicted, and a domino effect ensued that brought the U.S. economy to its knees.

What did President Obama do to try to get the United States out of the Great Recession?

Obama signed into law the American Recovery and Reinvestment Act of 2009, colloquially called "the stimulus bill." The law was designed to create jobs, pump money into the economy, and increase consumer spending. The law contains provisions on infrastructure investing, aid to the unemployed and low-income persons, and housing. Obama said upon signing the measure: "The American Recovery and Reinvestment Act that I will sign today—a plan that meets the principles I laid out in January—is the most sweeping economic recovery package in our history."

When did Osama bin Laden die?

Bin Laden died in May 2011. He was shot by U.S. operatives from the U.S. Naval Special Warfare Development Group and the Central Intelligence Agency in Abbottabad, Pakistan. A group of Navy SEALS carried out the covert mission called Operation Neptune Spear. Ordered by President Obama, the mission called for a nighttime raid on the residential compound inhabited by the al-Qaeda leader.

At a press conference, President Obama stated: "For over two decades, bin Laden has been al-Qaeda's leader and symbol and has continued to plot attacks against our country and our friends and our allies. The death of bin Laden marks the most significant achievement to date in our nation's effort to defeat al-Qaeda. Yet his death does not mark the end of our effort. There is no doubt that al-Qaeda will continue to pursue attacks against us. We must and we will remain vigilant at home and abroad."

What hate crimes law did Obama sign?

In October 2009, Obama signed into law the Matthew Shepard and James Byrd, Jr. Hate Crimes Prevention Act of 2009. It expanded the existing federal hate crimes law to include crimes motivated by a victim's actual or perceived gender, sexual orientation, gender identity, or disability.

"You understood that we must stand against crimes that are meant not only to break bones but to break spirits—not only to inflict harm but to instill fear," Obama said. "You understand that the rights afforded every citizen under our Constitution mean nothing if we do not protect those rights—both from unjust laws and violent acts. And you understand how necessary this law continues to be."

What is "ObamaCare"?

President Obama signed into law the Patient Protection Affordable Care Act (often called "ObamaCare"), which expands Medicaid coverage, prohibits insurance companies from denying care based on pre-existing illnesses, and supports medical research. There is a four-year window on the implementation of many of the law's major measures.

"The bill I'm signing will set in motion reforms that generations of Americans have fought for and marched for and hungered to see," Obama said upon signing the measure into law. "It will take four years to implement fully many of these reforms, because we need to implement them responsibly."

The law contains a controversial requirement known as "the individual mandate" that requires private individuals to purchase health care or to pay a "shared responsibility payment" to the government. Many lawsuits were filed challenging the constitutionality of the law, including the individual mandate requirement.

However, in June 2012, the U.S. Supreme Court upheld the law by a 5–4 vote in its decision in *National Federation of Independent Business v. Sebelius*. Conservative Chief Justice John G. Roberts, Jr. joined the four more liberal members of the Court in upholding the law. Roberts reasoned that the law fell within the U.S. Congress's broad taxing powers. The Court's decision upheld both the individual mandate provision and the so-called Medicaid expansion provision, which provides federal funds for states as long as they provide Medicaid coverage to individuals below a certain income level.

Chief Justice Roberts wrote: "The Affordable Care Act's requirement that certain individuals pay a financial penalty for not obtaining health insurance may reasonably be characterized as a tax. Because the Constitution permits such a tax, it is not our role to forbid it or to pass upon its wisdom or fairness."

Justice Antonin Scalia authored the primary dissenting opinion, contending that the health care law's individual mandate was clearly a penalty, not a tax, and thus beyond the reach of Congress's tax and spend powers.

TECHNOLOGY AND THE RISE OF SOCIAL MEDIA

What was Napster?

Napster was one of the original peer-to-peer file-sharing software systems used by millions to share music. The company was founded by John Fanning (1963–), his nephew Shawn Fanning (1980–), and Sean Parker (1979–). The primary use of Napster was to allow individuals to share audio music files in the MP3 file. It operated from 1999 until 2001. Lawsuits accused the company of contributing to widespread online piracy. The rock group Metallica and hip-hop producer Dr. Dre filed suit against Napster, alleging copyright violations. The Recording Industry Association of America also filed suit against Napster. Some critics alleged the lawsuits were more of a challenge to file-sharing software than to actual music piracy. Napster later merged with Rhapsody.

What is Google?

Google is the leading web-based search engine cofounded by Larry Page (1973–) and Sergey Brim (1973–) in the 1990s. Page and Brim were computer science Ph.D. students at Stanford University, who became friends and began working on creating a search engine. Their initial project was known as "Backrub."

In September 1997, Page and Brim registered "google" as a domain name. Google's website explains that the term google comes from the mathematical concept "googol," the number 1 followed by one hundred zeros, which represents infinity.

In September 1998, the two men incorporated Google in California and hired their first employee. By 2000, Google won web awards (Webbys) and was considered a technological breakthrough success. Later that year, Google Toolbar was released. The company Google has continued to expand and innovate through the years by creating Google Maps, acquiring YouTube, creating Android, and releasing Google Voice and Google Glass.

As Google says on its website, "We do search." Their number-one mantra is "Focus on the user, and everything else will follow." Google has become an essential part of everyday life for millions. It is the number-one way that most people first look up information online.

What is Facebook?

Facebook is an online social networking site founded by several Harvard University students, most prominently Mark Zuckerberg (1984–), in February 2004. Zuckerberg founded Facebook with fellow students Eduardo Saverin (1982–), and Andrew McCollum, Dustin Moskovitz (1982–), and Chris Hughes (1983–). Zuckerberg's original project was called Facemash.com. Facebook originally allowed students at Harvard and other Ivy League schools to connect with each other. This caused some trouble for Zuckerberg at Harvard. In February 2004, while a sophomore at Harvard, Zuckerberg started thefacebook.com.

Several Harvard seniors sued Zuckerberg, alleging that he intentionally misled them while they were creating Harvard-connection (later called ConnectU). The three men—Tyler Winklevoss (1981–), Cameron Winklevoss (1981–), and Divya Narenda (1981–)—later settled that suit.

Facebook remains the most popular social networking network in the world

Mark Zuckerberg is the wunderkind who made the social media website Facebook such a success and cultural phenomenon.

and Zuckerberg the world's youngest billionaire. A hit movie was inspired by the creation of Facebook and its spawning lawsuits—*The Social Network*.

When did Twitter launch?

Twitter, another popular online social networking platform, launched in March 2006. Created by Jack Dorsey (1976–), Twitter enables users to send text messages of up to 140 characters in messages known as "tweets." Twitter has more than 500 million registered users. People on Twitter then have followers—or other subscribers on Twitter—who receive their messages. Twitter has become a popular mode of communication for celebrities and other famous people to communicate to their fan base and the world at large.

Who founded YouTube?

YouTube, the popular video-sharing website, was founded by Steve Chen (1978–), Chad Hurley (1977–), and Jawed Karim (1979–). The three young men met as co-employees at PayPal, an e-commerce business that allows individuals to make online money transfers. Google purchased YouTube in October 2006 for $1.65 billion. YouTube has had its share of controversies, particularly when users post material that is offensive, defamatory, or that infringes on copyrights. YouTube has had an indelible impact on popular culture and music, winning a Peabody Award in 2008.

Who founded Wikipedia?

American entrepreneurs Jimmy Wales (1966–) and Larry Sanders (1968–) founded Wikipedia in January 2001. Wikipedia is a free online encyclopedia that provides a wealth of information in different languages on the global medium. Wikipedia comes from the Hawaiian "wiki," meaning quick, and "pedia," as in encyclopedia. There have been some notable controversies with Wikipedia, including false information provided by persons for particular entries. For example, an anonymous person managed to edit

a Wikipedia entry on prominent American journalist John Seigenthaler, Sr. (1927–) and post false comments, such as that Seigenthaler was implicated in the deaths of John F. Kennedy and Robert Kennedy. The information was patently false, as Seigenthaler was close friends with both Kennedys. Later, it was revealed that a young man in Nashville, Tennessee, had posted the material as a joke. Seigenthaler, a strong First Amendment advocate, urged Wikipedia to tighten its content controls. Despite certain controversies, Wikipedia has gained traction as a leading reference starting point.

Chad Hurley (left) and Steve Chen are the founders of YouTube, the video-sharing website.

SPORTS HISTORY

AUTO RACING

When was the first major organized automobile race in the United States, and what made it important?

The first widely publicized auto race in the United States occurred on Thanksgiving Day, 1895, and was organized by the *Chicago Times Herald*. The race was won by an American vehicle made by Charles and Frank Duryea, who in 1896 would be credited as the first American manufacturers of gasoline-powered automobiles. The Duryea car finished ahead of a Benz, the most noted carmaker in the world at the time, further inspiring many American tinkerers—including Henry Ford, Ransom Olds, and others—to continue their experiments with the newfangled horseless carriage. The first American race was preceded in early November 1895 by a reliability demonstration that ran from Chicago to Waukegan, Illinois, and back (ninety-two miles). The official race of fifty-two miles on Thanksgiving Day was won with an average speed of 5.1 miles per hour.

Which legendary auto racer was the first to break the one-minute mile in a gasoline-powered vehicle?

Barney Oldfield reached the speed of 64 mph in 1903 in a car called the 999, built by Henry Ford. The next year, Louis E. Rigolly, a Frenchman driving a Gabron-Brille, became the first to exceed 100 mph when he reached a top speed of 103 in Ostend, Belgium.

When was the first long-distance auto race held in the United States, and why was it stopped?

The Automobile Club of America organized the first long-distance race—five hundred miles, from Cleveland to New York—in 1901. News that President William McKinley had been assassinated led to the race being canceled as the leaders reached Buffalo, New York. McKinley, incidentally, had been the first American president to ride in an automobile.

What were the first American car and driver to win an international auto-racing event?

George Robertson drove a 16.2–liter Locomobile to victory in the 1908 Vanderbilt Cup, held on Long Island, New York. He posted an average speed of 64.3 miles per hour over the 258-mile course.

What is the history of the Pikes Peak hill-climb event?

A treacherous dirt road winds through 154 turns in 12.5 miles on its way to the top of the 14,110-foot Pikes Peak in Colorado's Rocky Mountains. It was inevitable that men and machines would race to see who could climb the hill the fastest. The first organized event took place in 1916 and was won by Rea Lentz in an aircraft-engined Romano Special. Racing's famous Unser family—who lived at the base of the mountain in Colorado Springs before moving to Albuquerque, New Mexico—claimed more than half the early Pikes Peak titles.

Why was the twenty-four-hour race at Daytona canceled in 1974?

The oil-producing countries of the Middle East had raised prices dramatically, leading to a national energy crisis. Race officials decided that it wouldn't look good to have a bunch of cars zooming around a track at 100 miles per hour for twenty-four hours when many Americans were forced to wait in line at the gas pumps. When the race resumed in 1975, five-time winner Hurley Haywood and four-time winner Peter Gregg teamed up to win it for the second time in three years in a Porsche Carrera.

How many Americans have won the Formula One World Drivers' Championship?

Two. Well-known endurance racer Phil Hill claimed the title in a Ferrari in 1961, and Mario Andretti won it in 1978 in a black John Player Special Lotus.

Which driver won an Indianapolis 500, a Daytona 500, the Twelve Hours of Sebring, a Formula One World Championship, and four USAC Indy Car championships?

Mario Andretti, who first began racing competitively during the late 1950s in a 1948 Hudson he and his brother, Aldo, adapted for racing, is among racing's most versatile drivers. His family, who had been interred in a displaced person's camp during World War II in Italy, emigrated to the United States in 1955. Since their father forbade the brothers to race, Mario and Aldo tinkered and raced secretly but were exposed when Aldo was injured in a crash. Mario kept racing against his father's wishes; he himself proved a more encouraging father when it came to auto racing, considering the successes of his race-driver sons Michael, Jeff, and John. Mario was USAC Champion and Rookie of the

Year in 1965. He finished third at Indy that year but won the race in 1967, and two years later he won at Daytona.

What is the largest sporting venue in the United States?

The Indianapolis Motor Speedway has room for more than 300,000 fans. For years, the Indianapolis 500 was the main attraction at the track, but in 1994, NASCAR brought its stock cars to the historic site and ran the inaugural Brickyard 400, won by Jeff Gordon.

When did Indianapolis Motor Speedway open, and why is it dubbed "the Brickyard"?

Indianapolis was opened in 1909 as a testing ground. The oval track surface was laid with 3.2 million bricks. The first Indianapolis 500 was run in 1911; even though the race is run in one day, testing, practice, and qualifying occur over a three-week period preceding the race.

Race car legend Mario Andretti has won over one hundred races in his career, including the Daytona 500, Indianapolis 500, the Formula One World Championship, the Indy Car National Championship, and at the Sebring International Raceway, among others.

Who was the first four-time winner of the Indianapolis 500?

Three drivers have won the race four times: A.J. Foyt, Jr., Al Unser, and Rick Mears, with Foyt the first to win four times. Foyt also won two Daytona 500s, the Twenty-Four Hours of LeMans, the Twenty-Four Hours of Daytona, and the Twelve Hours of Sebring, as well as races on the dirt and midget circuits. Foyt's feats were encouraged by his father, a garage owner and racer of midget cars, who gave his son an engine-equipped red racer at about the time young Foyt learned to walk. After years of experience racing around the yard, Foyt, at age five, competed and won against an established midget car driver in a three-lap exhibition.

Who is the only driver to run in the Indianapolis 500 and a Winston Cup stock car race on the same day?

In May 1994, John Andretti, nephew of racing legend Mario Andretti, finished tenth at the Indianapolis 500. Not content with running just one race that day, Andretti hopped in a waiting helicopter and flew to Charlotte, North Carolina, where he suited up for

Who was the first African American driver to compete in the Indianapolis 500?

Willy T. Ribbs made his way up through the racing ranks to qualify for the big race in 1991, thus becoming the first African American driver to be included in the field. Unfortunately, he failed to finish the race.

the Coca-Cola 600. His long day had an early finish when he crashed and ended up thirty-sixth at Charlotte.

When was the first NASCAR race held?

Until 1948, stock car racing was full of uncertainty: Would the next race be held? Would the track owner be able to afford to pay the winning driver? Would there be enough drivers to hold a race? With no governing body, there was chaos. Into that disorganized scene stepped Bill France, Sr., who founded the organization known as the National Association of Stock Car Auto Racing in late 1947. France had some success running races in 1948 with what were known as Modified cars, but on June 19, 1949, he hit pay dirt when he held a race in Charlotte, North Carolina, for fresh-off-the-showroom-floor "stock" cars. Crowds showed up in record numbers to watch Jim Roper claim victory in that race. The Strictly Stock races, as they were known, evolved into the Grand National East series and then into today's wildly popular Winston Cup circuit.

Who won the most races in a single NASCAR season?

In 1967, Richard Petty was already known as "The King" and was widely considered one of the top stock car drivers in the country. That season, however, he made it clear that he was the unquestioned best driver when he won twenty-seven of the forty-eight races he started, finishing in the top five eleven other times and the top ten once. To top all that off, Petty is also considered one of the nicest people in the world of sports. His easy-going manner and great sense of humor made him a fan favorite and helped turn NASCAR into the huge sport it is today.

Who is the youngest man to win the Winston Cup championship?

Jeff Gordon, the "Rainbow Warrior," was twenty-four when he claimed his first Winston Cup title in 1995. Gordon—loved by many fans and probably hated by just as many—won his second title in 1997.

Who was the first woman ever to win a major NASCAR race?

Shawna Robinson claimed this honor in 1988, when she won the AC Delco 100 in Asheville, North Carolina, driving in the Dash division. Later that year, she was named

Most Popular Driver in her division, and her winning Pontiac Sunbird was placed in the International Motorsports Hall of Fame.

Who was the first woman ever to qualify for the pole position in a NASCAR Grand National race?

Shawna Robinson achieved this feat in 1994, when she set a new track record lap speed of 174.330 miles per hour in qualifying for the Busch Light 300 in Atlanta, Georgia. But her hopes of becoming the first woman to win on the Grand National circuit were dashed on the very first lap. Fellow driver Mike Wallace hit her car from the side, causing her to hit another car. Although her car suffered serious damage in the crash, Robinson got back into the race and managed to complete sixty-three laps before a bad radiator ended her day. Some racers suggested Wallace hit her intentionally, but there was no way to know for sure. Still, Robinson was very dis-

Racer Jeff Gordon has been a fan favorite since he won the Winston Cup at the age of twenty-four in 1995.

appointed with the outcome of the race. "How many fans were taking bets, 'Is the girl going to crash on the first lap?'" she said in *Sports Illustrated*. "By starting on the pole and racing well, I hoped I could have changed those attitudes."

Why is the 1976 Daytona 500 considered one of the most memorable races ever?

It featured an epic battle between two of the best and most popular racers of their day—Richard Petty and David Pearson (the Silver Fox). They were the only drivers in contention for the checkered flag with twenty laps to go, and they ran each of those laps with only inches between their cars. Pearson held a slight lead going into the last lap, but Petty made a desperate attempt to pass in the final turn. Unfortunately, he couldn't quite hold his line and tapped Pearson's car, sending both of them careening into the wall. Both cars were nearly destroyed and rolled to a stop just short of the finish line. Pearson, who had managed to keep his engine running, radioed his crew to ask, "Has Richard crossed the line?" When they responded that Petty had not yet finished the race, Pearson put his car in gear and agonizingly nursed it across the line for the victory. Petty had to wait for a push-start from his crew and settled for second place.

BASEBALL

When did baseball originate?

People have been playing stick and ball games since the early days of civilization. On that premise, baseball can be traced back to games played in ancient Egypt, China, and Persia. But if we recognize baseball as a game played with four bases in a diamond configuration and a few other definite particulars, the organized sport we recognize as baseball began on June 19, 1846, on the Elysian Fields in Hoboken, New Jersey. Two amateur teams of nine players played a game umpired by Alexander J. Cartwright, a surveyor and athlete, who established guidelines for a game that most closely resembles modern baseball.

Games somewhat similar to baseball were played before that date in North America. The English sport of cricket was played in the early 1800s, but another game brought over from England called rounders is even more similar to baseball. In rounders, a batter strikes a ball and runs around bases. Balls caught on the fly are outs, and fielders can put runners out by hitting them with the ball as they run between bases. Clubs began forming to play this game, which they called baseball, based on those rules.

Legend has it that Abner Doubleday invented baseball in Cooperstown, New York, in 1839. However, while several varieties of baseball were played then and prior to 1846, and though Doubleday helped popularize them, there is little evidence that his game resembles baseball as we know it, even though a baseball-type game thrived in Cooperstown, which became the home for baseball's Hall of Fame. Alexander Cartwright is recognized as founding the first true organized baseball club, the Knickerbocker Base Ball Club, in 1842 in New York City. Cartwright and his Knickerbockers developed a set of twenty rules in 1845: The rules called for nine-player teams and a playing field with a home base and three additional bases set apart at specific distances (forty-two paces, later standardized to ninety feet); instead of hitting runners with the ball, they introduced the new rule of having fielders tag runners or forcing runners out by tagging the base to which a runner has to advance after a batter puts the ball in play; and they created foul lines that marked a distinct field of play, differing from the rounders and cricket formats, where the ball could be hit anywhere. The Knickerbocker-styled game (popularly called the New York Game) began spreading. During the Civil War, Union soldiers from New York City introduced the game in places they were stationed, and by 1865 the game with the Knickerbocker rules had become the most popular style of baseball.

When did professional baseball begin?

By the 1850s, baseball parks were rented to clubs, and teams would collect donations from fans to cover costs. The National Association of Base Ball Players (NABBP) was formed in 1858. After restricting members from taking payment for playing baseball—even though ballpark owners earned profits by renting the field and by selling food and beverages—the NABBP changed its policy in 1868. The first professional baseball team, the Cincinnati Red Stockings, began play in 1869.

Elysian Fields in Hoboken, New Jersey, is usually considered the place where the first games of organized baseball began. The Knickerbocker Club of New York City began playing there in 1845.

What were some of the first teams and leagues?

The Cincinnati Red Stockings barnstormed around the country in 1869, winning sixty games without a loss. In 1871, The NABBP became the National Association of Professional Base Ball Players (NAPBBP), representing players from ten clubs that made up the first professional baseball league. The teams played each other, and the best teams met for a championship series. In 1876, the National League of Professional Base Ball Clubs, known as the National League, was created with teams in Boston, Massachusetts; Chicago, Illinois; Cincinnati, Ohio; Hartford, Connecticut; Louisville, Kentucky; New York City; Philadelphia, Pennsylvania; and St. Louis, Missouri. The rival American Association was founded in 1882. In 1883, the two leagues formed an agreement that included playing exhibition games between the leagues' best teams following the regular season and adopting the reserve clause, which required players to obtain permission from their club's owner before joining another club. The American Association folded after the 1891 season, and its four best teams joined the National League. Before it went defunct, the American Association was considered a Major League.

What was the Federal League?

The Federal League was created when a minor league elevated itself and attempted to lure star major leaguers to jump ship in the process. The first player to sign a contract with the fledgling league was George Stovall of the St. Louis Browns. Future Hall of Famers Joe Tinker and Walter Johnson also signed with the Feds, although Johnson changed his mind when the owner of the Washington Senators gave him a nice raise and bonus to stay put. The Federal League's history was short-lived, lasting a mere two seasons (1914–1915), but its legacy lives on in Chicago's Wrigley Field, originally built for the Windy City's Federal League entry.

When were the Major Leagues formed?

In 1900, Ban Johnson, president of the minor league Western League, renamed the organization the American League, and teams began play the following year. Along with the established National League, which had begun play in 1876, they became recognized as the Major Leagues, ushering in the modern era of baseball.

What is the World Series?

The World Series is the championship series of Major League Baseball, the professional baseball league based in the United States (with two teams from Canada). Major League Baseball consists of two leagues—the American League and the National League. The winner of the American League plays the winner of the National League in the World Series. It consists of a best-of-seven format. The first World Series was won in 1903 by the Boston Red Sox (then called the Boston Americans) over the Pittsburgh Pirates.

What team has won the most World Series championships?

The New York Yankees have won twenty-seven World Series—far more than any other team in Major League Baseball. The next closest team is the St. Louis Cardinals, who have won eleven championships.

What was the Black Sox Scandal?

The Black Sox Scandal is the name given to the controversy associated with the 1919 World Series, where several members of the Chicago White Sox allegedly fixed the series by purposefully performing poorly against the victorious Cincinnati Reds. Eight White Sox players were banned for life from baseball, although they were acquitted of criminal charges.

The eight players were first baseman Chick Gandil (1888–1970), shortstop Charles Risberg (1894–1975), outfielder Oscar Felsch (1891–1964), pitcher Edward Cicotte (1884–1969), utility infielder Fred McMullin (1891–1952), pitcher Claude Williams (1893–1959), third baseman Buck Weaver (1890–1956), and star outfielder "Shoeless" Joe Jackson (1887–1951).

This picture of the eight shamed White Sox players ran in papers across the country in 1920. The Black Sox scandal sullied the good, wholesome name of the national pastime for many years.

Gandil was the leading player in the scandal, with ties to the underworld. The scheme was allegedly funded by Arnold "the Brain" Rothschild (1882–1928). A grand jury investigated the controversy in 1920, and a jury acquitted the players. However, newly installed baseball commissioner Kenesaw Mountain Landis (1866–1944), a federal judge, banned the eight players for life from Major League Baseball.

A big controversy, popularized in book and film, is whether star player "Shoeless" Joe Jackson really participated in throwing games in the series. Jackson was a great player who had led the White Sox to the World Series championship in 1917. Jackson's supporters point out that he batted .375 in the "Black Sox" series—the highest of any player—and he committed no errors in the field. It was reported that Jackson initially confessed to the grand jury of his involvement in the scandal, but he later recanted it consistently for more than thirty years. Other players involved in the scandal also supported Jackson's claims. It remains a controversy to this day.

Who was George Herman Ruth?

George Herman Ruth (1895–1948) was a larger-than-life figure who arguably became the nation's greatest sports figure. Known by his nickname "the Babe" or "the Bambino," Ruth was known for his colossal home runs and carefree lifestyle. He played twenty-two seasons in the major leagues from 1914 until the 1930s. He began his big league career with the Boston Red Sox as a pitcher but later moved to the Yankees, where he played right field. He clobbered 714 home runs in his illustrious career. His personal charisma made him a household name in the "Roaring Twenties."

When was the first All–Star Game?

The first All–Star Game was part of Chicago's Century of Progress Exposition in 1933. It was founded by *Chicago Tribune* sports editor Arch Ward as the featured sports event for the celebration. Comiskey Park hosted the event.

When was the Baseball Hall of Fame established?

The Baseball Hall of Fame was established in 1936 for two purposes: to honor the greatest players of the past and as part of the celebration of baseball's upcoming "centennial." The first induction class of Ty Cobb, Christy Mathewson, Honus Wagner, Babe Ruth, and Walter Johnson was elected in 1936 (none unanimously). The

Legendary baseball player "Babe" Ruth played from 1914 to 1935, hitting over 700 home runs.

1937 class consisted of Cy Young, Tris Speaker, and Nap Lajoie. The Hall itself didn't open formally until 1939.

How did World War II impact baseball?

The recruitment of Major League Baseball players into military service during World War II severely affected the game. Many players had precious years shaved off their careers as a result of the war. Stars such as Joe DiMaggio, Ted Williams, Bob Feller, and Hank Greenberg lost some of their most productive years—and possibly some major league records—to the war. The All-Star Game was even canceled in 1945. In 1943, Chicago Cubs owner Philip K. Wrigley formed the All-American Girls Professional Baseball League (AAGPBL) to fill the void and provide entertainment during this time. The league consisted of four teams in its first year (1943), growing to ten in its final season (1954). In 1988, the National Baseball Hall of Fame and Museum opened the "Women in Baseball" permanent exhibit. It quickly became one of the museum's most popular attractions.

Wartime travel restrictions limited where teams could conduct spring training. Most stayed close to home, where the weather wasn't very conducive to baseball-related activities. Equipment was harder to obtain, and the quality of play suffered with the infusion of players not yet ready for the big time or well past their primes. The 1945 World Series was described as "the fat guys vs. the tall guys at the company picnic." Joe Nuxhall made his major league debut at age fifteen; one-armed outfielder Pete Gray patrolled the outfield for part of the 1945 season; and players who had been retired for years came back to fill the void left by those who went to fight. One of the oddest developments of wartime baseball was the ascendance of the perennial doormat St. Louis Browns, who won their first and only pennant in 1944.

The war also served to change baseball's previous stand about race. While the Armed Forces were still segregated, African Americans played a major part in the Allied victory. Also, the hypocrisy of fighting people who considered themselves the "Master Race" while treating a large number of Americans as second-class citizens began to hit home. Shortly after the war, the Dodgers signed Jackie Robinson to a minor league contract.

What was baseball's "Shot Heard 'Round the World"?

On October 3, 1951, the New York Giants' Bobby Thomson hit a three-run homer in the bottom of the ninth inning of the third playoff game to decide the National League pennant.

In an era before the League Championship Series, the Brooklyn Dodgers and New York Giants needed a three-game playoff to decide the pennant after a furious race in the last weeks of the regular season. Brooklyn had led most of the year before a late–season collapse.

After splitting the first two games, the two teams returned to the Polo Grounds to finish the series. Don Newcombe of the Dodgers took a 4–1 lead into the ninth, but he got tired. Giants' shortstop Alvin Dark opened the ninth inning with an infield single, followed by Don Mueller's single. After Monte Irvin popped out, Whitey Lockman doubled Dark home. Mueller went to third, breaking his ankle on the slide (Clint Hartung ran for him). Charlie Dressen, the Brooklyn manager, brought in Ralph Branca to pitch to Thomson. On Branca's 2–1 pitch, Thomson deposited the ball into the Polo Grounds's cozy (256 feet), left-field corner stands.

The World Series, which that year seemed a bit anticlimactic, wasn't as kind to the Giants. They were beaten by the powerhouse Yankees. However, that Series marked the World Series debuts of Willie Mays (who was on deck when Thomson hit his blast) and Mickey Mantle.

Branca was also the losing pitcher in the first playoff game ever. In 1946, the Dodgers and St. Louis Cardinals ended the season deadlocked. Branca started and lost Game One 4–2.

What were the Negro Leagues?

The Negro Leagues refers to various professional baseball leagues reserved for black players. Major League Baseball had a color ban that prohibited blacks from playing with whites. Thus, many black baseball players played in separate leagues against one another. Perhaps the most prominent of these leagues was the National Negro League, which existed from 1933 until 1948—the year after Major League Baseball was finally integrated.

The Negro Leagues featured many outstanding talents. One of the lingering questions is how well many of the Negro League stars would have fared in the major leagues.

Who was Jackie Robinson?

Jack Roosevelt Robinson (1919–1972) was the first black man to cross the color barrier and play in a Major League Baseball game in the modern era. A multisport star athlete at the University of California, Los Angeles (UCLA), Robinson integrated baseball by playing with the Brooklyn Dodgers in 1947. He began his career at first base, but then moved to second base. The president and general manager of the Dodgers, Branch Rickey (1881–1965), sought to integrate baseball both for idealistic and pragmatic reasons. Rickey never forgot the sight of former black teammate Charley Thomas's humiliation at being denied basic public accommodations. Rickey vowed he would do something to change that harsh reality. Also, Rickey realized that the Negro Leagues were brimming with top talent, and he simply wanted to improve the Dodgers' changes to succeed.

Rickey hired Robinson and first placed him with the minor league Montreal Royals. Robinson dominated that league, leading the Royals to the championship. In 1947, Robinson made his major league debut with the Dodgers. He earned Rookie of the Year honors for his successes that year. He endured taunts from opposing players and fans but endured the hostility to become an American hero. He helped lead the Dodgers to the 1955 World Series championship.

There is little doubt that the stars of the Negro Leagues would have been stars in the major leagues if given the chance to participate. Josh Gibson (1911–1947) was a star catcher with the Homestead Grays who was called "the Black Babe Ruth" (although some Negro League supporters called Babe Ruth "the white Josh Gibson"). Like many black players of his day, Gibson also played in baseball leagues in Puerto Rico, the Dominican Republic, and Mexico.

Who was Willie Mays?

Willie Mays (1931–) may have been the greatest all-around player in professional baseball history. Mays hit 660 home runs, batted over .300, batted in more than nineteen hundred runs, and perennially won Golden Glove awards for his stellar defensive play in the outfield. He would hit a monstrous home run and make a diving,

The "Say Hey Kid," Willie Mays was a versatile, popular player who played from 1951 to 1973, hitting 660 home runs and batting over .300.

breathtaking catch in the outfield in the same game. Many of his contemporaries insist he was the best all-around player in the history of the game. *Sporting News*'s 100 Greatest [Baseball] Players listed Mays as the number-two-ranked player of all time—behind only Babe Ruth. He played most of his career with the San Francisco Giants, leading them to a World Series title in 1954.

What is the Cy Young Award?

Named after Denton True "Cy" Young (1867–1955), a record-setting pitcher (who still holds some of those records), the Cy Young Award is given each year to one pitcher in the National League and one pitcher in the American League.

Who was the last Major League Baseball player to hit .400 as a batting average for a full season?

Ted Williams (1918–2002) was the last Major League Baseball player to hit .400 in a professional Major League Baseball season. Williams, who was sometimes called "the Greatest Hitter Who Ever Lived," hit .406 in 1941 while playing for the Boston Red Sox—the only team for which Williams played in his career. Williams had a career batting average of .344 and also hit more than five hundred home runs. Since Williams' feat in 1941, several players have come tantalizingly close to a .400 batting average: Tony Gwynn (1960–) hit .394 in 1994; George Brett (1953–) hit .390 in 1980; and Rod Carew (1945–) hit .388 in 1978.

Who was the only rookie to be named Most Valuable Player?

Fred Lynn of the Boston Red Sox hit .331 with twenty-one homers and 105 runs batted in (RBIs), led the league in doubles (forty-seven), runs (103), and slugging percentage (.566), and stole ten bases to lead Boston to the pennant and earn American League Rookie of the Year and MVP honors in 1975.

Who was the first player to collect five hundred hits with four different teams?

Rusty Staub started with the Houston Colt .45s/Astros, where he collected 792 hits. He then went to Montreal, where, in the first of two tours with the Expos, he had 508 hits. New York was another two-time destination (1972–1975 and closing out his career from 1981–1985), where he tallied 709 hits. In Detroit from 1976–1978, he added 524 more safeties. Staub ended up with a career total of 2,716 major league hits.

Who was "Mr. October"?

Mr. October was the nickname of celebrated and charismatic baseball slugger Reggie Jackson (1946–), who won World Series championships with the Oakland Athletics and the New York Yankees. Jackson earned the moniker for his penchant of clutch hitting—including several memorable home runs—in the playoffs and the World Series. He is best known for his performance in Game Six of the 1977 World Series as a member of the Yankees. Jackson hit three home runs in that game off three different pitchers from the opposing Los Angeles Dodgers. Jackson was also known for his confident persona and for his open battles with teammates and coaches. He once said that he was "the straw that stirred the drink."

Why is baseball associated with steroids?

The modern era of baseball, from the 1990s to the early part of the twenty-first century, has been pejoratively dubbed the "steroid era." This is because numerous players—including high-profile players—used steroids during their career. For example, popular sluggers Mark McGwire (1963–) and Sammy Sosa (1968–)—who re-energized baseball in the late 1990s with their chase for the single-season home run record—are both believed to have used steroids. McGwire later admitted he used steroids and other banned substances during his career. Sosa has denied steroid use.

The Mitchell Report—a more than four-hundred-page report led by a committee by former U.S. Senator George Mitchell—contained detailed documentation of widespread steroid use in baseball. The report named nearly ninety Major League Baseball players who used steroids or other performance-enhancing drugs in their careers.

What active Major League Baseball player was the first to win the Cy Young Award four times in a row?

Atlanta Braves pitcher Greg Maddux won his first Cy Young Award in 1992 with the Chicago Cubs. After joining the Braves via free agency, Maddux continued to dominate the National League in 1993 and the strike-shortened seasons of 1994 and 1995. Twice during that span, his ERA was under 2.00 (1.56 in 1994 and 1.63 in 1995). His record for those four years was an amazing 75–30.

Who was George Steinbrenner?

George Steinbrenner (1930–2010), a.k.a. "the Boss," was the controversial managing partner and owner of the New York Yankees for more than thirty years. During his tenure, the Yankees won seven World Series. He was known for his controversial comments, meddling into coaching decisions, and trying to hire someone to uncover dirt on one of his former star players, Dave Winfield (1951–). While he has a complicated legacy, no one can dispute that Steinbrenner and the Yankees enjoyed a huge degree of success during his reign.

Pete Rose was a talented player (career batting average .303), primarily for the Cincinnati Reds, from 1963 to 1986. Later, as manager for the Reds, he got into trouble for betting on games, which prevented him from being placed in the Hall of Fame.

Why is Pete Rose *not* in the Hall of Fame?

Pete Rose (1941–) is not in the Baseball Hall of Fame because he bet on baseball games while serving as a manager for the Cincinnati Reds. Rose holds the all-time record for hits (more than forty-two hundred), won three World Series championships, and played in seventeen All-Star Games. Known as "Charlie Hustle," Rose gave it everything he had and certainly ranks among the all-time great baseball players. Many believe Rose deserves a place in the Hall of Fame based on his incredible on-the-field accomplishments. However, others insist that because he bet on baseball, he should remain permanently banned from consideration for induction to the Hall of Fame.

Cal Ripken broke Lou Gehrig's streak of consecutive games, but whose streak did Gehrig break?

The Iron Horse (Gehrig) passed Everett Scott, a shortstop who played for Boston and New York in 1,307 straight games from 1916 through 1925; interestingly, his streak stopped on May 5, 1925, and Gehrig's started a few weeks later (on June 1, 1925). Scott was traded from the Yankees to the Senators on June 17, 1925. Cleveland player Joe Sewell had a streak of 1,103 games from 1922 to 1930, running ahead of Gehrig for five years, but Gehrig went on to play until 1939.

Even though Cal Ripken's streak continued into 1998 from May 30, 1982, and passed twenty-five hunded games, he never reached the top twenty all-time in games played.

(Gehrig isn't in the top twenty, either.) In fact, no player who appeared in over 1,000 straight games (there are six) is in the top twenty in career games played, which shows the value of an occasional day off. George Brett is 20th at 2,707 games played, and Pete Rose is first at 3,562.

BASKETBALL

Who invented basketball?

James Naismith (1861–1939) invented basketball while working at a Young Men's Christian Association ("YMCA") in Springfield, Massachusetts. Born in Canada, Naismith attended McGill University in Montreal, Canada. He later moved to the United States, where he taught physical education courses. He needed an indoor game to occupy his students. His ingenious solution was to affix a peach basket to a wall and to have players attempt to loft the ball into the basket. Thus was born the game of basketball.

Naismith later moved to Denver, where he earned a medical degree. He then transitioned to the University of Kansas, where he later coached its basketball team beginning in 1898. He compiled a losing record at Kansas (55–60) but created a game that became popular around the globe.

How did the early game of basketball differ from the modern game?

There were several differences between the early game of basketball and the way it is played today. When Dr. Naismith invented the game, players could advance the ball only by passing it. Today the ball is advanced by players dribbling the ball up the court and passing. Another key difference is scoring. In the early game, when a player scored a basket, the ball moved to half court, where each side would compete for a jump ball. Today, when a team scores a basket, the other team takes the ball out of bounds and immediately takes the ball up the court to try to match the other team and score its own baskets.

Originally, the game consisted of two fifteen-minute halves with a five-minute rest period in between. Now, the college game consists of two twenty-minute halves with a fifteen-minute halftime.

When did the NCAA basketball championships begin?

The National Collegiate Athletic Association (NCAA) began a competition for dif-

The inventor of basketball, James Naismith created the game to give his students an athletic activity that could be played indoors.

ferent colleges and universities in basketball in 1939. In the first year of competition, the University of Oregon defeated Ohio State 46–33 to win the championship. Today, the NCAA champion is determined by a sixty-eight-team tournament in a process popularly known as "March Madness." It is a single-elimination tournament, pitting the top teams from Division I of the NCAA.

What is the Final Four?

The Final Four refers to the four teams that reach the semifinals in the NCAA basketball championship. The top four teams advance through several rounds. The two teams that win the Final Four games on Saturday then advance to the title game, which is generally played on the first Monday night in April.

What is March Madness?

March Madness refers to the dizzying popularity of the NCAA basketball tournament that begins in the month of March every year. The term was used in the early 1980s by broadcaster Brent Musburger (1939–) and other television executives to describe the popularity of the televised tournament. But, according to the *New York Times*, the term originally arose in 1939 during the Illinois state basketball tournament. The *Times* reported that the Illinois state basketball association's executive secretary, Harry V. Porter, wrote: "A little March madness may complement and contribute to sanity and help keep society on an even keel."

What team was a dynasty in the 1960s and 1970s in men's college basketball?

The UCLA Bruins dominated men's college basketball, winning ten NCAA championships in a span of twelve years from 1964–1975. John Wooden (1910–2010), also known as the "Wizard of Westwood," coached the team to seven consecutive championships beginning in 1964. His teams featured such dominant players as Lew Alcindor (later Kareem Abdul-Jabbar; 1947–), Bill Walton (1952–), and Gail Goodrich (1943–). Four of his title teams (1963–1964, 1966–1967, 1972–1973, and 1973–1974) went undefeated during the entire season. At one point during the early 1970s, his team won eighty-eight straight games. No college basketball team could hope to match the Bruins' unparalleled success.

What was the significance of the 1966 NCAA title game?

On March 19, 1966, Texas Western defeated the University of Kentucky Wildcats to win the NCAA championship by a score of 72–65. The significance was the racial element of the game. Texas Western, coached by Don Haskins (1930–2008), started five black players in the title game against Kentucky's all-white team coached by the legendary Adolph Rupp (1901–1977). Especially through the lens of history, the game is seen as significant in tearing down walls of racial prejudice and leading to a much greater influx of blacks into college basketball. Noted author Frank Fitzpatrick later wrote a book about the famous title game, *And The Walls Came Tumbling Down* (1999).

What famous NBA coach and executive played in that 1966 title game for the Wildcats?

Pat Riley (1945–) played for the Wildcats when they lost to Texas Western in the aforementioned NCAA championship game. But Riley certainly has won far more games than he has lost, particularly as a professional player, coach, and executive. After graduating from Kentucky, Riley played nine seasons in the NBA for three different teams—the San Diego Rockets, the Los Angeles Lakers, and the Phoenix Suns. He was a role player who averaged about seven points a game.

Pat Riley is one of the most accomplished coaches in NBA history.

After his playing career ended, Riley served as a broadcaster for the Los Angeles Lakers. When the Lakers' head coach, Jack McKinney (1935–), was injured and could not coach that year, Riley became an assistant coach for the Lakers under coach Paul Westhead (1939–). Westhead, with Riley as his assistant, won the NBA title in his first season as head coach. However, when Westhead was fired early in the 1981–1982 season, Riley became head coach. He was the architect of the famed Los Angeles Lakers' "Showtime" team headed by point guard Earvin "Magic" Johnson, forward James Worthy, center Kareem Abdul-Jabbar, and other stars. Riley won four NBA championships.

Riley later coached the New York Knicks in the 1990s, nearly leading them to the NBA championship in 1994, falling in seven games to the Houston Rockets. Riley's next stop was with the Miami Heat as a coach and then executive. He led the team to the NBA championship in 2005. Riley now serves as president of the Heat, which won two more championships in 2012 and 2013. Riley is considered one of the best coaches and executives in NBA history. As an executive, he is best known for acquiring LeBron James (1984–) and Chris Bosh (1984–) to help Dwyane Wade (1982–) to form "the Big Three." The Heat went to four straight NBA finals and won back-to-back championships in 2012 and 2013.

Who were the "Fab Five"?

"The Fab Five" referred to the five freshmen of the University of Michigan's basketball team, who in 1991 all started and advanced to the NCAA championship game, where they lost to Duke University. "The Fab Five" consisted of Jalen Rose (1973–), Chris Webber (1973–), Juwan Howard (1973–), Jimmy King (1973–), and Ray Jackson (1973–).

They played a free-flowing brand of basketball marked by dominating dunks and flamboyant passing. The five players all returned for their sophomore seasons and once again made it to the championship game of the NCAA tournament, this time barely losing to the University of North Carolina after an untimely time-out by Webber near the end of the game. The team had no more time-outs but Webber called time-out, which led to the calling of a technical foul and a North Carolina victory.

The Fab Five only played together two years, as Webber left for the NBA after his sophomore year. Rose and Howard followed suit after their junior seasons. King and Jackson played all four years of college ball. Webber, Rose, and Howard had long and successful careers in the NBA. King played briefly in the NBA and then in the minor professional leagues. Jackson played professional basketball in the Continental Basketball League (CBA), earning Rookie of the Year honors in 1995–1996. He never played in the NBA.

PROFESSIONAL BASKETBALL

What is the NBA?

NBA stands for the National Basketball Association, the premier professional basketball league in the world. It consists of twenty-nine teams based in the United States and one team (the Toronto Raptors) from Canada. Founded in 1946 as the Basketball Association of America, the league became known as the National Basketball Association after a merger with a rival league known as the National Basketball League.

An NBA season consists of eighty-two regular-season games. Teams are divided into two conferences— Eastern and Western. Sixteen teams—eight from each conference—advance to the playoffs. Each playoff series consists of a best-of-seven format. The winners of the Eastern and Western conferences advance to the NBA Finals.

Who was the greatest professional basketball player in history?

It depends on which basketball historian you ask. Some would say Michael Jordan (1963–), who led the Chicago Bulls to six championships in the National Basketball Association (NBA), was the greatest player of all time. Jordan combined uncanny athleti-

What team has won the most NBA championships?

The Boston Celtics have won the most NBA championships: seventeen. Coached by legendary coach Arnold "Red" Auerbach (1917–2006), the team dominated the sport in the late 1950s and 1960s. They won the NBA title an astonishing eight consecutive years (1959–1966). Anchored by center Bill Russell (1934–), a dominating defense presence, and Bob Cousy (1928–), a creative passing point guard, the team simply dominated the league.

cism with an indomitable will to win. He routinely led the NBA in scoring and became a cultural icon worldwide.

Others may argue that Kareem Abdul-Jabbar (1947–) is the greatest player in NBA history. He won six NBA championships—one with the Milwaukee Bucks early in his career and five more with the Los Angeles Lakers. Abdul-Jabbar remains the NBA's all-time leading scorer, with more than 38,000 points. His skyhook is the most effective and dominating offensive weapon in the history of basketball.

Still others might point to Wilton Norman "Wilt the Stilt" Chamberlain (1936–1999). Standing more than seven feet tall, Wilt Chamberlain literally dominated the basketball game. He often led the NBA in rebounds. His physical talents were imposing and awe-inspiring.

However, critics of Chamberlain often point to his rival Bill Russell of the Boston Celtics as the greatest player in basketball history. Russell certainly was the greatest winner, as he led the Celtics to eleven championships in his thirteen NBA seasons—from 1956–1969. Russell played incredible defense and was the only player in the league who could present problems for Chamberlain.

What was Wilt Chamberlain's most impressive statistic?

This is a difficult question to answer; Chamberlain dominated opponents and made the NBA record book his personal playground. Chamberlain once averaged more than fifty

Kareem Abdul-Jabbar (left) was a basketball powerhouse in the 1970s and '80s, and Wilt "the Stilt" Chamberlain was a star on the floor in the 1960s and early '70s.

points per game in an NBA season. He scored more than a hundred points in a single game. Others believe his most impressive individual statistic was grabbing fifty-five rebounds in one game. Others may point to the fact that Chamberlain actually led the league in assists one year—the only center ever to do so. Despite his statistical dominance, Chamberlain's teams often fell short when he squared off against the Boston Celtics and his rival Bill Russell (1934–).

How many championships did Bill Russell win?

Russell was an unparalleled winner in basketball. In college basketball, he led the University of San Francisco to consecutive NCAA championships in 1955 and 1956. Russell then led the United States to an Olympic gold medal at the 1956 Melbourne Olympic Games. The American team defeated the Soviet Union 89–55 in the gold medal game. Russell then joined the Boston Celtics of the National Basketball Association, after the crafty Red Auerbach engineered a draft day trade with the St. Louis Hawks. His last championship he won as a player-coach.

What NBA player was known as "Mr. Clutch"?

Jerry West (1938–) was known as Mr. Clutch during his fifteen-year career with the Los Angeles Lakers. West earned his nickname with his penchant for late-game heroics. One of his more memorable moments was a last-second fifty-five-footer in Game Three of the NBA Finals against the New York Knicks to send the game into overtime. When he retired, West had the highest points-per-game scoring average in the playoffs. It took the great Michael Jordan to post a higher scoring average.

Who is the only player in NBA history to average a triple-double during a season?

Oscar Robertson (1938–), "the Big O," averaged double figures in three different categories during the 1961–1962 season: 30.8 points, 12.5 rebounds, and 11.4 assists per game. Many consider Robertson one of the best all-around players in NBA history. Robertson played for the Cincinnati Royals and the Milwaukee Bucks. He won an NBA championship with the Bucks in 1971.

What players have most successfully jumped from high school directly to professional basketball?

Moses Malone (1955–) was one of the earliest players to make the successful transition from high school to the pros. He played high school ball at Petersburg (Virginia) High School, where it was said he was "a man among boys." He signed a letter of intent to play at the University of Maryland but never went to college. Instead, Malone went to play for the Utah Stars of the ABA. He had an immediate impact at the professional level. He played only two years in the ABA before moving to the NBA, where he played for nineteen seasons. Along with Julius Erving, Malone led the Philadelphia 76ers to the NBA championship in 1983. Malone was a fearsome force down low, often simply too strong for opponents. He frequently led the NBA in offensive rebounding.

Kevin Garnett (1976–) graduated from the basketball powerhouse Farragut Career Academy (Illinois) High School and entered the 1995 NBA draft. He was selected fifth in the draft that year by the Minnesota Timberwolves. He played twelve seasons with the Timberwolves and became one of the NBA's perennial all-star players. In 2007, he was traded to the Boston Celtics. Along with Ray Allen (1975–) and Paul Pierce (1977–), Malone helped lead the Celtics to the NBA championship. Garnett not only possessed excellent offensive skills for a big man but was a fierce defender. He is well known for the passion for which he plays the game. He continues to exhibit that passion—along with his former teammate Pierce—for the New Jersey Nets.

Kobe Bryant (1978–) graduated from Lower Merion High in Philadelphia, Pennsylvania, and went straight to the professional ranks. He first entered the NBA with the Los Angeles Lakers in 1996, and, as of the end of 2014, still plays for the Lakers. Bryant made minimal contributions in his first season, but as a sixth man in his second year was averaging more than fifteen points per game. He then blossomed into one of the league's true superstars, sometimes averaging more than thirty points per game. He scored eighty-one points in a single NBA game—second only to the great Wilt Chamberlain. Nicknamed "the Black Mamba," Bryant can singlehandedly dominate a basketball game. He has won five NBA championships.

LeBron James (1984–) entered the 2003 NBA draft after starring at St. Vincent–St. Mary's High School in Akron, Ohio. James played his first seven seasons with the Cleveland Cavaliers before his much-publicized (and sometimes much-maligned) move to the Miami Heat in 2010. However, the move paid great dividends for James, as he won back-to-back NBA championships in 2012 and 2013. He may be the most physically gifted basketball player in history. There is a reason he is known as "King James."

What player was known for breaking backboards?

Darryl Dawkins (1957–) was a muscular 6'10" center best known for his charismatic personality and his penchant for powerful dunks. Nicknamed "Chocolate Thunder," Dawkins dunked so hard that he shattered several backboards in NBA games. The NBA began using breakaway rims largely because of Dawkins' game-delaying dunks. Dawkins was a character in the truest sense of the word, saying that he was a resident of the planet Lovetron and naming some of his dunks. In November 1979, when he shattered a backboard and made a dunk running by an opposing player named Bill Robinzine, Dawkins named the dunk "the Chocolate-Thunder-Flying, Robinzine-Crying, Teeth-Shaking, Glass-Breaking, Rump-Roasting, Bun-Toasting, Wham-Bam, Glass-Breaker-I-Am-Jam."

What player literally changed his first name to World?

Lloyd Free (1953–) changed his name to World B. Free in 1981 at the height of his basketball prowess. Free averaged more than thirty points a game during the 1979–1980 season for the Los Angeles Clippers. Free was known for his unlimited range and penchant for taking—and often making—difficult shots. Another of his nicknames was "the Prince of Midair."

Who is Michael Jordan?

Many consider Michael Jordan (1963–) the greatest player in NBA history. A 6'6" shooting guard, Jordan possessed incredible athleticism and an even more indomitable competitive drive. As a freshman, he nailed the game-winning shot to lead the University of North Carolina Tar Heels over the Georgetown Hoyas to the NCAA championship in 1982. After his junior year, he turned pro and was drafted by the Chicago Bulls. He attained individual success but

Michael Jordan, who played primarily for the Chicago Bulls in the 1980s and '90s, is considered by many to be the greatest basketball player of all time.

not much team success in his early years. However, he later led the Bulls to six NBA championships during his NBA career. He led the NBA in scoring ten times. He earned the NBA Finals' Most Valuable Player Award during each of his team's six championships. He also was a perennial top defender, along with his teammate Scottie Pippen (1965–). Because of his aerial athleticism, he was often referred to as "Air Jordan" or "His Airness."

Who was Allen Iverson?

Allen Iverson (1975–) was a talented, mercurial guard blessed with phenomenal quickness who led the NBA in scoring in four different seasons and averaging more than thirty points per game in five different seasons. He regularly led the league in minutes played per game and also led the league in steals in four different seasons.

Iverson grew up in Hampton, Virginia, becoming a standout athlete in both football and basketball at Bethel High School. He literally dominated football games from both the quarterback and cornerback positions. Some say he was even better at football than basketball.

His early life featured controversy, as he was convicted of a felony for participating in a racially charged fight at a bowling alley. He received a fifteen-year prison sentence (with ten years suspended). After serving four months, he received clemency from Virginia Governor Douglas Wilder.

Iverson then attended Georgetown University for two years, where he excelled on the court. He entered the NBA in 1996, doing it his own way and in his own style. He wore his hair braided, clashed with his coach, and never backed down from the media. He famously—or infamously—derided the idea that he could become better or make his teammates better by attending practice.

Despite his controversial bravado, Iverson played hard and played with injuries on the court. He led the Philadelphia 76ers to the NBA finals in the 2000–2001 season, where they lost to the Los Angeles Lakers. He remains an iconic figure in basketball history for his patented player, his embrace of hip-hop culture, and his do-it-my-way attitude.

What player holds the record for most points in one quarter of an NBA playoff game?

One might expect the answer to be an all-time great scorer such as Michael Jordan, Jerry West, Oscar Robertson, or LeBron James, but the answer is Eric "Sleepy" Floyd (1960–). In 1987, the Los Angeles Lakers were facing the Golden State Warriors in Game Four of the playoffs. The Lakers were ahead 3–0 and looking for a sweep of the series. The Lakers led by fourteen points heading into the fourth quarter. However, Floyd—a shooting guard for the Warriors—literally could not miss. Floyd scored twenty-nine points in the quarter, including nineteen points in the first five minutes.

What NBA player was known as "Downtown"?

Fred Brown, or "Downtown Freddie Brown," was a guard with the Seattle Supersonics, known for his nearly unlimited shooting range. Brown literally could shoot from downtown. When he got on a roll, Brown was hard to stop. Brown helped the Supersonics to the 1978 NBA championship as its sixth man. His coach, Lenny Wilkins (1937–), referred to him as "instant offense." He once scored fifty-eight points in a playoff game for the Sonics.

What NBA guard was known as the "Microwave"?

Vinnie "the Microwave" Johnson (1956–) was a shooting guard for the Detroit Pistons, known for his ability to come off the bench and heat up the scoreboard quickly. Because

What was the ABA?

The American Basketball Association (ABA) was a professional men's basketball league that existed in the United States from 1967 until 1976, when it merged with the NBA. The ABA was a wild, free-flowing league filled with creative players, some eccentric owners, and an overall free spirit. It featured a red, white, and blue basketball, a shot clock, and the three-point shot. Terry Pluto immortalized the league and many of its players in his book *Loose Balls*. Many greater players—who later achieved fame in the NBA—began their professional careers in the ABA, including Julius "Dr. J." Erving (1950–), Artis Gilmore (1949–), and George "the Iceman" Gervin (1952–).

Four ABA teams merged into the larger NBA: the Denver Nuggets, the Indiana Pacers, the San Antonio Spurs, and the New York Nets.

of his penchant for getting hot and taking over games, he was known as the Microwave. He was a key member of the Pistons' championship teams in 1989 and 1990. Johnson hit the game-winning and series-winning shot in Game Five of the 1990 NBA championship series against the Portland Trailblazers.

Who was "Dr. J."?

Dr. J. was the nickname of Julius Winfield Erving II (1950–), a popular player best known for his amazing dunks and athleticism on the fast break. After two years at the University of Massachusetts, Erving joined the ABA—first with the Virginia Squires and then with the New York Nets. He led the Nets to two ABA championships and thrilled audiences with his gravity-defying slam dunks. It was said that people came to see "the Doctor" put on a show.

Julius "Dr. J." Erving, shown here in a recent photo, was a key player to the success of the Philadelphia 76ers from 1976 to 1987.

When the ABA merged with the NBA, Dr. J. joined the Philadelphia 76ers. He enjoyed an eleven-year career with the 76ers, including a championship season in 1982–1983, where he played alongside center Moses Malone (1955–), shooting guard Andrew Toney (1957–), and point guard Maurice Cheeks (1956–). That team lost only one game in the entire playoffs and swept the Los Angeles Lakers for Erving's lone NBA championship. Erving's immense popularity helped the league survive during some bleak financial times.

Who was the "Iceman"?

George Gervin (1952–) was known as the "Iceman" for his cool demeanor on the court and his ability to score points from all over the court. Gervin, a slender 6'8" shooting guard, could hit shots from all over the court. He was best known for his patented finger roll. Gervin led the NBA in scoring for several seasons. During one season, Gervin scored more than thirty-three points per game. He scored more than 25,000 points during his fourteen-year career in the ABA and NBA, averaging more than twenty points per game in twelve of his fourteen seasons.

What two players' great rivalry took the NBA to new heights in 1979 and the 1980s?

The rivalry between Earvin "Magic" Johnson (1959–) of the Los Angeles Lakers and Larry Joe Bird (1956–) literally saved professional basketball, taking the game to new and greater heights. Johnson and Bird had stoked their rivalry in college basketball, when

Who are the Harlem Globetrotters?

The Harlem Globetrotters are a popular exhibition basketball team known for their theatrical and entertainment skills on the court. Founded in the late 1920s, Abe Saperstein (1902–1966) guided the team in the early years as its coach and promoter. He later chose the name Harlem Globetrotters to signify the team as an all-black squad. The team wears red, white, and blue to signify it as America's team. Through the years, the team has had some players with incredible skills—men such as Curly Neal, Meadowlark Lemon, and Reece "Goose" Tatum.

Johnson's Michigan State Spartans defeated Bird and the Indiana State Sycamores for the NCAA championship.

The two renewed their rivalry in the NBA, as each played for one of the two great winning teams of the league—the Lakers and the Celtics. They won eight NBA titles between them (Johnson won five with the Lakers; Bird won three with the Celtics). Not only were Johnson and Bird fierce rivals, but they became very close friends. They both are frequently in the discussion when people talk about all-time greatest basketball players.

FOOTBALL

When did American football begin?

American football—just called football in the United States—began in the nineteenth century. It evolved from the sport of rugby. The first game was played in November 1869 between Rutgers and Princeton. Today it is probably the most popular sport in the United States.

When did NCAA football begin?

College football had several fatalities in the late nineteenth and early twentieth centuries. Between 1890 and 1905, more than three hundred college athletes died from playing football. As a result, many leaders—including President Theodore Roosevelt— urged for the creation of a body that could bring stability and safety to the sport. In 1906, the Intercollegiate Athletic Association of the United States was formed. In 1910, the name was changed to the National Collegiate Athletic Association.

What is the Heisman Trophy?

The Heisman Trophy is the top individual award in college football. Named after former college football coach John Heisman (1869–1936), the award was created by the Manhattan-based Downtown Athletic Club in 1935, where Heisman was its director at the time. When Heisman died in 1936, the award was renamed in his honor. Heisman had won a championship in 1917 as coach of Georgia Tech. The award has been dominated by quarterbacks and running backs.

The award has honored a "Who's Who" list of great players, including Roger Staubach from the Naval Academy (1963), O.J. Simpson from the University of Southern California (1968), Earl Campbell from the University of Texas (1977), Her-

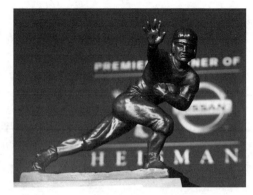

The Heisman Trophy is the top individual award in college football history.

schel Walker from the University of Georgia (1982), Barry Sanders from Oklahoma State University (1988), Tim Tebow from the University of Florida (2007), and Cam Newton from Auburn University (2010).

The only person to win the Heisman Trophy more than once was Ohio State running back Archie Griffin (1954–), who won in 1974 and 1975. Only one defensive player—or predominantly defensive player—has ever captured the award: Charles Woodson (1976–) from the University of Michigan in 1997.

What is the National Football League?

The National Football League (NFL) is the premier professional football league. It began in 1922, although for two years it operated under different names—the American Professional Football Conference and the American Professional Football Association.

The NFL currently consists of thirty-two professional football teams—sixteen in the National Football Conference (NFC) and sixteen in the American Football Conference (AFC). Twelve teams advance to the playoffs. The NFC and AFC winners then advance to play in the Super Bowl for the NFL championship.

What was the Ice Bowl?

The Ice Bowl was a famous playoff game between the Green Bay Packers and the Dallas Cowboys in December 1967, played in frigid, below-zero temperatures. With only seconds remaining, the Packers won the game 21–17. The Packers would then face and defeat the Oakland Raiders in the Super Bowl. The game featured teams led by two future Hall of Fame coaches: Vince Lombardi (1913–1970) for the Packers and Tom Landry (1924–2000) for the Cowboys.

What is the Super Bowl?

The Super Bowl is the biggest sporting event in the United States and one of the most widely watched sporting events in the world. It crowns the champion of the National

Football League (NFL). The winner of the American Football Conference (AFC) squares off against the winner of the National Football Conference (NFC) after surviving early playoff games.

The first Super Bowl took place on January 15, 1967, between the Green Bay Packers of the NFC and the Kansas City Chiefs of the AFC. The mighty Packers, coached by the legendary Vince Lombardi (1913–1970), won the game handily (35–10).

Why was Vince Lombardi considered such a great coach?

Vincent T. Lombardi led the Green Bay Packers to become a football dynasty. Lombardi once said, "Winning isn't everything; it is the only thing." He coached the Packers to six championships, including five in seven years. His Packers won the first two Super Bowls. He never had a losing season during his years as an NFL coach. The trophy for the winner of the Super Bowl is named in his honor.

What NFL team won the most Super Bowls?

The Pittsburgh Steelers have won six Super Bowls—the most of any team in NFL history. They captured titles in 1974, 1975, 1978, 1979, 2005, and 2008. The Dallas Cowboys and the San Francisco 49ers have each won five Super Bowls.

What former running back is often called the greatest football player in the history of the game?

Jim Brown (1936–) only played nine years in professional football—all for the Cleveland Browns. But he left a body of accomplishments and many bodies in his wake. Brown simply outran and overpowered opposing defenders, often inspiring opponents to refer to him as "Superman" or even "superhuman." Brown gained more than twelve thousand

Who was Jim Thorpe?

Jim Thorpe (1888–1953) was a former great football player in the 1910s and 1920s, known as the "World's Greatest Athlete." He not only played college and professional football, but also he won gold medals in the 1912 Olympic Games in the Pentathlon and the Decathlon. The 1912 Games were held in Stockholm, Sweden. Allegedly, King Gustav V of Sweden told Thorpe at the competition, "You, sir, are the world's greatest athlete."

Thorpe also played professional baseball and basketball. Thorpe earned All-American honors in college football while playing for Carlisle Indian Industrial School in Carlisle, Pennsylvania. He played professional football with the Canton Bulldogs. He was also named the greatest male athlete of the first half of the twentieth century.

years in his career, averaged more than five yards per carry, and averaged more than one hundred yards per game—the only running back in NFL history to eclipse that mark. He reached the Pro Bowl in each of his professional seasons. In 2002, in its listing of one hundred greatest players, *Sporting News* ranked him as the greatest football player of all time. As they wrote: "He was a physical masterpiece, a gift from the football gods."

Who was "The Juice"?

"The Juice" was the nickname of Buffalo Bills star running back Orenthal James Simpson, better known as O.J. Simpson (1947–). Simpson rushed for more than 11,000 yards in his ten-year career. In 1973, Simpson ran for a then-record 2,003 yards in only fourteen games, averaging a record 143 yards per game. He led the NFL in rushing in four different seasons. Sadly, O.J. Simpson today is remembered less for his gridiron achievements than for his alleged involvement in the murder of his former wife, Nicole Brown Simpson, and her friend Ronald Goldman. Simpson was found not guilty by a criminal jury in 1995. However, a civil jury in 1997 found him liable for the wrongful deaths of Simpson and Goldman. A judgment of more than $35 million was imposed on Simpson. He is currently in prison in Nevada on felony charges for armed robbery and kidnapping.

Who was "Sweetness"?

"Sweetness" was the nickname of former all-time great running back Walter Payton (1954–1999), who played his entire career with the Chicago Bears. Payton rushed for more than 16,000 yards in his thirteen-year NFL career. Payton's years of perseverance with the Bears paid off, as he won a Super Bowl with the Bears' mighty 1986 team. Mike Ditka (1939–) famously said that Payton was not only among the greatest of football players but also an even better human being. Football fans everywhere mourned his premature death in 1999 at age forty-five.

Who is the NFL's all-time rushing leader?

Emmitt Smith (1969–) is the NFL's all-time leading rusher, gaining more than 18,000 yards in his fifteen NFL seasons. He played the vast majority of his career with the Dallas Cowboys, with whom he won three Super Bowls. He ended his career with the Arizona Cardinals in 2004. Smith also scored more than 160 touchdowns in his Hall of Fame career.

NFL star Emmitt Smith ran over 18,000 yards with the football during his career and was on three Super Bowl-winning teams.

Who was Jerry Rice?

Jerry Rice (1962–) is generally considered the greatest wide receiver in NFL history and one of the greatest—if not *the* greatest—player in the league's history. Rice's accomplishments are staggering. In twenty NFL seasons, he grabbed more than fifteen hundred catches, scored 208 touchdowns, and garnered nearly 23,000 receiving yards. Rice, who was from Mississippi, was known for his Spartan work ethic and his amazing hands. Rice claimed that he developed his great hands while working for his father as a youngster doing brick masonry.

What was the "Immaculate Reception"?

The "Immaculate Reception" was a most unlikely game-winning touchdown catch in a playoff game between bitter rivals the Oakland Raiders and the Pittsburgh Steelers in December 1972. Oakland scored a touchdown with just more than a minute remaining in the fourth quarter to take a 7–6 lead. The Steelers were down to their last gasp, facing fourth down. Pittsburgh quarterback Terry Bradshaw (1948–) threw a pass to John Fuqua (1946–). Fuqua likely would have caught the pass, but fearsome Oakland safety Jack Tatum (1948–2010) delivered a vicious hit that caused the football to ricochet into the air. Pittsburgh running back Franco Harris (1950–) caught the ball in the air and ran for a game-winning touchdown. It remains one of the strangest, yet most spectacular, plays in NFL history.

What is the controversy over concussions?

More than four thousand former players have sued the NFL for concussion-related injuries they suffered as a result of blows to the head during their professional football careers. Many have suffered a variety of medical problems—such as Alzheimer's, chronic traumatic encephalopathy, and dementia—that they attribute to lack of safety procedures in place for players. Some famous former football stars have joined in these lawsuits, including former Dallas Cowboy defensive tackles Randy White (1953–) and Bob Lilly (1939–).

The controversy over concussion-related injuries has only increased in the wake of the suicide of another football great, linebacker Junior Seau (1969–2012), who shot himself at age forty-three. The National Institutes of Health has indicated that Seau suffered from chronic traumatic encephalopathy.

BOXING

Who was the first world heavyweight boxing champion?

John L. Sullivan (1858–1918), the "Boston Strong Boy," was the first world heavyweight champion under the modern Marquis de Queensbury Rules, requiring boxers to wear gloves. Previously, Sullivan had reigned as the champion of bare-knuckled bouts. Sullivan was a larger-than-life champion and even a cultural hero. He reputedly would walk into taverns and loudly proclaim, "I can lick any son-of-a-bitch in the house"—and then often did.

In 1892, Sullivan lost his world championship to a younger, more skilled boxer—James "Gentleman Jim" Corbett (1866–1933) stopped Sullivan in the twenty-first round.

Who was the first African American to win the heavyweight title?

John Arthur "Jack" Johnson (1878–1946) was the first black man to capture the world heavyweight championship. Johnson possessed superior boxing skills, including advanced defensive skills for the early twentieth century. Johnson was the "uncrowned champion" for several years, as a series of top white heavyweights refused to face him. He literally chased heavyweight champion Tommy Burns halfway around the world before finally receiving his title shot in Australia in December 1908. He punished Burns before the referee mercifully stopped the contest in the fourteenth round. Johnson held the championship until losing the belt to the much larger and younger Jess Willard in Havana, Cuba, in April 1915.

Johnson's most significant bout was his July 4, 1910, clash in Reno, Nevada, with former champion James J. Jeffries (1875–1953). The popular Jeffries had retired undefeated. The public talked him out of retirement to win back the title for white America. There was a significant amount of racial violence after Johnson defeated Jeffries. It caused authorities to ban the distribution of films showing the fight.

Johnson was a controversial figure, as many in White America resented the fact that a black man held the sport's most coveted crown. For his part, Johnson openly taunted opponents and flaunted his romances with white women. Prosecutors initiated a racially motivated prosecution of Johnson for an alleged violation of the Mann Act, because he cavorted with a white woman who was a former prostitute. Johnson had to flee the country for a period of years to avoid imprisonment.

What heavyweight champion was a symbol of the Roaring Twenties?

The popular Jack Dempsey (1895–1983) held the heavyweight title from 1919 until 1926, capturing great public acclaim for his slugging prowess. The so-called "Man-

One of the greatest champs in boxing was Jack Dempsey, who held the heavyweight title from 1919 to 1926.

SPORTS HISTORY

assa Mauler" (because he was born in Manassa, Colorado) would bob and weave his way to and through opponents, often winning with devastating punching power. Dempsey earned a shot at the title in 1919 against the mammoth Jess Willard (1881–1968), the man who had bested the great Jack Johnson. Dempsey's combination of speed and power was too much for Willard, who fell to the canvas seven times in the first round alone. Dempsey did not fight very frequently, but his fights were box office bonanzas. Dempsey held the title until 1926, when he lost a decision to the masterful boxer Gene Tunney (1897–1978). Dempsey fought Tunney in a rematch at Soldier's Field in Chicago and nearly recaptured his title in the seventh round. Dempsey dropped Tunney, who was down for about fourteen seconds. However, the referee did not start the count until Dempsey went to a neutral corner. Tunney rose at the official count of nine and won the rematch known as "the Long Count."

Who was the longest-running champion in boxing history?

Joe Louis (1914–1981) held the world heavyweight championship for nearly twelve years—the longest reign of any champion in boxing history. He defended his title twenty-seven times and is considered one of the greatest champions in the sport. Louis became the second black man to capture the heavyweight championship after the controversial Jack Johnson.

Louis became a national hero after he defeated the former world champion, German Max Schmeling, whom German leader Adolf Hitler had used to propagate his Aryan race white supremacy doctrines. For his part, Schmeling was a good and decent man who later forged a lifelong friendship with his former rival Louis. Schmeling actually provided Louis with his first professional loss in July 1936. Louis later captured the title with a victory over James J. Braddock the next year. But Louis wanted to avenge his only defeat.

In October 1938, Louis stopped Schmeling in the first round at Yankee Stadium to become a true American hero. He initially retired in March 1949 after defeating Jersey Joe Walcott for the second time. Louis made an ill-advised comeback and could not regain his past glory.

What fighter was known as the "Cinderella Man"?

James J. Braddock (1905–1974) was known as the "Cinderella Man" for his unlikely comeback and rise, culminating in his capturing the heavyweight championship over the heavily favored Max Baer in 1935. Braddock began his career as a light heavyweight and earned a shot at the world title against Tommy Loughran (1902–1982) in 1929. Braddock lost a unanimous decision, fracturing his powerful right hand in the process. Braddock, depressed after the loss and the injuries, lost six of seven fights at one point. He and his family suffered through terrible economic strife during the Great Depression.

In 1934, Braddock entered the ring as a heavyweight, facing the talented contender Corn Griffin (1911–1973). Braddock stopped the bigger man in the third round with

307

his powerful right hand, which seemed to be stronger after having healed. He then also upset two more favored fighters, John Henry Lewis (1914–1974)—who had beaten Braddock previously—and Art Lasky (1908–1980). The string of three straight upsets earned Braddock a shot at Baer, the heavyweight champion. Baer was a talented, if not at times unmotivated, champion who possessed terrific power. But Braddock beat him over fifteen rounds to capture the title. He lost his championship in his first defense against the great Joe Louis, although he managed to drop Louis in the first round.

Author and newspaper writer Damon Runyon (1880–1946) famously gave Braddock his nickname.

What boxer scored the most knockouts in boxing history?

Former world light heavyweight champion Archie Moore (1913–1998) won 130 bouts by knockout or technical knockout, more than any fighter in history. Known as the "Old Mongoose," Moore fought professionally for twenty-seven years. Born in Mississippi, Moore moved to St. Louis, Missouri, as a youth, where he went to reform school for stealing. His time in reform school was well spent, as he learned to box there. He turned professional in 1935 and quickly built a reputation as a tough fighter. Many top fighters and champions avoided facing Moore in the ring. For many years, he was known as an "uncrowned champion." Finally, he received his first title shot in 1952 at age thirty-nine, defeating Joey Maxim over fifteen rounds. He retained his title numerous times through the years.

Moore had a powerful left hook, a deadly right cross, and a feared body attack that he used to fell many opponents. Moore also tried his hand at heavyweight against larger opponents. In 1955, he challenged undefeated heavyweight champion Rocky Marciano for the title. Moore actually dropped Marciano early in the fight, but Marciano's relentless attack eventually overwhelmed Moore. The cagey veteran even fought the young Muhammad Ali in 1962. Moore is the only fighter to have fought both Marciano and Ali as a professional. Moore later became a highly respected boxing trainer.

Who was the only undefeated champion in heavyweight boxing history?

Rocky Marciano (1923–1969) is the only undefeated heavyweight champion in boxing history, with a perfect record of 49–0. Born Rocco Francis Marchegiano, he later changed his name to Marciano when he began his boxing career. Marciano's first love was baseball, but he soon discovered that he possessed natural power in his fists.

Tutored by the wily trainer Charley Goldman, Marciano overcame his awkward style to become a dominant heavyweight champion. During his career, he defeated several world champions, including Ezzard Charles (1921–1975), Jersey Joe Walcott (1914–1994), Archie Moore, and a past-his-prime Joe Louis.

Who was "The Greatest"?

The boxer known as "The Greatest" was the incomparable Muhammad Ali (1942–). Born Cassius Marcellus Clay in Louisville, Kentucky, he first garnered worldwide attention by capturing the gold medal in the light heavyweight division at the 1960 Rome Olympics. He turned professional, turning heads with his incredible speed and his lofty boasting. Clay often would accurately predict in what round he would stop his opponent.

He "shook up the world" by defeating the vaunted Charles "Sonny" Liston (d. 1970) to win the world heavyweight title in 1964. He later earned the scorn of many for changing his name and converting to the Nation of Islam, a black separatist group led by Elijah Muhammad.

He inspired even greater enmity when he refused induction into the U.S. draft. Authorities stripped him of his world championship. He suffered a three-and-a-

Muhammad Ali (left) with formal boxing rival George Foreman in a recent photo.

half-year exile from boxing as a result of his pacifist beliefs. Amazingly, he returned to the ring in 1970, losing to undefeated champion Joe Frazier in "the Fight of the Century" at Madison Square Garden.

But he shocked the world again when he upset George Foreman in Kinshasa, Zaire, to regain the heavyweight title in 1974. He later lost and then regained the title in 1978 in bouts with Leon Spinks.

But Ali did something even more special than regaining heavyweight glory. He became a worldwide hero. The former pariah became a beloved global ambassador—the most recognizable face on the planet. He carried the Olympic torch at the 1996 Olympic Games in Atlanta and earned the Presidential Medal of Freedom from President George W. Bush in 2005.

What fighter captured the heavyweight title at age forty-five?

George Foreman (1949–) won the Olympic gold medal at the 1968 Mexico City Olympics and then turned professional. Possessing devastating power, Foreman marched through the division like General William T. Sherman through Atlanta. He won his first thirty-seven fights before challenging "Smokin'" Joe Frazier for the heavyweight crown in Kingston, Jamaica. Foreman demolished Frazier in two rounds. However, he lost his world title to the incomparable Ali in Zaire in 1974. Foreman tried to regain the title but retired after losing a decision to Jimmy Young (1948–2005).

Foreman stayed retired for a decade, becoming a preacher and changing his outlook in certain aspects. Foreman returned to the ring in September 1987, initially to make more money for his church. However, Foreman had another goal in mind—to recapture heavyweight glory. Some critics scoffed at the notion that the forty-something Foreman could win the title, calling him "the Great, Fat Hope." But Foreman persisted.

He lost in his first attempt to regain the title when he dropped a decision to Evander Holyfield (1962–) in 1991. Many thought his dreams vanished when he later lost a decision to Tommy Morrison (1969–2013) in 1993, but Foreman managed to land a title shot against the undefeated Michael Moorer (1967–) in 1994. The younger and quicker Moorer won nearly every round of the fight, beating the bigger but older man to the punch. However, in the tenth round, Foreman caught Moorer with a straight right hand to the chin. Foreman knocked out the younger champion and regained the championship at age forty-five. For many years, Foreman worked as a boxing analyst for HBO, the channel that broadcast the Moorer–Foreman fight. Foreman's colleague Jim Lampley probably spoke for millions of Americans when he announced, "He did it. My God, he did it!"

What great fighter won three of four bouts against the great Willie Pep?

Willie Pep was an all-time great boxer, known for his brilliant boxing and defensive skills. Pep began his career by winning 134 of his first 136 professional bouts and captured the world featherweight championship. However, he lost his title in 1948 to a tall, young challenger named Sandy Saddler (1926–2001). Pep regained his title, winning a fifteen-round decision. However, Saddler won the last two fights between the two, stopping Pep in the tenth round in their fourth bout. Saddler was considered one of the greatest punchers in boxing history.

Who was the "Golden Boy"?

"The Golden Boy" is the nickname of talented boxer and current boxing promoter Oscar De La Hoya (1973–), who won an Olympic gold medal at the 1992 Barcelona Games. He

Who is generally considered the greatest boxer pound-for-pound in boxing history?

There have been numerous great boxers in the sport's history. Joe Louis, Muhammad Ali, Willie Pep (1922–), and others frequently appear in sport's listing of top pound-for-pound lists. But the boxer most experts view as the best in the history of the sport was former welterweight and middleweight champion Sugar Ray Robinson (1921–1989).

Born Walker Smith, Robinson became Ray Robinson when his coach used the card of another boxer, Ray Robinson, to enter him in an amateur tournament. Robinson had all the skills—pure boxing skills, one-punch power, endurance, and a great chin. He never lost a bout in his amateur career. He lost only one professional bout in his first 132 professional bouts. He was simply the best.

turned professional amidst great fanfare and did not disappoint. He won his first professional world championship in only his twelfth pro bout, stopping Denmark's Jimmy Bredahl (1967–) to win the World Boxing Organization ("WBO") super featherweight championship. He also won world titles in the lightweight, junior welterweight, welterweight, junior middleweight, and middleweight divisions.

De La Hoya captured the welterweight title with a decision victory over Pernell "Sweet Pea" Whitaker (1964–) in 1997. He won his first thirty-one pro bouts before suffering a controversial decision loss to Felix Trinidad (1973–) in 1999. He defeated numerous world champions in his illustrious career, finally retiring in 2008 with a one-sided loss at the hands of Philippine sensation Manny Pacquiao.

What American boxer is widely considered the sport's current pound-for-pound king?

Floyd "Money" Mayweather (1977–) is widely considered the sport's current pound-for-pound king. He has won world titles in five different weight classes and has not lost a professional bout, holding a record at the time of this writing of 46–0. Mayweather possesses uncanny defensive skills, quickness, and overall ring generalship. He won his first world title in the 130 lb. super featherweight division and has won titles as high as the 154 lb. junior middleweight division. He has defeated the likes of Oscar De La Hoya, Ricky Hatton, Diego Corrales, José Luis Castillo, Shane Mosley, and Juan Manuel Marquez in his career.

MIXED MARTIAL ARTS

What is Mixed Martial Arts?

Mixed Martial Arts, or MMA, is a combat sport that features many different fighting disciplines—boxing, wrestling, jiu-jitsu, judo, karate, and others. Fighters try to either knock out their opponents or defeat them by decision. Once referred to as "human cockfighting," MMA has become the fastest growing sport in North America over the past fifteen years. Once relegated to the fringes, major media outlets regularly cover the leading MMA bouts, most principally the fights in the Ultimate Fighting Championship (UFC).

When did the UFC begin?

The UFC began in 1993 in Denver, Colorado, with an eight-man, winner-take-all tournament. The "no-holds-barred" tournament featured fighters of different disciplines. The winner was a relatively slight Brazilian named Royce Gracie (1966–), who used his superior grappling and jiu-jitsu skills to defeat his much larger opponents. He submitted three straight opponents to capture the championship. His opponents were boxer Art Jimmerson, shoot fighter Ken Shamrock, and savate specialist Gerard Gordeau. Gracie's performance educated many sports fans to the prowess and importance of ground-fight-

ing skills. Now the UFC is the most popular and powerful brand and promotional
force in mixed martial arts in the world.

Who was the "Iceman"?

"The Iceman" was the moniker of former
UFC light heavyweight champion Chuck
Liddell (1969–), arguably the most popular MMA fighter in his prime. Liddell possessed strong punching power in his right
hand, excellent kicking skills, and an excellent take-down defense. He was known
for knocking out his opponents with his
patented right hand bombs. He is probably best known for his trilogy of bouts with
Randy "the Natural" Couture (1963–). Lid-

Chuck "The Iceman" Liddell was one of the most
popular MMA fighters from 1998 to 2010.

dell won two of the three bouts against Couture. He also faced the likes of Quinton
"Rampage" Jackson, Wanderlei Silva, and Rich Franklin.

GOLF

Where was the first golf club in the United States?

The South Carolina Golf Club was formed in Charleston in 1786. As early as 1743, a
shipment of ninety-six clubs and 432 balls arrived in Charleston from the Port of Leith
in Scotland.

When was the first U.S. Open played?

The first U.S. Open Championship was held in 1895 on the Rocky Farm Course at the
Newport (Rhode Island) Golf Club, founded by Theodore Havermeyer. He was president
of the United States Golf Association and reportedly covered all expenses to ensure that
the best golfers would compete. The first Open was originally scheduled for early September but was moved back to October so it wouldn't be overshadowed by the America's
Cup yacht races being held in a huge water hazard near the course. An Open competition
for professionals was held at St. Andrews Golf Club in Yonkers, New York, in 1894, and
both St. Andrews and Newport Golf Clubs held Amateur Open competitions that year as
well. The United States Golf Association was formed late in 1894 by representatives from
those two clubs, as well as The Country Club (Brookline, Massachusetts), Shinnecock
Hills (Southampton, New York), and the Chicago Golf Club to conduct national golf
championships in the United States. The first U.S. Open was won by Horace Rawlins,
who shot a 173 for the tournament and played in four nine-hole rounds during one day.

When was the Ryder Cup competition established?

In 1926, an unofficial match between a group of professionals from the United States and a team made up of golfers from England and Ireland was played in Wentworth, England. British seed merchant Samuel Ryder, an avid golfer, was so impressed with the competition that he donated the Ryder Cup to be awarded to the winning side in the biennial Ryder Cup competition. The first official Ryder Cup match was played at the Worcester Country Club in Massachusetts and was won by the host U.S. team.

In 1979, the competition changed to a United States vs. European team format. The competition had been dominated by the U.S., but the European team won four and tied another competition while only losing twice from 1979 to 1997.

Who is arguably the most popular male golfer?

Arnold Palmer (1929–) was the sport's first superstar in the television era. He had a great personality to go along with his marvelous game. Nicknamed "the King," Palmer had a legion of fans—"Arnie's Army"—who followed and cheered him along the golf course. He became the first golfer to earn $1 million in his career (1968). Palmer could also play some golf, winning sixty-two PGA titles and seven majors. He became part of the sport's "Big Three" with his rivals Jack Nicklaus and Gary Player.

Who was the first woman golfer to amass $1 million in lifetime earnings? Who was the first to do it in a single year?

Kathy Whitworth was a dominant force on the LPGA Tour from 1962 (when she won her first tournament) to 1981, when she became the first woman golfer to surpass $1 million in career earnings. She won the most LPGA tournaments from 1965–1968, taking thirty-five during that span and never fewer than eight in a season.

In 1996, Karrie Webb became the first woman to win $1 million in a single year, reflecting her great talent as a twenty-two-year-old rookie and also the tremendous growth in purses on the LPGA Tour. Webb won three tournaments that year and finished second in five others.

What American male golfer won the most major tournaments?

Jack Nicklaus, "the Golden Bear" (1940–), won eighteen career major championships—more than anyone else in the sport. The four major championships are

Golfing legend Arnold Palmer is shown here in a recent photo.

the Masters, the U.S. Open, the British Open, and the PGA Championships. Nicklaus won six Masters, four U.S. Opens, three British Opens, and five PGA titles. He also finished second in major tournaments an astonishing nineteen times.

He won his first title at the 1962 U.S. Open—in only his second year as a professional. His most famous victory occurred at the 1986 Masters—when he rallied on the final round to win the title at age forty-six.

Much recent talk in the golf world has focused on whether Tiger Woods—who has won fourteen major titles at the end of 2014—would overtake Nicklaus.

What male golfer won the Grand Slam?

Bobby Jones (1902–1971) captured the Grand Slam in 1930 by winning all four major titles in a single calendar year. In Jones's day, the four major tournaments were the U.S. Open, the British Open, the U.S. Amateur, and the British Amateur. Jones won all four of these tournaments in 1930. He retired from competition shortly after that amazing year. Jones has the greatest winning percentage of any golfer competing in Grand Slams. He competed in only thirty-one majors and won thirteen of them. It is unlikely anyone will ever approach that record of success.

What Hall of Fame golfer had the greatest final round comeback in U.S. Open history?

During the first three rounds of the 1960 Open, Arnold Palmer had turned in a respectable, but not spectacular, performance, 72–71–72, that left him seven strokes behind the tournament leader, Mike Souchak. Palmer started out the fourth round by driving the green on the 346-yard Par–4 first hole; he missed the eagle putt but left himself a tap-in for birdie. On the 410-yard second hole, he hit another long drive and just missed the green with his pitch but chipped in for another birdie. Palmer smashed his tee shot again on the next hole, a 348-yard dogleg left, and put a wedge shot a foot from the pin: birdie. His fourth consecutive birdie came on the 426-yard fourth hole when he sank an eighteen-foot putt. He settled for par on the Par–5 fifth hole but came back with another birdie with a twenty-five-foot putt on the Par–3 sixth hole. On the 411-yard Par–4 seventh hole, Palmer hit a wedge shot six feet from the pin and holed out for his sixth birdie in seven holes. Parring the eighth and ninth holes, he turned in a 30 for the front nine and solidified his reputation for final round charges, with "Arnie's

Army" vigorously cheering him on. Arnie's Army was a term coined by sportswriter Johnny Hendrix to describe the swarm of fans cheering Arnold Palmer on to victory at the 1958 Masters. Even after this spectacular front nine performance in the 1960 Open, Palmer's win was far from a done deal. At this point in the tournament, Souchak was tied for the lead, and several other players had a chance to win the Open, including young Jack Nicklaus (still in college) and the legendary Ben Hogan, who were playing together two groups ahead of Palmer. Arnie arrived at the seventeenth hole, needing pars on the last two holes to win. He played the Par–5 seventeenth conservatively, laying up short of the water with his second shot to ensure the par. Then, although he missed the green with his second shot on the Par–4 eighteenth, his neat little chip and four-foot putt won the Open for him. Palmer's final-round 65 (30 for the front and 35 on the back) was the lowest ever score by an Open winner on the last round of the tournament to that time.

Where does golf sensation Tiger Woods rank among the greats?

Eldrick "Tiger" Woods (1975–) ranks among the best players of all time. Most experts consider him either the greatest or second only to the great Jack Nicklaus. Golfing historians and the public often focus on major championship wins. As of the end of 2014, Woods has won fourteen major championships, trailing only Nicklaus' eighteen career

When it comes to who is the greatest American golfer in history, opinions vary between Jack Niklaus (left) and Tiger Woods (right).

major titles. Many assumed that Woods would not only break Nicklaus's record but crush it. However, Woods suffered a high-profile dissolution of his marriage with revelations that he had carried on an assortment of affairs. The marital discord seemed to impact Woods's golf game, as he has not won a major championship since the 2008 U.S. Open. Routinely ranked the number-one player in the world for several years, his ranking dropped for a period of time, although part of this can be explained by injuries.

In 2013 Woods regained his form, winning several titles. He has won seventy-nine career PGA titles—second only to "Slammin'" Sam Snead's (1912–2002) eighty-two titles.

What American female golfer may be the greatest female athlete in history?

Babe Didrikson Zaharias (1911–1956) was not only one of the great female golfers in history but also may have been the most accomplished female athlete of all time. She won all of golf's three female major tournaments in 1950. In her career, she won ten major titles and forty-one professional golf titles.

But "the Babe" was more than just a great golfer. She dominated every sport she ever played. She won gold medals in the 1932 Olympics in the 80-meter hurdles and the javelin. She literally dominated the court in women's basketball in her early days.

What female golfer captured the most major championships?

Patty Berg (1918–2006) won fifteen major championships—more than any female golfer in history. Berg was a founding member of the Ladies Professional Golf Association (LPGA) in a career that spanned decades. She won her first major championship at the Western Open in 1941 and her last major title at the LPGA championship in 1959. She won a total of sixty tournaments in her career, her last in 1962.

HOCKEY

What are the origins of hockey in the United States?

The first professional hockey team found a home in the United States, taking shape in 1903 in the city of Houghton, Michigan. Frank and Lester Patrick later brought professional franchises to the Pacific Northwest, including Portland, Oregon (the Rosebuds, 1914–1915), and Seattle, Washington (the Metropolitans, 1915–1916). The Seattle Metropolitans of the Pacific Coast Hockey Association (PCHA) defeated the Montreal Canadiens of the National Hockey Association (NHA) in 1917 to claim the Stanley Cup. (They were not the first American team to have their names engraved on the Cup, however. Towards the end of the 1915–1916 season, the PCHA champion Portland Rosebuds prematurely engraved their names on the trophy before they played against the National Hockey Association champion Montreal Canadiens. The Canadiens won the series three games to two, claiming the Cup.)

The first U.S.-based NHL club still in existence is the Boston Bruins, founded in 1924. Three other U.S. clubs—the Detroit Cougars (later the Red Wings), Chicago Blackhawks, and New York Rangers—began play in 1926–1927.

What was the first amateur hockey league in America?

The American Amateur Hockey League (AAHL) formed in November 1896. The teams included the St. Nicholas Hockey Club, the New York Athletic Club, the Crescent Athletic Club, and the Skating Club of Brooklyn. One year later, the Baltimore Hockey League was formed, as the game began to spread down the East Coast.

When did the National Hockey League begin?

On November 22, 1917, the NHL was organized, and on November 26, its five member clubs received charters. Those teams were the Montreal Canadiens, the Montreal Wanderers, the Ottawa Senators, the Quebec Bulldogs, and the Toronto Arenas. According to legend, the NHL was formed by the leaders of four former NHA clubs in a calculated attempt to oust Toronto Blueshirts owner Eddie Livingstone from professional hockey. There had been such animosity between Livingstone—who was angry in part because the league would not allow him to run two clubs—and the other NHA owners that in 1916–1917 the league cancelled Toronto's games and reassigned its players to other clubs. Although Livingstone took legal action against the new league, he lost his court case.

When it comes to hockey, the grand prize is winning the coveted Stanley Cup. In this photo, goalie Jonathan Quick of the L.A. Kings celebrates winning the 2014 championship and getting his chance to hold the Cup.

When did the Rangers, Blackhawks, and Red Wings begin?

The NHL continued its aggressive expansion into the 1926–1927 season and awarded three new franchises to New York, Chicago, and Detroit. With the Western Canada Hockey League—the only other major pro league—on the brink of folding, there would be plenty of players available for these new teams.

After the financial success of the Americans in their inaugural season, Tex Rickard and the Madison Square Garden management wanted a team of its own and figured New York City could manage two teams. They were granted a franchise named the Rangers. The team was assembled by Conn Smythe, but he had a falling-out with the Garden management and was dismissed before the team ever played a game. Lester Patrick, co-founder of the old Pacific Coast Hockey Association, managed and coached the team for its first seasons.

The Chicago team was originally owned by a group led by former football star Huntington Hardwick but was sold after only one month to the city's coffee tycoon, Frederic McLaughlin. During World War I, Blackhawks owner Frederic McLaughlin served in a machine gun battalion nicknamed the Black Hawks. When he returned home, he named the team after his old service battalion, and his wife drew the famous Native American head logo. The team was composed of players from the WCHL's Portland Rosebuds, whom Hardwick had purchased for $100,000 when he owned the team.

The NHL received five applications from five different groups for the Detroit franchise: it awarded the franchise to Wesley Seybourn and John Townsend, who represented a large group of investors formed by sports promoter Charles Hughes. The team was composed of players from the WCHL's Victoria Cougars, whom the team purchased in similar fashion to Chicago. The Detroit franchise was called the Cougars, just like the team of the players from which they had come.

Why did the Detroit Cougars change their name in 1930?

Detroit fans found "cougars" too difficult to say, so they became the Detroit Falcons in 1930. Two seasons later, they became the Red Wings.

How successful were the Rangers?

As soon as they stepped onto the ice in the 1926–1927 season, the Rangers became an immediate hit in New York City. They quickly overtook their fellow housemate Americans in the box office, and on the ice, and became known as "the classiest team in hockey."

In their first season, the Blueshirts took the league by storm, finishing first in the American Division with a 25–13–6 record before losing in the semifinals to Boston. In the following season, the Rangers again were among the top teams in the league, finishing second in their division and winning the Stanley Cup.

From that point on, the Rangers continued to do well on the ice, as well as at the box office. Until the 1941–1942 season, they missed the playoffs only once and won two more Stanley Cups (1933 and 1940). In the 1939–1940 season, the team averaged nearly ten thousand people per game in attendance. The architect of these teams was Lester Patrick, who had taken over the club after Conn Smythe was fired before the team played a game.

In the early days of the franchise, the team was headlined by the A line, one of the best of its day. The line consisted of Frank Boucher centering the Cook brothers, Bill and Bun. On defense, the team was led by the hard-hitting Ching Johnson. As those players aged out, they were eventually replaced by the likes of forwards Bryan Hextall and Neil Colville, defensemen Ott Heller and Muzz Patrick, and goaltender Davey Kerr.

Who was the first American to win the Hart Trophy?

Yonkers, New York, native Billy Burch of the Hamilton Tigers scored twenty goals in twenty-seven games in the 1924–1925 season to win the second Hart Trophy ever awarded.

Who made the difference in the 1928–1929 season for the Bruins, when they finally won their first Stanley Cup?

Cecil "Tiny" Thompson joined the Bruins just in time for the team to move to Boston Garden, where the team won its first Stanley Cup in 1929. The team also included stars like the shutdown defensive pair of Hall of Famer Eddie Shore and captain Lionel Hitchman. The team also included Harry Oliver, Dit Clapper, and Dutch Gainor.

Thompson started a ten-year run between the pipes for Boston with a 1.15 goals-against average and then nearly halved that during the playoffs! His GAA over a five-game sweep was 0.60. He went 3–0 versus the Montreal Canadiens, and 2–0 over the New York Rangers in the league's first all-American Stanley Cup final.

However, Cecil Thompson was not as "tiny" as his nickname suggested, standing 5'10" and weighing 160 pounds.

What was the first hockey franchise in Pittsburgh, and how successful were they?

The Pittsburgh Pirates existed in the NHL from 1925 to 1930. The Pirates can be traced back to the Pittsburgh Yellow Jackets of the U.S. Amateur Hockey Association. The Jackets were eventually sold to attorney James F. Callahan. In 1925, the NHL granted a franchise to Pittsburgh. When the team moved to Pittsburgh, Callahan renamed his franchise the Pittsburgh Pirates, after receiving permission from the owner of the Pittsburgh Pirates baseball team.

The Pirates played their inaugural season in 1925–1926, led by team captain Lionel Conacher and goaltender Roy Worters. In their very first NHL game, they defeated the Boston Bruins 2–1. Two days later, the Pirates stunned the mighty Canadiens 1–0 in what would be the legendary Georges Vézina's final game. However, they lost their home opener to the New York Americans 2–1 in overtime. In thirty-six games, they posted an admirable record of 19–16–1, finishing third in the league.

Their first season, however, would arguably be their best. In their second season, they finished fourth and missed the playoffs. The next year they earned a playoff spot but lost in the semifinals to the New York Rangers. This was the last time the Pittsburgh Pirates made the playoffs. Due to financial reasons, Callahan was forced to sell the team. It was relocated for one season before permanently disbanding.

In the 1935–1936 Stanley Cup playoffs, what record did the Detroit Red Wings and the Montreal Maroons establish that has never been broken?

In the first game of the playoffs, the Detroit Red Wings and the Montreal Maroons went scoreless through regulation and ended up playing almost two full games of overtime. The game went until 16:30 of the sixth overtime, which was—and still is—the longest game in league history at 176 minutes and 30 seconds.

How did the longest game in history end?

At 2:25 A.M. on Wednesday, March 25, 1936, at the Montreal Forum, a Detroit Red Wings rookie named Modere "Mud" Bruneteau picked up an errant pass from teammate Hec Kilrea. He then fired a low shot past the Maroons' goaltender, Lorne Chabot.

Between periods, Red Wings staff massaged players with rubbing alcohol and fed them teaspoons of sugar dipped in brandy to keep them going. Detroit goalie Normie Smith stopped eighty-nine shots and Montreal goalie Chabot stopped sixty-five shots before Bruneteau went out onto the ice.

What players formed the NHL's Production Line?

The Detroit Red Wings line of Gordie Howe, Sid Abel, and Ted Lindsay was formed on November 1, 1947, and played together through the 1951–1952 campaign. The trio reigned as the highest-scoring forward unit in the NHL in the early 1950s. The name was also a reference to the city's automotive industry, which Henry Ford had revolutionized by implementing the assembly line.

What players made up the famed "French Connection" line?

Gilbert Perreault, Richard Martin, and Réne Robert formed the high-scoring line

Gordie Howe (shown here) of the Detroit Red Wings was part of the famous Production Line that also included Ted Lindsay and Sid Abel.

> ## Why do fans in Detroit toss octopi onto the ice during playoff games?
>
> The tradition—which has been discouraged by the NHL by allowing referees to penalize a home team when fans interrupt a game by tossing items onto the ice—began during a 1952 playoff game: An octopus was tossed onto the ice to symbolize the eight playoff wins needed to capture the Stanley Cup at that time.

that helped take the Buffalo Sabres to the Stanley Cup finals in 1975, a mere five years after entering the league. The Sabres have not reached the finals since.

The 1973–1974 season marked the first time an expansion team won the Stanley Cup. What was that team?

The Philadelphia Flyers—known as the "Broad Street Bullies" for their rugged play—was the first expansion team to win the Cup. Proving it was no fluke, they repeated the feat the very next season.

What was so amazing about the hockey gold medal game during the 1980 Winter Olympics?

One of the most incredible upsets in sports history occurred in Lake Placid, New York, on February 2, 1980, when the U.S. hockey team, led by coach Herb Brooks, defeated the Soviet Union and won gold in a 4–3 victory. What made it such an upset was that the American team was made up of amateurs and collegiate players, while the Soviets had coaches from professional teams and trained at a world-class facility. Going into the game, the Soviets had won the previous four Olympics. Everyone was amazed the Americans had reached the final game, and no one believed they could defeat the Soviets. The victory has entered sports history annals as "the Miracle on Ice."

What team has currently gone the longest without winning the Stanley Cup?

In 1994, the New York Rangers won the Stanley Cup for the first time in fifty-three years; in 1997, the Detroit Red Wings won their first Cup in forty-one years; in 2010, the Chicago Blackhawks won their first Cup in forty-nine years. Currently, the Toronto Maple Leafs have not won since 1967. Of the original six expansion teams, Pittsburgh, Philadelphia, Los Angeles, and Dallas (originally Minnesota) have won Cups. St. Louis and San Jose remain Cup-less. Although they began play in the 1990s, the San Jose Sharks' lineage includes the original expansion California Golden Seals franchise, which relocated to Cleveland, then merged with Minnesota, then began play in San Jose after being allowed to take several Minnesota players with them.

Who is the only coach to win an NCAA college hockey championship and a Stanley Cup?

Bob Johnson won three NCAA titles with the University of Wisconsin (1977, 1981, 1983) and led the 1990–1991 Pittsburgh Penguins to the Stanley Cup eight months later before dying from a brain hemorrhage.

OLYMPICS

When did the United States first host the modern Olympic Games?

The modern Olympic Games first took place in April 1896, when the city of Athens, Greece, hosted the first modern Olympiad. The first time the Olympics took place in the United States occurred at the 1904 Summer Olympic Games in St. Louis, Missouri. The United States also has hosted the Summer Olympic Games in Los Angeles in 1936 and 1984 and Atlanta in 1996. The U.S. has hosted more Summer Olympic Games than any other nation.

What sports were featured in the 1904 Summer Olympic Games in St. Louis?

The 1904 St. Louis Summer Olympic Games featured archery, boxing, cycling, diving, fencing, golf, gymnastics, lacrosse, roque, soccer (called "football" by most of the world), swimming, tennis, track and field, tug of war, water polo, weightlifting, and wrestling.

Who was Jesse Owens?

Jesse Owens (1913–1980) was an American track and field athlete who won four gold medals at the 1936 Berlin Olympics. He captured gold in the 100 meters, the 200 meters, the long jump, and the 4 × 100 100-meter relay team, which he anchored. Owens achieved international acclaim at the Olympics, shattering German leader Adolf Hitler's misguided notions of Aryan supremacy.

What great American athlete later equaled Owens' performance at a later Olympics?

Carl Lewis (1961–), arguably the greatest male track and field athlete in history, equaled Owens's mark by winning gold

Track star Jesse Owens outraged German racist leader Adolf Hitler at the 1936 Berlin Olympics by winning four gold medals.

medals in the same four events as Owens at the 1984 Los Angeles Olympic Games. Lewis later added two more gold medals at the 1988 Seoul Olympics, two at the 1992 Barcelona Olympics, and one at the 1996 Atlanta Olympics for a total of nine gold medals.

What famous symbol of protest occurred at the 1968 Mexico City Olympics?

American sprinters Tommie Smith (1944–) and John Carlos (1945–) made the Black Power salute on the medal stand at the 1968 Mexico City Olympics. Smith captured the gold medal in the 200-meter dash, Carlos the bronze medal. On the podium, they donned black gloves and raised their fists while bowing their heads during the playing of the American national anthem. The two also wore black socks and no shoes on the podium to protest poverty among the black community in the United States.

The black gloves were a key part of the Olympic Project for Human Rights, a brainchild of sociologist Dr. Harry Edwards (1942–), who met Smith and Carlos at San Jose State (where the sprinters went to college on track scholarships).

In 2012, Smith said in an interview the black gloves were not meant to support the Black Panthers, a political group in the United States, but to support the principle of freedom in general. He referred to it as "the cry for freedom."

What American boxer did not win a gold medal but still was voted the most outstanding boxer of the 1988 Seoul Olympics?

Roy Jones, Jr. (1969–) dominated all his opponents en route to the gold medal match at the Seoul Olympics against Korean fighter Park Si-Hun. Jones dominated the three-round contest, landing more than eighty punches to only thirty for the Korean fighter. However, three judges voted for Park Si-Hun instead of Jones, meaning that the Korean fighter won the gold medal.

The referee said he was befuddled by the decision, and Park Si-Hun allegedly apologized to Jones for the bad decision. The terrible decision caused a change in the scoring system. For his performance at the games, Jones was awarded the prestigious Val Barker trophy—given to the best performing boxer at the Olympic Games.

What was special about the U.S. boxing team at the 1976 Olympic Games?

The 1976 U.S. Olympic boxing team was arguably the greatest team ever assembled by the United States—and perhaps in the history of the sport. It featured five gold medalists—flyweight Leo Randolph (1958–), lightweight Howard Davis, Jr. (1956–), light welterweight Sugar Ray Leonard (1956–), middleweight Michael Spinks (1956–), and light heavyweight Leon Spinks (1953–). The team also featured bantamweight Charles Mooney (1951–), who won a silver medal, and heavyweight John Tate (1955–1998), who won a bronze medal.

The team also included welterweight Clint Jackson (1954–), who lost in the quarterfinals but had a solid career as a professional, and featherweight Davey Armstrong

(1954–), who lost in the quarterfinals to eventual gold medalist Angel Herrera in a disputed 3–2 decision.

Many members of this team turned professional and won world championships. These included Randolph, who won a world title in the super bantamweight division; Leonard, who won world titles in numerous weight classes beginning with a welterweight championship in 1979; Michael Spinks, who won world titles at light heavyweight and heavyweight; Leon Spinks, who defeated Muhammad Ali for the heavyweight title in 1978; and Tate, who won the World Boxing Association championship in 1979.

What is the most decorated men's Olympic boxing team?

The U.S. 1984 Olympic team won more medals than any team in the country's history, with nine gold medals: light flyweight Paul Gonzalez (1964–); flyweight Steve McCrory (1964–2000); featherweight Meldrick Taylor (1966–); lightweight Pernell Whitaker (1964–); light welterweight Jerry Page (1961–); welterweight Mark Breland (1963–); light middleweight Frank Tate (1964–); heavyweight Henry Tillman (1960–); and super heavyweight Tyrell Biggs (1960–). Middleweight Virgil Hill (1964–) won a silver medal, and light heavyweight Evander Holyfield (1962–) won a bronze medal.

Many boxers from this team turned professional and won world titles, including Taylor, Whitaker, Hill, and Holyfield. However, this team's accomplishments occurred when many of the countries with top boxing teams—such as the Soviet Union and Cuba—boycotted the Olympics because it took place in Los Angeles.

What two American boxers won the Val Barker trophies at the 1976 and the 1984 Olympic Games, respectively?

It is somewhat surprising that the winners of the Val Barker trophies were won by Howard Davis, Jr. (1976) and Paul Gonzalez (1984). Davis and Gonzalez had excellent amateur careers and performed incredibly at the Olympics. However, neither man captured a world title at the professional ranks.

Meanwhile, some of their teammates—such as Sugar Ray Leonard, Michael Spinks, Virgil Hill, and Evander Holyfield—won multiple world championships and surely had Hall of Fame careers as professional pugilists.

Who defeated Floyd Mayweather at the 1996 Atlanta Olympic Games?

At the 1996 Olympic Games, Floyd Mayweather lost a semifinal match to Bulgaria's Serafim Todorov (1969–). Todorov represented Bulgaria in the Olympics in both 1992 and 1996. He lost in the quarterfinals in 1992 but defeated Mayweather in a disputed decision in 1996. He lost to a fighter from Thailand named Somluck Kamsing in the gold medal match. Todorov later turned professional but had only six pro bouts, retiring with a 5–1 record.

HORSE RACING

What is the Triple Crown?

The Triple Crown refers to the three major races for three-year-old horses in the United States: the Kentucky Derby, run at Churchill Downs in Louisville, Kentucky; the Preakness Stakes, run at Pimlico in Baltimore, Maryland; and the Belmont Stakes, run at Belmont Park in Elmont, New York. Only eleven horses have ever captured the vaunted Triple Crown: Sir Barton in 1919; Gallant Fox in 1930; Omaha in 1935; War Admiral in 1937; Whirlaway in 1941; Count Fleet in 1943; Assault in 1946; Citation in 1948; Secretariat in 1973; Seattle Slew in 1977; and Affirmed in 1978.

What Triple Crown winner was prone to erratic and wayward racing?

Whirlaway (1938–1953) endeared himself to racing fans all over the world for his distinctive racing style. Whirlaway, a free spirit, would often veer off to the very outside of the track, allowing slower horses to win races. Whirlaway also had a penchant for running in the back or middle of the pack and then exploding forward to win races. In the Triple Crown races, Whirlaway ran straight enough to run away with all three races, capturing the Kentucky Derby by eight lengths, the Preakness by five lengths, and the Belmont by three lengths.

What popular racehorse would sometimes win races when he was thirty lengths behind?

One of the most popular horses in American thoroughbred racing history was Silky Sullivan (1955–1977), who made a career out of coming out of nowhere to win races. Silky Sullivan won the 1958 Santa Anita Derby even though he trailed at one point by twenty-eight lengths. He once won a race when he was forty lengths off the leader. The horse became an eponym, as the term "Silky Sullivan" refers to a sports figure or a politician who comes out of nowhere to win a race.

What thoroughbred horses won the first two legs of the Triple Crown but could not win the Belmont?

Many horses have won both the Kentucky Derby and the Preakness yet failed to capture the Belmont—the longest of the three races at a mile and a half. Some of the more notable include Tim Tam in 1958, Majestic Prince in 1969, Spectacular Bid in 1979, Smarty Jones in 2004, Big Brown in 2008, and I'll Have Another in 2012.

Who was Man O'War?

Man O'War (1917–1947) is arguably the greatest thoroughbred racehorse in the history of horse racing. He won twenty of twenty-one career starts, including the Preakness and Belmont Stakes in 1920. Ironically, his only loss occurred at the 1919 Sanford

Memorial Stakes to a horse named Upset. Many horse racing experts have dubbed this horse the greatest of all time.

Many consider Man O'War to have been the greatest thoroughbred racehorse in history.

If not Man O'War, what other horse may be the greatest?

Secretariat (1970–1989) may be the greatest racehorse of all time. He won the Triple Crown in 1973, capping off an amazing season with the greatest performance of all time. Secretariat won the Belmont that year by an astonishing thirty-one lengths. The horse set time records at all three Triple Crown races that year. Secretariat won back-to-back Horse of the Year honors in 1972 and 1973. He also won the 1973 Marlboro Cup with a convincing win over his stablemate, Riva Ridge.

What great female horse was known as "the Queen"?

Zenyatta (2004) was known as "the Queen" or the "Queen of Racing" for her dominant performances on the racetrack. Standing more than seventeen hands tall, Zenyatta literally towered over her competition. She won nineteen of twenty career races, often crushing the opposition. The only loss of her racing career occurred in her last race—the 2010 Breeders Cup Classic, where she lost by a nose to Blame.

What horse won the Kentucky Derby as a 90:1 longshot?

Donerail entered the 1913 Kentucky Derby having performed in mediocre fashion as a two-year-old. However, Donerail surprised nearly everyone by winning the race over the favored Ten Point.

What three fillies have won the Kentucky Derby?

Only three fillies have ever won the Kentucky Derby: Regret in 1911, Genuine Risk in 1980, and Winning Colors in 1988. Regret raced only eleven times in her career and won nine times. She never lost to another female horse. Genuine Risk may have been the best-performing filly in terms of competing with the male horses. She not only won the Kentucky Derby in 1980 as a 13:1 underdog, but she finished second in both the Preakness and Belmont Stakes. Winning Colors also ran the Preakness, where she finished third, and the Belmont Stakes, where she finished sixth.

What famous filly had to be euthanized after a match race?

Ruffian was an undefeated filly who drew comparisons to Secretariat in terms of speed. "The Queen of the Fillies" won her first ten races. In her eleventh race, she competed in a match race with Foolish Pleasure, who had won the 1975 Kentucky Derby. Ruffian actually led by half a length when she broke two bones in her right ankle. The great filly had to be euthanized.

What two great rivals battled for supremacy in the 1977 Triple Crown races?

Affirmed and Alydar were both great horses who battled in all three Triple Crown races. Affirmed won all three races over his rival—although just barely. Affirmed won the three races over second-place Alydar by a combined total of two lengths. He only defeated Alydar in the Belmont by a neck. The two rivals raced against each other ten times; Affirmed won seven. However, Alydar won their last race at the 1978 Travers Stakes, after Affirmed was disqualified.

SWIMMING

What American swimmer has won more medals in Olympic history than anyone?

Michael Phelps (1985–) won a total of twenty-two Olympic medals—more than anyone in the history of the Games. He won six gold medals at the 2004 Athens Games, a record eight gold medals at the 2008 Beijing Games, and then four more gold medals at the 2012 London Games. At 6'4" with a long wingspan, Phelps devoured his competition over the years. He set many world records—most often in the butterfly and individual medley races.

Who previously held the most Olympic swimming medals?

Although recently surpassed by Phelps, it is definitely worth noting the record of Mark Spitz (1950–), who won seven gold medals in the 1972 Olympics in Munich, Germany. He had previously won two team golds in the 1968 Mexico City Olympics and also won silver and bronze medals. During his prime years, he set thirty-three official world records.

What American swimmer won Olympic gold and then became a major motion picture star?

Johnny Weismuller (1904–1984) won five Olympic gold medals in swimming at the 1924 Paris and the 1928 Amsterdam

Swimmer Michael Phelps, with eighteen gold medals to his credit, has won more Olympic gold than anyone in history.

Olympic Games. He was also part of the 1928 U.S. bronze medal-winning water polo team. After finishing his stellar athletic career, Weismuller played Tarzan in *Tarzan the Ape Man* (1932). He later played the character Jungle Jim in a series of hit movies.

What three American swimmers have each won a total of twelve Olympic medals in the sport?

Natalie Coughlin (1982–), Dana Torres (1967–), and Jenny Thompson (1973–) each won twelve Olympic Gold medals.

Couglin won two gold medals at the 2004 Athens Games and one at the 2008 Beijing Games. But she also won four silver and five bronze medals in her career. She added her twelfth medal at the 2012 London Games. Torres competed in an amazing five Olympic Games—the 1984 Los Angeles Games, the 1988 Seoul Games, the 1992 Barcelona Games, the 2000 Syndey Games, and the 2008 Beijing Games. At age 41, she won three silver medals in Beijing. Thompson won eight gold medals—two at the 1992 Barcelona Games, three at the 1996 Atlanta Games, and three at the 2000 Sydney Games. She also competed at the 2004 Athens Games.

TENNIS

What American tennis players captured the Grand Slam?

Only two American tennis players captured all four Grand Slam tournament titles in a calendar year. The first was Don Budge (1915–2000), who won all four tournaments in 1938. The only other American tennis player to accomplish the feat was Maureen "Little Mo" Connolly (1934–1969), who won all four titles in 1953. The only other tennis players to win the Grand Slam were not Americans—Australian Rod Laver in 1962 and 1969, Australian Margaret Court in 1970, and German Steffi Graf in 1988.

What American tennis player dominated tennis in the 1920s?

Bill Tilden (1893–1953) dominated men's tennis for much of the 1920s, winning many tournaments and rarely losing. Tennis historian Bud Collins estimated Tilden's winning percentage at greater than 90 percent. He won the U.S. Open seven times. Tilden's incredible athletic achievements sadly are now sometimes overshadowed by arrests he suffered in the 1940s and 1950s for inappropriate contact with minors. Nevertheless, "Big Bill," as he was known, was a phenomenal tennis player with historic accomplishments.

What American male tennis player posted a record of 82–3—the best in the modern era of men's tennis?

John McEnroe (1959–) dominated men's tennis in 1984—the last year he reigned as the #1 player in the world. The talented, temperamental McEnroe overwhelmed the competition with his lefty serve and amazing volleys. He often served and volleyed, forcing his competitors to try to hit passing shots. Usually, they could not convert enough of them to withstand McEnroe's consistent pressure.

McEnroe's amazing hand-eye coordination and reflexes at the net made him a dominant force in men's doubles. It was often said that the best men's doubles team in the world was John McEnroe and anyone else. During his career, he won seven Grand Slam titles in singles—four U.S. Open titles and three Wimbledon championships.

The winner of three Wimbledon and four U.S. Open titles, John McEnroe is considered one of the greatest tennis players to have played the game.

What other American tennis great of the 1970s and 1980s frequently competed with McEnroe for Grand Slam titles?

James Scott Connors (1952–), better known as "Jimmy" or "Jimbo," was the epitome of a fiery competitor. Connors stormed onto the scene in the early 1970s with his own unique brass-and-crass style. The left-handed Connors had a fearsome, two-handed backhand, which he could use to hit precise passing shots. He dominated the men's tour in 1974, winning three Grand Slams. He won eight Grand Slam titles in his career, including five U.S. Opens and two Wimbledon titles. He still holds the record for most professional tournament titles for men on the ATP tour at 109.

Connors outraged many with his antics on the court, arguing with umpires and grabbing his crotch. But he epitomized hard work, perseverance, and a never-say-die attitude. He became the darling of men's tennis in 1991, when at age thirty-nine, he won five matches at the U.S. Open—often in thrilling comeback fashion—to reach the semifinals.

What two American female tennis greats produced perhaps the greatest personal rivalry in all of sports?

Chris Evert (1954–) and Martina Navratilova (1956–) produced the greatest personal rivalry in all of women's sports. They played an astonishing eighty times in their career: Navratilova finished with a 43–37 lifetime edge. They also had contrasting styles: Evert relied on superb technical strokes from the baseline, while Navratilova employed an attacking, serve-and-volley game.

Both Evert and Navratilova won eighteen career major titles. Evert's most successful tournament was the French Open, where she won seven titles. The clay surface allowed Evert to display her consistent groundstroke game. Meanwhile, Navratilova's best

329

tournament was Wimbledon. The grass court tournament most favored Navratilova's attacking style of play. Navratilova captured the Wimbledon title nine times.

Who competed in the famous (or infamous) "Battle of the Sexes" match in 1973?

Billie Jean King (1943–), the top female tennis player in the world, defeated former male number-one player Bobby Riggs (1918–1995) at the Houston Astrodome in 1973. More than fifty million people watched this match live from thirty-seven different countries. There was a significant age difference between the two competitors: King was under thirty years old at the time; Riggs was fifty-five. Still many expected Riggs to win the match, as he formerly held the number-one ranking in men's tennis for part of the 1940s. Some doubted King would prevail, because earlier in the year, Riggs had easily defeated Margaret Court with an assortment of drop shots and junk balls. King then accepted Riggs' challenge. Always a believer in gender equality and women's rights, King took the match very seriously, believing a loss would be devastating for women in sports and society. She defeated Riggs 6–4, 6–3, 6–3.

What two sisters took tennis by storm in the late 1990s and the early twenty-first century?

Venus (1980–) and Serena (1981–) Williams took women's professional tennis by storm in the late 1990s. Reared in Compton, California, the sisters learned tennis from their

Serena (left) and Venus Williams are shown here playing doubles at the 2013 Australian Open. Together, the sisters have won over twenty Grand Slam titles.

eccentric father, Richard. The elder Williams had his daughters avoid the rigors of amateur tennis. Instead, they practiced against older women and men, developing devastating power games.

As of the end of 2014, Venus has won seven Grand Slam singles titles, while younger sister Serena has won eighteen Grand Slam singles titles. The two sisters have formed one of the great doubles teams in tennis history, capturing thirteen Grand Slam doubles titles. They still participate on the women's tour. Serena remains the number-one ranked female singles player.

TRACK AND FIELD

What American hurdler won more than 120 consecutive races in competition?

Edwin Moses (1955–) won 122 consecutive races in his specialty, the 400-meter hurdles. Moses won gold medals in the event at the 1976 Montreal Olympics and the 1984 Los Angeles Olympics. He likely would have won gold at the 1980 Moscow Olympics if the United States had not boycotted that event. He later won a bronze medal at the 1988 Seoul Olympics. Moses's amazing streak lasted from 1977 to 1987.

Moses was also known for his academic prowess. He took an academic scholarship to Morehouse College in Atlanta. He later received induction into the U.S. National Track and Field Hall of Fame.

What other great hurdler later played professional football?

Renaldo Nehemiah (1959–) was the dominant hurdler at the 110-meter distance—ranked number one in the world for several years in his prime in the late 1970s and early 1980s. He was the first hurdler to run the 110-meter hurdles in under thirteen seconds. Nehemiah was the hands-down favorite to win gold at the 1980 Moscow Olympics, but his chances ended when the United States boycotted those Olympic Games because of serious international tension with the host country, the Soviet Union. Nehemiah then turned his attention to professional football, joining the San Francisco 49ers as a wide receiver for three years. He had limited success in professional football. He later returned to track and field but was no longer the dominant force he had been in his prime.

What great sprinter was dominant at the 60-meter dash?

Houston McTear (1957–) literally tore up the competition in the 60-meter dash—an event not in the Olympics but that used to be a major event in the track and field world. (The event is still used for indoor track competitions.) In the mid- to late-1970s, McTear was the unquestioned king of the 60-meter dash. He simply had blazing speed, running the 100-yard dash in high school in Florida at nine seconds flat. At one meet, he was clocked running the distance in 6.38 seconds—although the timing was questioned. He held the official world record in the event from 1978–1986.

McTear also ran the longer 100-meter dash. He qualified for the 1976 Olympic Games but suffered an injury and could not compete. He was favored to medal at the 1980 Moscow Games but fell victim to the boycott.

What American male sprinter won ten Olympic medals?

Carl Lewis (1961–) won nine gold medals and one silver medal in his illustrious career that spanned four Olympic Games—the 1984 Los Angeles Games, the 1988 Seoul Games, the 1992 Barcelona Games, and the 1996 Atlanta Games. He was dominant in the long jump for more than a decade. He won gold medals in the event at all four Olympics.

Lewis also won gold medals in the 100-meter and 200-meter dashes. His only silver medal came at the 1992 Barcelona Olympics, where he finished second to fellow American Joe DeLoach. In 1999, the International Olympic Committee dubbed Lewis "Sportsman of the Century."

Olympic track star Carl Lewis in a recent photograph.

What great female sprinter competed in four Olympic Games?

Evelyn Ashford (1957–) completed in five Olympic Games—the 1976 Montreal Games, the 1984 Los Angeles Games, the 1988 Seoul Games, the 1992 Barcelona Games, and the 1996 Atlanta Games. She won four gold medals—one in the 100-meter dash and three in the 4 × 100 meter relay.

What two American women won gold medals in sprint events at consecutive Olympics?

Wyomia Tyus (1945–) and Gail Devers (1966–) each won gold medals in the 100-meter dash at consecutive Olympics. Tyus won gold medals at the 1964 Tokyo Games and the 1968 Mexico City Games. Devers captured gold at the 1992 Barcelona Games and the 1996 Atlanta Games in her great career.

What famous team did Ed Temple coach?

Ed Temple (1927–) coached the legendary (Nashville) Tennessee State University (TSU) Tigerbelles, the name of the vaunted female track and field team. Temple coached the team for more than forty years. The team was so dominant, it was dubbed "the Notre Dame of women's track and field." He guided such legendary female sprinters as Wyomia Tyus, Wilma Rudolph (1940–1994), Barbara Jones (1937–), Edith McGuire (1944–), and Chandra Cheeseborough (1959–).

What American athlete is the only man to win gold medals in the decathlon in consecutive Olympic Games?

Bob Mathias (1930–2006) is the only athlete to win gold medals in the decathlon in two consecutive Olympic Games. He captured his first gold at the 1948 London Olympics at age seventeen. Four years later, he dominated the event at the 1952 Helsinki Games, winning by more than nine hundred points. He later parlayed his athletic prowess into careers in both acting and politics. He served five terms as a member of the U.S. House of Representatives in California.

What high jumper completely changed the dominant technique in the event?

Dick Fosbury (1947–) revolutionized the technique high jumpers used to clear the bar. Previously, most jumpers used the straddle method or the upright scissors method. After experimenting with these techniques, Fosbury did something completely different. He ran at the bar and then away from the bar and led with his head and an arched back. Under this method, the high jumper turns away from the bar and clears his head, his body, and finally his legs over the bar.

This method became known as the "Fosbury Flop." Fosbury used the method to capture the gold medal at the 1968 Mexico City Games. Most dominant high jumpers ever since have used the "Fosbury Flop."

SOCCER

Who is Mia Hamm?

Mia Hamm (1972–) is arguably the greatest female American soccer player in history. She began playing on the United States Women's national soccer team when she was only fifteen—the youngest in history. A forward with a penchant for scoring goals, Hamm helped lead the U.S. Women's team to international glory with wins at the 1991 FIFA Women's World Cup, a gold medal at the 1996 Olympics, the 1999 FIFA Women's World Cup, and the 2004 Olympics. She retired in 2004 at age thirty-two with 158 goals in international competition.

How has the U.S. men's soccer team fared in the World Cup?

The U.S. men's team fared the best in the inaugural FIFA World Cup, finishing third in 1930. From 1954–1986, the U.S. did not even advance to the group stage. This means the squad lost many preliminary qualifying matches. Finally, the U.S. qualified for the 1990 World Cup. Since then, the best the U.S. men's team has done is a quarterfinal finish in the 2002 World Cup, losing 1–0 to Germany. The U.S. men's team reached the Round of Sixteen in the 2014 World Cup, losing to Belgium 2–1. On the positive side, the U.S. men's team has qualified for the world stage at every World Cup since 1990. Whether the U.S. men's team can advance into the elite level of teams—such as Brazil, West Germany, Spain, and Italy—remains to be seen.

Why was such praise heaped on U.S. goalkeeper Tim Howard in the 2014 World Cup?

Tim Howard (1979–) earned praise for his high number of saves during the World Cup, particularly in the Round of Sixteen game against a superior Belgian team. Howard singlehandedly kept the U.S. in the game with Belgium, making numerous diving saves. He set a record with sixteen saves in a single FIFA World Cup game. He earned the moniker "Secretary of Defense" after the performance.

MUSIC

Was the song "Yankee Doodle" actually written to make fun of Americans?

Yes. Composed during the French and Indian War by British physician Dr. Richard Schuckberg, "Yankee Doodle" contained lyrics to mock Americans as a bunch of dumb country bumpkins. After the original was written, however, American soldiers rewrote the lyrics in a more flattering manner, praising General Washington and using it as a rallying cry against the British.

At Yorktown, the Americans had the last say on the matter, when the British surrendered. The troops from England insulted the Americans by refusing to look at them and, instead, faced the Americans' French allies led by the Marquis de Lafayette. Lafayette, incensed by the snub, ordered his band in the light infantry brigade to play "Yankee Doodle," causing the startled Brits to unintentionally turn their heads toward the Americans.

Is it true that the music to the U.S. national anthem actually came from a British song?

Yes. When Francis Scott Key wrote the words to "The Star–Spangled Banner" after celebrating that Fort McHenry had not fallen to the British during the War of 1812, he used the meter and rhythm of a popular British tune, "To Anacreon in Heaven," which was a song often sung in British pubs.

Who wrote "This Land Is Your Land"?

Woodrow Wilson "Woody" Guthrie (1912–1967) was a folk and protest music writer who composed "This Land Is Your Land" in 1940 as a reaction to the Irving Berlin song "God

Bless America," which he found annoying and unrealistic. Guthrie, who lived through the Great Depression and the Dust Bowl, tried to capture the true spirit of hard-working Americans in his music. One of his eight children, Arlo Guthrie (1947–), has carried on the folk music tradition of his father.

Who was Pete Seeger?

A folk singer and activist, Pete Seeger (1919–2014) was famous for writing songs such as "Where Have All the Flowers Gone?," "Turn! Turn! Turn!," and "If I Had a Hammer." Many of his songs became even more well known after they were performed by other musicians such as the Byrds, the Kingston Trio, and Peter, Paul and Mary.

What is blues music?

Blues music is a form of music popularized in the late nineteenth and early twentieth centuries that arose out of the tradition of so-called Negro spirituals, work songs, and other music that arose from African Americans in the American south. Blues music often features many instruments, specific and repetitive lyrics, and bass lines. Blues music often features the musical depiction of a sad or mellow mood. Blues music inspired many later genres of music—most notably rock and roll. It has been said that "the blues had a baby, and they named it rock 'n' roll."

What are some different types of blues music?

Types of blues music include Delta Blues, Chicago Blues, electric blues, and Jump blues. Delta Blues was an early form of blues music that originated in the Mississippi Delta region. This type of blues music is known for its use of the harmonica and the guitar. Some well-known Delta Blues musicians include John Lee Hooker (1917–2001) and Chester Arthur Burnett (1910–1976)—better known as Howlin' Wolf.

The Chicago Blues, as the name suggests, originated in Chicago, Illinois. It featured amplified music, electric guitars, drums, and saxophones. A few of the better-known Chicago Blues musicians were Muddy Waters (1913–1983), Otis Spann (1930–1970), and the incomparable Buddy Guy (1936–).

The electric blues also became popular in Chicago. It features bass guitars and heavy amplification of the guitar and other instruments. Some leading electric blues artists include T. Bone Walker (1910–1975) and the contemporary Kenny Wayne Shepherd (1977–).

Jump blues is an uptempo form of blues music popular in the 1940s. It featured groups of musicians playing horns, the saxophone, and other instruments. It was a progenitor of both rhythm and blues and rock 'n' roll music. LaVern Baker (1929–1997) and Roy Milton (1907–1983) were popular in this genre.

Who is Buddy Guy?

Buddy Guy (1936–) is an inspiring and energetic blues vocalist and guitarist who still performs to audiences in his seventies. One of the pioneers of the Chicago blues sound, he has inspired a host of guitarists, such as Jimmy Page, Eric Clapton, and Stevie Ray Vaughan. He also served as a key influence on the late, great Jimi Hendrix.

Guy still has a blues club in Chicago—Buddy Guy's Legends. Born in Louisiana, Guy eventually moved to Chicago in part because of the racial climate in the South. He played frequently with Muddy Waters and other popular blues musicians. His career really took off again in earnest in the late 1980s and early 1990s. His brand of performing distinguishes Guy from other musicians, as he often strolls out into the crowd and mingles with his audiences. He often freelances and certainly has his own unique style.

It is somewhat sad that Guy did not receive mainstream recognition for his musical genius until the twenty-first century. He won a Grammy for Best Traditional Blues Album in 2003 and another Grammy in 2010 for Best Contemporary Blues Album. He was inducted into the Rock and Roll Hall of Fame in 2005.

Who invented jazz?

Ferdinand "Jelly Roll" Morton (1885–1941), a New Orleans pianist, claimed credit for having invented jazz. And to some degree, it was fair of him to think so—after all, his recordings with the group The Red Hot Peppers (1926–1930) are among the earliest examples of disciplined jazz ensemble work. But in truth, the evolution of jazz from ragtime and blues occurred thanks to many musicians in several cities. Most regard Morton as one of the founders of jazz; others include Bennie Moten (1894–1935), Eubie Blake (1883–1983), Duke Ellington (1899–1974), and Thomas "Fats" Waller (1904–1943).

Some would go back even further to trace the roots of jazz: From 1899–1914, Scott Joplin (1868–1917) popularized ragtime, based on African folk music. Even astute music critics may not be able to draw a clear-cut distinction between ragtime and early jazz. Both musical forms rely on syncopation (the stressing of the weak beats), and either style can be applied to an existing melody to transform it. The definitions and boundaries of the two terms have always been subject to debate, further complicated by the fact that some musicians of the time considered ragtime synonymous with early jazz.

But there are important—albeit not strict—differences between the two genres: Ragtime was composed and written down in the European style of notation; early jazz was learned by ear (players would simply show one another how a song went by playing it). Jazz encourages and expects improvisation; ragtime, for the most part, did not. The basic rhythms are also markedly different, with jazz having a swing or "hot" rhythm that ragtime does not.

Whatever its origins, jazz became part of the musical mainstream by the 1930s and influenced other musical genres as well—including classical. American composer George Gershwin (1898–1937) was both a songwriter and composer of ragtime, as well as a composer of symphonic works. Many of his works—including *Rhapsody in Blue* (1924) and his piano preludes—contain ragtime and jazz elements.

Perhaps more than any other composer and musician, Miles Davis (1926–1991) expanded the genre. Through decades of prolific work, Davis constantly pushed the bound-

337

aries of what defines jazz and in so doing set standards for other musicians.

Who was Satchmo?

Satchmo was the nickname of the legendary Louis Armstrong (1901–1971), a jazz pioneer from New Orleans, Louisiana, known as much for his stellar playing of the trumpet as his singing. In his day, jazz music focused on the collective group. Armstrong's improvisational talents allowed him to showcase his considerable individual talents. He learned to play the trumpet and the cornet in his days as a juvenile at the New Orleans Home for Colored Waifs, where he was sent after getting into trouble. In the early 1920s, he joined the Creole Jazz Band. He later became a pop star with hits such as "Hello, Dolly!" (from the musical of the same name) in 1964.

Jazz trumpeter Louis Armstrong took his childhood experiences in New Orleans and turned it into a stellar musical career.

What famous female jazz musician was nicknamed "Lady Day"?

"Lady Day" was the nickname of the incomparable Billie Holiday (1915–1959), a leading jazz musician and one of the pioneers of popular music. Some music critics consider her one of the greatest singers of all time. Some of her songs are legendary, including *Lady Sings the Blues*, *God Bless the Child*, and *Fine and Mellow*. Born in Philadelphia in 1915, she overcame an incredibly difficult childhood—including being raped by a relative—to become a musical icon.

What great protest song did Holiday sing?

Holiday performed the song "Strange Fruit" in 1939. Written by Jewish teacher Abel Meeropol (1903–1986), the song dealt with the lynchings of young African Americans. Holiday recorded the song in 1939, and it became a national hit. Selling more than a million copies, it was inducted into the Grammy Hall of Fame in 1978. It was said that Holiday's powerful vocals and the stirring lyrics of the song would drive many audience members to tears.

When did the Big Band Era begin?

On December 1, 1934, Benny Goodman's *Let's Dance* was broadcast on network radio, effectively launching the swing era, in which Big Band music achieved huge popularity. Goodman (1909–1986) was a virtuoso clarinetist and bandleader. His jazz-influenced dance band took the lead in making swing the most popular style of the time.

What composer is often considered a quintessential songwriter of classic American songs?

That honor goes to Russian-born composer Irving Berlin (1888–1989), who penned such timeless songs as "White Christmas," "There's No Business Like Show Business," "God Bless America," "Alexander's Ragtime Band," and "Happy Holidays," many of which were featured in Hollywood films in the 1940s and 1950s.

How did George and Ira Gershwin affect the American music landscape?

Like Irving Berlin, the Gershwins wrote many songs for Hollywood films that gained wide popularity. Pianist and composer George Gershwin (1898–1937) was famous for such orchestral works as *Rhapsody in Blue, An American in Paris,* and the opera *Porgy and Bess.* His brother Ira (1896–1983) was a lyricist who contributed to his brother's works, penning the words to such popular songs as "Someone to Watch over Me," "Embraceable You," and "I Got Rhythm." These and many other songs are musical mainstays in the American lexicon to this day.

How old is country music?

Old-time music or "hillbilly music"—both early names for country music—emerged in the early decades of the 1900s. By 1920, the first country music radio stations had opened, and healthy record sales in rural areas caused music industry executives to take notice. But it was an event in 1925—in the middle of the American Jazz Age—that put country music on the map: On November 28, WSM Radio broadcast the *WSM Barn Dance,* which soon became known as The Grand Ole Opry when the master of ceremonies, George D. Hay, took to introducing the program that way (it aired immediately after an opera program). The show's first performer was Uncle Jimmy Thompson (1848–1931). Early favorites included Uncle Dave Macon (1870–1952), who played the banjo and sang, and Roy Acuff (1903–1992), the Opry's first singing star. Millions tuned in, and soon the Nashville-based show had turned Tennessee's capital city into Music City U.S.A. In the 1960s and again in the late 1980s and 1990s, country music reached the height of its popularity while holding on to its small-town, rural-based audience, who were the show's first fans.

What country music icon was known as the "Man in Black"?

Johnny Cash (1932–2003) was a country music legend whose outlaw image, deep voice, and ability to thrive in several genres of music endeared him to millions. Cash is primarily known for his country music, but he also performed gospel, blues, rockabilly, and rock music. Some of his more famous songs are "I Walk the Line," "Folsom Prison Blues," and "Ring of Fire." Cash often performed his music behind prison walls. He performed a concert at San Quentin and followed this up with several other concerts at different prisons. He even performed at a prison in Sweden. He often performed music while dressed all in black.

Who was the first female solo artist inducted into the Country Music Hall of Fame?

Patsy Cline (1932–1963) holds this distinction—albeit posthumously, as she was inducted in 1973—a decade after her untimely death at age thirty in a plane crash. Born Virginia Patterson Hensley in Westminster, Virginia, she became a star after appearing on the Grand Ole Opry in 1955 and Arthur Godfrey's (1903–1983) television variety show in 1957. Some of her most well-known songs were "Crazy," "I Fall to Pieces," and "Walkin' After Midnight."

Who is the "First Lady of Country Music"?

The "First Lady of Country Music" is the moniker of Loretta Lynn (1932–). During her career, she had sixteen number-one hits, including "Coal Miner's Daughter,"

Country music star Loretta Lynn has had sixteen number-one hits in her career.

"Fist City," "Don't Come Home A-Drinkin'," and "You Ain't Woman Enough." She was born in Kentucky, the daughter of a coal miner. Her 1975 autobiography was entitled *Coal Miner's Daughter*. It was later made into a hit movie by the same title, starring Sissy Spacek (1949–) and Tommy Lee Jones (1946–). Lynn credited Patsy Cline as her mentor during her early years in the country music business, as she ascended into star status. She later created an album entitled *I Remember Patsy*, performing some of Cline's top hits. Her youngest sister Crystal Gayle (1951–) became a country music star in her own right.

Is bluegrass music a distinctly American genre?

Yes, the style of music developed out of country music during the late 1930s and throughout the 1940s. Bill Monroe (1911–1996), a country and bluegrass singer-songwriter, altered the tempo, key, pitch, and instrumentation of traditional country music to create a new style—named for the band that originated it—Bill Monroe and the Blue Grass Boys (Monroe's home state was Kentucky). Bluegrass was first heard by a wide audience when, in October 1939, Monroe and his band appeared on the popular country music radio program *The Grand Ole Opry*.

Although bluegrass evolved through several stages and involved a host of contributors, through it all, Bill Monroe remained the guiding and inspirational force and therefore merits the distinction of being the "father of bluegrass."

What was *American Bandstand*?

American Bandstand was a very popular American music variety show that ran from 1952 until 1989. For most of its years, Dick Clark (1929–2012) hosted the show as its ageless, iconic guide. The show featured Top 40 artists performing their top hits to an admiring audience. The show first aired regionally in Philadelphia, hosted by Bob Horn (1916–1966). The show featured the popular "Rate a Record" segment, where teenage audience members would give their impression of top record hits.

What was *Soul Train*?

Soul Train was an American music show that appeared on syndicated television from 1971–2006. Created by Don Cornelius (1936–2012), the show featured a literal Who's Who of rhythm and blues ("R&B"), soul, and disco music. Cornelius served as the show's host from 1971–1993. It often featured a dizzying array of dance performances as well. One of the most popular features of the show was the "Soul Train line," where audience members would form a dance line and then one person or couple would perform various dance moves while everyone else danced in a line. Many top musicians performed on Soul Train over the years.

What was "Rockabilly"?

Rockabilly was a music style associated with rural white America. It was heavily influenced by African American blues music. It largely became subsumed by rock music as it became more popular in the 1950s and 1960s.

What are the origins of rock and roll?

There is no universally accepted explanation for the origins of rock 'n' roll music. Many believe it began in the 1940s and 1950s, inspired from a combination of blues music, R&B, jazz, and gospel. Rock and roll infused many elements traditionally associated with blues and jazz music but incorporated a greater and louder use of drums, saxophones, and guitars. Rock and roll music is now generally called rock music and features a steady diet of electric guitar, electric bass guitar, and the energetic playing of the drums.

Who popularized the term "rock 'n' roll"?

Popular Cleveland-based disc jockey Alan Freed (1921–1965) popularized the use of the term "rock and roll" in the early 1950s. Known by the nickname "Moondog," Freed was

What were race records?

Race records were large phonograph records marketed to African Americans in the 1920s and 1930s. Race records predominantly consisted of blues, jazz, and gospel music. The term sounds pejorative today, but the records were popular and helped to inspire newer generations of musicians—both white and black.

341

known for playing the music of many different types of artists—both black and white. He appeared as himself in the 1956 film *Rock, Rock, Rock*. He also had his own television show. He ran into trouble for the practice of payola—accepting payments from record companies to play specific records.

Who was the "King of Rock and Roll," or just "the King"?

Elvis Presley (1935–1977) was a cultural icon, dynamic music performer, and arguably the most popular musician of all time. Born in Tupelo, Mississippi, Presley moved to Memphis with his family in his teens. He worked with record producer Sam Phillips and essentially brought African American-style music to white America. Many of his rock 'n' roll songs are classics, including "Hound Dog," "Jailhouse Rock," and "Don't Be Cruel." Presley acknowledged that he drew inspiration from a litany of African American performers. He once referred to Fats Domino as the "real king of rock and roll." Presley lived on an estate in Memphis known as Graceland. Millions still flock to Graceland, which remains a top tourist attraction.

What two great British bands came to America, becoming arguably the great rock bands of all time?

The Beatles and the Rolling Stones are considered perhaps the two greatest rock and roll bands in music history. Formed in Liverpool in 1960, the Beatles led the so-called "British invasion" of the music charts in America. The Beatles appeared on *The Ed Sullivan Show* in February 1964, and the phenomenon of "Beatlemania" hit the country. The Beatles played rock and roll, psychedelic rock, and pop ballads. At the height of their popularity, the foursome included John Lennon (1940–1980), Paul McCartney (1942–), Ringo Starr (1940–), and George Harrison (1943–2001). They remain the best-selling band in music history.

The Rolling Stones formed their band in London in 1962. Two of their original members still perform with the band—lead vocalist Mick Jagger (1943–) and guitarist

What happened "the day the music died"?

On February 3, 1959, three talented and influential musicians—Buddy Holly (1936–1959), Ritchie Valens (1941–1959), and J. P. "the Big Bopper" Richardson—died in a plane crash, along with the pilot, near Clear Lake, Iowa. Holly, who was only twenty-two, is still considered by many to have been one of the most important influences on early rock and roll with such songs as "Peggy Sue" and "That'll Be the Day." Valens, also incredibly young, pioneered Chicano rock with his song "La Bamba." Richardson (1930–1959), the oldest of the three, was a disc jockey and rockabilly star best known for "Chantilly Lace." In 1971, songwriter and musician Don McLean (1945–) immortalized the tragic event in his song "American Pie."

The undisputed King of Rock and Roll was, and will always be, Elvis Presley.

Keith Richards (1943–). Some of their greatest songs include "Miss You," "Brown Sugar," "Jumpin' Jack Flash," and "Satisfaction."

Who was Jimi Hendrix?

Jimi Hendrix (1942–1970) was perhaps the greatest electric guitarist in the history of music. He became famous for his memorable performances headlining music festivals, including Woodstock in 1969. He had a unique and unusual style—playing the guitar with his teeth, behind his back, and with a variety of other circus tricks. His 1967 album *Are You Experienced* has been described as revolutionary and the album that radically changed people's perceptions of music. Sadly, Hendrix's career in the spotlight lasted only a few years, as he died at age twenty-seven of a drug overdose.

Who is "the Boss"?

"The Boss" is the nickname for popular rock musician Bruce Springsteen (1949–), who still performs with his E Street Band. He is known for his energetic concert performances. He has released eighteen studio albums, sold more than 120 million records worldwide, and won twenty Grammy Awards in his career. His career exploded in 1984 with the release of his seventh album, *Born in the U.S.A.*, which became a worldwide phenomenon. Seven songs on the album became hits. While considered a rock and roll musician, Springsteen's influences include folk, blues, and country music. He has been called an American icon.

Who was the "King of Pop"?

The "King of Pop" was none other than the brilliant but enigmatic Michael Jackson (1958–2009). Jackson is considered one of the greatest—if not *the* greatest—entertainer of all time. He began his career as a young child as the youngest member of the Jackson Five—with his brothers Jackie, Tito, Jermaine, and Marlon. He later became a mega-superstar with his solo career in the early 1980s. His dance moves—and his signature "moonwalk"— were shown on music videos, and he parlayed his talents into best-selling albums and a litany of #1 hits. His album *Thriller* remains the best-selling album of all time, featuring such hits as "Thriller," "Billie Jean," and "P.Y.T." It has sold more than one hundred million copies worldwide, according to some estimates.

"King of Pop" Michael Jackson is shown here meeting President Ronald Reagan and First Lady Nancy Reagan in 1984 at the time of the peak of his popularity.

Jackson's personal life took a downturn in the 1990s, when allegations of child sexual abuse first surfaced. In 2005, he faced child sexual abuse charges in court, but a jury acquitted him of the charges. He died in 2009 from cardiac arrest, just as he was preparing for another world tour. His younger sister Janet (1966–) also became—and remains—a mega-superstar.

Is there a "Queen of Pop"?

Yes. Madonna Louise Ciccone (1958–), who as a performer goes simply by Madonna, achieved stardom in the 1980s and 1990s, often with such risque songs as "Like a Virgin" and "Vogue." Also acclaimed for her glitzy stage performances, she is a Grammy Award winner who parlayed her ability to perform into an acting career as well. She has starred in movies such as *A League of Their Own* and won a Golden Globe for Best Actress for starring in the Broadway musical *Evita*.

Who is Prince?

Prince is Prince Rogers Nelson (1958–), a talented, enigmatic musician who is wildly popular among his legion of fans. He writes and produces his own music, plays numerous musical instruments, and has promoted the careers of various talented female artists such as Sheila E. (1957–) and Carmen Electra (1972–). Born in Minneapolis, Minnesota, Prince became a star in his late teens. His lyrics often are sexually charged and his music

heavily infused with funk and rock. He has a wide vocal range and is known for his incredibly entertaining live performances. He has sold more than one hundred million records in his career. He has been called several names during his career. The last two names by which he referred to himself have been "The Artist Formerly Known as Prince" or just "The Artist."

When did rap music hit the music scene?

Rap music—sometimes called hip-hop music—can be traced to forms of blues, jazz, and rock. But rap music developed in the 1970s in the Bronx and New York City with legends such as Afrika Bambaataa (1957–), Kool Herc (1955–), and Grandmaster Flash (1958–). These disc jockeys would spin records and create funky beats. Later, these beats were accompanied by the signature of what came to be known as rap music—rhythmic, rhyming speech.

At one point going by the name of an unpronounceable syllable, singer and musician Prince has proven a popular, though enigmatic, talent.

345

Early groups had a disco music influence, as characterized by Grandmaster Flash and Furious Five, the Sugar Hill Gang, and the Treacherous Three. Some early rap musicians were very socially conscious, as the Furious Five's Message and New York New York attest.

Later, rap music became more hardcore, as a genre known as gangsta rap developed. Many criticize some versions of rap or hip-hop as too sexually explicit and filled with racially derogatory language, including excessive use of the N-word. Rap music was initially dismissed by some as a fad.

That turned out to be dead wrong, as rap music created *bona fide* music superstars, including M.C. Hammer (1962–), Tupac Shakur (1958–1996), and Eminem (1972–).

What rapper's real name is James Todd Smith?

James Todd Smith (1968–) is the real name of longtime successful rapper LL Cool J. He released his first album—*Radio*—in 1985 and has followed that with a dozen other albums. He is perhaps best known for his mastery of ballad rap songs and for high-energy raps "I'm Bad" and "Mama Said Knock You Out." At the end of 2014, LL Cool J is a very successful actor with a leading role on the hit television show *NCIS: Los Angeles*.

Who is Public Enemy?

Public Enemy is a rap group known for its politically conscious raps and unwillingness to flinch in the face of controversy. Popular in the late 1980s and early 1990s, Public Enemy began in 1982. It was led by its lead singer Chuck D. (1960–), hype man Flavor Flav (1959–), and Terminator X (1966–) (who left the group in 1999). The group's album *Fear of a Black Planet* was a megahit, including perhaps the group's best-known song— "Fight The Power." Public Enemy had some crossover appeal and was inducted into the Rock and Roll Hall of Fame in 2013.

What record producer cofounded Def Jam?

Rick Rubin (1963–) cofounded Def Jam with Russell Simmons (1957–) and worked with many of the leading rap artists in the 1980s and beyond. Rubin worked with such groups as Run DMC, the Beastie Boys, Public Enemy, and LL Cool J. But Rubin's influence extends far beyond rap music. As a co-president of Columbia Records until 2012, Rubin is

When did Emile Berliner invent the gramophone?

Berliner obtained his first patent for what he termed the "gramophone" in 1887. He later invented the Berliner Gramophone Company. Berliner was a prolific inventor, even creating a type of helicopter in his career.

a major player in the music industry. He has worked with groups as diverse as the Dixie Chicks, Red Hot Chili Peppers, and Slayer.

What is a Grammy?

A Grammy is a prestigious award given by the National Academy of Recording Arts and Sciences in the United States for outstanding achievement in music. The academy first presented the awards in May 1959. The name "Grammy" comes from the disc record gramophone invented by Emile Berliner (1851–1929).

What are the four major Grammy Awards given each year, irrespective of music genre?

The four major Grammy awards given regardless of genre are Album of the Year, Record of the Year, Song of the Year, and Best New Artist.

What artist has won the most Grammy awards?

Sir Georg Solti (1912–1997) won thirty-one Grammy Awards—thirty-two if you count a lifetime achievement award—in his career as an orchestral musical director. He began his career in Europe but fled Nazi Germany before World War II. He later came to the United States, where he gained fame as a conductor and as the long-standing musical director of the Chicago Symphony Orchestra.

Which artists have won the most Grammys for Album of the Year?

Frank Sinatra (1915–1998) and Stevie Wonder (1950–) have each won three times for Album of the Year. Sinatra won in 1960 for *Come Dance with Me!*, in 1966 for *September of My Years*, and in 1967 for *A Man and His Music*. Wonder won the award in 1973 for *Innervisions*, 1974 for *Fulfillingness' First Finale*, and 1976 for *Songs in the Key of Life*. Paul Simon (1941–) also has won Album of the Year three times, but his first award in 1971 for *Bridge Over Troubled Waters* was shared with his co-performer Art Garfunkel.

What female artist has won the most Grammys of any living performer?

Alison Krauss (1971–) has won twenty-seven Grammy Awards, second in history only to Sir Georg Solti. Krauss performs bluegrass and country music. She also has written numerous hit songs in her career. She has been playing music since she was five years old, when she began playing classical violin. Soon she turned to bluegrass, where she earned acclaim.

Who is the youngest person to win a Grammy?

LeAnn Rimes (1982–) is the youngest person to win a Grammy Award at age fourteen in 1997, when she won Grammys for Best New Artist and Best Female Country Vocal Performance for her rendition of the Bill Mack song "Blue."

Who won the first Grammy for Best Rap Performance?

DJ Jazzy Jeff & The Fresh Prince won the inaugural Grammy for Best Rap Performance in 1989 for their song "Parents Just Don't Understand." The Fresh Prince was the stage name for Will Smith, now a major movie star. In 1989, Smith led a boycott of the Grammy Awards, in part because the Academy refused to televise the awarding of the rap Grammy.

What rap artist has won the most Grammy Awards for Best Rap Album?

Eminem—born Marshall Bruce Mathers III (1972–)—has won five Grammys for Best Rap Album. He won in 2000 for *The Slim Shady LP*, in 2001 for *The Marshall Mathers LP*, in 2003 for *The Eminem Show*, in 2010 for *Relapse*, and in 2011 for *Recovery*. Eminem has won a total of thirteen Grammys in his career.

LeAnn Rimes is the youngest person to ever win a Grammy, which she did in 1997 at the age of fourteen for the song "Blue."

MOVIES

What are some early milestones in the U.S. motion picture industry?

Motion pictures continue to develop, as new, sophisticated technologies are introduced to improve the movie-going experience for audiences. In the decades following their rudimentary beginnings, there were many early milestones, including not only advancements in technology but improvements in conditions for those working in the then-fledgling industry:

Great U.S. Movie Milestones, 1900 to 1940

Year	Milestone
1903	Edwin S. Porter's *The Great Train Robbery* was the first motion picture to tell a complete story. Produced by Edison Studios, the twelve-minute epic established a pattern of suspense drama that was followed by subsequent movie makers.
1907	Bell & Howell Co. was founded by Chicago movie projectionist Donald H. Bell and camera repairman Albert S. Howell with $5,000 in capital. The firm went on to improve motion picture photography and projection equipment.

Great U.S. Movie Milestones, 1900 to 1940

Year	Milestone
1910	*Brooklyn Eagle* newspaper cartoonist John Randolph Bray pioneered animated motion picture cartoons using a "cel" system he invented that was subsequently used by all animators.
1912	*Queen Elizabeth*, starring Sarah Bernhardt, was shown July 12 at New York's Lyceum Theater, the first feature-length motion picture seen in America.
1915	D. W. Griffith's *The Birth of a Nation* provided the blueprint for narrative films.
1925	The new editing technique used in *Battleship Potemkin* revolutionized the making of motion pictures around the world. Soviet film director Sergei Eisenstein created his masterpiece by splicing film shot at many locations, an approach subsequently adopted by most film directors.
1926	The first motion picture with sound ("talkie") was demonstrated.
1927	The Academy of Motion Picture Arts and Sciences was founded by Louis B. Mayer of MGM Studios. The first president of the Academy was Douglas Fairbanks.
1927	The first full-length talking picture, *The Jazz Singer*, starring vaudevillian Al Jolson, was released. By 1932, virtually all movies talked.
1928	Hollywood's major film studios signed an agreement with the American Telephone & Telegraph Corporation (AT&T) to use their technology to produce films with sound, leading to an explosion in the popularity of motion pictures.
1929	The first Academy Awards ceremony (for 1928 films) was held. Winners were William Wellman for Best Picture (*Wings*), Emil Jannings for Best Actor (in *Last Command*), and Janet Gaynor for Best Actress (in *Sunrise*). Movie columnist Sidney Skolsky dubbed the awards "the Oscars."
1929	Eastman Kodak introduced 16-millimeter film for motion picture cameras.
1933	The Screen Actors Guild (SAG) was formed when six actors met in Hollywood to establish a self-governing organization of actors. The first organizing meeting yielded eighteen founding members.
1935	The first full-length Technicolor movie, *Becky Sharp*, was released. The technology, however, was still in development, and the colors appeared garish.
1939	*Gone with the Wind* was released in Technicolor, which had come a long way since its 1935 debut.

Who was Cecil B. DeMille?

A film director and producer whose name has become as legedary as his epic films, Cecil B. DeMille (1881–1959) was a giant in Hollywood, working under the aegis of the studio Metro-Goldwyn-Mayer. Making a name for himself in the silent film era, his vision became more and more grand, producing such big-budget movies as *Cleopatra* (1934), *Samson and Delilah* (1949), *The Greatest Show on Earth* (1952), and *The Ten Commandments* (1956). In 1952, the Golden Globe Awards created the Cecil B. DeMille Award for "outstanding contributions to the world of entertainment." DeMille, of course, was the first recipient.

What studio created the first full-length animated movie?

Walt Disney Studios produced the first full-length cartoon, *Snow White and the Seven Dwarfs,* in 1937, which became a huge hit. Disney (1901–1966) would follow it up with a string of other such features, including *Bambi, Pinocchio, Alice in Wonderland, Sleeping Beauty,* and *Cinderella.* Today, Disney is a household name, continuing to produce television shows and movies, as well as running theme parks.

What was the "Hollywood Blacklist"?

In 1947, studio executives assembled at New York's Waldorf-Astoria Hotel put together a list of alleged Communist sympathizers, naming some three hundred writers, directors, actors, and others known or suspected to have Communist Party affiliations or of having invoked the Fifth Amendment against self-incrimination when questioned by the House Un-American Activities Committee. The "Hollywood Ten" who refused to tell the Committee whether or not they had been Communists were Alvah Bessie, Herbert Biberman, Lester Cole, Edward Dmytryk, Ring Lardner, Jr., John Howard Lawson, Albert Maltz, Samuel Ornitz, Adrian Scott, and Dalton Trumbo. The film industry blacklisted the Hollywood Ten on November 25, and all of them drew short prison sentences for refusing to testify.

What is the "Oscar"?

The Oscar refers to the most prestigious award issued by the Academy of Motion Picture Arts and Sciences for those in the movie and film industries. The Oscar is the name for the actual award, but they are also called Academy Awards. The five major Oscar awards are for Best Picture, Best Actor, Best Actress, Best Supporting Actor, and Best Supporting Actress.

Who has won the most Oscars?

The incomparable Walt Disney (1901–1966) won twenty-two Academy Awards, far more than anyone in history. He won most of his awards for Best Short Subject, Cartoons. The iconic figure remains a dominant force in the entertainment industry. He won his first Academy Award in 1932 for the cartoon *Flowers and Trees*.

Who is the only performer to win four acting Oscars?

Katharine Hepburn (1907–2003) won four Academy Awards in a career that spanned

Actress Reese Witherspoon holds an Oscar she won in 2006.

> ## How did the awards come to be known as Oscars?
>
> There are many explanations for the origin of the term "Oscar" to designate an Academy Award winner. What is known is that the Academy of Motion Picture Arts and Sciences began dubbing the awards Oscars in 1939. Bette Davis claimed she named her award after her late husband, Harmon Oscar Nelson. Another theory is that the executive secretary of the Academy, Margaret Herrick, dubbed the awards Oscars after her cousin, Oscar Pierce. Whatever the origin, the name has become a cultural fixture.

more than sixty years. She won Best Actress awards for *Morning Glory* (1934), *Guess Who's Coming to Dinner* (1968), *The Lion in Winter* (1969), and *On Golden Pond* (1982). She received eight other nominations for Best Actress in her career.

What two American men have won three acting Oscars?

Walter Brennan (1894–1974) and Jack Nicholson (1937–) each won three Oscars. Brennan won three Best Supporting Actor Oscars: *Come and Get It* (1936), *Kentucky* (1938), and *Westerner* (1940). Nicholson won a Best Actor award for *One Flew Over the Cuckoo's Nest* (1975), a Best Supporting Actor award for *Terms of Endearment* (1983), and another Best Actor award for *As Good As It Gets* (1997). The English actor Daniel Day-Lewis is the only other male actor to capture three Academy Awards.

Who is the youngest person to win an acting Oscar?

Tatum O'Neal (1963–) remains the youngest person to win an Academy Award for acting, winning as Best Supporting Actress in 1973 at age ten in *Paper Moon*. Justin Henry (1971–) received an Oscar nomination for Best Supporting Actor at eight years old for his performance in *Kramer vs. Kramer* (1978). Quvenzhané Wallis (2003–) received an Oscar nomination for Best Actress for her performance in *Beasts of the Southern Wild* (2012). But Henry and Wallis did not win, making O'Neal still the youngest to win the prestigious award.

What performer has received the most Oscar nominations?

Meryl Streep (1949–) has received an astounding nineteen Academy Award nominations in her career as of the end of 2014. She has won three times: Best Supporting Actress in *Kramer vs. Kramer* (1979), Best Actress for *Sophie's Choice* (1982), and Best Actress for *Iron Lady* (2011).

What films have won the most Academy Awards?

Three films won eleven Academy Awards: (1) *Ben-Hur* (1959), (2) *Titanic* (1997), and (3) *The Lord of the Rings: The Return of the King* (2003). All three films won Best Picture.   351

Two films received fourteen Oscar nominations—*All About Eve* (1950) and the afore-mentioned *Titanic*.

What space/fantasy movie became an instant success, spawning numerous sequels and prequels?

Star Wars (1977) grossed more than $460 million in the United States alone, passing *Jaws* as the most successful movie ever made until that time. Written and produced by George Lucas (1944–), the movie featured classic clashes between good and evil, spectacular special effects, and some intriguing characters. The movie was later renamed *Star Wars Episode IV: A New Hope*. Even though it was the fourth volume in the eventual series, *Star Wars* was the first movie filmed in the Star Wars series. It was followed by *The Empire Strikes Back* (1980) and *Return of the Jedi* (1983).

Years later, Lucas produced three "prequels" to Star Wars: *The Phantom Menace* (1999), *Attack of the Clones* (2002), and *Revenge of the Sith* (2005). As of the end of 2014, Lucas is working on a sequel trilogy, which will be episodes seven, eight, and nine in the series.

To many, the original movie *Star Wars* remains the series' best, as it first introduced the public to the likes of Luke Skywalker, Darth Vader, Princess Leia, Han Solo, and many other characters that have entered the cultural pantheon.

What *Star Wars* actor also played in the hit Indiana Jones series?

Harrison Ford (1942–) is one the most successful actors in motion picture history in terms of box office success. He burst to fame in the role of Han Solo in the Star Wars trilogy. He then catapulted to even greater fame by playing the lead character Henry "Indiana" Jones in the 1981 classic *The Raiders of the Lost Ark*. The roles of Han Solo and Indiana Jones arguably make Ford among the greatest actors in action movie roles in history. He also has participated in numerous other box office successes, such as *Blade Runner* (1982), *Witness* (1985), *Patriot Games* (1992), and *The Fugitive* (1993).

What was *E.T.: The Extraterrestrial?*

E.T. was a 1982 movie that became the highest-grossing movie in American his-

Steven Spielberg first made it big as a director and producer with 1975's *Jaws,* about a great white shark terrorizing a New England coastal town.

tory to that time. It told the poignant story of an extraterrestrial named E.T. who befriended a young boy named Elliott. The movie tugged at audiences' heartstrings. The movie was produced and directed by the acclaimed Steven Spielberg (1946–).

What other hit movies have been produced by Steven Spielberg?

Steven Spielberg is arguably the most successful producer/director in Hollywood history. He won Oscars for Best Director for *Schindler's List* (1997), a movie about the Holocaust, and *Saving Private Ryan* (1998), a movie about the Vietnam War. He also worked on *Jaws* (1975) and *E.T.* (1982), which both set box office records when they were produced. He was executive producer of the popular *Men in Black* series, starring Will Smith and Tommy Lee Jones. Spielberg most recently earned accolades for his film *Lincoln* (2012), which garnered a dozen Oscar nominations. His films have grossed more than $8.5 billion worldwide.

What epic about a disaster at sea became the biggest blockbuster of all time?

1997's *Titanic,* directed by James Cameron, is a fictionalized version based on the true story of the 1912 sinking of the *RMS Titanic.* With a budget of $200 million, the movie was, fortunately, a big hit, grossing over $600 million domestically its first year and over $1.2 billion internationally. Cameron would later also make great strides in filmmaking with the 2009 science-fiction film *Avatar,* which represented huge technical achievements in computer-generated imagery (CGI).

RADIO AND TELEVISION

What was radio's immediate cultural impact?

During the 1930s, radio—pioneered in the late 1800s—was woven into the fabric of everyday American life. People across the country—in cities, suburbs, and on farms—tuned in for news and entertainment, including broadcasts of baseball games and other sporting events, as well as comedy and variety shows, dramas, and live music programs. President Franklin D. Roosevelt used the new medium to speak directly to the American public during the trying times of the Great Depression, broadcasting his "fireside chats" from the White House. Between the 1920s and the 1950s, gathering around the radio in the evenings was as common to Americans as watching television is today. Networks offered advertisers national audiences, and corporate America eagerly seized the opportunity to speak directly to people in their own homes. The advent of television in the 1950s and its growing popularity over the next two decades changed the role of radio in American life. Having lost its audience to TV, radio programmers seized upon rock music as a way to reach a wide—albeit a very young—audience. Many argue that the rise of the musical genre kept radio alive. In the decades since, radio programming has become increasingly music-oriented; talk and news programming are also popular.

What was the immediate impact of television?

The publicity surrounding the television broadcast of the World's Fair (April 30, 1939) inspired a flurry of broadcasting activity but reached limited audiences. On May 17, 1939, the National Broadcasting Company (NBC) televised a baseball game between Princeton University and Columbia University, which NBC billed as the world's first televised sporting event. On August 26, NBC telecast a professional baseball game between the Brooklyn Dodgers and the Cincinnati Reds. More NBC broadcasts from Radio City featured live opera, comedy, and cooking demonstrations. Crowds waiting outside the 1939 New York premiere of *Gone With the Wind* were also televised. Feature films were aired, including a dramatization of *Treasure Island*, *Young and Beautiful*, and the classic silent film *The Great Train Robbery* (1903). Soon television stations proliferated: by May 1940, twenty-three stations were broadcasting.

In 1941, after considerable deliberation on its part and that of the industry itself, the Federal Communications Commission (FCC) adopted transmission standards. Commercial operations were approved effective July 1, and two New York stations (a National Broadcasting Company [NBC] and a Columbia Broadcasting System [CBS] affiliate), went on the air. By the end of that year, the first commercial on television, financed by watch manufacturer Bulova, was aired. In December, with the bombing of Pearl Harbor and the entrance of the United States into World War II, commercial development of television was put on hold while American industry devoted its resources to the war effort.

But the television industry was eager, and as soon as Allied victory appeared certain, Radio Corporation of America (RCA) reopened its NBC television studio on April 10, 1944. CBS followed suit, reopening its operations on May 5. At the war's end in 1945, nine part-time and partly commercial television stations were on the air, reaching about 7,500 set owners in the New York, Philadelphia, Pennsylvania, and Schenectady, New York, areas.

By 1947, the four networks that then existed—ABC, CBS, NBC, and DuMont (a short-lived competitor)—could still provide only about ten hours of prime-time programming a week, much of it sporting events. In late 1948, it was estimated that only ten percent of the population had even seen a television show. However, as the networks stepped up their programming with live drama programs, children's shows, and variety shows (a format that was familiar and popular to the American radio-listening audience), interest in television grew rapidly. By the spring of 1948, industry experts estimated that 150,000 sets were in public places such as bars and pubs, accounting for about half of the total number of sets in operation. Just a year later, 940,000 homes had televisions. And by 1949, production of sets had jumped to three million.

Which was the first TV network?

It was the National Broadcasting Company (NBC), founded November 11, 1926, by David Sarnoff (1891–1971), then President of Radio Corporation of America (RCA). Sarnoff, considered one of the pioneers of radio and television broadcasting, created NBC to provide a program service to stimulate the sale of radios. In the 1940s, he reorganized the network to provide TV programming, again to stimulate sales of RCA products—this time, televisions. It was Sarnoff who demonstrated television at the World's Fair in New York in 1939.

Next came the Columbia Broadcasting System (CBS) on September 26, 1928, established by William S. Paley (1901–1990), an advertising manager for Congress Cigar Company. Paley sold some of his stock in the cigar company in order to raise $275,000 to buy into the beleaguered United Independent Broadcasters (which controlled Columbia Phonograph, hence the name). He built the floundering radio network into a powerful and profitable broadcasting organization.

The American Broadcasting Corporation (ABC) television network was last, in 1943. It was only by government order that the third network, ABC, was created at all. In 1943, when RCA was ordered to give up one of its two radio networks, it surrendered the weaker of the two (NBC Blue), which was bought by Edward J. Noble, the father of Life Savers candy. In 1945, Noble formally changed the name to the American Broadcasting Company, which three years later began broadcasting television from its New York flagship station.

Was there a "Golden Age" of television?

People commonly refer to the 1950s as TV's Golden Age, which is the decade when Americans embraced television and the networks responded with a rapid expansion of programming. Critics still hail the programs of the Golden Age to be the most innovative programming in television history. It was during this decade that anthology programs such as *Kraft Television Theatre, Playhouse 90,* and *Studio One* made live drama part of the nightly fare on prime-time television. Americans could tune in to watch original screenplays such as *Twelve Angry Men* (1954), *Visit to a Small Planet* (1955), and *The Miracle Worker* (1957). And tune in they did, prompting the production of more than thirty anthology programs sponsored by the likes of Goodyear, Philco, U.S. Steel, Breck, and Schlitz. Since the production work was based in New York, the anthologies drew young playwrights, including Gore Vidal, Rod Serling, Arthur Miller, and A. E. Hotchner. A new group of prominent television directors and producers emerged. And the studio dramas attracted the talents of actors George C. Scott, James Dean, Paul Newman, Grace Kelly, Eva Marie Saint, Sidney Poitier, Lee Remick, and Jack Lemmon.

The other cornerstone of 1950s television programming was the variety show—also performed live. Comedians Jack Benny, Red Skelton, Jackie Gleason, George Burns, Sid Caesar, and "Mr. Television" Milton Berle thrived in the format.

But the cost of producing live programs and the growing popularity of television—which created a new mass market that demanded even more programming—combined to spell the end of television's Golden Age. Soon, live dramas and variety shows were replaced by situation comedies, westerns, and other set-staged programs that could be taped in advance and produced in quantity.

355

What was the most influential comedy series of the 1950s?

The comedy *I Love Lucy* remains one of the most iconic shows ever produced. Starring Lucille Ball and her husband, Desi Arnaz, the program ran from 1951–1957 and featured some of the best writing and slapstick humor ever produced. Even today, many Americans will recall such scenes as Lucy and her pal Ethel (Vivian Vance) trying to wrap chocolates in a factory, or Lucy becoming drunk on an alcohol-laden concoction as the Vitameatavegamin girl. The show became a model for many sitcoms featuring husbands and wives in later years.

Who was the first female anchor of a nightly news television show?

Barbara Walters (1929–) became the first female co-anchor of a major television news show in 1976 on *ABC Evening News* with Harry Reasoner (1923–1991). For twenty years, 1984 to 2004, she was the host of the popular newsmagazine television show *20/20*. She gained even more fame in the late 1990s for creating the popular daytime talk show *The View*, which continues to be extremely popular.

Walters is best known for her detailed and personal interviews with the leading personalities of the world. She has interviewed kings, queens, presidents, movie stars, sports figures, and other celebrities and famous people. In the process, she has become a famous personality in her own right.

Who was "Mr. Television"?

Milton Berle (1908–2002) was known as "Mr. Television" during the Golden Age. He hosted NBC's *Texaco Star Theater* and brought his vaudeville comedy act to the new medium. The show dominated the Nielsen ratings and earned Berle an Emmy Award. He refused to deny spots to deserving black performers. When his show declined in ratings, he eventually turned his comedic talents to Las Vegas, performing there for many years.

Who is Norman Lear?

Norman Lear (1922–) is an American television producer and writer who produced some of the most groundbreaking television shows in the 1970s and 1980s. He created *All in the Family*, *The Jeffersons*, *Good Times*, *Sanford and Son*, and *Maude*. His shows often poked fun at racial stereotypes, tackled difficult racial themes, and addressed political controversies. The pioneering Lear founded the civil liberties group People for the American Way in 1981. He is a staunch supporter of First Amendment/free-speech rights and causes.

Lear served in World War II, flying in more than fifty combat missions. In the 1950s, he worked as a writer for various television series. In 1971, he produced *All in the Family*, a hit comedy series revolving around the bigoted Archie Bunker and his family. The show produced a popular spin-off series, *The Jeffersons*, featuring Bunker's former black neighbor George Jefferson. *All in the Family* was television's most popular sitcom for four to five years, topping the Nielsen ratings. It ran from 1971 to 1979 before spinning off into *Archie Bunker's Place*.

Possibly one of the greatest comedy shows of all time, *I Love Lucy* starred (clockwise from top right) Desi Arnaz; his wife, Lucille Ball; Vivian Vance; and William Frawley. Many of the episodes are considered TV classics.

Who were the stars of *All in the Family*?

All in the Family's principal character was Archie Bunker, played memorably by Carroll O'Connor (1924–2001). Bunker was considered almost a "loveable bigot"—despite his racist sentiments, he had good qualities in his character—loving his family, opposing the Klan, and carrying on a good relationship George Jefferson's son Lionel.

Archie Bunker's wife, Edith, was played by Jean Stapleton (1923–2013). Archie constantly insulted her as a "dingbat" but also deeply loved her. Kindhearted Edith often tried to bridge family conflicts. She was very good friends with George Jefferson's wife Louise.

Norman Lear is the talented writer and producer behind such groundbreaking television shows as *All in the Family* and *The Jeffersons*.

Archie and Edith had one daughter, Gloria Stivic—played by Sally Struthers (1947–). Gloria, a proponent of women's rights, often found herself trying to mediate conflicts between her father and her husband, Mike.

Mike Stivic, Archie's son-in-law, was politically and socially liberal, infuriating Archie. Mike also frequently had problems earning a living but instead went to school—something that also seemed to bother blue-collar Archie. Mike was played by Rob Reiner (1947–), who later achieved even greater fame as a producer. Archie constantly referred to Mike as "Meathead."

What was the most successful spin-off of *All in the Family*?

The most successful show spawned from *All in the Family* was *The Jeffersons*—another show developed by Norman Lear. *The Jeffersons* lasted eleven seasons (1975–1985), with more than 250 episodes. George and Louise Jefferson initially appeared as Archie and Edith Bunker's neighbors. However, George—who owns dry cleaning stores—becomes more affluent and moves his family to a high-rise complex in New York City.

George Jefferson, played memorably by Sherman Hemsley (1938–2012), was prejudiced, often calling white men "honky." He also opposed his son Lionel's dating and marriage to Jenny Willis, the daughter of interracial couple Tom and Helen Willis. The show was not as explicitly political as *All in the Family*, but it still tackled some tough racial issues during its successful run.

What was significant about the Willis family on the show?

The Willis family on *The Jeffersons* was one of the first interracial couples depicted on television. White banker Tom Willis was married to Helen Willis, a strong black female.

The two often were the butt of jokes made by George Jefferson. Franklin Cover (1928–2006) played Tom Willis, and Roxie Roker (1929–1995) played Helen Willis. Interracial couples remain rarely depicted on major television shows. The Willises were a groundbreaking couple during the 1970s and 1980s.

Who was Johnny Carson?

Johnny Carson (1925–2005) was an American comedian best known for hosting the most popular nighttime television talk show—*The Tonight Show Starring Johnny Carson*, which ran from 1962–1992. The show featured his sidekick Ed McMahon (1923–2009), who would intone the famous entrance—"Here's Johnny!"

Carson received six Emmy Awards, was inducted in the Television Hall of Fame, and even earned a Presidential Medal of Freedom. Later late-night television talk show hosts, such as Jay Leno, David Letterman, Jimmy Fallon, and Conan O'Brien, have all cited Carson's influence over their work.

What is an Emmy?

The Emmy is the premier award given to the best in television. It is television's equivalent to the Oscar for movies, the Grammy for music, and the Tony for theater. First awarded in 1949, Daytime Emmys and Primetime Emmys are now awarded.

What HBO series dominated the Emmys?

The Sopranos was arguably the most popular series in the history of cable television, garnering numerous Emmy awards. The show began airing in 1999 and ended in 2007 after six seasons and eighty-six episodes. Created by David Chase (1945–), the show revolved around the life of New Jersey-based mob boss Tony Soprano, played by actor James Gandolfini (1961–2013). Soprano struggles with depression while being faced with competing mob bosses, marital struggles, infidelity issues, and other personal problems. Much of the show focused on Soprano's ability to deal with stress by meeting with his psychiatrist, Dr. Jennifer Melfi, portrayed by Lorraine Bracco (1954–).

The Sopranos became the first cable television series to win the Emmy for Best Drama Series in 2004 and then won again in 2007. Both Gandolfini and Edie Falco (1963–), who played Soprano's wife, Carmela, earned Emmy nominations six times and won three Emmys. Many other actors and actresses on the show earned Emmy nominations during the show's historic run.

What other HBO drama series has been called "the best show on television"?

The Wire may be the one of the best series ever created in television history. *The Wire*, based in Baltimore, Maryland, focused on the corruptibility of many American institutions and policies. The show, a police crime drama, delves into the issues and problems of society much deeper than typical police crime dramas. The show ran on HBO for five seasons and sixty episodes, from 2002–2008.

Created by David Simon (1960–), the show focused as much on the people in the drug trade as on the police. It depicted not only the drug kingpins but lowlier drug runners and even a fascinating stick-up artist named Omar Little, played by actor Michael K. Williams (1966–). There are college courses on *The Wire* at Ivy League schools. A law school professor wrote a criminal law textbook based on the show. It has had an incredibly broad and deep cultural impact.

Who is Oprah Winfrey?

Oprah Winfrey (1954–) is one of the most successful people in the world, rising from poverty to become perhaps the leading television personality of her time. She is best known as the host of her own talk show, *The Oprah Winfrey Show*, which ran in syndication from 1986–2011. Born in poverty in Mississippi, Winfrey moved as a teenager to live with her father Vernon in Nashville. She attended East Nashville

Now one of the richest people in the United States, Oprah Winfrey made it big as a talk show host and now owns a television network.

High School and Tennessee State University. After college, she worked as a local news anchor in Nashville before eventually moving to Chicago.

She eventually hosted a morning show in 1983 and then in 1986 began the show bearing her own name. She soon displaced Phil Donahue (1935–) as the number-one daytime talk show in the country. Winfrey was a key figure in Barack Obama's successful run for the presidency in 2008, particularly the hotly contested Democratic primary against Hillary Clinton.

What is reality television?

Reality television is a popular type of television programming that features undocumented scripts and focuses on capturing the real lives of its protagonists—who often are regular people, as opposed to famous celebrity actors. Reality television is a staple of MTV—and its iconic show *The Real World*, which began in 1992 and still runs today. *The Real World* examines the lives of several young people who come from different backgrounds and live together in a house. The show gets up and close and personal into the lives and problems of the cast.

Reality television became even more popular with the success of the show *Survivor*, which began airing in the United States in 2000. The show has been featured in more than twenty countries around the globe, but the United States version became an instant success. In *Survivor*, contestants are placed on an island, normally with little food and no shelter. They literally must endure the elements, while participating in challenges to survive elimination. The show features two teams and literally proceeds, as contestants are eliminated one by one, until there is only one cast member left standing. In the so-called "tribal counsel," past members of the show vote on who should remain as the winner. Of the sixteen contestants, corporate trainer Richard Hatch (1952–) narrowly won the first U.S. competition with a 4–3 vote over whitewater rafting guide Kelly Wiglesworth (1977–).

What is *American Idol*?

American Idol is a reality television show and singing competition that achieved top ratings for many years, beginning with its debut in the United States in 2002. The show begins with tryouts by tens of thousands across the country to be selected for participation on the show. At various cities around the country, contestants sing briefly before a panel of judges who determine whether the participant has enough skill and talent to deserve a flight to Las Vegas. At the Vegas auditions, the singers compete to make the top 32 or top 20.

The winner of the competition receives a record deal with a major label. Some winners of the show have become household names and significant stars. For example, Season Four winner was Carrie Underwood (1983–), now one of the biggest stars in country music, who has won six Grammys.

The show features host Ryan Seacrest (1974–), who has been with the show since Season One, and a panel of three judges. For many years, the three judges were singer Paula Abdul (1962–), British music producer Simon Cowell (1959–), and American musician and record producer Randy Jackson (1956–). Much of the show's popularity was inspired by the interaction of the three judges, including Cowell's biting sarcasm and wit. The show still features three star judges, including pop music icon Jennifer Lopez (1969–), country music star Keith Urban (1967–), and jazz musician Harry Connick, Jr. (1967–).

Ryan Seacrest, host of the singing competition *American Idol*, has made a name for himself in the music industry as a television and radio personality.

LITERATURE

Who was born Samuel Langhorne Clemens?

Samuel Langhorne Clemens (1835–1910) was the birth name of Mark Twain, perhaps the most famous of all American novelists. Born in 1835 in Florida, Missouri, Twain moved with his family to Hannibal, Missouri. His father, a local judge, died when Twain was twelve; one year later, Twain served as a printer's apprentice. Twain discovered his love for writing at this job.

He left printing for the more physically adventurous job of river pilot's apprentice. He later became a licensed river pilot. Beginning in the late 1860s, Twain began to earn fame for his writing. His book *The Adventures of Tom Sawyer* was published in 1876, and *The Adventures of Huckleberry Finn* was published in 1885.

Who was Ernest Hemingway?

Ernest Hemingway (1988–1961) was an American novelist, essayist, and writer who won the Nobel Prize for Literature in 1954. Hemingway committed suicide at age sixty-one while living in Idaho. Some of his best-known works include *A Farewell to Arms* (1929), *For Whom the Bell Tolls* (1940), and *The Old Man and the Sea* (1951). Before achieving fame as a novelist, Hemingway worked as a journalist. Hemingway lived life to the fullest, serving in World War I, going on a safari in Africa, reporting on the Spanish Civil War, and living in Paris. Hemingway was known for his economical and clear writing style. He believed in positive construction and short sentences. Several of his works are considered classics of American literature.

Who was the first African American novelist in the United States?

Harriet E. Wilson (1825–1900) was the first African American to have a novel published in North America. She published her novel *Our Nig* (also known as *Sketches from the Life of a Free Black*) anonymously in 1859. It discusses the life of a slave named Mag Smith and her daughter Frado. The novel was forgotten about for decades until African American scholar Henry Louis Gates, Jr. (1950–) discovered it in 1982.

What were the lasting effects of the Harlem Renaissance?

The Harlem Renaissance (1925–1935) marked the first time that white Americans (principally intellects and artists) gave serious attention to the culture of African Americans. The movement, which by some accounts began as early as 1917, was noted in a 1925 *New York Herald-Tribune* article that announced, "We are on the edge, if not in the midst, of what might not improperly be called a Negro Renaissance." The first African American Rhodes scholar, Alain Locke (1886–1954), a professor of philosophy at Howard University, led and shaped the movement, during which Upper Manhattan became a hotbed of creativity in the post–World War I (1914–1918) era.

Not only was there a flurry of activity, but there was a heightened sense of pride as well. The movement left the U.S. with a legacy of literary works, including those by Jean Toomer (his 1923 work, *Cane,* is generally considered the first work of the Harlem Renaissance), Langston Hughes (*The Negro Speaks of Rivers,* 1921; *The Weary Blues,* 1926), Countee Cullen (*Color,* 1925; *Copper Sun,* 1927), Jessie R. Fauset (novelist and editor of *The Crisis,* the journal of the National Association for the Advancement of Colored People, or NAACP), Claude McKay (whose 1928 novel, *Home to Harlem,* evoked strong criticism from W. E. B. Du Bois and Alain Locke for its portrayal of black life), and Zora Neale Hurston (the author of the highly acclaimed 1937 novel *Their Eyes Were Watching God,* who was the first black woman to be honored for her creative writing with a prestigious Guggenheim Fellowship).

The Harlem Renaissance was not only about literature but also about music. The genres of jazz and blues flourished during the prosperous times of the postwar era. During the 1920s and 1930s, Louis Armstrong, "Jelly Roll" Morton, Duke Ellington, Bessie Smith, and Josephine Baker rose to prominence. Their contributions to music performance are still felt by artists and audiences today, regardless of color.

What is the Pulitzer Prize?

The Pulitzer Prize is a prestigious award given to the best in journalism, poetry, literature, and musical composition. Named after American newspaper publisher Joseph Pulitzer (1847–1911), the awards are administered by New York City's Columbia University. Columbia hosts what is generally considered the country's best journalism school. It arguably is the most prestigious award given to American creators of different forms of writing.

What poet won four Pulitzer Prizes?

The great American poet Robert Frost (1874–1963) won four Pulitzer Prizes in poetry (1924, 1931, 1937, and 1943). Many of his poems featured depictions of rural New England. Born in San Francisco, Frost and his family moved to New England in 1885 after the death of Frost's father. Frost attended Dartmouth University for a couple of months. He later attended Harvard University for two years but left due to illness. For many years, he taught English at Amherst (Massachusetts) University. He also taught at Middlebury College for many years. Some of his better-known poems include "The Road Not Taken," "Mending Wall," "Stopping by Woods on a Snowy Evening," and "Acquainted with the Night."

Who was Tennessee Williams?

One of America's most famous playwrights, Thomas Lanier ("Tennessee") Williams (1911–1983) is best known for such works as *A Streetcar Named Desire* (1947), *Cat on a Hot Tin Roof* (1955), and *Orpheus Descending* (1958).

363

What reclusive author wrote *Catcher in the Rye*?

J. D. Salinger (1919–2010) was an immensely popular American writer who—for whatever reason—retreated from public view and stopped publishing his work for public consumption in the 1960s. He achieved lasting fame for his novel *Catcher in the Rye*, depicting the adventures and plight of teenager protagonist Holden Caulfield. It has sold more than sixty-five million copies worldwide, remaining an immensely popular book. It remains a favorite among teenagers and young adults. The book was controversial in some quarters because of its use of profanity and discussion of sexual themes.

Author Toni Morrison won the Nobel Prize in literature in 1993.

Who is the last American to win a Nobel Prize in Literature?

Toni Morrison (1931–) is the last American to win a Nobel Prize in Literature. She won the prestigious honor in 1993. African American, Morrison's best-known novels include *Beloved, The Bluest Eye*, and *Song of Solomon*. Her works often depict African American females dealing with difficult circumstances. She also teaches and serves on the editorial board of the political magazine *The Nation*. In 2012, she won the Presidential Medal of Freedom.

Is there an American Poet Laureate?

In 1985, the U.S. Congress authorized the naming of a national Poet Laureate. In 1986, Kentucky-born man of letters Robert Penn Warren (1909–1989) became the country's first Poet Laureate. Among his works are the novels *All the King's Men* (1946, Pulitzer Prize) and *A Place to Come To* (1977); several volumes of poetry; and essays published in the anthology *I'll Take My Stand* (1930). He was also the editor of the literary journal *The Southern Review* (1935–1942). Warren's successors have included Joseph Brodsky, Mona Van Duyn (the first woman to receive the honor), and Rita Dove (the first African American to receive the honor).

What has been called our "national novel"?

Harper Lee's (1926–) brilliant book *To Kill a Mockingbird* is considered a national treasure and has been called our "national novel" by Oprah Winfrey. The book tells the story of a young girl named Scout Finch, who learns about the dignity and goodness of her father, Atticus Finch, a lawyer who defends a black man, Tom Robinson, from unjust charges of rape against a white woman. It is perhaps the most widely read book in high schools across the country. Many still consider the book their all-time favorite. Lee, who earned a law degree herself, never wrote another published novel.

Who are some other influential writers in American history whose works are now considered literary classics?

Some major figures in American literature not already named above include those listed in the following table.

Author	Birth/Death Dates	Accomplishments

Washington Irving 1783–1859
Irving's stories *Rip Van Winkle* and *The Legend of Sleepy Hollow* are timeless classics.

James Fenimore Cooper 1789–1851
Cooper is widely acknowledged for creating the first hero in American literature, Natty Bumppo, who appears in his "Leatherstocking" series of five novels, including *The Last of the Mohicans.* Cooper's stories embraced the adventurous spirit of the early American frontier.

Ralph Waldo Emerson 1803–1882
An Transcendentalist philosopher and essayist who encapsulated his beliefs in the essay *Nature* (1836), in which he maintained that the mysteries of life could be grasped through the study of the natural world.

Nathaniel Hawthorne 1804–1864
Now required reading in most American high schools, Hawthorne is the author of such classics as *The Scarlet Letter* (1850) and *The House of the Seven Gables.* His fiction typically addresses themes concerning sin, guilt, and their consequences.

Edgar Allan Poe 1809–1849
The undisputed master of spooky stories, Poe wrote horror, mysteries, poetry, criticism, and even science fiction. Among his beloved stories are "The Fall of the House of Usher" (1839), "The Murders in the Rue Morgue" (1841), "The Tell-Tale Heart" (1843), "The Cask of Amontillado" (1846), and the poem "The Raven" (1845).

Henry David Thoreau 1817–1862
A protegé of Ralph Waldo Emerson's, Thoreau was similarly a naturalist and philosopher. He expressed his Transcendental beliefs and philosophy of "living deliberately" most famously in his *Walden; or, Life in the Woods* (1854), which relates his efforts and thoughts while living in the wilderness outside of Concord, Massachusetts.

Herman Melville 1819–1891
Melville's masterpiece is undoubtedly his 1851 novel, *Moby-Dick,* which is about a captain of a whaling ship so obsessed with killing a white whale that he destroys everything in his life.

Walt Whitman 1819–1892
An influential poet who influenced the rising popularity of the free verse form, Whitman was influenced by Transcendentalism but also was interested in realism and humanism. His masterpiece is the poetry collection *Leaves of Grass,* which he worked on until his death.

Author	Birth/Death Dates	Accomplishments

Emily Dickinson — 1830–1886

A reclusive woman who almost never left her family home in Amherst, Massachusetts, she wrote over 1,700 poems but rarely published them. Almost all of her works were printed after her death. She had a unique style of writing, experimenting with punctuation, slant rhyme (words that almost rhyme, but not quite), and meter.

Willa Cather — 1873–1947

Spending most of her life in Nebraska, Cather embraced her environment and time with stories about the frontier and life on the prarie in such books as *O Pioneers!* (1913) and *My Antonia* (1918).

Robert Frost — 1874–1963

A four-time winner of the Pulitzer Prize, Frost was a poet who wrote realistically about life in rural New England. His poems are often concerned with questions about existence and how one can live in an indifferent universe. Also the poet laureate of Vermont and winner of a Congressional Gold Medal, he is the author of such oft-quoted poems as "Stopping by Woods on a Snowy Evening," "The Road Not Taken," and "Mending Wall."

Jack London — 1876–1916

Also an author of frontier tales, London wrote about the American West and especially life in Alaska and the Klondike in such books as *The Call of the Wild* (1903), *White Fang* (1906), and *The Sea Wolf* (1904).

F. Scott Fitzgerald — 1896–1940

Fitzgerald's books epitomized the themes and concerns of the 1920s Age of Jazz, most famously in his 1925 masterpiece, *The Great Gatsby.*

William Faulkner — 1897–1962

Faulkner is best known for his books set in his native state of Mississippi, though he made up Yoknapatawpha County. The winner of the 1949 Nobel Prize in Literature, Faulkner is the author of such works as *The Sound and the Fury* (1929), *Absalom, Absalom!* (1936), and *The Reivers* (1962).

Margaret Mitchell — 1900–1949

Although she only wrote one novel in her lifetime, Mitchell was the author of *Gone with the Wind* (1936), a romantic tale of the Old South before and during the American Civil War, which won a Pulitzer in 1937.

John Steinbeck — 1902–1968

Often concerned with the lives of migrant workers and sharecroppers during the Great Depression, Steinbeck is best known for *Of Mice and Men* (1937), *The Grapes of Wrath* (1939), and *East of Eden* 1952. He won a Pulitzer in 1940 and the Nobel Prize in Literature in 1962.

Bibliography

Alter, Jonathan. *The Defining Moment: FDR's Hundred Days and the Triumph of Hope*. New York: Simon & Schuster, 2006.

Amar, Akhil Reed. *America's Constitution: A Biography*. New York: Random House, 2005.

Ambrose, Stephen E. *Undaunted Courage: Meriwether Lewis, Thomas Jefferson, and the Opening of the American West*. New York: Simon & Schuster, 1997.

———. *Eisenhower: The President*. New York: Simon & Schuster, 1984.

Banner, Stuart. *The Death Penalty: An American History*. Cambridge: Harvard University Press, 2002.

Barone, Michael. *Our Country: The Shaping of America from Roosevelt to Reagan*. New York: The Free Press, 1990.

Bennett, William J. *America The Last Best Hope,* two volumes. Nashville: Thomas Nelson, 2006.

Beschloss, Michael R. *Eisenhower: A Centennial Life*. New York: HarperCollins Publishers, 1990.

———. *Kennedy and Roosevelt: The Uneasy Alliance*. New York: W.W. Norton & Company, 1980.

Bowen, Catherine Drinker. *Miracle at Philadelphia: The Story of the Constitutional Convention, May to September, 1787*. Boston: Little, Brown, 1966.

Brinkley, Douglas. *American Heritage History of the United States*, New York: Viking Penguin, 1998.

Burger, Warren E. *It Is So Ordered: A Constitution Unfolds*. New York: William Morrow and Company, 1995.

Bush, George W. *Decision Points*. New York: Crown, 2010.

Carter, Jimmy. *White House Diary.* New York: Farrar, Strauss & Giroux, 2010.

Clinton, Bill. *My Life*. New York: Alfred A. Knopf, 2004.

Collier, Christopher, and James Lincoln Collier. *Decision in Philadelphia: The Constitutional Convention of 1787*. New York: Random House, 1986.

Drew, Elizabeth. *Richard M. Nixon: The American Presidents Series: The 37th President, 1969–1974*. New York: Times Books, 2007.

Flexner, James Thomas. *Washington: The Indispensable Man*. Boston: Little, Brown, 1974.

Foner, Eric. *The Story of American Freedom*. New York: W.W. Norton, 1998.

Gilbert, Martin. *The First World War: A Complete History*. New York: Henry Holt, 1994.

Higginbotham, A. Leon, Jr. *Shades of Freedom: Racial Politics and Presumptions of the American Legal Process*. New York: Oxford University Press, 1996.

Hofstadter, Richard. *The American Political Tradition: And the Men Who Made It*. New York: Vintage Books, 1948.

Isaacson, Walter. *Benjamin Franklin: An American Life*. New York: Simon & Schuster, 2003.

Kaplan, Fred. *John Quincy Adams: American Visionary*. New York: HarperCollins, 2014.

Keegan, John. *Fields of Battle: The Wars for North America*. New York: Random House, 1995.

Ketcham, Ralph. *James Madison: A Biography*. Charlottesville: University of Virginia Press, 1990.

Kluger, Richard. *Simple Justice: The History of Brown v. Board of Education and Black America's Struggle for Equality*. New York: Alfred A. Knopf, 2004.

Leckie, Robert. *The Wars of America*. New York: Harper & Row, 1981.

Lewis, John (with Michael D'Orso). *Walking with the Wind: A Memoir of the Movement*. New York: Harcourt Brace, 1998.

Maraniss, David. *First in His Class: A Biography of Bill Clinton*. New York: Simon & Schuster, 1996.

McCullough, David. *1776*. New York: Simon & Schuster, 2005.

———. *Truman*. New York: Simon & Schuster, 1992.

McPherson, James M. *The Illustrated Battle Cry of Freedom: The Civil War Era*. New York: Oxford University Press, 2003.

McWhorter, Diane. *Carry Me Home: Birmingham, Alabama: The Climactic Battle of the Civil Rights Revolution*. New York: Simon & Schuster, 1996.

Morgan, Edmund S. *The Birth of the Republic: 1763–1789*. Chicago: University of Chicago Press, 1956.

Peters, Charles. *Lyndon B. Johnson: The American Presidents Series: The 36th President, 1963–1969*. New York: Times Books, 2010.

Rakove, Jack. *James Madison and the Creation of the American Republic*. New York: Longman, 2002.

Rehnquist, William H. *Centennial Crisis: The Disputed Election of 1876*. New York: Alfred A. Knopf, 2004.

Remini, Robert V. *The Life of Andrew Jackson*. New York: Penguin Books, 1988.

———. *John Quincy Adams*. New York: Henry Holt & Company, 2002.

Rodell, Fred. *55 Men: The Story of the Constitution, Based on the Day-by-Day Notes of James Madison*. Harrisburg, PA.: Stackpole, 1986.

Schlesinger, Arthur M., ed. *The Almanac of American History*. New York: G.P. Putnam's Sons, 1983.

Seigenthaler, John. *James K. Polk: The American Presidents Series*. New York: Times Books, 2003.

Sitkoff, Harvard. *The Struggle for Black Equality 1954–1980*. New York: Hill & Wang, 1981.

Smith, Jean Edward. *FDR*. New York: Random House, 2008.

Tocqueville, Alexis de. *Democracy in America*, trans., ed., with an introduction by Harvey Mansfield. Chicago: The University of Chicago Press, 2000.

Ward, Geoffrey C. *The Civil War: An Illustrated History*. New York: Alfred A. Knopf, 1990.

Williams, Harry T. *Lincoln and His Generals*. New York: Vintage Books, 1952.

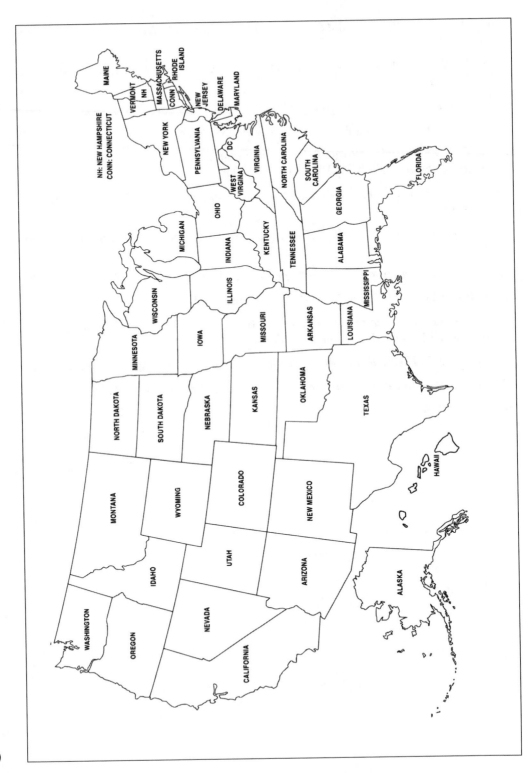

The American States

(note: populations are 2014 estimates)

Alabama

Admitted: December 14, 1819
22nd State
Capital: Montgomery
Largest City: Birmingham
Nickname: Yellowhammer State
Electoral Votes: 9
Population: 4.8 million

Alaska

Admitted: January 3, 1959
49th State
Capital: Juneau
Largest City: Anchorage
Nickname: The Last Frontier
Electoral Votes: 3
Population: 735,000

Arizona

Admitted: February 14, 1912
48th State
Capital: Phoenix
Largest City: Phoenix
Nickname: The Grand Canyon State
Electoral Votes: 11
Population: 6.6 million

Arkansas

Admitted: June 15, 1836
25th State
Capital: Little Rock
Largest City: Little Rock
Nickname: The Natural State
Electoral Votes: 6
Population: 2.95 million

California

Admitted: September 9, 1850
31st State
Capital: Sacramento
Largest City: Los Angeles
Nickname: The Golden State
Electoral Votes: 55
Population: 38.3 million

Colorado

Admitted: August 1, 1876
38th State .
Capital: Denver
Largest City: Denver
Nickname: Centennial State
Electoral Votes: 9
Population: 5.27 million

Connecticut
Admitted: January 9, 1788
5th State
Capital: Hartford
Largest City: Bridgeport
Nickname: Constitution State
Electoral Votes: 7
Population: 3.6 million

Delaware
Admitted: December 7, 1787
1st State
Capital: Dover
Largest City: Wilmington
Nicknames: The First State, the Blue
    Hen State, the Diamond State, Small
    Wonder
Electoral Votes: 3
Population: 925,000

Florida
Admitted: March 3, 1845
27th State
Capital: Tallahassee
Largest City: Jacksonville
Nickname: Sunshine State
Electoral Votes: 29
Population: 19.5 million

Georgia
Admitted: January 2, 1788
4th State
Capital: Atlanta
Largest City: Atlanta
Nickname: Peach State
Electoral Votes: 16
Population: 10 million

Hawaii
Admitted: August 21, 1959
50th State
Capital: Honolulu
Largest City: Honolulu
Nickname: Aloha State
Electoral Votes: 4
Population: 1.4 million

Idaho
Admitted: July 3, 1890
43rd State
Capital: Boise
Largest City: Boise
Nickname: Gem State
Electoral Votes: 4
Population: 1.6 million

Illinois
Admitted: December 3, 1818
21st State
Capital: Springfield
Largest City: Chicago
Nickname: Prairie State
Electoral Votes: 20
Population: 12.9 million

Indiana
Admitted: December 11, 1816
19th State
Capital: Indianapolis
Largest City: Indianapolis
Nickname: Hoosier State
Electoral Votes: 11
Population: 6.6 million

Iowa
Admitted: December 28, 1846
29th State
Capital: Des Moines.
Largest City: Des Moines
Nickname: Hawkeye State
Electoral Votes: 6
Population: 3.1 million

Kansas
Admitted: January 29, 1861
34th State
Capital City: Topeka
Largest City: Wichita
Nickname: Sunflower State
Electoral Votes: 6
Population: 2.9 million

Kentucky
Admitted: June 1, 1792
15th State
Capital City: Frankfort
Largest City: Louisville
Nickname: Bluegrass State
Electoral Votes: 8
Population: 4.4 million

Louisiana
Admitted: April 30, 1812
18th State
Capital City: Baton Rouge
Largest City: New Orleans
Nickname: Pelican State
Electoral Votes: 8
Population: 4.6 million

Maine
Admitted: March 15, 1820
23rd State
Capital City: Augusta
Largest City: Portland
Nickname: Pine Street State
Electoral Votes: 4
Population: 1.3 million

Maryland
Admitted: April 28, 1788
7th State
Capital: Annapolis
Largest City: Baltimore
Nickname: Old Line State
Electoral Votes: 10
Population: 5.9 million

Massachusetts
Admitted: February 6, 1788
6th State
Capital: Boston
Largest City: Boston
Nickname: Bay State
Electoral Votes: 11
Population: 6.7 million

Michigan
Admitted: January 26, 1837
26th State
Capital: Lansing
Largest City: Detroit
Nicknames: Wolverine State; Great Lake
    State
Electoral Votes: 16
Population: 9.9 million

Minnesota

Admitted: May 11, 1858
32nd State
Capital City: St. Paul
Largest City: Minneapolis
Nicknames: North Star State; Land of
    10,000 Lakes
Electoral Votes: 10
Population: 5.4 million

Mississippi

Admitted: December 10, 1817
20th State
Capital: Jackson
Largest City: Jackson
Nickname: Magnolia State
Electoral Votes: 6
Population: 3 million

Missouri

Admitted: August 10, 1821
24th State
Capital: Jefferson City
Largest City: Kansas City
Nickname: Show Me State
Electoral Votes: 10
Population: 6 million

Montana

Admitted: November 8, 1889
41st State
Capital: Helena
Largest City: Billings
Nickname: Treasure State
Electoral Votes: 3
Population: 1 million

Nebraska

Admitted: March 1, 1867
37th State
Capital City: Lincoln
Largest City: Omaha
Nickname: Cornhusker State
Electoral Votes: 5
Population: 1.9 million

Nevada

Admitted: October 31, 1864
36th State
Capital City: Carson City
Largest City: Las Vegas
Nicknames: Silver State; Sage State;
    Sagebrush State
Electoral Votes: 6
Population: 2.8 million

New Hampshire

Admitted: June 21, 1788
9th State
Capital City: Concord
Largest City: Manchester
Nickname: Granite State
Electoral Votes: 4
Population: 1.3 million

New Jersey

Admitted: December 18, 1787
3rd State
Capital: Trenton
Largest City: Newark
Nickname: Garden State
Electoral Votes: 14
Population: 8.9 million

New Mexico
Admitted: January 6, 1912
47th State
Capital: Santa Fe
Largest City: Albuquerque
Nickname: Land of Enchantment
Electoral Votes: 5
Population: 2.1 million

New York
Admitted: July 26, 1788
11th State
Capital: Albany
Largest City: New York City
Nickname: Empire State
Electoral Votes: 29
Population: 19.6 million

North Carolina
Admitted: November 21, 1789
12th State
Capital: Raleigh
Largest City: Charlotte
Nicknames: Old North State; Tarheel
State
Electoral Votes: 15
Population: 9.8 million

North Dakota
Admitted: November 2, 1889
39th or 40th (Admitted on same day as
South Dakota)
Capital: Bismarck
Largest City: Fargo
Nicknames: Peace Garden State; Flicker-
tail State; Roughrider State
Electoral Votes: 3
Population: 723,000

Ohio
Admitted: March 1, 1803
17th State
Capital: Columbus
Largest City: Columbus
Nickname: Buckeye State
Electoral Votes: 18
Population: 11.6 million

Oklahoma
Admitted: November 16, 1907
46th State
Capital: Oklahoma City
Largest City: Oklahoma City
Nickname: Sooner State
Electoral Votes: 7
Population: 3.8 million

Oregon
Admitted: February 14, 1859
33rd State
Capital: Salem
Largest City: Portland
Nickname: Beaver State
Electoral votes: 7
Population: 3.9 million

Pennsylvania
Admitted: December 12, 1787
2nd State
Capital: Harrisburg
Largest City: Philadelphia
Nickname: Keystone State
Electoral Votes: 20
Population: 12.8 million

Rhode Island

Admitted: May 29, 1790
13th State
Capital: Providence
Largest City: Providence
Nicknames: Ocean State; Plantation State
Electoral Votes: 4
Population: 1 million

South Carolina

Admitted: May 23, 1788
8th State
Capital: Columbia
Largest City: Columbia
Nickname: Palmetto State
Electoral Votes: 9
Population: 4.8 million

South Dakota

Admitted: November 2, 1889
39th or 40th (Admitted on same day as
    North Dakota)
Capital: Pierre
Largest City: Sioux Falls
Nickname: Mount Rushmore State
Electoral Votes: 3
Population: 845,000

Tennessee

Admitted: June 1, 1796
16th State
Capital: Nashville
Largest City: Memphis
Nicknames: The Volunteer State; Big Bend
    State; Hog and Hominy State; The
    Mother of Southwestern Statesmen
Electoral Votes: 11
Population: 6.5 million

Texas

Admitted: December 29, 1845
28th State
Capital: Austin
Largest City: Houston
Nickname: Lone Star State
Electoral Votes: 38
Population: 26.4 million

Utah

Admitted: January 4, 1896
45th State
Capital: Salt Lake City
Largest City: Salt Lake City
Nickname: Beehive State
Electoral Votes: 6
Population: 2.9 million

Vermont

Admitted: March 4, 1791
14th State
Capital: Montpelier
Largest City: Burlington
Nickname: Green Mountain State
Electoral Votes: 3
Population: 626,000

Virginia

Admitted: June 25, 1788
10th State
Capital: Richmond
Largest City: Virginia Beach
Nicknames: Old Dominion State;
    Mother State
Electoral Votes: 13
Population: 8.2 million

Washington
Admitted: November 11, 1889
42nd State
Capital: Olympia
Largest City: Seattle
Nickname: Evergreen State
Electoral Votes : 12
Population: 6.9 million

Wisconsin
Admitted: May 29, 1848
30th State
Capital: Madison
Largest City: Cheyenne
Nickname: Badger State
Electoral Votes: 10
Population: 5.76 million

West Virginia
Admitted: June 20, 1863
35th State
Capital: Charleston
Largest City: Charleston
Nickname: Mountain State
Electoral Votes: 5
Population: 1.8 million

Wyoming
Admitted: July 10, 1890
44th State
Capital: Cheyenne
Largest City: Cheyenne
Nickname: Equality State
Electoral Votes: 3
Population: 584,000

Presidents

1. George Washington
(1732–1799)
Years in office: 1789–1797
Political Party: Independent
Election Opponent: None
Home State: Virginia
Vice President: John Adams

2. John Adams
(1735–1826)
Years in office: 1797–1801
Political Party: Federalist
Election Opponent: Thomas Jefferson
Home State: Massachusetts
Vice President: Thomas Jefferson

3. Thomas Jefferson
(1743–1826)
Years in office: 1801–1809
Political Party: Democratic-Republican
Election Opponents: John Adams in 1800; Charles Pinckney in
    1804
Home State: Virginia
Vice Presidents: Aaron Burr; George Clinton

4. James Madison

(1751–1836)

Years in office: 1809–1817

Political Party: Democratic-Republican

Election Opponents: Charles Pinckney in 1808; DeWitt Clinton in 1812

Home State: Virginia

Vice Presidents: George Clinton; Elbridge Gerry

5. James Monroe

(1758–1831)

Years in office: 1817–1825

Political Party: Democratic-Republican

Election Opponent: Rufus King in 1816; unopposed in 1820

Home State: Virginia

Vice President: Daniel D. Tompkins

6. John Quincy Adams

(1767–1848)

Years in office: 1825–1829

Political Party: Democratic–Republican

Election Opponents: Andrew Jackson, Henry Clay, and William Crawford

Home State: Massachusetts

Vice President: John C. Calhoun

7. Andrew Jackson

(1767–1845)

Years in office: 1829–1837

Political Party: Democratic

Election Opponent: John Quincy Adams in 1828; Henry Clay and William Wirt in 1832

Home State: Tennessee

Vice Presidents: John C. Calhoun; Martin Van Buren

8. Martin Van Buren
(1782–1862)
Years in office: 1837–1841
Political Party: Democratic
Election Opponents: Daniel Webster and Hugh White
Home State: New York
Vice President: Richard Mentor Johnson

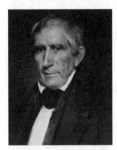

9. William Henry Harrison
(1773–1841)
Years in office: 1841
Political Party: Whig
Election Opponent: Martin Van Buren
Home State: Ohio
Vice President: John Tyler

10. John Tyler
(1790–1862)
Years in office: 1841–1845
Political Party: Whig
Election Opponent: None—assumed office as vice president
    after the death of President William Henry Harrison
Home State: Virginia
Vice President: None

11. James K. Polk
(1795–1849)
Years in office: 1845–1849
Political Party: Democratic
Election Opponents: Henry Clay and James Birney
Home State: Tennessee
Vice President: George Dallas

12. Zachary Taylor
(1784–1850)
Years in office: 1849–1850
Political Party: Whig
Election Opponents: Martin Van Buren and Lewis Cass
Home state(s): Virginia and Kentucky
Vice President: Millard Fillmore

13. Millard Fillmore
(1800–1874)
Years in office: 1850–1853
Political Party: Whig
Election Opponents: None—assumed office after the death of
    President Taylor
Home State: New York
Vice President: None

14. Franklin Pierce
(1804–1869)
Years in office: 1853–1857
Political Party: Democratic
Election Opponents: Winfield Scott and John Pitale
Home State: New Hampshire
Vice President: William R. King

15. James Buchanan
(1791–1868)
Years in office: 1857–1861
Political Party: Democratic
Election Opponents: Millard Fillmore and John C. Freemont
Home State: Pennsylvania
Vice President: John Breckenridge

16. Abraham Lincoln
(1809–1865)
Years in office: 1861–1865
Political Party: Republican
Election Opponents: Stephen Douglas, John C. Breckenridge
    and John Bell in 1860; George B. McClellan in 1864
Home State: Illinois (born in Kentucky)
Vice Presidents: Hannibal Hamlin; Andrew Johnson

17. Andrew Johnson
(1808–1875)
Years in office: 1865–1869
Political Party: Democratic
Election Opponent: None—assumed office as vice president
    after the assassination of President Lincoln
Home State: Tennessee
Vice President: None

18. Ulysses S. Grant
(1822–1885)
Years in office: 1869–1877
Political Party: Republican
Election Opponent: Horace Seymour in 1868; Horace Greeley
    in 1872
Home State: Ohio
Vice Presidents: Schuyler Colfax; Henry Wilson

19. Rutherford B. Hayes
(1822–1893)
Years in office: 1877–1881
Political Party: Republican
Election Opponent: Samuel Tilden
Home State: Ohio
Vice President: William Wheeler

20. James A. Garfield

(1833–1881)
Year in office: 1881
Political Party: Republican
Election Opponent: Winfield Scott Hancock
Home State: Ohio
Vice President: Chester A. Arthur

21. Chester A. Arthur

(1829–1886)
21st President
Years in office: 1881–1885
Political Party: Republican
Election Opponent: None—assumed office after the assassination of President Garfield
Home State: New York
Vice President: None

22 & 24. Grover Cleveland

(1837–1908)
Years in office: 1885–1889; 1893–1897
Political Party: Democratic
Election Opponent: James Blaine in 1884; Benjamin Harrison and James B. Weaver in 1892
Home State: New York
Vice Presidents: Thomas Hendricks; Adlai Stevenson I

23. Benjamin Harrison

(1833–1901)
Years in office: 1889–1893
Political Party: Republican
Election Opponent: Grover Cleveland
Home State: Ohio
Vice President: Levi Morton

25. William McKinley

(1843–1901)

Years in office: 1897–1901

Political Party: Republican

Election Opponents: William Jennings Bryan, Thomas Watson, and John Palmer in 1896; William Jennings Bryan in 1900

Home State: Ohio

Vice President: Theodore Roosevelt

26. Theodore Roosevelt

(1858–1919)

Years in office: 1901–1909

Political Party: Republican

Election Opponent: initially assumed office as vice president under President McKinley; Alton Parker in 1904

Home State: New York

Vice President: Charles W. Fairbanks

27. William Howard Taft

(1857–1930)

Years in office: 1909–1913

Political Party: Republican

Election Opponent: William Jennings Bryan

Home State: Ohio

Vice President: James Sherman

28. Woodrow Wilson

(1856–1924)

Years in office: 1913–1921

Political Party: Democratic

Election Opponents: William Howard Taft, Theodore Roosevelt and Eugene Debs in 1912; Charles Evans Hughes in 1916

Home State: New Jersey

Vice President: Thomas R. Marshall

29. Warren G. Harding

(1865–1923)

Years in office: 1921–1923

Political Party: Republican

Election Opponents: James Cox and Eugene Debs

Home State: Ohio

Vice President: Calvin Coolidge

30. Calvin Coolidge

(1872–1933)

Years in office: 1923–1929

Political Party: Republican

Election Opponents: initially assumed office after the death of President Harding; Robert LaFollette, Burton Wheeler and John Davis in 1924

Home State: Massachusetts (born in Vermont)

Vice President: Charles G. Dawes

31. Herbert Hoover

(1874–1964)

Years in office: 1929–1933

Political Party: Republican

Election Opponent: Alfred E. Smith

Home State: New York (born in Iowa)

Vice President: Charles Curtis

32. Franklin D. Roosevelt

(1882–1945)

Years in office: 1933–1945

Political Party: Democratic

Election Opponents: Herbert Hoover in 1932; Alfred Landon in 1936; Wendall Wilkie in 1940; and Thomas Dewey in 1944

Home State: New York

Vice Presidents: John Nance Garner; Henry A. Wallace; Harry Truman

33. Harry S. Truman
(1884–1972)
Years in office: 1945–1953
Political Party: Democratic
Election Opponent: initially assumed office after the death of
    President Roosevelt; Thomas Dewey, Strom Thurmond, and
    Henry Wallace in 1946
Home State: Missouri
Vice President: Alben W. Barkley

34. Dwight D. Eisenhower
(1890–1969)
Years in office: 1953–1961
Political Party: Republican
Election Opponent: Adlai Stevenson in 1952 and 1956
Home State: Kansas (born in Texas)
Vice President: Richard Nixon

35. John F. Kennedy
(1917–1963)
Years in office: 1961–1963
Political Party: Democratic
Election Opponent: Richard Nixon
Home State: Massachusetts
Vice President: Lyndon Johnson

36. Lyndon B. Johnson
(1908–1973)
Years in office: 1963–1969
Political Party: Democratic
Election Opponent: initially assumed office as vice president
    after the assassination of President Kennedy; Barry Goldwa-
    ter in 1964
Home State: Texas
Vice President: Hubert Humphrey

37. Richard M. Nixon
(1913–1994)
Years in office: 1969–1974
Political Party: Republican
Election Opponents: Hubert Humphrey and George Wallace in
    1968; George McGovern in 1972
Home State: California
Vice Presidents: Spiro Agnew; Gerald Ford

38. Gerald Ford
(1913–2006)
Years in office: 1974–1977
Political Party: Republican
Election Opponent: assumed office as vice president after the
    resignation of President Nixon
Home State: Michigan (born in Nebraska)
Vice President: Nelson Rockefeller

39. Jimmy Carter
(1924–)
Years in office: 1977–1981
Political Party: Democratic
Election Opponent: Gerald Ford in 1976
Home State: Georgia
Vice President: Walter Mondale

40. Ronald Reagan
(1911–2004)
Years in office: 1981–1989
Political Party: Republican
Election Opponents: Jimmy Carter and John Anderson in 1980;
    Walter Mondale in 1984
Home State: California (born in Illinois)
Vice President: George W. Bush

41. George H.W. Bush

(1924–)
Years in office: 1989–1993
Political Party: Republican
Election Opponent: Michael Dukakis in 1988
Home State: Texas (born in Massachusetts)
Vice President: Dan Quayle

42. Bill Clinton

(1946–)
Years in office: 1993–2001
Political Party: Democratic
Election Opponents: George Bush and Ross Perot in 1992; Bob
   Dole in 1996
Home State: Arkansas
Vice President: Al Gore Jr.

43. George W. Bush

(1946–)
Years in office: 2001–2009
Political Party: Republican
Election Opponents: Al Gore and Ralph Nader in 2000; John
   Kerry in 2004
Home State: Texas (born in Connecticut)
Vice President: Dick Cheney

44. Barack Obama

(1961–)
Years in office: 2009–2017
Political Party: Democratic
Election Opponents: John McCain in 2008; Mitt Romney in
   2012
Home State: Illinois (born in Hawaii)
Vice President: Joe Biden

U.S. Constitution

We the People of the United States, in Order to form a more perfect Union, establish Justice, insure domestic Tranquility, provide for the common defence, promote the general Welfare, and secure the Blessings of Liberty to ourselves and our Posterity, do ordain and establish this Constitution for the United States of America.

ARTICLE I.

SECTION 1. All legislative Powers herein granted shall be vested in a Congress of the United States, which shall consist of a Senate and House of Representatives.

SECTION 2. The House of Representatives shall be composed of Members chosen every second Year by the People of the several States, and the Electors in each State shall have the Qualifications requisite for Electors of the most numerous Branch of the State Legislature.

No Person shall be a Representative who shall not have attained to the Age of twenty five Years, and been seven Years a Citizen of the United States, and who shall not, when elected, be an Inhabitant of that State in which he shall be chosen.

Representatives and direct Taxes shall be apportioned among the several States which may be included within this Union, according to their respective Numbers, which shall be determined by adding to the whole Number of free Persons, including those bound to Service for a Term of Years, and excluding Indians not taxed, three fifths of all other Persons.

The actual Enumeration shall be made within three Years after the first Meeting of the Congress of the United States, and within every subsequent Term of ten Years, in such Manner as they shall by Law direct. The Number of Representatives shall not exceed one for every thirty Thousand, but each State shall have at Least one Representative; and until such enumeration shall be made, the State of New Hampshire shall be entitled to chuse three, Massachusetts eight, Rhode Island and Providence Plantations one, Connecticut five, New York six, New Jersey four, Pennsylvania eight, Delaware one, Maryland six, Virginia ten, North Carolina five, South Carolina five and Georgia three.

When vacancies happen in the Representation from any State, the Executive Authority thereof shall issue Writs of Election to fill such Vacancies.

The House of Representatives shall chuse their Speaker and other Officers; and shall have the sole Power of Impeachment.

SECTION 3. The Senate of the United States shall be composed of two Senators from each State, chosen by the Legislature thereof, for six Years; and each Senator shall have one Vote.

Immediately after they shall be assembled in Consequence of the first Election, they shall be divided as equally as may be into three Classes. The Seats of the Senators of the first Class shall be vacated at the Expiration of the second Year, of the second Class at the Expiration of the fourth Year, and of the third Class at the Expiration of the sixth Year, so that one third may be chosen every second Year; and if Vacancies happen by Resignation, or otherwise, during the Recess of the Legislature of any State, the Executive thereof may make temporary Appointments until the next Meeting of the Legislature, which shall then fill such Vacancies.

No person shall be a Senator who shall not have attained to the Age of thirty Years, and been nine Years a Citizen of the United States, and who shall not, when elected, be an Inhabitant of that State for which he shall be chosen.

The Vice President of the United States shall be President of the Senate, but shall have no Vote, unless they be equally divided.

The Senate shall chuse their other Officers, and also a President pro tempore, in the absence of the Vice President, or when he shall exercise the Office of President of the United States.

The Senate shall have the sole Power to try all Impeachments. When sitting for that Purpose, they shall be on Oath or Affirmation. When the President of the United States is tried, the Chief Justice shall preside: And no Person shall be convicted without the Concurrence of two thirds of the Members present.

Judgment in Cases of Impeachment shall not extend further than to removal from Office, and disqualification to hold and enjoy any Office of honor, Trust or Profit under the United States: but the Party convicted shall nevertheless be liable and subject to Indictment, Trial, Judgment and Punishment, according to Law.

SECTION 4. The Times, Places and Manner of holding Elections for Senators and Representatives, shall be prescribed in each State by the Legislature thereof; but the Congress may at any time by Law make or alter such Regulations, except as to the Place of Chusing Senators.

The Congress shall assemble at least once in every Year, and such Meeting shall be on the first Monday in December, unless they shall by Law appoint a different Day.

SECTION 5. Each House shall be the Judge of the Elections, Returns and Qualifications of its own Members, and a Majority of each shall constitute a Quorum to do Business; but a smaller number may adjourn from day to day, and may be authorized to compel the Attendance of absent Members, in such Manner, and under such Penalties as each House may provide.

Each House may determine the Rules of its Proceedings, punish its Members for disorderly Behavior, and, with the Concurrence of two-thirds, expel a Member.

Each House shall keep a Journal of its Proceedings, and from time to time publish the same, excepting such Parts as may in their Judgment require Secrecy; and the Yeas and Nays of the Members of either House on any question shall, at the Desire of one fifth of those Present, be entered on the Journal.

Neither House, during the Session of Congress, shall, without the Consent of the other, adjourn for more than three days, nor to any other Place than that in which the two Houses shall be sitting.

SECTION 6. The Senators and Representatives shall receive a Compensation for their Services, to be ascertained by Law, and paid out of the Treasury of the United States. They shall in all Cases, except Treason, Felony and Breach of the Peace, be privileged from Arrest during their Attendance at the Session of their respective Houses, and in going to and returning from the same; and for any Speech or Debate in either House, they shall not be questioned in any other Place.

No Senator or Representative shall, during the Time for which he was elected, be appointed to any civil Office under the Authority of the United States which shall have been created, or the Emoluments whereof shall have been increased during such time; and no Person holding any Office under the United States, shall be a Member of either House during his Continuance in Office.

SECTION 7. All bills for raising Revenue shall originate in the House of Representatives; but the Senate may propose or concur with Amendments as on other bills.

Every Bill which shall have passed the House of Representatives and the Senate, shall, before it become a Law, be presented to the President of the United States; If he approve he shall sign it, but if not he shall return it, with his Objections to that House in which it shall have originated, who shall enter the Objections at large on their Journal, and proceed to reconsider it. If after such Reconsideration two thirds of that House shall agree to pass the Bill, it shall be sent, together with the Objections, to the other House, by which it shall likewise be reconsidered, and if approved by two thirds of that House, it shall become a Law. But in all such Cases the Votes of both Houses shall be determined by Yeas and Nays, and the Names of the Persons voting for and against the Bill shall be entered on the Journal of each House respectively. If any Bill shall not be returned by the President within ten Days (Sundays excepted) after it shall have been presented to him, the Same shall be a Law, in like Manner as if he had signed it, unless the Congress by their Adjournment prevent its Return, in which Case it shall not be a Law.

Every Order, Resolution, or Vote to which the Concurrence of the Senate and House of Representatives may be necessary (except on a question of Adjournment) shall be presented to the President of the United States; and before the Same shall take Effect, shall be approved by him, or being disapproved by him, shall be repassed by two thirds of the Senate and House of Representatives, according to the Rules and Limitations prescribed in the Case of a Bill.

SECTION 8. The Congress shall have Power To lay and collect Taxes, Duties, Imposts and Excises, to pay the Debts and provide for the common Defence and general Welfare of the United States; but all Duties, Imposts and Excises shall be uniform throughout the United States;

To borrow money on the credit of the United States;

To regulate Commerce with foreign Nations, and among the several States, and with the Indian Tribes;

To establish an uniform Rule of Naturalization, and uniform Laws on the subject of Bankruptcies throughout the United States;

To coin Money, regulate the Value thereof, and of foreign Coin, and fix the Standard of Weights and Measures;

To provide for the Punishment of counterfeiting the Securities and current Coin of the United States;

To establish Post Offices and Post Roads;

To promote the Progress of Science and useful Arts, by securing for limited Times to Authors and Inventors the exclusive Right to their respective Writings and Discoveries;

To constitute Tribunals inferior to the supreme Court;

To define and punish Piracies and Felonies committed on the high Seas, and Offenses against the Law of Nations;

To declare War, grant Letters of Marque and Reprisal, and make Rules concerning Captures on Land and Water;

To raise and support Armies, but no Appropriation of Money to that Use shall be for a longer Term than two Years;

To provide and maintain a Navy;

To make Rules for the Government and Regulation of the land and naval Forces;

To provide for calling forth the Militia to execute the Laws of the Union, suppress Insurrections and repel Invasions;

To provide for organizing, arming, and disciplining the Militia, and for governing such Part of them as may be employed in the Service of the United States, reserving to the States respectively, the Appointment of the Officers, and the Authority of training the Militia according to the discipline prescribed by Congress;

To exercise exclusive Legislation in all Cases whatsoever, over such District (not exceeding ten Miles square) as may, by Cession of particular States, and the acceptance of Congress, become the Seat of the Government of the United States, and to exercise like Authority over all Places purchased by the Consent of the Legislature of the State in which the same shall be, for the Erection of Forts, Magazines, Arsenals, dock-Yards, and other needful Buildings; And

To make all Laws which shall be necessary and proper for carrying into Execution the foregoing Powers, and all other Powers vested by this Constitution in the Government of the United States, or in any Department or Officer thereof.

SECTION 9. The Migration or Importation of such Persons as any of the States now existing shall think proper to admit, shall not be prohibited by the Congress prior to the Year one thousand eight hundred and eight, but a tax or duty may be imposed on such Importation, not exceeding ten dollars for each Person.

The privilege of the Writ of Habeas Corpus shall not be suspended, unless when in Cases of Rebellion or Invasion the public Safety may require it.

No Bill of Attainder or ex post facto Law shall be passed. No capitation, or other direct, Tax shall be laid, unless in Proportion to the Census or Enumeration herein before directed to be taken.

No Tax or Duty shall be laid on Articles exported from any State.

No Preference shall be given by any Regulation of Commerce or Revenue to the Ports of one State over those of another: nor shall Vessels bound to, or from, one State, be obliged to enter, clear, or pay Duties in another.

No Money shall be drawn from the Treasury, but in Consequence of Appropriations made by Law; and a regular Statement and Account of the Receipts and Expenditures of all public Money shall be published from time to time.

No Title of Nobility shall be granted by the United States: And no Person holding any Office of Profit or Trust under them, shall, without the Consent of the Congress, accept of any present, Emolument, Office, or Title, of any kind whatever, from any King, Prince or foreign State.

SECTION 10. No State shall enter into any Treaty, Alliance, or Confederation; grant Letters of Marque and Reprisal; coin Money; emit Bills of Credit; make any Thing but gold and silver Coin a Tender in Payment of Debts; pass any Bill of Attainder, ex post facto Law, or Law impairing the Obligation of Contracts, or grant any Title of Nobility.

No State shall, without the Consent of the Congress, lay any Imposts or Duties on Imports or Exports, except what may be absolutely necessary for executing its inspection Laws: and the net Produce of all Duties and Imposts, laid by any State on Imports or Exports, shall be for the Use of the Treasury of the United States; and all such Laws shall be subject to the Revision and Controul of the Congress.

No State shall, without the Consent of Congress, lay any duty of Tonnage, keep Troops, or Ships of War in time of Peace, enter into any Agreement or Compact with another State, or with a foreign Power, or engage in War, unless actually invaded, or in such imminent Danger as will not admit of delay.

ARTICLE II.

SECTION 1. The executive Power shall be vested in a President of the United States of America. He shall hold his Office during the Term of four Years, and, together with the Vice-President chosen for the same Term, be elected, as follows:

Each State shall appoint, in such Manner as the Legislature thereof may direct, a Number of Electors, equal to the whole Number of Senators and Representatives to which the State may be entitled in the Congress: but no Senator or Representative, or Person holding an Office of Trust or Profit under the United States, shall be appointed an Elector.

The Electors shall meet in their respective States, and vote by Ballot for two persons, of whom one at least shall not lie an Inhabitant of the same State with themselves. And they shall make a List of all the Persons voted for, and of the Number of Votes for each; which List they shall sign and certify, and transmit sealed to the Seat of the Government of the United States, directed to the President of the Senate. The President of the Senate shall, in the Presence of the Senate and House of Representatives, open all the Certificates, and the Votes shall then be counted. The Person having the greatest Number of Votes shall be the President, if such Number be a Majority of the whole Number of Electors appointed; and if there be more than one who have such Majority, and have an equal Number of Votes, then the House of Representatives shall immediately chuse by Ballot one of them for President; and if no Person have a Majority, then from the five highest on the List the said House shall in like Manner chuse the President. But in chusing the President, the Votes shall be taken by States, the Representation from each State having one Vote; a quorum for this Purpose shall consist of a Member or Members from two-thirds of the States, and a Majority of all the States shall be necessary to a Choice. In every Case, after the Choice of the President, the Person having the greatest Number of Votes of the Electors shall be the Vice President. But if there should remain two or more who have equal Votes, the Senate shall chuse from them by Ballot the Vice President.

The Congress may determine the Time of chusing the Electors, and the Day on which they shall give their Votes; which Day shall be the same throughout the United States.

No person except a natural born Citizen, or a Citizen of the United States, at the time of the Adoption of this Constitution, shall be eligible to the Office of President; neither shall any Person be eligible to that Office who shall not have attained to the Age of thirty-five Years, and been fourteen Years a Resident within the United States.

In Case of the Removal of the President from Office, or of his Death, Resignation, or Inability to discharge the Powers and Duties of the said Office, the same shall devolve on the Vice President, and the Congress may by Law provide for the Case of Removal, Death, Resignation or Inability, both of the President and Vice President, declaring what Officer shall then act as President, and such Officer shall act accordingly, until the Disability be removed, or a President shall be elected.

The President shall, at stated Times, receive for his Services, a Compensation, which shall neither be increased nor diminished during the Period for which he shall have been elected, and he shall not receive within that Period any other Emolument from the United States, or any of them.

Before he enter on the Execution of his Office, he shall take the following Oath or Affirmation: "I do solemnly swear (or affirm) that I will faithfully execute the Office of President of the United States, and will to the best of my Ability, preserve, protect and defend the Constitution of the United States."

SECTION 2. The President shall be Commander in Chief of the Army and Navy of the United States, and of the Militia of the several States, when called into the actual Service of the United States; he may require the Opinion, in writing, of the principal Officer in each of the executive Departments, upon any subject relating to the Duties of their respective Offices, and he shall have Power to Grant Reprieves and Pardons for Offenses against the United States, except in Cases of Impeachment.

He shall have Power, by and with the Advice and Consent of the Senate, to make Treaties, provided two thirds of the Senators present concur; and he shall nominate, and by and with the Advice and Consent of the Senate, shall appoint Ambassadors, other public Ministers and Consuls, Judges of the supreme Court, and all other Officers of the United States, whose Appointments are not herein otherwise provided for, and which shall be established by Law: but the Congress may by Law vest the Appointment of such inferior Officers, as they think proper, in the President alone, in the Courts of Law, or in the Heads of Departments.

The President shall have Power to fill up all Vacancies that may happen during the Recess of the Senate, by granting Commissions which shall expire at the End of their next Session.

SECTION 3. He shall from time to time give to the Congress Information of the State of the Union, and recommend to their Consideration such Measures as he shall judge necessary and expedient; he may, on extraordinary Occasions, convene both Houses, or either of them, and in Case of Disagreement between them, with Respect to the Time of Adjournment, he may adjourn them to such Time as he shall think proper; he shall receive Ambassadors and other public Ministers; he shall take Care that the Laws be faithfully executed, and shall Commission all the Officers of the United States.

SECTION 4. The President, Vice President and all civil Officers of the United States, shall be removed from Office on Impeachment for, and Conviction of, Treason, Bribery, or other high Crimes and Misdemeanors.

ARTICLE III.

SECTION 1. The judicial Power of the United States, shall be vested in one supreme Court, and in such inferior Courts as the Congress may from time to time ordain and establish. The Judges, both of the supreme and inferior Courts, shall hold their Offices during good Behavior, and shall, at stated Times, receive for their Services a Compensation which shall not be diminished during their Continuance in Office.

SECTION 2. The judicial Power shall extend to all Cases, in Law and Equity, arising under this Constitution, the Laws of the United States, and Treaties made, or which shall be made, under their Authority; to all Cases affecting Ambassadors, other public Ministers and Consuls; to all Cases of admiralty and maritime Jurisdiction; to Controversies to which the United States shall be a Party; to Controversies between two or more States; between a State and Citizens of another State; between Citizens of different States; between Citizens of the same State claiming Lands under Grants of different States, and between a State, or the Citizens thereof, and foreign States, Citizens or Subjects.

In all Cases affecting Ambassadors, other public Ministers and Consuls, and those in which a State shall be Party, the supreme Court shall have original Jurisdiction. In all the other Cases before mentioned, the supreme Court shall have appellate Jurisdiction, both as to Law and Fact, with such Exceptions, and under such Regulations as the Congress shall make.

Trial of all Crimes, except in Cases of Impeachment, shall be by Jury; and such Trial shall be held in the State where the said Crimes shall have been committed; but when not committed within any State, the Trial shall be at such Place or Places as the Congress may by Law have directed.

SECTION 3. Treason against the United States, shall consist only in levying War against them, or in adhering to their Enemies, giving them Aid and Comfort. No Person shall be convicted of Treason unless on the Testimony of two Witnesses to the same overt Act, or on Confession in open Court.

The Congress shall have power to declare the Punishment of Treason, but no Attainder of Treason shall work Corruption of Blood, or Forfeiture except during the Life of the Person attainted.

ARTICLE IV.

SECTION 1. Full Faith and Credit shall be given in each State to the public Acts, Records, and judicial Proceedings of every other State. And the Congress may by general Laws prescribe the Manner in which such Acts, Records and Proceedings shall be proved, and the Effect thereof.

SECTION 2. The Citizens of each State shall be entitled to all Privileges and Immunities of Citizens in the several States.

A Person charged in any State with Treason, Felony, or other Crime, who shall flee from Justice, and be found in another State, shall on demand of the executive Authority of the State from which he fled, be delivered up, to be removed to the State having Jurisdiction of the Crime.

No Person held to Service or Labour in one State, under the Laws thereof, escaping into another, shall, in Consequence of any Law or Regulation therein, be discharged from such Service or Labour, But shall be delivered up on Claim of the Party to whom such Service or Labour may be due.

SECTION 3. New States may be admitted by the Congress into this Union; but no new States shall be formed or erected within the Jurisdiction of any other State; nor any State be formed by the Junction of two or more States, or parts of States, without the Consent of the Legislatures of the States concerned as well as of the Congress.

The Congress shall have Power to dispose of and make all needful Rules and Regulations respecting the Territory or other Property belonging to the United States; and nothing in this Constitution shall be so construed as to Prejudice any Claims of the United States, or of any particular State.

SECTION 4. The United States shall guarantee to every State in this Union a Republican Form of Government, and shall protect each of them against Invasion; and on Application of the Legislature, or of the Executive (when the Legislature cannot be convened) against domestic Violence.

ARTICLE V.

The Congress, whenever two thirds of both Houses shall deem it necessary, shall propose Amendments to this Constitution, or, on the Application of the Legislatures of two thirds of the several States, shall call a Convention for proposing Amendments, which, in either Case, shall be valid to all Intents and Purposes, as part of this Constitution, when ratified by the Legislatures of three fourths of the several States, or by Conventions in three fourths thereof, as the one or the other Mode of Ratification may be proposed by the Congress; Provided that no Amendment which may be made prior to the Year One thousand eight hundred and eight shall in any Manner affect the first and fourth Clauses in the Ninth Section of the first Article; and that no State, without its Consent, shall be deprived of its equal Suffrage in the Senate.

ARTICLE VI.

All Debts contracted and Engagements entered into, before the Adoption of this Constitution, shall be as valid against the United States under this Constitution, as under the Confederation.

This Constitution, and the Laws of the United States which shall be made in Pursuance thereof; and all Treaties made, or which shall be made, under the Authority of the United States, shall be the supreme Law of the Land; and the Judges in every State shall be bound thereby, any Thing in the Constitution or Laws of any State to the Contrary notwithstanding.

The Senators and Representatives before mentioned, and the Members of the several State Legislatures, and all executive and judicial Officers, both of the United States and of the several States, shall be bound by Oath or Affirmation, to support this Constitution; but no religious Test shall ever be required as a Qualification to any Office or public Trust under the United States.

ARTICLE VII.

The Ratification of the Conventions of nine States, shall be sufficient for the Establishment of this Constitution between the States so ratifying the Same.

DONE in Convention by the Unanimous Consent of the States present the Seventeenth Day of September in the Year of our Lord one thousand seven hundred and Eighty seven and of the Independence of the United States of America the Twelfth. In Witness whereof We have hereunto subscribed our Names.

Go. Washington
President and deputy from Virginia

New Hampshire
John Langdon
Nicholas Gilman

Massachusetts
Nathaniel Gorham
Rufus King

Connecticut
Wm Saml Johnson
Roger Sherman

New York
Alexander Hamilton

New Jersey
Wil Livingston
David Brearley
Wm Paterson
Jona. Dayton

Pennsylvania
B Franklin
Thomas Mifflin
Robt Morris
Geo. Clymer
Thos FitzSimons
Jared Ingersoll
James Wilson
Gouv Morris

Delaware
Geo. Read
Gunning Bedford jun
John Dickinson
Richard Bassett
Jaco. Broom

Maryland
James McHenry
Dan of St Tho Jenifer
Danl Carroll

Virginia
John Blair
James Madison Jr.

North Carolina
Wm Blount
Richd Dobbs Spaight
Hu Williamson

South Carolina
J. Rutledge

Charles Cotesworth Pinckney
Charles Pinckney
Pierce Butler

Georgia
William Few
Abr Baldwin

Attest: William Jackson, Secretary

AMENDMENT I.

Congress shall make no law respecting an establishment of religion, or prohibiting the free exercise thereof; or abridging the freedom of speech, or of the press; or the right of the people peaceably to assemble, and to petition the Government for a redress of grievances.

AMENDMENT II.

A well regulated Militia, being necessary to the security of a free State, the right of the people to keep and bear Arms, shall not be infringed.

AMENDMENT III.

No Soldier shall, in time of peace be quartered in any house, without the consent of the Owner, nor in time of war, but in a manner to be prescribed by law.

AMENDMENT IV.

The right of the people to be secure in their persons, houses, papers, and effects, against unreasonable searches and seizures, shall not be violated, and no Warrants shall issue, but upon probable cause, supported by Oath or affirmation, and particularly describing the place to be searched, and the persons or things to be seized.

AMENDMENT V.

No person shall be held to answer for a capital, or otherwise infamous crime, unless on a presentment or indictment of a Grand Jury, except in cases arising in the land or naval forces, or in the Militia, when in actual service in time of War or public danger; nor shall any person be subject for the same offense to be twice put in jeopardy of life or limb; nor shall be compelled in any criminal case to be a witness against himself, nor be deprived of life, liberty, or property, without due process of law; nor shall private property be taken for public use, without just compensation.

AMENDMENT VI.

In all criminal prosecutions, the accused shall enjoy the right to a speedy and public trial, by an impartial jury of the State and district wherein the crime shall have been committed, which district shall have been previously ascertained by law, and to be informed of the nature and cause of the accusation; to be confronted with the witnesses against him; to have compulsory process for obtaining witnesses in his favor, and to have the Assistance of Counsel for his defence.

AMENDMENT VII.

In Suits at common law, where the value in controversy shall exceed twenty dollars, the right of trial by jury shall be preserved, and no fact tried by a jury, shall be otherwise re-examined in any Court of the United States, than according to the rules of the common law.

AMENDMENT VIII.

Excessive bail shall not be required, nor excessive fines imposed, nor cruel and unusual punishments inflicted.

AMENDMENT IX.

The enumeration in the Constitution, of certain rights, shall not be construed to deny or disparage others retained by the people.

AMENDMENT X.

The powers not delegated to the United States by the Constitution, nor prohibited by it to the States, are reserved to the States espectively, or to the people.

AMENDMENT XI.

The Judicial power of the United States shall not be construed to extend to any suit in law or equity, commenced or prosecuted against one of the United States by Citizens of another State, or by Citizens or Subjects of any Foreign State.

AMENDMENT XII.

The Electors shall meet in their respective states, and vote by ballot for President and Vice-President, one of whom, at least, shall not be an inhabitant of the same state with themselves; they shall name in their ballots the person voted for as President, and in distinct ballots the person voted for as Vice-President, and they shall make distinct lists of all persons voted for as President, and of all persons voted for as Vice-President and of the number of votes for each, which lists they shall sign and certify, and transmit sealed to the seat of the government of the United States, directed to the President of the Senate;

The President of the Senate shall, in the presence of the Senate and House of Representatives, open all the certificates and the votes shall then be counted;

The person having the greatest Number of votes for President, shall be the President, if such number be a majority of the whole number of Electors appointed; and if no person have such majority, then from the persons having the highest numbers not exceeding three on the list of those voted for as President, the House of Representatives shall choose immediately, by ballot, the President. But in choosing the President, the votes shall be taken by states, the representation from each state having one vote; a quorum for this purpose shall consist of a member or members from two-thirds of the states, and a majority of all the states shall be necessary to a choice. And if the House of Representatives shall not choose a President whenever the right of choice shall devolve upon them, before the fourth day of March next following, then the Vice-President shall act as President, as in the case of the death or other constitutional disability of the President.

The person having the greatest number of votes as Vice-President, shall be the Vice-President, if such number be a majority of the whole number of Electors appointed, and if no person have a majority, then from the two highest numbers on the list, the Senate shall choose the Vice-President; a quorum for the purpose shall consist of two-thirds of the whole number of Senators, and a majority of the whole number shall be necessary to a choice. But no person constitutionally ineligible to the office of President shall be eligible to that of Vice-President of the United States.

AMENDMENT XIII.

1. Neither slavery nor involuntary servitude, except as a punishment for crime whereof the party shall have been duly convicted, shall exist within the United States, or any place subject to their jurisdiction.

2. Congress shall have power to enforce this article by appropriate legislation.

AMENDMENT XIV.

1. All persons born or naturalized in the United States, and subject to the jurisdiction thereof, are citizens of the United States and of the State wherein they reside. No State shall make or enforce any law which shall abridge the privileges or immunities of citizens of the United States; nor shall any State deprive any person of life, liberty, or property, without due process of law; nor deny to any person within its jurisdiction the equal protection of the laws.

2. Representatives shall be apportioned among the several States according to their respective numbers, counting the whole number of persons in each State, excluding Indians not taxed. But when the right to vote at any election for the choice of electors for President and Vice-President of the United States, Representatives in Congress, the Executive and Judicial officers of a State, or the members of the Legislature thereof, is de-

nied to any of the male inhabitants of such State, being twenty-one years of age, and citizens of the United States, or in any way abridged, except for participation in rebellion, or other crime, the basis of representation therein shall be reduced in the proportion which the number of such male citizens shall bear to the whole number of male citizens twenty-one years of age in such State.

3. No person shall be a Senator or Representative in Congress, or elector of President and Vice-President, or hold any office, civil or military, under the United States, or under any State, who, having previously taken an oath, as a member of Congress, or as an officer of the United States, or as a member of any State legislature, or as an executive or judicial officer of any State, to support the Constitution of the United States, shall have engaged in insurrection or rebellion against the same, or given aid or comfort to the enemies thereof. But Congress may by a vote of two-thirds of each House, remove such disability.

4. The validity of the public debt of the United States, authorized by law, including debts incurred for payment of pensions and bounties for services in suppressing insurrection or rebellion, shall not be questioned. But neither the United States nor any State shall assume or pay any debt or obligation incurred in aid of insurrection or rebellion against the United States, or any claim for the loss or emancipation of any slave; but all such debts, obligations and claims shall be held illegal and void.

5. The Congress shall have power to enforce, by appropriate legislation, the provisions of this article.

AMENDMENT XV.

1. The right of citizens of the United States to vote shall not be denied or abridged by the United States or by any State on account of race, color, or previous condition of servitude.

2. The Congress shall have power to enforce this article by appropriate legislation.

AMENDMENT XVI.

The Congress shall have power to lay and collect taxes on incomes, from whatever source derived, without apportionment among the several States, and without regard to any census or enumeration.

AMENDMENT XVII.

The Senate of the United States shall be composed of two Senators from each State, elected by the people thereof, for six years; and each Senator shall have one vote. The electors in each State shall have the qualifications requisite for electors of the most numerous branch of the State legislatures.

When vacancies happen in the representation of any State in the Senate, the executive authority of such State shall issue writs of election to fill such vacancies: Provided, That the legislature of any State may empower the executive thereof to make temporary appointments until the people fill the vacancies by election as the legislature may direct.

This Amendment shall not be so construed as to affect the election or term of any Senator chosen before it becomes valid as part of the Constitution.

AMENDMENT XVIII.

1. After one year from the ratification of this article the manufacture, sale, or transportation of intoxicating liquors within, the importation thereof into, or the exportation thereof from the United States and all territory subject to the jurisdiction thereof for beverage purposes is hereby prohibited.

2. The Congress and the several States shall have concurrent power to enforce this article by appropriate legislation.

3. This article shall be inoperative unless it shall have been ratified as an Amendment to the Constitution by the legislatures of the several States, as provided in the Constitution, within seven years from the date of the submission hereof to the States by the Congress.

AMENDMENT XIX.

The right of citizens of the United States to vote shall not be denied or abridged by the United States or by any State on account of sex.

Congress shall have power to enforce this article by appropriate legislation.

AMENDMENT XX.

1. The terms of the President and Vice President shall end at noon on the 20th day of January, and the terms of Senators and Representatives at noon on the 3d day of January, of the years in which such terms would have ended if this article had not been ratified; and the terms of their successors shall then begin.

2. The Congress shall assemble at least once in every year, and such meeting shall begin at noon on the 3d day of January, unless they shall by law appoint a different day.

3. If, at the time fixed for the beginning of the term of the President, the President elect shall have died, the Vice President elect shall become President. If a President shall not have been chosen before the time fixed for the beginning of his term, or if the President elect shall have failed to qualify, then the Vice President elect shall act as President until a President shall have qualified; and the Congress may by law provide for the case

wherein neither a President elect nor a Vice President elect shall have qualified, declaring who shall then act as President, or the manner in which one who is to act shall be selected, and such person shall act accordingly until a President or Vice President shall have qualified.

4. The Congress may by law provide for the case of the death of any of the persons from whom the House of Representatives may choose a President whenever the right of choice shall have devolved upon them, and for the case of the death of any of the persons from whom the Senate may choose a Vice President whenever the right of choice shall have devolved upon them.

5. Sections 1 and 2 shall take effect on the 15th day of October following the ratification of this article.

6. This article shall be inoperative unless it shall have been ratified as an Amendment to the Constitution by the legislatures of three-fourths of the several States within seven years from the date of its submission.

AMENDMENT XXI.

1. The eighteenth article of Amendment to the Constitution of the United States is hereby repealed.

2. The transportation or importation into any State, Territory, or possession of the United States for delivery or use therein of intoxicating liquors, in violation of the laws thereof, is hereby prohibited.

3. The article shall be inoperative unless it shall have been ratified as an Amendment to the Constitution by conventions in the several States, as provided in the Constitution, within seven years from the date of the submission hereof to the States by the Congress.

AMENDMENT XXII.

1. No person shall be elected to the office of the President more than twice, and no person who has held the office of President, or acted as President, for more than two years of a term to which some other person was elected President shall be elected to the office of the President more than once. But this Article shall not apply to any person holding the office of President, when this Article was proposed by the Congress, and shall not prevent any person who may be holding the office of President, or acting as President, during the term within which this Article becomes operative from holding the office of

President or acting as President during the remainder of such term.

2. This article shall be inoperative unless it shall have been ratified as an Amendment to the Constitution by the legislatures of three-fourths of the several States within seven years from the date of its submission to the States by the Congress.

AMENDMENT XXIII.

1. The District constituting the seat of Government of the United States shall appoint in such manner as the Congress may direct: A number of electors of President and Vice President equal to the whole number of Senators and Representatives in Congress to which the District would be entitled if it were a State, but in no event more than the least populous State; they shall be in addition to those appointed by the States, but they shall be considered, for the purposes of the election of President and Vice President, to be electors

appointed by a State; and they shall meet in the District and perform such duties as provided by the twelfth article of Amendment.

2. The Congress shall have power to enforce this article by appropriate legislation.

AMENDMENT XXIV.

1. The right of citizens of the United States to vote in any primary or other election for President or Vice President, for electors for President or Vice President, or for Senator or Representative in Congress, shall not be denied or abridged by the United States or any State by reason of failure to pay any poll tax or other tax.

2. The Congress shall have power to enforce this article by appropriate legislation.

AMENDMENT XXV.

1. In case of the removal of the President from office or of his death or resignation, the Vice President shall become President.

2. Whenever there is a vacancy in the office of the Vice President, the President shall nominate a Vice President who shall take office upon confirmation by a majority vote of both Houses of Congress.

3. Whenever the President transmits to the President pro tempore of the Senate and the Speaker of the House of Representatives his written declaration that he is unable to discharge the powers and duties of his office, and until he transmits to them a written declaration to the contrary, such powers and duties shall be discharged by the Vice President as Acting President.

4. Whenever the Vice President and a majority of either the principal officers of the executive departments or of such other body as Congress may by law provide, transmit to the President pro tempore of the Senate and the Speaker of the House of Representatives their written declaration that the President is unable to discharge the powers and duties of his office, the Vice President shall immediately assume the powers and duties of the office as Acting President.

Thereafter, when the President transmits to the President pro tempore of the Senate and the Speaker of the House of Representatives his written declaration that no inability exists, he shall resume the powers and duties of his office unless the Vice President and a majority of either the principal officers of the executive department or of such other body as Congress may by law provide, transmit within four days to the President pro tempore of the Senate and the Speaker of the House of Representatives their written declaration that the President is unable to discharge the powers and duties of his office. Thereupon Congress shall decide the issue, assembling within forty eight hours for that purpose if not in session. If the Congress, within twenty one days after receipt of the latter written declaration, or, if Congress is not in session, within twenty one days after Congress is required to assemble, determines by two thirds vote of both Houses that the President is unable to discharge the powers and duties of his office, the Vice President shall continue to discharge the same as Acting President; otherwise, the President shall resume the powers and duties of his office.

AMENDMENT XXVI.

1. The right of citizens of the United States, who are eighteen years of age or older, to vote shall not be denied or abridged by the United States or by any State on account of age.

2. The Congress shall have power to enforce this article by appropriate legislation.

AMENDMENT XXVII.

No law, varying the compensation for the services of the Senators and Representatives, shall take effect, until an election of Representatives shall have intervened.

Index

Note: (ill.) indicates photos and illustrations.

409

413

417

419

421